Scaling the Ivory Tower

Scaling the Ivory Tower:
Your Academic Job Search Workbook

Hillary Hutchinson

Mary Beth Averill

MarshFlower Publishing
Mount Pleasant, SC

Also by Mary Beth Averill & Hillary Hutchinson

How to Become an Academic Coach: What you need to know

By Hillary Hutchinson

Confidence: The Real McCoy

Change: From Surviving to Thriving

The EDUCO System: Your guide to becoming a happy, productive, thriving academic

Go forth and set the world on fire.
~ Ignatius of Loyola, on sending Jesuits out to create universities.

I think there's going to need to be a drastic change in how these universities work.
~Alexis Ohanian, a founder of the website Reddit

Copyright © 2019 Hillary Hutchinson and Mary Beth Averill

All rights reserved.

No part of this publication may be reproduced, stored in a retrieval system, or transmitted in any form or by any means, electronic, mechanical, photocopying, recording, scanning or otherwise except as permitted under Section 107 or 108 of the 1976 United States Copyright Act, without the prior written permission of the authors.

Requests for permission should be addressed to either:

    Mary Beth Averill (writeonmba at gmail.com), or

    Hillary Hutchinson (hillary at transitioningyourlife.com).

Limit of Liability/Disclaimer of Warranty: While the authors have made every effort in preparing this book to provide the best information possible, no warranties or representations with respect to the contents of this book are made regarding the completeness of this book, and we specifically disclaim any implied warranties of the merchantability or fitness for a particular purpose. The advice and strategies contained herein may not be applicable to your situation. You should consult with a professional where appropriate.

First Edition

MarshFlower Publishing,
Mount Pleasant, South Carolina

Book cover design and illustration by Katherine Morter.

ISBN: 9781794609303

DEDICATION

To our academic coaches' mastermind group, the Brainiacs, who supported the idea of creating an academic job search workbook, and particularly to Kate Duttro, for constantly encouraging us to write it.

ACKNOWLEDGEMENTS

Hillary and Mary Beth would like to acknowledge each other for the accountability we provided each other in getting this book finished. The fact that this book has been written at all is a testimonial to the power of accountability and coaching.

We would also like to acknowledge the many job-seeking clients we have worked with over the years. You have taught us what you need to know.

We also thank Carol Mejia for her diligence in formatting and preparing the manuscript for publication. Many hands make light work!

TABLE OF CONTENTS

HOW TO USE THIS BOOK	xiv
Contact Us	xv
FOREWORD	xvi

PART 1: JOB SEARCH OVERVIEW 1
The Job Search Cycle 2
    Community College Hiring Cycle and Job Expectations 3
Variations on Hiring 4
    The Tenure Track 5
    Misleading Ads 6
    Year to Year Contracts and Contingent Work 7
    Visiting Professor (Also Known As VAP) 7
    Considering an Adjunct Job Worksheet 8
    Teaching at a Distance 10
    Postdoctoral Teaching and Research 10
    Research Appointments 11
    Cluster Hiring 11
    Postdoctoral Position Worksheet 12
    What Is the Explanation for When Jobs Are Taken Off the Market? 12
Other Things To Consider before You Start Your Job Search 13
    Month by Month "To Do" List Worksheet 14
    Self-care 15
    Job Search Timeline Worksheet 16
    Considerations in Applying for Full-Time Academic Job Worksheet 17
    Self-care Worksheets 22
    Building Confidence 25
    Confidence Worksheet 26
    Imposter Syndrome Worksheet 30

PART 2: STAYING ON TOP OF YOUR ACADEMIC JOB SEARCH 33
Beginning the Process of Looking for Work 33
    Professional Print Sources and Online Professional Sources 33
    Headhunters and Recruiting Firms in Higher Education 37
    Using Social Media 39
    Application Tracking for Job Sources Worksheet 40
    Salary Information 48
    Expand Your General Networking 48
    Elevator Speech Worksheet, Part 1 53

Elevator Speech Worksheet, Part 2	54
Start Attending and Presenting at Conferences	57
Networking/Connecting Worksheet	58
Conference Attendance Worksheet	63
Why Publishing Sooner Instead of Later Is a Good Idea	64
What To Do between Your PhD and Your New Job	65
Publish	65
Publishing—Pre-PhD Plan Worksheet Coursework, Comps, or Preliminary Research	68
Publishing—Pre-PhD Plan Worksheet From Presentations and Conferences	69
Publishing—Dissertation and Post-PhD Publishing Plan Worksheet	70
Publishing—Continued Plan Worksheet	71
Sample Publishing—Publication Plan Worksheet	72
Find Work That Pays	73
Prepare for a Teaching Career (If You Want To Go to a Teaching Institution)	75
Be Clear about What You Want from an Academic Job	75
General Job Search Preparation Worksheet	76

PART 3: ORGANIZING YOUR JOB SEARCH — 78

Why Keep Paper Copies?	78
Systems You Can Use to Organize Your Job Search	80
Use a Log or Spreadsheet for the Big Picture Look at Your Job Search Efforts	80
Use the Notebook Method for Tracking Job Searches with Hard Copies	81
Sample Job Log for Academic Position Search	82
Job Log for Academic Position Search Worksheet	82
Job Log Face Sheet—Optional Worksheet	83
Set Up Your Own Simple System for Electronic Files	84
How to Stay Organized if Spreadsheets Are Not Your Thing?	84
There's an App for That! Organizing Electronically	86
Sites for Help with Your Academic Job Search	88
Website Evaluation Worksheet	89

PART 4: YOUR ACADEMIC JOB PORTFOLIO — 91

Timing of Submission	91
Written Materials	91
The Ten Elements of Your Academic Job Portfolio	92
The Cover Letter	93
Key Competencies or Contributions to Research Worksheet	97
Cover Letter for Interdisciplinary Positions	99
Postdoc Application Cover Letter	99
Curriculum Vitae (CV)	100
Sample Academic Cover Letter	101

Table of Contents

Cover Letter Planning Worksheet	103
Cover Letter Worksheet	105
Cover Letter Checklist Worksheet	106
Other CV Details	109
CV Checklist Worksheet	111
Action Words for Cover Letters and CVs Worksheet	113
CV Worksheet	115
Recommendations/Professional References	116
Teaching Philosophy Statement	118
Recommendations Worksheet	119
Recommendation Letter Worksheet	120
Sample Recommendation Letter	121
Sample Syllabi	122
Teaching Philosophy Statement Worksheet	123
Research Statement	125
Syllabus Worksheet	126
Research Presentation, aka 1st Job Talk	127
Research Statement Worksheet	128
Research Talk Questions & Answers Worksheet	130
Sample Class, aka 2nd Job Talk	132
Class Preparation Worksheet	135
Equity and Diversity Statement	137
Equity and Diversity Statement Worksheet	138
Teaching Evaluations	139
Teacher Evaluation Form (Your Own) Worksheet	140
Job Application Feedback	141
Sample Postcard/Email Application Follow-up	141

PART 5: YOUR JOB SEARCH INTERVIEWS — 143

Types of Interviews for Academics	143
General Interview Preparation	143
Research—Most Important Considerations to Me Worksheet	144
Telling My Story Worksheet	145
Background Preparation: Know Your Institution	146
Links to Particularly Useful Articles about Interviewing	148
Basic Interview Etiquette	148
General Considerations before an Actual Academic Interview	152
Things You Might Need To Do During an Academic Job Interview	154
Traits You Want To Project During the Actual Interview	156
How To Handle a Variety of Types of Interviews	157

Interview—Videoconference (Skype, Zoom, or Other Service) and Telephone Considerations Worksheet	162
Interview—Basic Questions Worksheet	164
Preparation before an On-site Interview	166
Sample On-campus Interview Schedule	167
What To Keep in Mind during the Campus Interview	170
Interview—In-depth Questions Related to Teaching Worksheet	172
Interview—In-depth Questions Related to Research Worksheet	174
Interview—In-depth Questions Related to Writing Worksheet	175
Interview—In-depth Questions Related to Other Duties Worksheet	176
As the Interview Is Ending	182
After the Interview	182
Interview—On-campus Worksheet	183
Interview Checklist Worksheet	185
When the Hiring Process Does Not Include a Final On-campus Interview	187
If You Receive a Job Offer	188
Negotiating	189
Considering a Job Offer Worksheet	191
Negotiating Your Job Offer Worksheet	194
Negotiation Checklist Worksheet	195
Complications	196
PART 6: ADDITIONAL CONSIDERATIONS	198
Failure to Track PhDs' Career Outcomes	198
Number of Academic Job Applicants	201
What Are the Chances of Being Offered a Tenure-track Job?	203
Alternatives to the Professoriate	209
Inside Academia	209
Leaving Academia	214
Grieving Your Losses	215
Post Academia	216
Transferable Skills Acquired or Sharpened in Graduate School Worksheet	220
Summary	222
PART 7: CONCLUSION	223
How Long To Look for a Faculty Job Worksheet	225
Epilogue	227
APPENDIX A: Tips for Organizing To Deal with Overload	228
APPENDIX B: List of Worksheets and Sample Documents	235
ENDNOTES	237

Table of Contents

INDEX	280
ABOUT THE AUTHORS	287

HOW TO USE THIS BOOK

We wrote this book because as academic coaches we have seen so many clients be completely befuddled regarding the job search process. Graduate school provides you with an expertise in an academic field but rarely does anyone talk about how you actually get a job working in the world of higher education. Too often, even when graduate students know they should be looking for work while finishing their dissertations, they feel completely overwhelmed by tackling these two huge projects simultaneously. We have heard many say, "If I think about looking for a job now, I will never get this dissertation done."

We get it. Many people would prefer to concentrate on the side of the equation where they have a bit more control over the outcome, finishing the dissertation. However, the current reality surrounding academic employment means that both projects must be handled simultaneously, although your job search may continue after you have defended your dissertation.

In **Part 6: Additional Considerations**, we have provided some incredibly depressing statistics about how few people can land a full-time academic job, let alone a tenure-track job. We did this because we felt offering a workbook like this without providing information about the realistic prospects for a job would be both unfair and unethical. We have frequently heard how few graduate programs ever discuss these statistics or offer any help on alternative pathways for PhDs who find themselves unable to get the kind of job they want. Therefore, we have included a section on alternatives to the professoriate, inside and out of academia. Information that is not attributable to a particular source comes from our own experiences working in academia or with clients.

If you are a newly minted or soon-to-be minted PhD, we want you to use this book to identify both problems and possible remedies to any area of the academic job search troubling you. Academia is a peculiar world, with rules of its own and unusual denizens who often have no sense of how things all fit together. Too many of those already entrenched in the old tenure-track system are still unaware of the realities facing academic job applicants today and of how to approach the academic job search process now. We designed this workbook as a resource to help you by providing context and a wide variety of self-paced exercises to better prepare you for the search. This workbook is for those of you committed to at least trying to get that full-time academic job. It lays out the job search cycle and the *how-to* for all the various stages of the search. While other books also illuminate the process, this book provides worksheets to help you craft your own story for an admittedly intimidating endeavor.

Skim the Table of Contents to find the information that most pertains to your situation. You can read the chapters or sections in any order that suits you. We recommend completing the applicable worksheets early on in your job search process, since they may save you some time. As you can tell from the copious citations, a lot of research has gone into this book; however, we encourage you to keep up to date, to tweak the worksheets to meet your needs, and to contact us with any questions.

How to use this book

We have made this book available both electronically and in hard copy since many people prefer the hard copy version for worksheets. If you are using the electronic version, you will be able to immediately click on any links we have referenced; if this does not work for you, go to the referenced Endnote where you will find the complete URL address. If you are using a hard copy, you can also find all referenced links with the full internet address in the Endnotes. Please note, if you are working from the electronic version, you may find white space or odd page breaks around the worksheets depending on the device and font size you are using to read this book.

Whether you are using an electronic or hard copy of this workbook, you may download all the worksheets by going to the link at **Appendix B.**

Contact Us

We welcome suggestions and additions. The world of academia is changing rapidly with the inclusion of more electronic resources and publications, which in turn is impacting both the work and the work product produced by academics beyond the traditional in-classroom delivery of lectures, testing, and grading. We are greatly appreciative of any suggestions our readers may have for improving the content or adding any new items we have not considered to aid in the job search process.

Contact Mary Beth by emailing writeonmba at gmail.com or Hillary by emailing hillary at transitioningyourlife.com with your suggestions, concerns, or desire to connect for a complimentary session.

FOREWORD

Congratulations! You've defended your dissertation or your defense is on the near horizon. You're completing a postdoc and want a more permanent position. You're not happy with your current academic job and want to move on. All these are reasons for being on the academic job market. To help you, we have organized this book in seven sections: Part 1 introduces the academic job search cycle and outlines the various categories for hires. Part 2 helps you stay on top of your academic job search. Part 3 is about staying on top of your job search—ways to organize. Part 4 outlines important pieces of your academic job search portfolio. Part 5 presents the ins and outs of your academic job search interview. In Part 6 we discuss additional considerations around applying for an academic job, including the chances of being offered a tenure-track job and alternatives to applying for a job in the academy. In Part 7 we conclude by reiterating some of the most important items to consider as you go through a month by month academic job search process.

We've crafted the attached worksheets to be specific to academics. *Nature's* 2017 PhD survey of 5,700 graduate science students from diverse scientific fields in Asia, Europe, and North America indicated that 52% of new PhDs still wanted a career in academia. Fifty-nine percent expected the process of finding work to take up to three years. However, 18% said they did not have useful conversations about careers with advisors or mentors inside academia and 60% reported they have turned to the internet for career advice along with guidance provided by supervisors (34%), colleagues (30%), or other researchers (30%).[1]

As a confidence builder for your job search process, remember: You are already in a very elite group. Only 1-2% of the entire population holds a PhD degree. No matter what field you are in, from humanities to engineering or science, 40-50% enrolled in a doctoral program will never finish.[2]

Even if you no longer want a job in the academy after you have finished your doctoral program, plenty of the information in this book can help you as you conduct your alternative job search. Learning to present yourself in a positive light, telling your story so it is oriented toward the future and not the past, crafting a resume that highlights the skills you *want* to use, rather than focusing on the ones you have, are all essential elements for any employment seeker. The exercises provided here can help you shine as a job candidate in or out of academia.

So, let's get started!

PART 1: JOB SEARCH OVERVIEW

What do we mean when we speak about an academic job these days?

Traditionally academic jobs have been full-time tenure-track jobs that required some measure of teaching, research, and service. Junior faculty and tenured faculty had offices at a college or university and met with students face-to-face in lecture halls, seminar rooms, labs, studios, and in their offices. The landscape of higher education has changed so dramatically that now at least 75% of university teaching faculty are contingent, contract, or adjunct employees with some part-time and some full-time adjuncts usually teaching a 4-4 class load.[3]

Adjuncts and contingent faculty (contract worker, term-limited instructor, or sessional lecturer) may or may not have offices. They may or may not get benefits along with their pay. They may get less pay than a colleague in the same department. They may meet with students face to face weekly, or just several times a year, or not at all if students and faculty interact mainly in online courses.

The process of obtaining a full-time tenure-track academic appointment is extremely difficult and long. As one faculty member put it: "…the first thing you should know is that academics are brutal, and academia encourages brutality."[4] She was referring to the emphasis placed on research over teaching, the fear people have that their ideas will be stolen, or that they will not get their work published but this statement also applies to the job search process. Rejection is an unenviable but inevitable part of the job search.

Conducting a job search can also be costly. You may need to budget for mailing hardcopy materials, attending conferences, and physically getting to a campus interview if the institution is not paying. Fordham University's English Department estimated that a doctoral student in the sixth and final year of funding may need $4,500 for all job search related costs.[5] Fordham's English Department now provides that amount in addition to a regular fellowship specifically designed to defray the job search costs for graduate students on a tight budget. This enlightened approach has not yet been replicated elsewhere.

This workbook is meant to normalize the academic job search process, give you pragmatic steps to take, and remove some of the fear of the unknown. It is for people finishing or recently finished with a graduate degree, usually a PhD, who want to join the full-time academic workforce. In Part 6, Additional Considerations, we provide some of the employment statistics and the alternatives to the professoriate available to you which you may benefit from reading *before* you prepare your job search materials.

In this chapter, we give you an overview of the annual academic job search cycle for four-year and two-year institutions. You may want to consider whether you really want to work at a research institution, or would be more comfortable with a primarily teaching institution more oriented to serving and helping undergraduates.[6] We cover some of the variations in hiring including tenure-track jobs, adjuncting, online or distance teaching, shared positions, research, and administration, as well as what may be happening behind the scenes when jobs are taken off the market. Finally, we discuss a few other things you may want to consider before you start your job search, including self-care and dealing with the imposter syndrome.

The Job Search Cycle

Understanding the academic job search cycle is imperative for preparing your portfolio to submit to a search committee. Academic hiring has a much longer time cycle than any other industry sector. From the institution's perspective, the process may begin with an advertisement submitted to relevant journals in the early fall for a position to start the following fall, with a deadline for submission of materials as early as mid-October, or more typically by mid-December. In some fields, search committee members may do initial screenings of potential candidates at a conference in December or January. However, the entire search committee may not convene until after winter break in late January or early February, with the expectation of bringing in candidates or conducting final interviews over the internet, by conference call, or even in person during Spring Break (often in March) or even later in the spring.

In general, for a non-tenure-track position, you will *not* be granted an on-campus interview. You will most likely be interviewed at a conference, or later by phone or video. You may not even talk to anyone at all: a decision could be made to hire you on the basis of your submitted written materials.

If you are a tenure-track candidate, after you have already undergone the grueling process of providing all the application materials, doing a preliminary interview at a conference, or later by phone or video, and find yourself still in the running, you will likely be one of 3 to 4 candidates invited to interview on campus. Once candidates have been interviewed, the name of the search committee's top choice may need to be submitted to a higher-level administrator such as the department chair, the dean, president or even provost for approval before a contract can be offered. Sometimes every one of these people has to sign off on the hiring decision, so at any point you can, unfortunately, be booted out of consideration. After you are offered a position, the final paperwork may not be finished until the June before the fall semester, with the expectation that successful candidate will move during the summer and get settled in before classes start in late August or early September.

As you begin this process, make sure you actually read the advertisement for the position. A remarkable number of people fail to read it carefully (i.e., "between the lines") in order to discern what the hiring committee is seeking. A surprising amount of time is devoted by the search committee [7] and those vetting the application, such as an HR department, and the wording is often the product of long negotiations and compromise. Search committees in the humanities may be looking for different things than in the sciences, but generally, research institutions emphasize on your publication record and/or your ability to bring in funding for your own research. The reputation of your primary advisor can also come into play, especially as you apply for assistant professor positions since often you cannot stand on your own record at this point in your career.[8] If you do not include a letter from your primary advisor in the recommendations, committees may view that as a "red flag" and assume you are the problem, or you are the person who is difficult to work with, rather than your advisor.

Remind yourself that "not all search committees are created equal," and be prepared to give the members information about yourself that will show off your potential. Treat them with respect, and make clear from your interactions that you expect to be treated professionally, too. Keep the reader/interviewer topmost in your mind as you move through the process, but never forget you are also interviewing them. That will keep you on track and reduce your anxiety.

The cover letter should reflect your interpretation of the original ad, and help tell the search committee "What's in it for them?" if they hire you. The submitted CV should also reflect the advertisement to some extent and, depending on position, may require a slight reorganization of the order or type of information presented. For instance, if teaching is the primary duty, then it makes sense to move teaching up to the top part of the CV; if research is being emphasized, that should be placed nearer to the top. Both the cover letter and CV need to immediately capture the attention of those in a hiring position.

Community College Hiring Cycle and Job Expectations

Community colleges are usually two-year institutions that award an Associate's degree or a certification in some job field (practical nursing, nurse's aide, dental assistant or dental technician, computer technician, food services, hospitality, etc.). Some students attend the community college to earn a professional certification. Others see the community college as a way to ease into college socially, financially, and workload-wise before they transfer to a four-year institution. Often community college students need remedial help. Faculty at community colleges are expected to be teaching and student-centered rather than research centered. Some community colleges require that faculty have a doctorate, and others hire long-term faculty with a Master's degree. Hiring requirements may also vary by department.

The hiring cycle at community colleges mimics that at larger institutions.[9] Most hiring is done for the start of fall term, but the process may be shorter and less formal than that of four-year institutions because departments are usually small and the emphasis is on teaching and other work with students. The hiring cycle may also be shorter since community colleges often do not know how many students will be enrolled until immediately prior to a semester, and those schools may suddenly find themselves scrambling to fill positions.

Reasons to choose to work at a community college may be a geographical preference, lack of research workload, love of teaching, less pressure, employment while looking for a university job, and so on. Since people teaching at community colleges may move on to other jobs at more prestigious institutions, job openings may appear at any time of the year. In the past few years, we've had clients who taught at a community college while finishing and defending a dissertation and then moved to another part of the country mid-year as well as clients who heard of a community college job opening for spring term about a week before spring classes started and were hired immediately.

An advantage of looking for work at a community college is that many community colleges of varying sizes exist. Faculty positions at one of 1,300 community colleges make up about one-third of the higher education positions in the United State.[10] One disadvantage is that many community colleges hire from the local graduate student pool so that they do not have to offer any sort of long-term employment, and graduate students will generally jump at the opportunity to get some experience no matter how low the pay, or how soon it is to the start date.[11]

In the blog *Tenure, she wrote*, "Dr. Klotz" explained three reasons why someone looking for an academic job that requires some teaching should consider a community college. She refers to competitive salaries, chances to do research, and variable teaching loads—things that don't necessarily come to mind when one thinks of a community college.[12]

So, do community colleges have tenure? According to Jenkins,[13] most community colleges either have tenure or some form of permanent faculty contracts. In some community colleges, the contracts are automatically renewed every year so long as the faculty member continues to meet the requirements of the job; other community colleges, especially in the eastern US have more stringent requirements that approach those of four-year institutions.

In a recent article,[14] Melissa Dennihy listed several things a person applying for a job at a community college should keep in mind: have a good understanding of the expectations of the job, emphasize teaching experience, enjoy collaborating with other faculty, and learn about the students at the institution. Spend time preparing a teaching portfolio that includes lessons, texts, and activities and plan a teaching demonstration that highlights these aspects of your portfolio. Teaching is of paramount importance at community colleges, and less specialized, more general education classes will be useful in your application package.

We summarize the interview process for a community college job in **Part 5: Your Job Search Interviews.**

Variations on Hiring

By now, even at the beginning of your job search, you are probably aware that a variety of kinds of positions exist in academia. For decades, doctoral candidates or new PhDs or post-docs have started their job searches looking for tenure-track positions. Some people look for post-doctoral research or research/teaching positions as a way to build their resumes before they compete for a tenure-track job. However, many find they end up in post-doc positions for many years, without ever being offered a permanent position.

A job as adjunct faculty, contingent faculty, contract faculty, or visiting lecturer or professor—none of which offer any job security—can still be a backup plan to getting a full time, tenured position. Community college teaching, university research or clinical appointments, and administrative positions are options that can become long-term jobs. Online teaching, blended classes, or flipped classes may be done by tenure track faculty or by adjuncts. Additionally, some opportunities exist in programs that are doing cluster hiring. The variety of jobs to apply for may seem overwhelming and most of them are not on the tenure-track. We review these options starting with tenure-track jobs and moving on to the others.

Part 1: Job Search Overview

The Tenure Track

Many new graduates look for tenure-track jobs because they assume that people with tenure cannot be easily fired for their personal, political, social, or religious beliefs. Tenure is supposed to provide an environment of academic freedom in which faculty largely determine the content of what they will teach and what they will research. This professional guarantee is unique to academia, and what people mean when they refer to "academic freedom." Faculty do not have the freedom to purposefully teach incorrect information or an excuse to rest on their laurels and never be productive again; rather, tenure is meant as an incentive for academic production by protecting the right to pursue one's research even if it takes an unexpected or political direction at odds with the current status quo. Until you have achieved tenure, however, you are not protected.

The tenure process usually takes up to seven years, and many people have found the process to be as challenging as completing their dissertations. A major expectation for tenure is having your work published in refereed journals over the course of your "probationary" time. Teaching and service are also taken into account, but not to the same degree as research and publications, especially at research-oriented institutions. While the full tenure process may take up to seven years, many universities review a candidate's work at three years. A good third-year review may be needed for one to continue on the tenure track. Junior faculty on the tenure track usually start at the (non-tenured) Assistant Professor level. Whether or not a person moves up to the (tenured) Associate Professor level as part of gaining tenure varies depending on the institution. A promotion to Full Professor may happen years later, depending on one's research, teaching, and service. Much like receiving a PhD, once you actually receive tenure, it is exceptionally hard to take it away.

Tenure-track jobs are relatively sparse these days and will become ever rarer. The *Inside Higher Education* website listed 2,334 tenure-track positions available as of October 2017, out of a total of 7,670 positions advertised, or roughly just one-third[15] of available positions. This total is overly optimistic because the vast majority of those advertising in this specialized forum are 4-year public universities, not 4-year private schools, community colleges and certainly not the over 3,000[16] for-profit entities that for the most part do not even have a tenure category. Studies have shown over and over again that most (at least ¾) of all working faculty are contingent or adjunct faculty operating on a *part-time* contract basis.[17] These faculty do not have, and likely will never get, a tenure-track job offer, let alone tenure, from their employing institution. The possibility of being offered a tenure-track job is close to 20%. The number who may actually get tenure at this moment in time is probably closer to 16% as overworked, underpaid, highly stressed professors are often unable to meet rigorous tenure requirements including a subjective component of "worthiness."

Depending on the institution, your teaching or your research may be more weighted in getting tenure. Some universities still value teaching more than research and publishing. Other institutions expect their faculty to do everything and are more likely to offer a tenure-track job to those who teach, research, publish, and do service work. And a surprising new twist: more and more institutions are requiring professors to bring in grant money to help fund their own positions, no matter the field, as a condition of granting tenure.

Some of our clients have tenure-track jobs where their teaching is highly valued and research is de-incentivized. Their complaints about this situation are that they are still interested in doing some research and their colleagues and departments aren't particularly supportive of that desire. They lack colleagues who are interested in staying current in their fields and they may experience what they feel is a lack of adequate library, lab, or professional development resources. Additionally, their teaching loads are heavy, which doesn't leave them a lot of time for research or writing.

People who are hired into tenure-track jobs at research-oriented universities also have very heavy workloads, maybe less teaching than at some other places, but the expectations of research and publishing start from year one and are very demanding. Depending on your field, cutting-edge work can look stale by the time it is published given the sluggishness of academic peer reviews—reviews done by people with equally demanding and time-consuming jobs.

The first year at a new faculty job, whether or not it is on the tenure track, is heavy with class preparation. You will also need to put in social time to get to know both your colleagues and the institutional culture. Making some friends and allies among the faculty and getting an understanding of the university's culture is especially important if you are on the tenure track. If for some reason you need help, whether covering a class while you attend a conference or because of a family emergency, you need to know whom you can ask without fear of punishment, not to mention that having friends and trusted colleagues is good for your mental health.

In your first year, if you have not already gotten a contract to publish your dissertation before graduating, you need to be seeking out places and ways to get your dissertation into the world. Once you have this underway, you want to be finding new doable, publishable research projects. If colleagues of outside your institution see you as contributing to your field, that will make you more valuable in the eyes of your home institution. While you are doing all these things, you probably will be getting comfortable with a new city or part of the country.

Misleading Ads

Some of our clients have asked us about what they see as misleading ads for "Assistant Professor" jobs—in other words, the job ad gives the indication that the job is for a tenure-track position, but a closer read of the advertisement indicates the job is actually being offered for a term of one to three years. In other words, it is actually a contract position and not a tenure-track position.

It has also happened that applicants have devoted quite a bit of time to an application for an ostensible tenure-track position, sometimes even interviewing, only to discover the job is actually a one to three-year appointment and not even a renewable contract job at that. In an article in *The Chronicle of Higher Education*, Rebecca Schuman detailed her research in response to such ads[18] in which the job title is for "Assistant Professor," but the job is *not* tenure track. Some institutions give people who are ABD the title Lecturer and anyone with a doctorate is titled an Assistant Professor. So, read those advertisements very, very carefully.

PhD Comics has weighed in on false tenure-track titles for non-tenure-track employees.[19] If you don't already know Jorge Cham's comic about life in academia, take a look, because it can inject some much-needed humor and perspective into this challenging profession.

Part 1: Job Search Overview

Year to Year Contracts and Contingent Work

Roughly 75% of all university teaching at the present time is done by people who are *not* on the tenure track; i.e., by adjuncts, contingent or contract hires, post-docs, or visiting faculty. Many terms exist for positions that involve year to year contracts,[20] such as adjunct faculty, contingent faculty, or contract faculty. People in these positions usually teach mainly lower level courses, especially for non-majors, although sometimes an adjunct is hired to teach upper-level courses in an area of expertise.

An adjunct may have a private office, may share an office, or may not have an office. Adjuncts are usually expected to hold office hours, but often they are not allowed to attend faculty meetings, and if they are invited, will not have a vote on policy issues or curricula matters are under consideration for change. They rarely serve on departmental or college committees, because they are not considered to be permanent employees. They may or may not have access to a lab or studio, office supplies, and clerical help.

While tenure-track faculty may have a university-supplied work computer and telephone, adjuncts usually have to supply their own, frequently lugging all their equipment and materials from home to campus and back again. Their teaching loads are usually higher than those of tenured or tenure-track faculty and their pay scales are often much lower than those of tenure-track faculty. An adjunct appointment is usually without benefits and does not include funds for faculty development like conferences. Such an appointment can be very difficult financially. Adjuncts have reported living in cars, using food banks, suffering from debilitating illnesses, and even turning to sex work to supplement their income. Debra Leigh Scott, who is working on a documentary about adjuncts, said, "We take a kind of vow of poverty to continue practicing our profession. We do it because we are dedicated to scholarship, to learning, to our students, and to our disciplines."[21]

Adjuncts often teach at more than one institution of higher education to cobble together enough work and pay to equal a full-time job, but the wear and tear of constantly commuting takes a toll. See the worksheet, **Considering an Adjunct Job,** for help in deciding whether to pursue an adjunct job and what questions to keep in mind if you go this route. The route from being a contingent worker to being on the tenure track at an institution is increasingly rare.

Adjuncts and contract hires are essentially the same, with all the same issues, though some institutions may specifically refer to a hire as a contract employee with the designation Lecturer, while others may hide the contract nature of the employment with the title Adjunct. Most students and people outside academia will not understand the term "adjunct professor" nor will they know that it translates to "non-tenure track" and that it is almost certainly considered only a part-time job. Contingent positions are usually those that begin with a set contract period, and once the institution feels satisfied with your work, the position may convert to an actual tenure-track path.

Visiting Professor (Also Known As VAP)

A visiting faculty member is generally someone with teaching and advising experience who fills in for one semester or one year to replace a tenured faculty person who is on sabbatical, medical leave, or taking course release to concentrate on research. Visiting faculty usually have an office

Considering an Adjunct Job Worksheet

Answer the questions honestly below to assess whether you really want to pursue an adjunct job.

Why do you want to accept an adjunct position?

    Family considerations: For instance, your spouse is the primary income-earner, and a move is required; you have very small children and do not currently want to pursue a full-time academic position; you do not want to leave academia behind even though you have not been able to secure a full-time position.

    Location: Is adjuncting attractive because it's located in a place you want to live or travel?

    Experience: Will the job increase your skills teaching, honing current class curricula, or developing syllabi for new courses?

    Is adjuncting a placeholder for you while you continue to seek a full-time position?

    Do you see adjuncting as a way to develop new colleagues or collaborators?

    Do you see adjuncting as a way to find time to write and submit writing for publication? If so, what is a realistic way to look at the time you will have available for this?

What are the expectations of the hiring institution concerning the adjunct position?

    What is the expected teaching load and schedule? [4-4, 4-3, 2-2, or other variation; is it M-W-F or T-Th?]

Part 1: Job Search Overview

Is there an opportunity for any possible course relief in the future?

What services or equipment is offered? This may include office, mailbox, email address, computer, phone, library privileges, parking, lab or studio space.

What expectations, if any, go beyond meeting classes and holding office hours?

What are the terms of employment being offered? [1, 2, 3-year contract? Potential to renew after the initial contract period?]

What are the expectations for research and publishing for an adjunct?

What are some other issues to consider?

Salary and other incentives:

Health benefits:

Commute time:

Need to work at more than one institution for financial reasons:

and computer and perhaps lab or studio space, will be asked to attend faculty meetings (though likely without voting privileges since they are temporary members of a department), and sometimes advise students. From the very start, they know their positions are time-limited, but the positions allow them to know new colleagues and make new contacts, all of which can help with seeking the next academic position.

A visiting professorship may provide health insurance and library access, both of which can be difficult to get without an academic appointment. Many former graduate students struggling to publish some portions of their dissertation suddenly find themselves without access to journals or databases they used while in graduate school. Some visiting faculty positions may involve only part-time teaching, but allow the appointees time and space for ongoing research in their areas of expertise while using an institutional affiliation.

Teaching at a Distance

Teaching at a distance usually means online teaching.[22] One recent study said that one of three students take at least one online course.[23] For this kind of position, you may be developing your own class syllabus and slides, lectures, and/or videos, or the curriculum may be supplied by the institution and your job is to interact with and grade the students. The type and amounts of contact with students may vary from video conferencing with them, to recording lectures for them to watch, to grading, to emails or phone contacts. Some online graduate programs hire distance teachers who have regular video conferencing or phone meetings with their advisees.

An advantage of distance teaching is that your schedule and dress code may be more flexible than what is expected for an on-campus job. A disadvantage is that you may lack the opportunity to develop colleagues and you may not have the intellectual stimulation of a campus job (e.g., colleagues, visiting lecturers, library access).

Frequently, one component of distance teaching is the requirement for online discussion, via Blackboard, Canvas, Moodle, or whatever module is currently used by the institution. Though moderating such discussions can be done on your own schedule, it can take a surprising amount of time. Just like any other form of written conversation, statements can easily be taken the wrong way, either intentionally or unintentionally. You may need to devote class time to clearing up such misunderstandings before moving forward with the class material. This process can be frustrating for both teachers and students.

Postdoctoral Teaching and Research

Postdoctoral appointments vary a lot—from one semester to renewable for many years; from all research or all clinical work to a combination of research, teaching, or clinical work; from well-funded, often by grants, to funding such as one would expect for graduate students. A post-doc may be a great way to get more research experience, often working with leaders in your field. It can also be a placeholder while you write up publications and look for a tenure-track job. In general, more post-docs are available in the sciences than there are in the humanities, though some humanities positions do exist. Applying for post-doc positions can take just as much time as applying for tenure-track positions. Every post-doc position has requirements and expectations unique to the specific department and institution. Read the criteria for a post-doc position carefully and ask yourself if this particular appointment will meet your needs. Use the **Postdoctoral Position Worksheet** for a list of questions to consider.

Research Appointments

If you like doing research or being a statistician, you may be happy with a job working in someone else's lab or on someone else's grant. We know PhDs who have chosen this path because they got computer, and perhaps lab or studio space, and asked to attend faculty meetings (though likely without voting privileges since they are temporary members of a department), and sometimes advise students. From the very start, they knew their positions are time-limited, but they wanted the flexibility to work and care for family, they wanted time for creative writing (essays, books), or they liked doing research but didn't enjoy teaching and departmental service. Although these jobs don't usually offer tenure, they may be long-term, almost permanent, positions with good pay as long as the grant money keeps coming in. Be aware of the danger, however, that when you are employed on soft-money, you can lose your job relatively quickly when funding dries up for whatever reason.

Cluster Hiring

Cluster hires have been around for about 20 years, but they are not common. Generally, they are related to programs that are large in scope and supported by "deep-pocketed" funders and may be managed at the level of the provost, president, or chancellor's office. Faculty from a variety of designated fields are hired to work on a research agenda outlined in a university's strategic plan. If you are being considered for employment as part of a cluster hire, whether a new initiative or one seeking new complementary hires, be clear about the expectations of the university for your position.

Hiring clusters are usually research-based. An example of a cluster hire would be "Health Disparities" where expertise may come from biology, medicine, environmental science, women's studies, and others. Typical language describing a cluster hire uses terms like "studying the intersection of ecology and human health" and will generally mention the appointment as "cross-disciplinary." Sometimes the cluster hire is a way to for a program to take a more holistic look at regional issues, such as practices around immunization across one entire state. Faculty hired in a cluster are expected to collaborate on publications and may even share some sort of collaborative space, such as a dedicated laboratory. Each hire is typically connected to a "home" department in which their specialty is located, and that may be the place where their own offices are located. Cluster hires are touted to increase faculty diversity and, in some cases, to lower costs. Though the emphasis is on research, some positions may also carry a small teaching load.

The hiring process for cluster hires is somewhat different from a departmental hiring process. While a faculty member may serve on, or even chair, the hiring committee, deans also often serve on the committee and final hiring decisions usually rest with the provost or a dean. Sometimes a hired faculty member will have certain strengths that may influence the jobs offered to people hired later in the cluster. "When you hire the first person, that may change what you want in the second and third person," said Laura R. Severin of North Carolina State University. "You may

> **Postdoctoral Position Worksheet**
>
> What are the specific criteria for this position?
>
> What are the dates of the position?
>
> Is this position renewable?
>
> Will I be working with someone I respect and like?
>
> What does this position pay?
>
> Will the funding be enough that I won't ultimately feel used and resentful?
>
> Will I be able to pursue my own research ideas or will I be working on someone else's project?
>
> What will this position offer in terms of skill building, publications, recommendations?
>
> If I have to move to take the post-doc, will the financial and educational benefits be more than the costs of moving and settling into a new city?

have some needs that are filled by the first person that you didn't anticipate. Then you have to rethink the skills and experiences needed for persons two and three."[24]

What Is the Explanation for When Jobs Are Taken Off the Market?

What a let-down! Finally, you see a listing for a job that you feel you fit well. The deadline for applications is at a reasonable interval from when you see the listing. You tweak your application materials and you are all set to submit them when the listing and link to apply for it completely disappear. Or, you have submitted your materials well ahead of the deadline, but you have not received a confirmation the materials were received, and the listing disappears. What happened and what, if anything, can you do about it?

Probably the funding for the position disappeared. The university may have decided not to renew this slot. The job may have been at least partially dependent on grant money. For instance, a course release for the person who usually taught certain classes may not be needed because the grant that person was expecting did not get funded or renewed. The university may have decided to reorganize by combining some departments so that existing faculty could teach the classes. Other scenarios are also possible.

Since search committees often don't have funding for clerical help, especially if the search has been discontinued, no one is available to send you a letter explaining what happened. Even if the job has not disappeared, the application and materials you sent in may not ever be acknowledged. This situation leaves you wondering what to do next. You have several options, depending on how attached you are to the idea of working at that institution:

- You can do nothing.
- You can call the department office and ask the administrative assistant what happened to the position and who the chair of the search was.
- You can call the chair of the now defunct search committee and ask if the job will be open in the future.
- You can send a letter or email with your CV, saying you would like to be kept in mind if the position becomes available later.
- If you know someone at the institution or in the department for which the job listing disappeared, you can ask that person what happened.
- You can look at online bulletin boards or list serves to see if others have had a similar experience with this job ad and if they have any inside information about what happened. We have clients who do this. Our caveat is that this kind of online activity may be a distraction from just attending to getting out applications for jobs that really exist.

Please note, getting answers to any of these questions is very difficult, in part because something may be going on, completely unrelated to you, and people are busy. Try not to take it personally. Be realistic. Getting a tenure-track job is hard (See Part 6, Additional Considerations, for some statistics on the chances of being offered a tenure-track job in various fields.) Keep applying elsewhere. It's easy to get discouraged or lose confidence. No matter what happens, you have finished a dissertation, no small achievement. You are not a failure.

Work toward finding that academic job of your dreams by using the **Month by Month "To Do" List Worksheet,** the **Job Search Timeline Worksheet,** and the **Considerations in Applying for Full-Time Academic Job Worksheet.**

Other Things To Consider Before You Start Your Job Search

As Rick Reis noted in one of his email installments [25] for *Tomorrow's Professor*, you must "Think about your job search, your participation in scholarly organizations, and the completion of your

Month by Month "To Do" List Worksheet		
Time Period	**Action To Take**	**Action Taken**
Summer, June-August	-Drafts or templates of the written materials - Request references -Set up application file tracking system with deadlines -Look for conferences to attend -Finish dissertation or write articles/book using dissertation -Support group and/or maintaining social connections	
August-September	-Review job listings (continue through May) Determine application strategy	
September	-Write conference papers -Create cover letter template -Update CV	
October	-Write teaching philosophy -Write research statement -Prepare job talk -Begin applying for jobs -Prepare "unofficial" evaluations for students -Start attending conferences	
November	-Prepare course descriptions -Organize sample syllabi -Prepare sample class to teach -Apply for jobs	
December	-Review official teaching applications -Review Rate My Professor -Determine response to criticism -Apply for jobs	
January	-Make any needed adjustments to application materials	

Part 1: Job Search Overview

	- Look for additional emotional support -Apply for jobs	
February	-Apply for jobs -Attend job interviews	
March-May	-Keep checking job ads -Attend job interviews -Negotiate offers -Negotiate actual contract -Start moving plans -Determine financial structure until first paycheck	
June-July	-Pack and move	
August	-Start new position -Get to know entering cohort group across the school -Begin a folder for collecting tenure materials	

research as a unified whole." Completion is certainly an important part of what you need to think about as you engage in this process: completing papers you can present and publish before graduation, finishing the dissertation itself, and being able to begin a new job without a major project looming over your head. In truth, given the very tight job market for academic positions, search committees will almost always choose a candidate with a degree over one that is still in process.

Before we move on to actual details of the job search, we cover handling self-care, building confidence, and dealing with the imposter syndrome.

This is a good time to fill out the **Considerations in Applying for Full-Time Academic Job Worksheet** which may provide you with some additional questions to consider. Applying for academic jobs is tedious, time-consuming, and frequently demoralizing work. You should also consider what alternatives to a tenure-track job appeal to you. Some people are happy as contract workers or adjuncts, others like working as administrators, and some PhDs find satisfying employment outside the academy. Be sure you really want to go down the tenure-track route before you expend your energy on it.

Self-care

Stress: Why we need to pay attention to self-care. Most people find that the dissertation process stressful and most PhDs searching for a job find that process stressful, too. Many things may contribute to the stress. You may be doing the additional work of applying for jobs while finishing your dissertation or supporting yourself (and for some of you, your families) with contract work as an academic or with other work. The job search process is one of uncertainty and waiting. You may experience wide vacillations of hope and disappointment: sometimes you feel

Job Search Timeline Worksheet
Now that you have looked at the sample job timeline above, think about how you need to adapt it to your particular situation. What do you want to add? What can you leave out? What will you tweak? Below you can create your own monthly TO DO list. You can indicate priorities for the month with color coding. Job Search: [year] June July August September October November December January [target job start year] February March April May June July August

Considerations in Applying for Full-Time Academic Job Worksheet

Before you begin:

How are the papers you are writing going to feed into your dissertation work? Are they potentially publishable in respected journals? [More on this in the section, "The importance of publishing early and often."

Have you determined which conferences will be best for you to attend in the two-three years leading up to graduation? [More on this under "Conferences."]

Are you attending job talks in your department to see how others prepare their job talks?

Who are you meeting that might be able to tell you about job postings? [More on this in "Expand your general networking."]

Are you clear about what is expected in your role as a faculty member? If not, make sure you spend some time understanding your prospective role.

How are your teaching skills? Do you have enough experience or training? What do your teaching evaluations say you do well or not so well?

Do you need a professional website? Many universities now require them of faculty, and some recommend them for graduate student. Make sure you know the norm is in your field.

Are you active on social media? Again, what is the expected norm for your field? [More on this in "Using social media."]

Is your committee set up and on board with your topic?

As you near your graduation time and review job postings:

What is the impact on any partner for jobs you would like to get? If applicable, how will you handle being a dual-career academic couple?

What other things do you need to consider before even beginning the application process, like where you will be located, or whether at a research or teaching institution, how being at that particular institution might further future research?

Do you have all your references lined up? Do you know for certain what they will say about you or your work?

Have you prepared your CV, research statement, teaching philosophy and typical cover letter that you can repurpose to any posted position? [More on each of these in separate sections below.]

If you do not succeed in landing an academic position in the first job cycle:

Have you got a realistic back up plan? Will you search for administrative job at a university or another institution? Are you willing to go outside the academic environment for employment while you keep looking?

Should you look for postdoctoral positions?

you have found the perfect position, other times you wonder what you will have to settle for; sometimes you feel sometimes you feel very capable and other times your gremlins just can't seem to stop whispering in your ear about what a loser you are. While you have control over the quality of your application materials, you have little to no control over how they are received. Job listings appear and are suddenly deleted from the realm of possibility. Just when you need to be most calm and confident, for example during an interview visit, you may find yourself quite anxious or seriously distracted. Sometimes you might feel overwhelmed with decisions to make or what priorities to set.

In this section, we want to help you understand that feeling stressed is normal. We offer some information and advice that may help keep you sane and whole as you work toward your ivory tower job. Start by reading through the list that follows and noticing which of the things on it you are doing or not doing. Follow that by reading the subsections on self-care and make time to take action in the areas that need attention. Begin with some basic practices:

- Identify your stressors.
- Look for positive progress every day.
- Celebrate every positive step forward.
- Get clear about what you can control and what you cannot control.
- Identify your gremlins, maybe literally name them, and know they are speakers of false truths.
- Take care of yourself—get enough good sleep, good nutrition, exercise, social time, fun, and relaxation.

Major components of self-care: Sleep, nutrition, and exercise. Many people think of self-care as being what is depicted in the "luxurious hand lotion" commercial on television, but self-care is more comprehensive and deeper than good hand skin health. For job seekers, graduate students, and even faculty, important components of self-care are enough restful sleep, good nutrition, and exercise. Although we are considering these items as separate categories, they are really intertwined.

Generally, we recommend seven to eight hours of sleep a night, but we've qualified that with the term restful. If you toss and turn a lot or if you wake up tired, your sleep is probably not restful. Exercise and nutrition, as well as your personal biorhythms, influence your sleep. Worry (about money, finishing your dissertation, your job search, family issues, etc.) can be a big sleep disrupter. A general recommendation for good sleep is to develop a sleep habit that includes going to bed at about the same time every night, getting up at about the same time every morning after seven to eight hours of sleep, and refraining from strenuous exercise and eating or drinking anything other than water after 8 pm (or two to three hours before bedtime). If you feel tired a lot, talk to your doctor to rule out physical causes for poor sleep. Finally, the investment in a good mattress is well worth it over the roughly 10-15 years you will be using the mattress.

We are using the word nutrition instead of diet to discuss what you eat because we don't believe in adding to your stress by suggesting that you diet. Some of our clients who are faculty members have talked about "eating like a graduate student" several times a year during the grading period, but graduate students don't necessarily have to have poor nutrition. The food you take in feeds your brain and gives you energy to perform the tasks you need to perform. Good nutrition also keeps your organ systems healthy and more able to ward off or recover from disease. General recommendations include going light on refined, white, starchy or sugary foods; eating enough fiber to stay regular; drinking plenty of water; and getting adequate fruit, vegetables, protein, and healthy fat. Books on good nutrition are abundant—check some out if you need more information.

Exercise is a great stress reducer and it makes your brain work better. We've had several clients who have reported taking a 15-minute walk before sitting down to write helps with idea and word flow. Put some time and thought into developing an exercise pattern that you enjoy: your exercise regime might include walking, running, hiking, swimming, working out at a gym, playing group sports, dancing, taking the stairs instead of the elevator, or something else. Build in aerobic exercise as well as exercise for strength and flexibility. Try to exercise every day and vary the type of exercise you do throughout the week. Do some kind of exercise every day, but don't overdo. If you can find time to watch TV or read, then you can find time to exercise. Some people find music playlists or podcasts entertaining and educational and used them to relieve the boredom of repetitive workouts.

Social time and fun. Taking time for interacting with other people or pets can also be an important part of your self-care. Many people have a need for connection and nonjudgmental acceptance, and most of us need physical touch on a regular basis. You may sometimes be able to combine your social time with meals or exercise. If you live alone, you may have to work harder at creating a schedule that includes nurturing social time. Work bonds may not be enough. If you live with other people, you may need to pay more attention to your and their affiliative needs during your job search: "too busy" and "too tired" tend not to lead to satisfaction. As with sleep, nutrition, and exercise, pay attention to what you need and have a plan to meet those needs. We often tell our clients to "take care of yourself first" because that will garner long-term rewards. This is akin to the spiel on the airplane about "first put on your own oxygen mask before you try to help anyone else." You aren't going to be of much help while struggling to breathe.

Fun and time out from work are also important. Both finishing a dissertation and a job search can be long slogs. Prevent or diminish burnout by building a balanced life that includes fun, laughter, and hobbies. Having something to talk about other than your research or your job search will help you maintain your enthusiasm and expanded topics may be a big relief to the other people in your life. This practice of having a life outside of work can help you build a bridge to the next phase of your life. You may notice that the time spent deliberately away from work actually rejuvenates your thought processes and the energy you can bring to bear on writing and filling out applications.

Mindfulness. A few years ago, Mary Beth noticed that when she had a cup of tea in the morning while sitting on her patio and watching the spiders spin, her whole day went better. She was calmer, more rested, and less likely to become irritated. Although for years she had resisted learning to meditate, she later discovered Loving Kindness Meditation as a practice that she could engage in while walking and she noticed that it conferred similar benefits. Hillary, for her part, reads meditative poetry early each morning in order to stay centered before drinking coffee and reading the newspaper. We recommend that you consider meditation, yoga, or some kind of spiritual practice to round out your self-care routine.

Handling inquiries from family and friends. Inquiries from family and friends are the bane of most graduate students and job seekers at any time in life. Once you have finished and defended your dissertation, your family and friends should stop asking you when your dissertation will be done. However, they may switch their worries about your writing life to your job search by asking "Why haven't you found a job yet?" Or they may ask how the job search is going in general, what jobs you have applied for, what you have heard from the places you've applied to, etc. Depending on the person inquiring, you might want to explain the extraordinarily slow hiring process in academia.

Sometimes the concerns and questions are very specific and may be unrealistic, especially coming from people unfamiliar with academic job searches. For example, we had a client who completed a dissertation in a very specialized field. Her fiancé, who lived across the country, only wanted our client to apply for academic jobs in the big city where he lived. Needless to say, this insistence by the fiancé did nothing to lower our client's job hunting stress level. Try these answers on for size: "I only recently finished my studies and just began the job search application process." "I am looking for the position that best fits my qualifications and interests." "I am seeking to mesh my academic career with that of my family (can be exceptionally useful when questioner knows you have an employed spouse)." And if it's true, here is a lovely answer: "I am interviewing/under consideration for a position now." With practice, these responses will become natural and put you and your interlocutor at ease.

Try to stay aware that your family and friends love and care about you. Most of them want to be supportive but may not know how to show their support. To help them share their concern in a positive way, think about some positive things you want from them and ask for those things. For example, you could specify what kinds of communication (texts, email, snail mail cards or letters, phone calls) you would like, and how often you would like to receive them during this time. If you can think of concrete items they can do for you, tell them. Some ideas: they can gift you with flowers or fruit of the month for a year, contribute to travel costs to home or for part of your job search, listen to your tales of job search woe, or anything else. Keeping them focused on what they can do will probably work better than wishing they would bother you less.

When and what you share about your job search and your progress in the search is up to you to decide. This is one area where you *can* exercise some control. Think of some stock phrases you can use in response to repeated inquiries about your job search. Here's an example: "I know you are concerned about what's happening in my career search, but you'll be the first to know when I know something."

Money worries. Money worry is a huge gremlin for most job seekers. And guess what? It's perfectly normal and probably won't go away when you get a job. That's just the nature of this particular beast. Just know that you are not alone in this feeling. Practicing self-care around this worry means making some practical plans for dealing with money. Create a budget if you don't have one. Figure out a payment plan for student loans. Keep a credit card only for emergencies. There are numerous ways to keep that money beast in a cage but taking action to address these concerns is far better than letting it roam around in your brain wreaking havoc. For more on handling money worries, see the section on "Find Work That Pays."

Self-care is a form of "paying yourself first." Take the time to invest in your future by eating right, getting restful sleep, exercising, and giving yourself permission to socialize and take time off from the job search. You'll be glad you did. Taking care of your body and your psyche is a prerequisite for taking of your brain, one of your most important assets as an academic. These practices will lay the groundwork for your continued life as a sane and balanced faculty member, employee, or entrepreneur.

Self-care Worksheets

Sleep

Describe your current sleeping habits:

    How many hours of sleep do you get on the average?

    What time do you go to bed?

    What time do you get up?

    Is your sleep restful and restorative?

    What disturbances, if any, intrude on your sleep?

    What do you want to change to improve your sleep?

    What steps do you need to take to do this?

Nutrition

Describe your daily nutrition. How much of each of the following do you get in an average day:

    Water: glasses or ounces

    Protein: servings

    Fruit: servings

    Vegetables: servings

    Healthy fat:

    Fiber:

    Non-sugar carbs:

    Sugar:

    Caffeine:

Part 1: Job Search Overview

Other (list)

What changes, if any, do you want to make in your daily nutrition?

What steps will you take to make these changes?

Exercise

How much aerobic exercise do you get in a week?

What activities do you use to get aerobic exercise?

What strength or flexibility exercise to you get weekly?

What changes, if any, do you want to make to your exercise regime?

What steps will you take to make these changes?

Social Time

Whom do you like to spend time with and what do you like to do during your social times?

How do you feel about the amount of social time in your daily or weekly life now?

What changes, if any, do you want to make in terms of social time?

What steps will you take to make these changes?

Fun

What do you do for fun?

How do you feel about the amount of fun time in your daily or weekly life now?

What changes, if any, do you want to make in terms of fun?

What steps will you take to make these changes?

Mindfulness or Spiritual Practice

How important is mindfulness or a spiritual practice to you?

What changes, if any, do you want to make in terms of mindfulness or spiritual practice?

What steps will you take to make these changes?

Handling Inquiries from Others about the Job Search

How do you feel about inquiries from others about your job search?

What kinds of communications and how often would work best for you?

What concrete things would you like your family or friends to do to be supportive of you during your job search?

How and when can you best communicate with your family and friends about the job search?

How you would like them to show their support for you during the search?

> List some stock phrases you can use to answer their questions about your job search before you have a contract for a job you want:
>
> 1.
>
> 2.
>
> 3.

Building Confidence

If you need some help building your confidence as you put yourself into your academic job search, take time to work on building confidence in your own abilities. Academia is filled with critiques and rejections. Because you will generally get more rejections than acceptances, the academy is one of the most difficult places to feel confident. You need to realize how much you have already accomplished. Know everyone else interviewing for that coveted position is probably suffering from their own set of insecurities, and you are completely normal.

Finishing a doctorate and preparing to move on is a major transition and can sometimes feel like stalling out intellectually. It is not. Be confident that ideas are percolating under the surface, and you will be able to pursue your ideas when there is not as much energy going toward the job search. As William Bridges so aptly noted in his many published works on transitions,[26] what may seem like unproductive time in academia that saps your confidence may really be the fallow period that allows for the sprouting of ideas after a period of gestation.

Confidence is not the same as self-esteem. True confidence grows from real successes. The best confidence arises from taking on challenges: the things you have done that felt difficult, or almost impossible, to do at the beginning. Confidence is the feeling of flow that emerges as you engage at a deeper level with what you are doing, enabling you to move forward. Self-esteem, on the other hand, is too often built on cheers for attempts, whether or not the activity in question was successful, like trophies for every member of a child's soccer team when the team did not, in fact, win the seasonal competition. We tend to be far more enthusiastic concerning our prospects when we believe we are capable of achieving acts of strength, intelligence, and endurance.

You may have heard of Amy Cuddy's "power postures," as her explanation of them is one of the most downloaded TED talks[27] ever. Though her theory has been subject to some criticism, it is true that your brain will believe what you tell it, whether through what you say to yourself or what you do to embody a belief. Exercising power postures can literally make you feel more balanced, strong, and confident. Many people have had success with practicing these stances privately in the restroom just before an interview. Build your confidence by taking a positive body stance at least once in the coming week, perhaps by simply asking a question rather than petitioning or apologizing for it.

Confidence Worksheet

Write 10 things you have done successfully at any stage in your life.

	Successes I have had	What I did to make it happen
1.		
2.		
3.		
4.		
5.		
6.		
7.		
8.		
9.		
10.		

Consider creating a list of "10 things I have done successfully in my life." It doesn't matter if a success was learning to ride a bike at age 6, riding the bus downtown alone at age 12, winning an essay contest at age 17, or graduating from college at age 22. For most academics, finishing the PhD is a huge success. Once you have finished your list, find a way to short-hand your accomplishments, and keep them with you on a piece of paper in your wallet or put them in the Notes section of your cell phone. Giving yourself a confidence boost by checking your list when writing job applications or interviewing for positions is very useful.

Part 1: Job Search Overview

If you would like to do a meditative visualization on *Creating Confidence*, we have prepared one for you.[28] It's a little over nine minutes long, so give yourself the time and space to enjoy it. If you feel like you need more help with gaining confidence, consider reading the information and doing the exercises in the following section on the imposter syndrome.

Imposter syndrome. What is the *imposter syndrome*? You have probably at least heard the term. Maybe you have even experienced it. High-achieving individuals, successful by all external standards including significant intellectual abilities, don't always credit their successes to their own efforts and achievements, but sometimes feel that their successes are flukes, mere luck, or being in the right place at the right time. They often express these feelings as "I feel like a fraud" and fear the people around them will discover they really don't know as much as they appear to know. If this description feels familiar, you may be experiencing imposter syndrome (IS) or imposter phenomenon (IP).

Some men and many women experience imposter syndrome. The term was coined in 1978 by clinical psychologists Dr. Pauline R. Clance and Suzanne A. Imes as a phenomenon of high-achieving women, though it is no longer limited to women. Clance wrote, "I experienced IP feelings in graduate school. I would take an important examination and be very afraid that I had failed. I remembered all I did not know rather than what I did." She recalls after beginning to teach that a colleague said to her "I feel like an imposter here with all these really bright people," and the seeds were sown for a career examining this issue.[29]

Valerie Young [30] described encountering the Clance and Imes article when another student began reading it aloud. She was four years into a graduate program in education at the University of Massachusetts in Amherst, "and procrastinating terribly on writing my dissertation."[31] As the students and the professor all began to nod in agreement with the article, she was astounded: "To learn that even they felt like they were fooling others rocked my world." She created a workshop with fellow student Lee Anne Bell to overcome imposter syndrome because "you can't share your way out of impostor syndrome." You have to take action and find new positive ways of thinking about yourself. Over 80,000 people have attended this workshop as of 2017. In *The secret thoughts of successful women: Why capable people suffer from the imposter syndrome and how to thrive in spite of it.*

Young has listed "Seven perfectly good reasons why you may feel like an imposter":

1. *You were raised by humans* [too much approval or not enough approval]
2. *You are a student*
3. *You work in an organizational culture that feeds self-doubt*
4. *You work alone*
5. *You work in a creative field:* "The very nature of creative work makes those who do it vulnerable to feeling inadequate, especially if you are not formally trained."
6. *You are a stranger in a strange land* [geography, class, gender, etc.]: "You feel it is an accident that you are where you are."
7. *You feel you represent your entire social group* (e.g., black women, gay men, disabled youth).[32]

Imposter syndrome tends to increase at times of transition (such as during job searching and being junior faculty) but it can persist long beyond those times. For some people, especially women and minorities, the more successful they are, the more likely they are to experience IS.[33] This phenomenon was confirmed in *Nature*'s recent survey of PhD students when nearly one in four respondents listed impostor syndrome as one of the many difficulties they face in graduate school and in seeking employment.[34]

Imposter syndrome is especially prevalent among newly minted PhDs seeking their first full-time jobs, but it is not limited to them. It's normal, in fact, to feel like an imposter, even when you are the expert in the room. I promise you that many of my clients experience imposter syndrome as they defend their dissertations to their committee members worrying, "Pretty soon they will know I am a fraud and don't know nearly as much about this subject as they do." Even the very best teachers, no matter the stage in their career wonder, "How am I going to teach this subject? I don't know nearly enough about it." Many experienced professors feel inadequate when they come across newly published information or new texts in their field they have not yet read and figured out how to incorporate into the course material. Valerie Sheares Ashby, Dean of Duke University's College of Arts and Sciences since 2015, now gives talks on how she overcame her own issues around imposter syndrome.[35] Clearly, this issue can affect you at any point in your academic career.

Overcoming imposter syndrome. And now the good news: You can overcome feeling like an imposter in a variety of ways. Start by looking at your beliefs about yourself that may be distorted. Focus on how you add value, look at your work from a different perspective, and see how you are making a genuine contribution. Here are some suggestions:

Avoid comparing yourself to others. Buying into a negative narrative is truly bad for your mental health. Comparing yourself to others and finding yourself wanting can lead to depression and paralyze you from acting. You are unique. You have different talents, different skills, different understandings. That's fine. You finished your dissertation, and now you are on the academic job market. No one can ever take that PhD away from you. You have already succeeded. You have already proven your abilities. You belong in academia.

Remind yourself that you have had a role in your own successes. Success didn't just happen to you. No one handed you a PhD on a silver platter. You earned it. You took on many challenges and learned a lot of content and new skills as part of finishing your doctorate. Even honorary degrees are given as recognition of some significant accomplishment.

Remember that you are not alone. Everyone else is struggling with feeling like a fraud, too, especially in academia.[36] The academic culture is critical: you are constantly being evaluated for your teaching, research, and administrative abilities, not to mention the reviews or rejections you receive for articles you submit. If you are a woman or in an ethnic minority that has few representatives in your field, that may contribute to the feeling of "I don't belong here." It's not you, it's a structural issue.

Develop a strategy for handling negative feedback. Most of the feedback you receive will be negative since critiques are valued in the academy. You will most likely get mainly negative feedback from students, who consider you a mere employee as they pay for their degrees, and no longer hold professors (let alone graduate assistants) in high esteem. Most undergraduates have no idea how badly a negative review can hurt both personally and professionally, and use end of semester reviews to vent any of their frustrations. Often when people treat you in a negative manner, they are projecting their own insecurities onto you. The challenge for you is to not take on their projections but handle them in a non-defensive way instead. Visualize success.

Flip your narrative around. In *The work*, Byron Katie [37] has suggested that you "describe who you would be without that story." Instead of "I'm a fraud," turn it around with just one word, "not," as in "I am not a fraud." Another turnaround might be, "The smart people around here believe in me. I must be doing something right." Or, "I am smart enough to figure out the solution, even if I do not know the answer now." This might help you separate your feelings from fact. There is real evidence that you know what you are doing.

Focus on adding value. What would you do if you were not afraid? Organize a panel at a conference. Submit an unfinished article to a trusted friend to ask if it makes sense? Find a partner to design a new experiment? Design a new experiment yourself? Think about how you can find a way to explore the issues that interest you. Write down your research questions. Look for allies, people who can support you in adding value through your work. Add value by mentoring someone who is not as far along in the process as you, whether an undergraduate or a peer struggling to finish the dissertation. What comes easily to you may not be as easy for someone else. You may just discover you know more than you thought you did. You have valuable experience to offer.

Recognize that periods of great productivity and periods of less productivity are a normal part of the creative cycle. Don't let that cycle stress you out. Your peers probably experience something similar. One professor who writes political analyses told me, "I think of myself as a puma. Much of the time I am at rest. Then something tasty comes along, and I pounce." For her, the metaphor is one of how long it takes to think something through before writing it down and letting it out into the world. You are entitled to rest between periods of high productivity. In fact, you are doing your brain a favor by letting it relax a bit. It's a three-pound muscle after all, and you will fatigue it if you never give it any breaks. Letting your mind wander may actually result in new ideas or insights.

Treat experience as an experiment. It's OK to be wrong. In the history of science, 99% of all experiments fail, before a researcher finds one answer that works. In the apocryphal version of an experiment story, when Thomas Edison's Menlo Park lab manager came to him to say, "We've tried a thousand times to make an incandescent light bulb [for commercial production] and it's just not possible," Edison supposedly told his lab manager to get back to work, because he was still looking for the one way that *would* work. Failure is far more common than success. That's exactly how we learn and produce new knowledge.

Keep a sense of humor. PhD Comics is a good place to start.[38] Another thing to try is taking your catastrophizing to its logical conclusion—consider where you want to live when you are a bag lady or a man sleeping on a grate. Or try SAS,[39] Academia Obscura,[40] or Lego Academics [41] (complete with photos) on Twitter for some fun.

29

Imposter Syndrome Worksheet

How do you relate to Jodi Foster's comments below?

> For Jodi Foster [feeling like an imposter] first happened when she put her acting career on hold to pursue an undergraduate degree and then again after she won the best actress Oscar for *The Accused*. "I thought it was a fluke," Foster explained in a *60 Minutes* interview. "The same way when I walked on the campus at Yale. I thought everybody would find out, and they'd take the Oscar back. They'd come to my house, knocking on the door. 'Excuse me, we meant to give that to someone else. That was going to Meryl Streep.' "(Young, 2011, p. 22).[42]

On a scale of 1-5, how closely does this story describe you? Why?

Referring back to Valerie Young's list below of *7 perfectly good reasons why you may feel like an imposter,* which do you feel most applies to you and why?

1. You were raised by humans
2. You are a student
3. You work in an organizational culture that feeds self-doubt
4. You work alone
5. You work in a creative field
6. You are a stranger in a strange land
7. You feel you represent your entire social group

    Why?

Which of the coping and protecting mechanisms listed below resonate with you most? In what way?

- Over-preparing and hard work
- Holding back (never letting go of a project)
- Maintaining a low or ever-changing profile
- Using charm or perceptiveness to win approval
- Procrastination
- Never finishing
- Self-sabotage
- Perfectionism

Related to the list above, what does your behavior help you avoid?

Related to the list above, what does your behavior protect you from?

Part 1: Job Search Overview

Related to the list above, what does your behavior help you get?

What is the price you pay? Include emotional, physical, psychological reactions.

Identify a situation in which you were fabulously adequate in the past week.

When have you done something difficult, and survived?

What wise choices have you made?

Where have you created value (past, present, future)?

Write down your most ludicrous beliefs about yourself. Now put them in perspective. Are any of them real, or just a story you are telling yourself? Whom would you be *without* that story?

Write down 10 good things people have said about you:
1.
2.
3.
4.
5.
6.
7.
8.
9.
10.

Name your fears. Naming fears can make them less scary. What exactly are your fears regarding this job search? That you won't interview well? That you will come across as arrogant when you want to merely project confidence? That you have not published enough in the right places? That you won't ever get offered a job? That you will get offered a job, but in a location where you or your partner do not want to be? That you will never earn enough money to be comfortable? Or pay off those student loans? It's also possible that you have the classic fear of success: What if I get the tenure-track job of my dreams, and I can't cut it?

All of these fears can be concretely dealt with by talking to someone about them (exposing fears to sunlight can shrink them), practicing interview techniques, thinking clearly before you apply whether the location is going to make the whole application process worthwhile or not, and being realistic about the money you need to earn to both live and pay off loans.

If what you have read here about IS/IP feels familiar to you, you might try answering the questions in the **Imposter Syndrome worksheet**. We have also created a meditative visualization on *Overcoming the Imposter Syndrome*. [43] It's almost 12 minutes long, so allow yourself the time to enjoy it.

You may also want to return to the **Confidence Worksheet** to list at least 10 accomplishments are you proud of, and the role you played in achieving success.

One last note about confidence and the imposter syndrome. Some people truly feel uncomfortable with the entire notion of projecting confidence they do not feel. If this is true for you, practice some compassion for yourself. We all have to deal with the inner critic, but remember that the role of the inner critic is to keep you safe and ensure your survival in the world. Recognizing that you are human, that you are imperfect, and that you will make mistakes, then remind yourself to be kind to yourself when you make a mistake to help you keep things in perspective. [44] You really don't have to beat yourself up, and you will be better off if you don't.

Researchers [45] have suggested that people who are compassionate with themselves view missteps more objectively and are more likely to take constructive action than people who lack self-compassion. When you are being kind to yourself, you are accepting of any shortcomings you feel you have. Self-compassion keeps you from exaggerating either your weaknesses or your strengths or from hiding self-doubt behind an artificial presentation of yourself. In other words, you get some of the benefits of being confident without being delusional about what you can do. As Kristin Wong wrote, "Pulling your shoulders back is easy. Learning to be kind to yourself takes considerably more effort."[46] Let go of the negative self-talk and find a more supportive and gentle voice in your head moving forward.

PART 2: STAYING ON TOP OF YOUR ACADEMIC JOB SEARCH

Your job search includes a lot of moving parts. You may have to begin by deciding whether staying in academia is for you. If you want some of the reasons people choose not to pursue an academic career, refer to **Part 6: Additional Considerations**, for some depressing but realistic statistics on how many people will be able to achieve the dream of a tenure-track job.

Once you have realistically assessed the odds, and decided you still want to pursue a full-time tenure-track position, you first need to figure out where you are going to look for those jobs. Next, you will need to think about how you will use social media, both to look for work and to present yourself and your skills to potential employers. You will need to expand your networks, find a way to quickly summarize your research, and tell a little bit about yourself. You will need to make decisions about attending conferences to promote yourself on your job search, not to mention working on publishing before you graduate. Once you actually start applying for jobs, you will need to find a way to track applications that work for you.

These are all things to consider *before* making sure you have a flawless and complete academic portfolio prepared. (See **Part 3: Your Academic Job Portfolio** for a full discussion of the various portfolio elements.)

Beginning the Process of Looking for Work

Looking for academic jobs can be a little daunting. No one we know enjoys going on the job market. The search is even more fraught for those hoping to enter the somewhat rarefied atmosphere of teaching in higher education. You've already put a large amount of resources, energy, and time into obtaining a graduate degree. As you are finishing your degree, you have to ramp up by adding the job search to the mix of tasks to do. Making sure that you have a plan for where to look and how to keep track of what you have found as well as what action you have taken can help lessen the anxiety and stress of the process.

The first step is thinking about where you might actually find academic job postings. You will probably need to explore professional sources, both in print and online. Also, never underestimate the power of actually asking people in your field if they know of any openings or where a position might be opening soon. You may just get a heads up to look for an upcoming announcement.

Finally, for questions you feel are best answered by your peers who may have the same or similar concerns, whether related to salary, publication submissions, networking, teaching, or anything else, consider joining the Academia Stack Exchange,[47] a question and answer site for academics.

Professional Print Sources and Online Professional Sources

Start your job search with the obvious, by going to the journals, newspapers, and websites specializing in higher education. All of the sources listed below have postings that change regularly. Check in periodically to see new job postings. Make sure you also look at any sites related to your own field. The **Application Tracking for Job Sources Worksheet** provided after the list of sources is designed to help you with a first pass at figuring out what type of positions, and their deadlines, you want to apply for in academia.

Basic sources. Following is a list of some of the basic sources for job postings in higher education in alphabetical order with a bit of information about each one.

The Chronicle of Higher Education [48]

A paid subscription site, with varying prices for students, faculty, and institutions. Online, *The Chronicle* is published every weekday. The print version comes out once per week. With approximately 51,000 subscribers and audited website traffic approximating 12.8 million pages a month, the Chronicle is widely read by people in higher education for news, advice, and thousands of current job listings. Clicking on the main page header "Jobs" will take you to the *ChronicleVitae*[49] page, where you can create a profile and access booklets, webinars, and set up job alerts for yourself. At *ChronicleVitae* after you have set up a profile, you can search jobs by keywords, position type location, or date posted. Each year *ChronicleVitae* issues the *Academic Year Kickoff* in early September with a cut-off date for those advertising new faculty jobs in late August and claims 92% of job seekers use it to seek faculty, administrative, and executive openings.[50] The section labeled "Jobs Outside Academe" are actually listings for non-research or non-teaching jobs, such as "data scientist" or "Vice President of Alumni Membership," jobs still tightly linked to academia. In addition, there is also a list of available reports on "Careers in Academe."

Higher Education Recruitment Consortium [51]

The Higher Education Recruitment Consortium (HERC) is a non-profit organization that uses fees from member institutions to support the website and job postings. Members of HERC comprise over 700 colleges, universities, hospitals, research labs, government agencies, and related non- and for-profit organizations. You will have to create an account and fill out a brief survey that helps the organization understand the demographics of those using the site. Once this is done, you can set up job alerts to your own specifications.

Inside Higher Ed [52]

A five-day per week online newsletter with news, opinion, and jobs for all of higher education. Subscriptions are free, and there is an extensive jobs section listing openings in order of most recently posted, with an interactive search capability for teaching or administrative work in the United States.

National Center for Faculty Development and Diversity [53]

You have to join this organization and pay annual dues. An individual membership is $240 for graduate students and post-docs. There is a "members only" section where you can:
- Search job openings;
- Subscribe to new posting notifications based in your field
- Access some Powerpoint presentations designed to decipher the academic job market.

Hirers can:
- Search potential candidates by résumé or CV, so post your CV there for hirers.
- Post a job opening, so you should scan for newly advertised positions.

There is also an excellent resources page [54] covering academic writing, teaching, diversity, time management, negotiation, and a few miscellaneous items. To access this page, you must be a member.

Times Higher Education[55]

The *Times Higher Education* abbreviated as "THE" was formerly *The Times Higher Education Supplement*, once a division of *The Times* newspaper in London. It is a weekly magazine specializing in reporting news and issues related to higher education. It is best known for its annual "World University Rankings" published since 2004. It includes a section on Jobs [56] that can be searched using keywords, or location by continent, or by academic discipline. The section on "professional services" runs the gamut from department heads to administrative assistants to departments. You can set up email alerts for new postings, and there is no fee to search the database.

Journals in your field. Many departments advertise for new hires in journals specific to their fields, rather than in the larger journals, as a way to reduce the flood of unqualified applicants. Therefore, you should be checking journals in your own field. For instance, the Modern Language Association (MLA) has a Job Information List [57] where hiring organizations can submit job postings, get information on all ads posted for the past several years, and find information on sites where there might be positions for MLA members with business, government, or non-profits. Member and non-members can search the database of job listings.

The American Anthropological Association [58] (AAA) has a section on its site simply called "Jobs" with listings. The *American Anthropologist,* a journal put out by the AAA, puts job advertisements online within 24 hours of receiving them, and for an additional fee, employers can also have them listed again in the print edition. Users do not have to be members of AAA to search the postings, and you can also create a profile for job alerts. The American Association for the Advancement of Science (AAAS) has a Careers section on its website with hundreds of job listings for a variety of job types both online and in print. Know the best place to look in your specialty area.

Honor societies. If you belong to an honor society, networking through that organization can be useful, as officers are frequently people with doctoral level education in their fields. They may know in advance of announced openings. In addition, some honor societies have job sites of their own where, surprisingly, you may find advertisements for academic tenure-track employment. For instance, in January 2016, Phi Kappa Phi [59] had advertisements for two tenure-track positions.

Some social media sites like Vitae [60] or Higher Education Professionals [61] are dedicated specifically to helping people find jobs in higher education. Though most of these jobs are posted in the areas we discussed above, these are other places to search for openings, particularly for higher education administrators. More information is provided in the section on sites related to academic job searches.

Additional places to look. Some additional sites for job hunting include AcademicJobs.Wikia.com [62] and HR job announcement lists from individual institutions, especially if you are targeting work at a specific institution. The wiki page provides yet another list of places you can search for work using various web portals such as Academic Careers Online.[63] This wiki lists Research Calls [64] as a job resource, but actually, it is more oriented toward finding publishers and funding.

You might also consider looking at some less-used job sources, such as *The Economist* or *The Guardian*. *The Economist* magazine has some advertisements for academic jobs, particularly higher education administration jobs, all over the world. Each periodically advertises academic positions, both administrative and professorial. Granted many of these positions may require you to leave the United States, but would you rather have a full-time teaching position overseas[65] with benefits or a part-time teaching gig as an adjunct in the US? There are a wide variety of places where jobs you may want can be advertised.

Considerations for an overseas position. Since we are on the topic of looking for employment outside the United States, here are some reasons to consider an overseas position:
- Given the paucity of higher education jobs available for recently minted PhDs, or even for those already holding post-doctoral positions, broadening the area where you are willing to work can open some new possibilities. Search committees in far-flung places do not receive a large number of US-trained applicants and may be very happy to give you an offer.
- Some countries are actively seeking to create high-quality university systems (Kazakhstan, Hong Kong, Vietnam) and would like to hire Western-trained PhDs.
- You may actually have fewer courses to teach and more time to write.
- Financial considerations may play a part. Depending on the cost of living where you go to teach, such as Asia, Latin America or the Middle East, even a modest salary could be worth more than a higher paying position in the United States. Student loan payments can be potentially lowered if you have an "income-driven repayment plan," especially if under your out-of-country salary your calculated repayment would not cover the interest on the loan. However, you must know the terms of your borrowing agreement first!
- Tax provisions may be lower, and there are US rules to lower the impact of "double taxation" in your first year abroad under the Foreign Earned Income Exclusion.[66]
- Family considerations may play a part in deciding to work overseas, but plenty of partners and children have agreed to go because of the learning opportunity being in a foreign country affords. It can be a chance to learn a new language, help children become bilingual, and experience a different culture. Concerning family, safety concerns also need to be addressed but consider that there are places in the US where crime and violence are high before dismissing another country out-of-hand.
- Instead of working at looking for an academic job, you could actually be working in an academic job. Instead of spending all your energy on searching and filling out applications, you might even have the energy to write the next article or two.

- You may find colleagues you never considered working with before, as you mingle with people in a different locale with a different agenda from your own. You may find your research ideas rejuvenated when examining them from a new perspective, or you may find new places to publish what was not on your radar before.

The Chronicle of Higher Education offers a PDF collection of articles on this topic titled "Teaching Abroad" [67] available for download.

For all these reasons, and more, if you are determined to stay on an academic career trajectory, consider widening the scope of your search beyond your own borders. Please note, in Europe, Australia, and the Middle East, universities are far more likely to hire their own graduates than universities in the US. For a more detailed tracking form that will help you monitor the entire application process, see the **Job Search Log for Academic Positions** worksheet in the **Organizing Your Job Search** section.

Headhunters and Recruiting Firms in Higher Education

One question we are often asked is "Should I contact a recruiter to find a position in higher education?" In general, the answer is "no." However, if you happen to be at a high-level administrative position, such as Provost, Academic Dean, or President, then the answer may be "yes." Recruiters are more likely involved in these high-level searches. Since we get asked this question so often, we have also provided a list of recruiters and their sites for you to explore.

Headhunters generally are quite secretive about candidates selected and the status of a search, and this holds true for higher education, too. Often potential candidates will not join an open search process, fearing it could alienate them in their current jobs. The flip side of this argument is that faculty at the hiring institution who may be affected by the choice of a particular high-level administrator are often shut out of the selection process. In general, the hiring institution sets the parameters of their desired candidate and the search firm works to fill it based on that profile. Universities that have worked with search firms believe that it professionalizes the process, and keeps the high profile job from being offered to someone through the "old boy network."

Recruiting firms also troll online in places like LinkedIn to see if they can discover people who may not actively be seeking alternative employment, but would not turn down the opportunity to investigate a new position. This increases the potential employment pool. Over one million US recruiting/HR professionals are on LinkedIn, accounting for 1 out of every 20 US LinkedIn profiles,[68] or a total of 5% of all LinkedIn users. If you want to connect with recruiters, The Undercover Recruiter with over 45,000 members allows job seekers to join and ask any questions about careers and recruiting.[69]

E-Recruitment, administered by a small staff, is a network of "senior" recruiters with nearly 200,000 members worldwide. Recruiters actually post their job listings on the job board in this group.[70] This board is mainly of use to those in higher education seeking to obtain higher level leadership positions such as Provost, President, or Academic Dean. It is not nearly so useful for those trying to get a job as a professor, as it is difficult to find a recruiter willing to work with new

PhDs. If you have decided to contact a recruiter, we suggest you put at least two academic positions on your profile to help show you do have some pertinent academic experience.

In 2016, LinkedIn finally helped job seekers connect with recruiters creating "Open Candidates" to make "it easier to connect with your dream job by privately signaling to recruiters that you're open to new job opportunities."[71] Because this is a private function, it's hard to know if any academic job seekers have found it of use.

If you are considering contacting a recruiter for yourself be aware of a few pitfalls:

1. The response time is frequently lengthy because recruiters may be looking to fill up to 20 different positions at any one time.
2. Young recruiters may be more common than older experienced ones because they are cheaper. 3) Recruiters may be less aware of the actual issues facing higher education generally, and higher education candidates in particular.
3. The actual customer is the hiring entity and not the position seeker.
4. Payment (for the recruiter) is usually a percentage of the person's salary of the first year, so money rather than talent may dictate who a recruiter pushes. This probably will mean that you will end up having to pay the recruiter for finding you a job.

To see a full description of various firms and what they specialize in, go to Higher Ed Jobs [72] where about 75 firms are currently listed. You will notice that most of them specialize in recruiting for "executive searches" or "senior scholars." This information may not be particularly helpful if you happen to be just starting out in your career as an academic often referred to as "an early career academic." In addition to those listed on the *Inside Higher Ed* site above, here are a few more:

The Babb Group [73]
This is a group more oriented to online educational platforms and to help adjuncts find a way to create a more stable living, than to helping someone find a permanent on-site tenure-track position. You can submit a package to them to send out to other institutions, or get help with your CV, or subscribe to their in-house network, ExclusiveEDU.

Diverse Jobs [74]
The description from their website: "Listings include both faculty jobs and college administrator jobs. Job seekers will soon be able to take advantage of new tools and resources for preparing resumes and academic portfolios."

The Hudson Group [75]
The description from their website: "…works with a network of Venture Capital/Private Equity Groups, publicly-traded education corporations, traditional higher education universities and colleges with an interest in top talent to manage their educational interests."

Isaacson, Miller [76] has a broad mandate to recruit "transformative leaders for education, healthcare, philanthropy, advocacy, and other endeavors that advance the public good." They have an excellent reputation, but again, are for high-level administrative positions, not necessarily for early career academics.

Opus Partners [77]
The description from their website: "we serve client organizations that are in the vanguard of education, patient care, research, and culture." Primarily for higher level administrators.

Parker Executive Search [78]
The description from their website: "Conducted more than 500 successful higher education searches for chancellor, president, vice president, provost, dean, chair and director positions."

Russell Reynolds [79]
From their website on the higher education practice: "Recruitment and assessment of transformational senior academic and non-academic administrators." Works primarily in the United States and Great Britain.

Shefrin & Associates [80]
The description from their website: "…a high-level recruiting, career college brokerage services and consulting exclusively tailored for the private career school sector."

Vector Careers [81]
The description from their website: "[we] focus strictly on companies that service the educational industry."

Witt/Keifer [82]
The description from their website: "Education recruiting includes presidents, provosts, deans, and officers for business and finance, advancement and development, student affairs, enrollment, IT, and more."

Academics 360 [83]
Last, we mention a site that does not belong to a particular search firm. Academia 360 provides mostly the same recruiter list as that on *Inside Higher Ed* website discussed above in the section on "Where to look for jobs." The description from their website: "Academic360 is a meta-collection of internet resources that have been gathered for the academic job hunter. It includes links to roughly 3,000 faculty, staff, and administrative announcements so is not restricted to teaching positions."

Using Social Media

Many new PhDs are active on social media, and some have been able to network there enough to at least be considered for a position, or find it a way to keep apprised in their own groups of job that may be opening up. As you read through the information provided on specific social media sites, keep in mind that recruiting is a two-way street: recruiters and hiring entities can and do use social media to look for potential candidates, and you can use social media sites to connect back to them.

Source	Date Advertised/Deadline	Job Posting Information (e.g., number)
Application Tracking for Job Sources Worksheet		
Use this worksheet to help you get started in looking at the various sources for academic job listings. It may help you narrow down the places where you want to continue to look. For a more detailed tracking form that will help you monitor the entire application process, see the "Job Search Log for Academic Positions" worksheet.		
Professional print sources and online professional sources		
Inside Higher Ed		
The Chronicle of Higher Education		
Journals in your own field		
Headhunters and recruiting firms in higher education		
Social media		
Facebook		
LinkedIn		
Twitter		
Specialized social media sites		
Additional places to look		
Professional social media sites/web pages for your specialty area		
Human Resources offices at colleges and universities		
Newspapers/magazines (e.g., *The Economist*)		

Colleges and universities are using social media, especially social networking sites, not only to recruit but to research prospective students and professors. So, you should, too, as long as you are careful about posting. Many academics use all manner of social media to shed light on thorny issues, world events, and their own research interests. However, since potential employers do view social media sites when considering a job candidate for a position, you must be circumspect in what you do and what you post. For instance, posting photos of yourself partying while scantily clad is not advisable. Even if you think the post is private, it may not be, as there are many work-arounds to record information even from sites purporting to destroy information immediately.

Part 2: Staying on Top of Your Academic Job Search

As far as hiring goes, a May 2017 blog entry reported that for self-reporting corporate recruiters, 92% have used LinkedIn, 24% have used Facebook, and 14% have used Twitter to find candidates.[84] In terms of the audience you are reaching, an article in *USA Today* reported that a 2016 Pew Research Center study found the majority of adults using the internet (nearly 80%) were on Facebook, 32% percent use Instagram, 31% use Pinterest, 29% use LinkedIn and 24% use Twitter.[85] That's a lot of potential exposure to other adults, some of whom may be helpful in your job search.

In terms of use by administrators in higher education, social media adoption among four-year accredited institutions in the United States continues to grow, as reported in a study by University of Massachusetts. Here a few of the key highlights from the most recently available data, 2012-2013:[86]

- Over half of college presidents studied are posting on Facebook (58%) and tweeting (55%), while 35% host their own blogs.
- Schools show an interest in new tools including Pinterest (31% adoption), Google+ (25% adoption) and Instagram (16% adoption).
- Over two-thirds of US colleges and universities have some official school blogging activity on their campus.

Another article reported that 41% of faculty now use social media as a teaching tool,[87] though the biggest use remains requiring students to view a particular video and comment on it. Facebook, Twitter, and LinkedIn remain the biggest social media sites for academics.

Issues that may arise when using social media. Before discussing *why* you may want to engage an audience on social media, we offer some caveats. This form of communication can be a major time sink, and it can also be addictive.[88] While no formal psychiatric definition for a general "social media addiction" exists, Eliene Augenbraun reported that the National Institutes of Health did add a 2012 study to its website stating "Internet Addiction Disorder (IAD) ruins lives by causing neurological complications, psychological disturbances, and social problems."[89] If you Google "blocking social media," you will immediately find at least 10 different apps for mobile and desktop computers, compatible with Windows, Mac, and Android depending on what you need. Some like Cold Turkey, Focus Lock, and Flipd are free, while others range in purchase price from $7.00-$30.00 and may offer year-long subscriptions.

Another issue with social media is that you might not be hired or you could later be fired for opinions you expressed on social media. Comments reflecting your own political opinion, if not expressed carefully, can be picked up by media outlets and taken entirely out of context. If you have just been hired as an adjunct professor, you are far more likely to be let go than if you are a tenure-track faculty member with some academic freedom protections.

A 2016 Faculty Tech Survey by *Inside Higher Ed* noted that 35% of 1,671 respondents strongly agreed with the statement "Recent attacks on scholars for views expressed on social media have led me to change the way I communicate on social media" while only 13% strongly agreed with the statement "Social media is a good way for professors to communicate with the broader public." [90]

For another excellent article on this topic, see Tressie Cottom's blog post, "Academic outrage: When the culture wars go digital." [91]

Even if you have had a long tenure in the same position, social media can still sabotage your career: Lecturer Lars Maischek, employed by California State University since 2006, was told he would not be returning in the fall of 2017 after he posted a controversial political opinion.[92] There have been incidents of faculty expressing opinions that were widely circulated and denounced; there have been cases of mistaken identity that caused harm to the wrong person; there have even been incidents where faculty have been disciplined for a social media response by someone they supervised.[93] Social media can become a world of instant fame and instant censure, and some of the policing communities can be quite harsh. Sadly, getting support from your employing institution may be unlikely when a firestorm occurs.[94]

Remind yourself: Social media are tools, not ends to themselves. Your best use of social media is for creating positive exposure to your work and ideas and to make connections (aka networking). For aspiring academics, knowing that colleges and universities will seek to protect their reputations on social media is important. Follow the advice that career counselors give all applicants in any sector of the economy: never speak badly of a former employer no matter how awful the experience may have been for you personally. Any possible employer may reconsider hiring you if they suspect you may someday speak badly about them on social media, or for that matter in an interview with someone else.

Building a social media presence. Here's one piece of advice that comes from industry marketing gurus and is generally given to new start-ups as they try to build their brand that may also be useful to you as a job seeker: Pick one social media platform as yours and ignore the rest of them. As sociologist Cottom wrote, "Social media platforms are designed to facilitate certain kinds of behaviors. Twitter amplifies. Facebook brands. Tumblr remixes. Instagram illustrates."[95] So, figure out where you fit. If you like Facebook, use it; if you prefer Twitter, use that. But don't waste your precious time trying to build a presence for every existing social media platform.

Be aware that the constant interruptions that staying current on social media may involve can seriously impede your academic productivity. Our advice to users of social media is to treat them like wading across a stream. See what's going on as you step into the water, wade across, then quickly get out of the water. If you know there are certain people or institutions you want to follow, check on them semi-regularly, but don't obsess.

Do not lie or exaggerate your accomplishments on social media. In a January 2016 *Inside Higher Ed* article, Colleen Flaherty wrote:

> Academic bios -- such as those for department or personal websites, conference proposals and social media -- are supposed to simultaneously explain scholars' work and "sell" their potential. While they aim to make one seem intellectually desirable and hirable, authenticity isn't usually a priority.[96]

Be cognizant that your discerning readers will take everything you say there with a grain of salt. Flaherty's essay went on to describe what real academic bios could look like using #realacademicbios. Some tweets by academics about what their lives really look like run the gamut from funny to sad. Amusing bios include: "She remains single and thus has no one to thank for running a household while writing this book" @Rebecca_Raphael or "Award-winning teacher on precarious 4-month contracts and 1/3 the salary of his 'research intensive' tenured counterparts"@AndrewR_Physics., take a look at the hashtag_#realacademicbios. The irreverence may inspire you to use Twitter to further engage with potential colleagues.

For individual academics looking for work, the best use of social media is to create their own web pages with basic information about who they are and what they are doing and then to blog about their own work. Blogging, designed to be interactive with most posts providing for a comment area, can require a great deal of monitoring, or response time. Unlike traditional academic publishing, the author is expected to engage with the reader quickly and to trade information or opinions. We caution you to be thoroughly aware of the potentially large amount of time blogging or creating podcasts for your basic website can require. Also, unlike traditional academic publishing, blogs don't have the prestige factor of peer-reviewed articles.

In Social Media for Academics,[97] Mark Carrigan, a sociologist and academic technologist from the University of Warwick, England, wrote that because social media platforms are ever-evolving, his cannot be the last word on the subject. His book is meant to help academics publicize their work, build networks, and manage information, all without falling into the "time sinkhole." Carrigan also coined the term "glass tower" to replace the "ivory tower" because he believes academia is now more visible to those outside it, and those inside more vulnerable to rock throwing, with all the attendant problems that suggests.

Carrigan also feels academics are more likely to experience problems of "context collapse," meaning the problem of interpretation by the outside world when social media as used by academics is taken out of context. As mentioned earlier, posting can actually destroy an academic career (even if the academic is not fired outright) with the speed and ferocity of a lightning strike when some comment that seemed relatively tame to the author goes viral. Carrigan suggests one strategy for limiting damage with regard to one's current institution is to include a disclaimer in the social media profile, no matter the platform, that "all views expressed here are my own."

Tracking your social media presence. Before we get into a discussion of several of the most widely used social media platforms, you might want to know about Altmetric.[98] Begun in 2012, the Altmetic "bookmarklet" uses badges to help individual researchers, institutions, and academic librarians see how often any piece of published research with a doi (digital object identifier) has been mentioned in a wide variety of channels. The "donut badges" at Altmetric are color coded for ease of reference. The overall number of mentions, such as 499, is provided within a colorful "donut" hole. This number is then divided into mentions on news platforms (red), blogs (yellow), tweets (turquoise), Facebook posts (blue), Google (gray), or a "research highlight platform," which could be an actual academic journal, (several different colors).

You can literally see how many tweeted about you (302) or mentioned what you wrote in blogs (15) or whether there was even one mention in a peer review site or journal article. The summary tab will also provide some information about user demographics and how much attention this research has gotten in comparison to other data released at about the same time. Altmetric is trying to find a new way to determine the impact or level of discussion for new research in an age of social media, beyond just collecting citations in a peer-reviewed journal. However, critics believe that sheer numbers do nothing to show whether or not a paper is important or has influence, especially if the majority of "shares" or "mentions" come from a single source.[99] In other words, the data produced by Altmetric may be just a different form of "echo chamber."

Social media platforms. You may be familiar with many of the social media platforms currently in use. Below we discuss some a few of them, and issues we have seen facing academics in regard to particular platforms.

Facebook: In our experience, individual academics are much more likely to use *Facebook* to share information with both their students and fellow researchers, but NOT to post the news that they are looking for a job. With over 2.13 billion active monthly users, and 1.37 daily active users as of 4th quarter 2017, Facebook is the most common form of social networking being used anywhere on the planet.[100] Ninety-eight percent of colleges and universities reported having a Facebook page (up from 87% in 2011). Compare this to all Google platforms combined (search engine, Android phone, and YouTube viewers), currently at 1.5 billion users.

Maintaining a Facebook page remains the 6th most common way that colleges and universities market themselves. Eighty percent of college admissions officers have received a friend request on Facebook, and Facebook pages are one of the most common ways admissions officers get information about potential students.[101] Given these statistics, you can bet university hiring authorities are looking at Facebook (and LinkedIn) when considering new employees. One issue of concern is how many "users" are actually businesses promoting a brand or accounts set up by people for their pets or other endeavors, like taking a gnome around the world and snapping photos in various locations. Facebook itself says there are approximately 83 million fake profiles.

Another issue of concern to academics with a Facebook page is whether you really want to use the site to publicize your work. Facebook has a license to use your work as soon as you agree to the Terms of Service in order to use the service. It does *not* have the copyright or own images you've posted. You can work via email to resolve an issue but it appears many Facebook employees believe any posted content is owned by Facebook, so deleting information when you believe copyright infringement may have taken place may be difficult. As noted by blogger Jonathan Bailey in *Plagiarism Today,* "If a creator submits a copyright notice to Facebook and Facebook declines to remove it, there isn't much further that most can do. The work, more or less, just stays online." Unless you have the money to sue Facebook, you don't have much recourse.[102]

Instagram: This is a free photo and video sharing application. It was acquired by Facebook in 2012 and is another way to create a social network for yourself. You instantly share information either publicly (the default setting) or privately and attach (mostly) picture types of files to other networks, including Facebook, Twitter, Tumbler, and Flickr. Instagram may be a way for you to connect with like-minded others who may be able to help you with your academic job search. It's not a place to look for advertisements for jobs; it's more of a tangential resource. Unlike Snapchat, which is designed to delete information immediately, Instagram allows you to choose a filter to save your photos or videos. With Instagram Stories, you can create up to a 60-minute video, which may be a way to publicize a project you are working on to a different audience. As of 2017, 500 million users were accessing the site per month.

LinkedIn: LinkedIn calls itself the biggest "professional network" in the world. It is a place where you can post your entire resume online and create a profile of yourself with the code phrase "looking for new opportunities" for "would like to have a new job." As of fourth quarter 2018, LinkedIn had 500 million members in 200 countries and territories.[103] If you are finishing a doctorate, you can upload your CV in its entirety. You also have the option of unloading projects, slide shares, or articles as part of your profile as well.

Make sure your LinkedIn profile is impeccable and up-to-date because connections will want to check you out. A headshot that looks professional is important, though you can do it yourself by having a friend take the photo, as long as you are dressed appropriately and there is nothing in the background, or you will immediately be pegged as an amateur. It's OK to connect with anyone who requests it. LinkedIn's advice to "connect with only people you know," is not especially useful when you are a job seeker. You can easily block someone if the connection turns out to be problematic, but you do not want to limit people looking at what you offer to only people who already know you. Strive for 500+ connections, because once you reach that number, LinkedIn no longer displays your number of connections.

In the academic world, the group that benefits most by using LinkedIn is administrators, particularly in the highest levels of administration such as President and Provost offices. If you are seeking a job at this level, be careful to keep your LinkedIn conversations private.

If you are still seeking your first academic job, you can make additional personal connections by joining LinkedIn groups. You are allowed to belong to 50 groups at a time. If you joined groups that are not working for you, leave the groups and find others: join as many as you think might be useful, follow the discussions for a while, then weed out the ones you haven't found of use. The best way to get known in groups is to respectfully share your expertise in a discussion—and remember, whatever you say will be out there forever for anyone to call up.

If you choose to use LinkedIn to look for academic work, here are a few tips:

- Search the site for people like yourself and see what your potential competition has created as a profile; this can be particularly useful when creating a resume or posting a CV to your LinkedIn site.
- If you don't know an individual and want to know them, in your request for connection message show things you have in common: same alma mater, similar subject area or even now living in the same geographical area. If you don't know them well, or at all, err on the side of addressing them formally, as "Dr. Smith" or "Rev. Jones." If you want to connect with someone in another country that is not a problem since LinkedIn is a huge network used by people worldwide.[104]
- Use the site to research institutions you are interested in joining. My alma mater, for instance, has an institutional web page as well as department web pages and pages for individual professors.
- Use the site for networking and look for a group where you can "link up" because someone you know, want to know, or know of, is participating. You can use generic search terms to find institutions of interest, like "art history" or simply "historian."

- Use the message function to get in touch with some people. There are two levels for messaging, one free and one paid—you can guess which one gives you more access.
- Check to see if, and who, is checking out your own profile. What you can see about "viewers" will depend on whether you have Basic (free) or Premium (subscription) service. Premium service is not generally necessary, but that is the only way you can currently see who is viewing your profile. LinkedIn tries to get you to upgrade by saying "35 people have looked at your profile this week," but you will have to pay to see them.

LinkedIn is a place to list particular elements of expertise as well as a place to post presentations or published papers. You can ask people to write very short (1 paragraph) recommendations about you and you can have your links endorse you for particular skills. Fewer and fewer people are doing the written recommendations as it is time-consuming for recommenders, so don't worry about getting a lot of those.

Snapchat: This was designed to be an ephemeral image service originally released in 2011, where images would disappear after a short period of time. As of 2017, there were an estimated 166 million daily users, primarily millennials. Most of the content was "comedic" rather than an effort to keep the conversation private. McDonald's used Snapchat to look for unskilled labor and included a lens to self-photograph what you would look like in a McDonald's uniform; 3 million used the lens, with at least 2,500 submitted "Snaplications." However, this may not be the best social media platform for an academic. Anything you put out on Snapchat can also be saved with a screenshot and may haunt you later.

Twitter: If you don't know what Twitter is, you must not be paying attention to the news. Twitter is simply a micro-blogging site, that for years limited communication to 140 characters per "tweet" (meaning posted communication). In September 2017, Twitter doubled the character limit to 280. The verdict is still out on how well that is working. Twitter had about 330 million active users as of the 3rd quarter of 2017,[105] with 500 million tweets per day and around 200 billion tweets per year.[106] Academics and potential academics need to be aware of two significant hazards with regard to Twitter: 1) Taken out of context, real-time tweeting can lead to mockery and distract a speaker; and 2) There may be inadvertent posting of data that are legally prohibited for various reasons.[107]

Twitter previously announced the closing of its video blogging site, Vine, in October 2016 because the app did not make money. Its live streaming video, Periscope, is on the decline with fierce competition from Facebook Live. All the cautionary statements made with regard to social media apply double to anything live. Workarounds to save such videos exist and what may seem like a good idea at the spur of a moment may not look like such a good idea 24 hours later. Eighty-four percent of institutions of higher education have a school Twitter account.

Social media could be getting more important. Social media, including Twitter, have even been proposed for inclusion in the tenure decision. The final report of the American Sociological Association subcommittee on the evaluation of social media and public communication in sociology, "What counts? Evaluating public communication in tenure and promotion" (August, 2016)[108] suggested a category should be added for tenure and promotion in the form of a "public communication criterion" showing engagement on the part of the academic with the wider community outside the educational institution. The report noted that social media engagement can substantially influence a current conversation in the media and that scholarly work elucidating one side of the argument or another can be especially important. Our caveats are that social media can be a time drain, a place where academics may be berated for airing the results of their research that do not fit current cultural norms, and incorporating social media increases the load professors must bear in justifying tenure and promotion.

Recruiters also use Twitter to find talent, and some academics have created profiles to help institutions find them. As of November 2011, roughly 30% of faculty in the US and UK scholars tweeted, according to Jason Priem at GitHub.[109] That number is surely much larger now. Glen Wright from Academia Obscura commented, "Hashtags, used to collate tweets on a particular subject, are great for community building, with regulars such as #PhDchat,#AcWri, and #ScholarSunday providing opportunities for academics to interact with and learn from each other. Others, such as #AcademicsWithCats or #AcademicsWithBeer, are a little more light-hearted, building communities around extra-curricular interests."[110]

A five-part guide for academics to using Twitter is available from Jojo Scoble, also known as The Online Academic.[111] Her book, *Twitter for Academics*, was published in 2016. *The Chronicle of Higher Education* also offers the "10 Commandments of Twitter for Academics".[112]

Specialized social media sites. A specialized social media site helpful to academic job seekers is Wiki Academic Job.[113] This is a Wiki for tracking searches in various categories for academic faculty positions. The home page lists job and postdoc categories and "interview experiences" includes a venting page. If you go to the category page, you can see people's anonymous posts about interviews and rejections and their comments about what's really going on with a job. The "word on the street" section lists rumors about jobs that may be posted. This site is also one way to find out when searches have been closed. We caution that the information available is quite hit and miss.

You can sometimes create an electronic profile at Human Resources departments for institutions where you would like to work. Such a profile can be especially helpful if you have narrow geographic limits on your job search so that when jobs come up on announcement lists meeting your qualifications, you will be among the first to be notified of the opening. These openings are not centralized, so you will have to create a profile with each institution.

Glassdoor and Idealist: Not recommended for academic job searches. We do not recommend using Glassdoor [114] unless you are planning to leave academia, or want to transition to a different type of career inside academia. Most of the jobs posted under the category "Higher Education" are not for professors, with names like "Account Executive, SciQuest" or "Manager of Scholar Support Services, Hispanic Scholarship Fund." You might find some postings related to jobs in educational publishing, essentially sales representative positions where you would travel from campus to campus, hawking textbooks and trade paperbacks for a particular publisher. The main usefulness of Glassdoor is the anonymous posting of real interview questions and salary information by people that upload to the site, though again, it seems to have limited use for those wanting to stay in academia.

We also do not recommend using Idealist.org. [115] We have seen discouraged job candidates look for academically-related work through this organization, thinking that they can find a good organization where their research and analytical skills will be valued. Many jobs are listed for non-profits and NGOs but they tend to be entry-level positions with very low salaries. If, for whatever reason, you have decided to stop pursuing an academic job, use Idealist to scan for the organizations that interest you, then begin to find ways to establish relationships with people inside the organization, perhaps using LinkedIn or informational interviews. If you want to stay in academia, you do not need to look on Idealist.

Salary Information

Finally, if you would like salary information for any advertised position, it is available for publically funded institutions in state budgets, often right down to the individual professor level. It takes time to sift through obtainable information, which is sometimes still only available on paper through your local reference library. You may have far more difficulty getting information on private institutions. One resource for determining salaries is the Chronicle of Higher Education's Data source,[116] allowing you to search by position, school name, or type of school. Most advertised positions use advertised a lowest to highest range offer.

The most recent 2017-18 compensation survey by the American Association of University Professors[117] shows comparative data from 1,018 institutions surveying 378,365 individuals and can give you information for both public and private institutions. The National Center for Education Statistics (NCES) at the US Department of Education averages salaries by state, position level held, and shows overall pay differences between public and private non-profit institutions through 2016.[118] NCES does not offer data on salaries at for-profit schools.

Expand Your General Networking

You've no doubt heard this advice before: network, network, network. It's not the best way to think about what you are trying to do, since it conjures up visions of standing at a cocktail party, desperately making small talk and trying to bring up your real worry: getting an academic job. Networking is not about passing your business card to everyone you know or adding someone to your LinkedIn profile. A better phrase for networking is actually *connecting*. You are honestly trying to make deeper connections with people who share common interests and goals and who might be interested in helping you. Strategies to connect include talking to departmental visitors, schmoozing at conferences, and sending (with permission) your papers to people you have cited, have met at conferences, or are otherwise professionally acquainted with. You may even make real friends in the process. In addition, you may eventually connect with an "information broker," someone that likes connecting people of like interests, who could help you.[119]

As an academic, you might not think you need a business card, so think of it as a "connection card" instead. The object is to have something easy to give to someone else so you are not both scrabbling for a piece of paper to jot information down. It should have your name, title (Dr.), current position, if applicable (and nothing if it is not), and how to contact you (phone number, email, webpage). Including some brief description of what you do, like "expert in medieval churchyards," is helpful for jogging the memory of the other person. If you are technologically adept, you may be able to share contacts via your mobile phone, where the descriptor becomes even more important so that you can be found by a keyword search, even when your contact does not remember your name, or you do not remember theirs.

People generally *do* want to help other people. Deeper connections lead to people's keeping you in mind when a job posting comes up. Sometimes people will refer you to a job they are not interested in themselves but are happy to pass along to a known colleague. Remember, all other things being equal, people are more likely to refer you if they know, like, and trust you. Your job in this equation is to present yourself professionally, to provide some information that allows your colleagues to understand what you do (perhaps, with their permission, in the form of a PDF article or paper you presented earlier), and to allow the relationship to unfold without being too pushy.

Networking can be especially daunting to introverts. Many self-selected academics fall into this personality type. People naturally drawn to research and writing, rather than to engaging socially with other people, often have a rich interior life that leads them to a career in academia. Roughly 50% of the total population are considered introverts, so plenty of others find networking a terrifying word. Remember, replace the word network with connection. Then begin by recognizing being socially cautious makes connecting hard for you, and practice a few approaches to increase your comfort level. Extroverts can practice connecting using the ideas below as well.

Start by engaging in conversations where the stakes are low: begin saying hello to the mail delivery person or the check-out clerk at the grocery store. Maybe even offer a sympathetic observation about their work, like "Must be hard to jump in and out of that delivery truck when it's raining," or "I bet your feet get tired standing at the register." They may or may not respond, but often such an observation will lead to a short conversational exchange. Great. You've practiced connecting.

A similar tack is offering a compliment or a thank you to someone you do not know very well. Maybe someone you work with has helped you get an assigned task finished earlier than if you had done it alone. Say "thanks" out loud and notice the response you get. Or compliment a classmate on her presentation skills. All these approaches are low stakes and possible conversation starters.

Next, find people who seem similar to you. They do not have to be in your field or share your same research interests. Look for something else you might have in common: do you both like to go to live music events? Perhaps you both went to the same concert already. Is there any similar background, like taking piano lessons as a kid, that you might have in common with your conversational partner? If so, you have something to talk about: how hard the music is to play, whether or not the performer trained formally or not, your own experience of learning to be an appreciative audience member. This is the basis for a shared, friendly conversation, which may go deeper once you've given yourself permission to freely engage. You may discover those with similar interests are not so scary to talk to after all.

If you are seriously introverted, you need to spend a little time actually engaging with others to the point that you are more relaxed and you can see more commonalities than differences with your fellow humans. Give yourself a week to just say "hello," and the next week to say, "Hello, I like your jacket," and the third week to offer open-ended statements inviting a short conversation. At this point, you may be ready to find people with similar interests, or be able to connect with people only tangentially aligned with your interests.

After you've had a bit of practice with low stakes relating, you can begin connecting with people you would like to know who could potentially further your career. Easy places to begin your forays into connection as a recent doctoral graduate are alumni organizations and your own honor society. Many of these hold monthly luncheons or other activities and may even be looking for a speaker. What better way to engage a wider audience on your academic expertise, feel comfortable about your role as an expert and know you have something to talk about with the people in the room than by speaking to them.

If you are still a graduate student, think about connecting with people you know in your field who are not at your university. Consider the following sources:

- Former grad students from your department who now work elsewhere;
- Graduate students and faculty in your field at nearby colleges, universities, and community colleges; and
- Outside member(s) of your committee, especially if they are in your field but at another institution.

If you are a junior faculty member looking to change jobs, having colleagues outside your department helps enormously. Now is a good time to start cultivating them by doing things like:

- Manuscript exchanges;
- Managing colloquia;
- Serving on editorial boards; and
- Serving on a site visit accreditation team.

Once you begin adding up the people you know, beginning with family and close friends, you will likely find 12-20 people in your own personal network. Now recognize that each of these people have 12-20 people in their circles, some of whom do not overlap with people you know, and your circle extends to 144-400 pretty quickly. The average number of extended social connections via social media for all ages in the US was 350 as of 2016.[120] Even people who claim they know hardly anyone actually have about 150 people in their extended circles before adding social media connections. As you think about reaching out, remind yourself, you never know who someone else knows, or where a connection might lead you.

As you begin to connect with others, think about what you might do for them as well as what they might do for you. Reciprocity is a fundamental in human relationships, found in such old adages as "Do unto others as you would have others do unto you," or more crassly, "You scratch my back and I'll scratch yours." A positive reciprocal social action is a common social expectation, no matter what culture you belong to in the world.

Remember to be clear about exactly what you want from someone else in your connecting circle. An introduction? Information about job openings? The opportunity to speak? This is about putting your best foot forward as you look for that ideal academic job for you. People will help you more easily if you can tell them specifically what you want from them. "I'd like to connect with someone in the English Department at the local community college; do you know anyone I can speak to?" is much better for the listener than "Can you help me? I'm not sure what I want exactly."

In the business world, you are encouraged to create an "elevator speech." No one knows exactly where the term originated, but the idea is to present yourself strongly and concisely in the time it takes to ride an elevator from the first floor to the 20th. Generally, you are working with 3-5 sentences, and certainly no longer than 60 seconds. This concept can be *extremely* useful for new PhDs that often need to abbreviate their research both succinctly and in a manner people uninitiated to their field can understand and appreciate quickly.

To sum up, here are the steps for making meaningful connections:
- Know what you want out of the connection
- Make sure you know who you really want to talk to, and why
- Connect with them, preferably in person or by social media (Twitter is good for this)
- If you are attending the same conferences, make sure you meet them there
- Exchange professional work, but only if the other person has agreed, not unsolicited
- Absolutely make sure you follow up, preferably in a timely manner

A useful article on this topic continues to be "Networking on the Network" by Phil Agre (2003, June 11).[121]

Crafting an elevator speech. Crafting an elevator speech is also extremely useful preparation for answering "Tell me about yourself," one of the most common standard questions in both interviews and just general conversation with job candidates. The person asking may literally know nothing about you, so be prepared to explain who you are quickly and succinctly, and also what makes you unique. Do not start telling them immediately about your research in detail. People are used to hearing and evaluating sound bites these days.

As Roberta Kwok wrote in "Two minutes to impress":

> ...Aside from fielding questions about their jobs at cocktail parties, researchers may need to summarize their work briefly while interviewing for a position, asking for money, taking a visiting politician on a lab tour or wooing a potential collaborator at a conference.[122]

Her example of an effective elevator speech comes from American Society for Cell Biology (ASCB) inaugural 2012 Elevator Speech Contest:

> Hi, my name is Cecilia Seixas, and I am a postdoc at the New University of Lisbon's Chronic Diseases Research Center in Portugal. I am studying how cells assemble an organelle, the cilium, that is like an antenna sticking out of the surface ..." [Seixas] then went on to explain that the cilium acts as a receptor for signals, often needs its parts replaced and can cause diseases when not functioning properly.[123]

The contest, which continues annually, also uses video pitches to help scientists learn how to explain their research.[124]

Here is another example for someone who wants to continue teaching, but not necessarily at the research university level:

I'm currently studying the biology of snails at [insert university]. One of my greatest strengths is my ability to make the abstract concepts tangible for students. I'm interested in working at [insert name of institution] to teach and develop curricula. Because I believe in education as an opportunity, I want to be in a position to help students develop to their highest potential.

This pitch could either be followed up with the speaker's responding to the listener's questions or, if this is an informal contact, the speaker could transition to "Enough about me: What do you do?"

Brevity is the soul of an elevator speech, and that's difficult for most academics to wrap their heads around, trained as they are to deal in nuances or complicated formulations. If you get only one short academic minute to influence how you are perceived, what's the most important thing for you to get across? Your elevator speech is often the big "why" you are interested in pursuing some particular pathway. Use the two-part **Elevator Speech Worksheets** to help you craft a statement on what you have to offer.

The idea behind an elevator pitch is to start a conversation about your work as a graduate assistant or young college teacher. A common mistake in crafting an elevator speech is to give a huge amount of information on the logistics of how you do whatever you do. Your audience is much more interested in "What can you do for me?" If you start by saying, "I lecture, give assignments to promote critical reasoning skills and give feedback on papers by students," you will have bored someone already in education. If the person is not in education, she most likely will not even understand what you are talking about.

Generally, people do not want to know *how* so much as *why* you do this. I've met many professors at community colleges who are actually passionate about helping students learn how to read and write so those students can find a better paying job and take care of their own families instead of literally struggling to read a menu or write out an order at a restaurant. Go back to the basics of what got you interested in this profession in the first place. After you've hooked them with the elevator speech with "I use my classes to help make the aspirations of young adults come true," you can elaborate the how when asked adding "by teaching critical reasoning and persuasive writing skills."

Once you have the basics down, practice until saying your elevator speech aloud feels natural. You do not need to memorize the statement word for word like an actor in a play. It may be enough to create a bullet point list of what you want to include so that you can adjust it for the audience. You will likely use a different version for people outside academia than you would for a colleague in your field, but do not underestimate the value of a succinct account of what you do when presenting for a poster session in a crowded exhibition hall. Remember, you do not have to tell them the complete story when you are delivering your elevator speech or reveal any limitations or caveats to your results. Save that information for a later follow-up discussion, if it occurs.

Elevator Speech Worksheet, Part 1

Part 2: Staying on Top of Your Academic Job Search

As you read the items below, think about the number of floors on the left-hand side of the page as the floor where you start and the floor where you get off.

1. Who am I? Introduce yourself using your name.

2. What do I do? What do I teach/research/administer?

3. Experience: What is my particular expertise? Area of education? [This is a place to show at what stage you are in your career. Do this avoiding graduate field jargon. Only 1% of the population every attends graduate school, so make your level of experience clear to the person outside the higher education arena-even if you are ultimately addressing people in higher education with the hiring power.]

4. Experience (continued): What benefits derive from my work? What are my skills, based on my proven accomplishments, that others will find of use? [This is a great place to use examples of how your research can be put to use.]

5. What group of people do I serve? Who benefits from my work?—Be specific: What position am I in? In what capacity do I serve? "The opportunity to do [x] is what really drew me to this field." For instance, "I help kids with cancer survive into adulthood."

6. Why do I do this? [Connections want to understand and will remember your why, especially if you give them a story: "My younger brother died of leukemia when he was only seven."]

7. What makes me unique? [In business, this is often referred to as your Unique Selling Proposition or USP—What makes you different from the competition? Why would anyone want to hire you specifically? Or think in broad terms: what is the main thing you want this person to

remember about who you are? Continue the example, "I was the first person in my lab to identify a new way to detect a lack of iron in DNA material."]

8. What do you want the other person to do? [Do you want a business card, a later meeting, a referral, or something else? Know what you want to you can ask directly.]

9. Show them you care: Wrap up with "Who are you? What do you do?" This is very important so that the person you are speaking to does not get the impression you are only out for yourself. No one likes to feel diminished by a conversation.

Elevator Speech Worksheet, Part 2

1. Very Basic Structure:

Hi, my name is _____. I'm in _____ [field], and I'm looking to _____ [teach/work at nearby community college or research university].

Fill in the last blank of the first sentence with your current career aspiration, whether it is to stay within your field, or move up, or even move into an alternate academic career like biotechnology.

Now work to make it more intriguing, providing a memorable sound bite version:

2. Sound bite version:

Hi, my name is _____. I use my classes to help make the aspirations of young adults come true, and I welcome the opportunity to learn more about how I could do more of this at [community college or research university], where I understand you work.

As you begin creating your spiel, imagine you are telling a favorite grade school teacher what you are doing now with your life. This may keep you from speaking too technically or using too much field-specific jargon. Stay away from the details and keep to the big picture. This is just a short interaction, not nearly as scary as being on display for an hour or more giving a presentation or doing an interview. Relax and have some fun fashioning your patter.

Just as you would for any other professional presentation, practice your words and delivery with a live human audience like a spouse, partner, or colleague you trust. Be willing to adjust what you say for maximum impact. If you have trouble touting your strengths and abilities, remember this speech is about authentically presenting yourself to someone new. If you have a good working relationship with your primary advisor, ask that person to listen and give feedback on whether you are hitting the high points strongly enough.

As you start delivering your spiel to people you do not know, make eye contact, express enthusiasm for your work, and speak authoritatively on your area of expertise. If you can see interest is waning, draw the person in by asking about what she or he does. See if you can tie their work to yours in a way that will keep them talking to you. "Oh, you work for a pharmaceutical company? This new gene therapy might be of interest to your employer." Do not lie about your experience, even at this early juncture, in an attempt to impress.

Links to information about networking. We provide a partial list of websites on "how to network" and descriptions of how they can best be used. Remind yourself as you think about networking that what you are really trying to do is "connect, connect, connect" with people you want to know in a deeper way or truly do have things in common with. The following list contains both internet sites and some classic books now available electronically:

- *Work It Daily* [125] is a site for basic information and regularly updated articles.
- For basic information about using LinkedIn, take a look at their "one-sheet" advice.[126]
- For STEM (especially Biomed) people, try *Cheeky Scientist*.[127]
- For samples of a different kind of "I want to connect" letter, sometimes called a "pain letter," you can look at a LinkedIn site [128] or subscribe to the newsletter at Human Workplace and get the downloadable 20-page E-Book "How to Write a Pain Letter" for free. For premium membership at $10.00 per month, you get access to a number of electronic publications on "reinventing yourself" from a career standpoint.[129]
- The paperback or Kindle book, *Smart networking: Attract a following in person and online*,[130] by Liz Lynch (2008) is aimed at business people, but applicable to anyone that wants to delve deep into the process and methods for networking.
- If you need to learn how to reach out, try this now relatively well-known book by Keith Ferrazzi (2014): *Never eat alone, expanded and updated: And other secrets to success, one relationship at a time*.[131]
- A timeless book to help the more introverted is Meghan Weir's (2009) *Confessions of an introvert: The shy girl's guide to career, networking and getting the most out of life*.[132]
- And if you need help understanding what introverts offer in order to explain that to someone else, try Susan Cain's (2013) *Quiet: The power of introverts in a world that can't stop talking*.[133]
- An oldie but goodie on connecting with people is Dale Carnegie's (1936; reissued 1998) classic book, *How to win friends & influence people*.[134]

You want to remember the avenues you are exploring to make connections (aka networking), including when you actually made contact, and with whom. Follow-up dates can also be entered into your calendar (paper or electronic) to remind you to get back to the person before the contact goes from "warm" to "cold" and you are forced to begin again.

Mind maps. Another potentially useful tool for figuring out your networking plan is to draw a mind map of all your connections. Invented by Tony Buzan,[135] mind maps are used for all kinds of projects, including writing, managing meetings, strategic planning, and evaluations. We've provided a template for a very neat (uncluttered) version, just to give you the idea. You can copy the one here or go directly to the source at Arjen ter Hoeve's website,[136] where the form is available for free.

Most mind maps are hand-drawn and are considerably messier than indicated on this template because the point is to start with yourself in the middle and then free associate connections. Often different colors are used to represent different directions. Think about branching nodes. Most of the people writing about mind maps recommend that each "trunk" be a different color so you carry that color forward as you "branch out" and as your branches sprout "twigs" in order to keep track of the main items. Search your browser using the phrase "mind map images" to see some examples.[137]

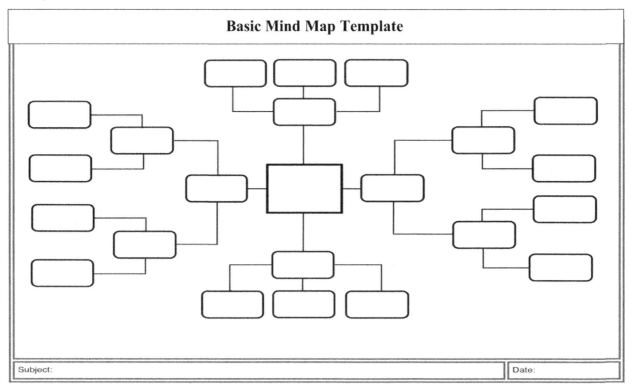

Here's how to do it: Start by putting yourself in the middle and work outward. Your first network connection could be your partner or your degree cohort members. Next, add the people you know through those people. You may have to ask them who they know to keep filling out your connections; however, one branch could be "where I will find people." The twigs branching off from this could be labeled with each of these categories: class, in coffee shops, at conferences, department gatherings, etc. It's free-form, so don't get too excited about trying to make it perfect. You can play with it later, adding on or taking off items. There are even mind map apps, such as Mindjet,[138] XMind,[139] or Coggle,[140] but beware the time it may take for you to figure out how to draw your ideas using them!

Part 2: Staying on Top of Your Academic Job Search

Start Attending and Presenting at Conferences

If you are considering an academic career, begin attending and presenting at conferences,[141] if you haven't already done so. In terms of thinking about networking, or better, thinking about connecting with like-minded people, begin attending conferences as soon as you can in graduate school. Initially, you may want to limit yourself to local or regional events in your field, so you can keep costs down. Do not wait to start attending until your last year in graduate school or until you have finished your dissertation. That will be too late. You should begin meeting and knowing the people who can help you AND the people you can help. Starting small will give you a sense of what to expect in your field, from how people dress to attend, to what kinds of topics draw the larger audiences. These observations will give you a big confidence boost when it is time to attend and present your own material.

To get to know people at the conference, use casual small talk, such as "How was your flight?" or "Which presentations are you most interested in attending?" to help both of you feel at ease. If they ask about your current research, be prepared with your elevator speech. Think of a memorable title for your research; your connections will not remember "A Socio-Economic Exploration of Political Groups in Turkey," but "Tanks and Scarves: Political Parties in Modern Turkey" tells a story people will remember. Images like this in a title help people remember your topic. Alliteration can also help make a title memorable: "Nuclear Knights," with the subtitle "A critical analysis of the pro-nuclear views of Sir Ernest Titterton and Sir Philip Baxter,"[142] or a real title for an article by Colleen Burke, "Tulips, tinfoil and teaching: Journal of a freshman teacher."[143] Have some fun and brainstorm catchy titles with a group of people you know. It's a great game for a graduate student happy hour, and you can offer to buy a drink for the best title devised. You can say "that's the working title" if your research is not finished. Writers will understand this idea.

By staying current in your field, you have an easy opening for a conversation: "Have you read Dr. Shaley's most recent article in *Neuroscience*? What did you think?" It's fine to have a few stock questions like this in your head to help you relax about meeting others in your field. Or if you meet scholars whose work you have already read, ask about where their recent research is leading them. If they seem reluctant to discuss this, they may be worried about their ideas being stolen, so be discerning about when to back off. You may have a more in-depth conversation about the research once trust has been established. Make them comfortable with you, and you may find you can relax, too.

Know how to end the conversation gracefully, with a simple acknowledgment such as, "I enjoyed speaking with you today;" "Hope to see you again sometime;" or "Thank you for your time." Then be prepared to actually move on. Others may be reluctant to seem rude by ending the conversation even when they want to and, by leaving, you let others move into the conversation circle and keep your own desired connection from avoiding you in the future because they "couldn't get away."

Networking/Connecting Worksheet			
Use this table to fill in the avenues you are exploring to make connections (aka networking).			
What connection?	When contacted	Who?	When was follow-up?
General			

Coffee shop			
Co-workers (current and former)			
Current work supervisor			
Fraternity/Sorority			
Friends, family & neighbors			
Medical community (doctor, dentist, specialist)			
Meet Up (groups of special interest to you)			
Political connections			
Religious connections			
Volunteer/charity work colleagues			
HiEd related special interest groups (e.g., hearing specialists, modernist literature groups)			
Committee members or professors from your institution			
Committee members from outside your institution			
Conference connections			
Editorial board colleagues			
Former graduate students			
Graduate student cohort members			
Manuscript exchangers			

Part 2: Staying on Top of Your Academic Job Search

Nearby institutions, students & faculty			
PhD/MA supervisor			
Site visit accreditation teams			
Social Media			
Facebook			
LinkedIn			
Pinterest			
Twitter			
Other			

Just to get you started, answer these questions:

- What conferences have you attended, where, and when?
- What networking wins did you have at each?
- What would you do differently next time?

How to choose a conference to attend. The first thing to consider when choosing a conference is *when* in the year the conference is held. In some fields, given the academic job cycle, December and January conferences often include job interviews. Interviewing faculty may find attending a conference and scouting prospective candidates to be easier for them during the winter holiday season than when conferences are held in the middle of a semester.

In some fields, conferences are held in the summer and fall and may be a good place to get your name and ideas out into the view of others in your discipline. These conferences may also include faculty scouting potential applicants, even if the search committee has not been formally established with a timeline for interviewing.

Ask yourself, "Is the conference large (national or international) or small (regional or local)?" Notice whether it is a general, widely-focused conference on a variety of topics or a small, themed conference around a specific topic. If the conferences that interest you rotate where they are held, attend local ones even if you are not presenting so that you can get a sense of what goes on and who attends.

Some of the larger conferences may actually include in-person workshops in your area of study, giving you a chance to interact more personally with others in your field. Think about who you expect to attend by looking at the advance programs, often online, and determine whether there are people attending or presenting whose work you have been following and whom you would like to meet from the keynote speaker to panelists to other attendees.

Ask yourself, "How prestigious is the conference?" and "How hard will it be to get a paper accepted there?" You want to be noticed in a good way and that can mean presenting a paper or poster session or organizing and moderating a panel. Build opportunities for conversation starters about your research or that of others. If you present early in your dissertation process, you may meet people with similar interests who can be helpful to you with your dissertation project, maybe even helping you get participants for your research or by serving as an outside committee member.

Consider the kinds of presentations the conference hosts. Some conferences or subgroups of conferences are designed for presentation of works in progress or for workgroups, with a simple goal of presenting your ideas and get feedback. Take all comments with a grain of salt; you can decide after further consideration whether the suggestions made are worth pursuing or not. Panel presentations, poster sessions, and individual presentations are all options for getting some experience and for getting known. We have known graduate students and junior faculty who presented as part of a panel and then a panel member or the moderator edited the papers for the session so they could be published as a special issue of the sponsoring organization's journal.

If you are anxious about presenting, start by presenting at smaller conferences several years before you are on the job market. Another option: Large conferences often have many sessions running simultaneously with opportunities to present to a relatively small audience. How many people are there really does not matter, since you are simply practicing what it feels like to talk about your subject in a formal way with people you do not already know. Many people actually find presenting to strangers easier than presenting to their cohort.

In picking your conference, determine whether the venue will make it easy for you to meet up with people, and connect informally over the beverage of your choice. Are there dinners or other networking opportunities built into the conference? Are there people whose work you have been following that you would like to meet? How will you do this? Consider whether the conference program affords you the opportunity to find new people interested in your area, and perhaps begin following their work using social media. You also want to keep an eye out for those you meet whose work you do not know about but should start following.

Perhaps you have already worked "virtually" with some of the people you want to meet and this would be a good time to meet them face to face, to get more extensive feedback in person than you might otherwise get. Maybe you want to find a place you can suggest to others for informal meetings: a coffee shop area or an empty conference room if you want to discuss future collaborations with someone.

One of our clients told us about meeting other graduate students in her field at a conference. They decided to form a writing group, which has been meeting regularly by Skype for a couple of years. Because they are all studying aspects of the same question, they can actually help each other with writing content and with reaching out to new contacts.

Money can be an issue in choosing what conference to attend. Your department may have a pool of money to help defray conference expenses or your doctoral chair may have a grant that will cover the costs of your travel or registration. Some conferences have scholarships to help students pay for their registration. You usually have to pay for your room and board and transportation. Carpooling with someone from your institution or rooming with someone you don't know from another institution can be another way to network and build deeper connections for the future.

When you have determined the "best fit" conference, you must at all times present yourself as a professional. This includes dressing professionally for travel to and from the conference. You literally do not know when someone sitting next to you on the plane will be someone you want to know. I once rode in a shuttle from the tarmac to the terminal and discovered that the woman sitting next to me was a leading edge researcher in an area that interested me. Whew. So glad I was wearing a black jacket and pants with a colorful scarf. I looked, and felt, like her peer, which made talking to her a whole lot easier. This advice goes for traveling *from* the conference as well. Megan Poorman (2017) offers some especially good tips on attending conferences. See her article about affording the conference, packing and travel, and getting the most out of your conference experience.[144]

Next, make sure you practice your paper or poster session explanation. Provide handouts with your name and contact information where it is appropriate. Take business cards and copies of your CV with you and be willing to hand them out. Share contact information via your cell phone, especially if you have a Twitter account. Even if you believe that most of the networking is done at the end of the day over drinks, remember that people may be assessing you as a potential colleague at any time.

To get started on picking out your conference, answer these questions:
- What have you learned about "conferencing" from this section that you did not already know?
- What conference will you consider attending in the next year? Why?
- What is your goal for that conference? (To practice presenting? To meet new people in your field? Anything else?
- What clothes will you wear while traveling and while attending the conference?

As we discussed in the networking section above, make sure to follow up after the conference with anyone you may have met there, whether by email, connecting through LinkedIn, with some sort of note saying, "I enjoyed meeting you" and mentioning something that will jog their memory about a conversation you may have had.[145] If you have promised anything like a reference to an article, make sure you provide it. You will see a column header on the **Conference Attendance Worksheet** "How and when am I following up?" to help you stay on top of this.

Proactive job searching at conferences. You can look proactively for academic jobs at conferences in a number of ways, but most will necessitate a long-term time investment. By proactive we mean getting involved in the conference itself, as well as attending. Here are some suggestions:

Organize a panel. If you know that you and several people you know who are working on the same topic plan to attend the conference, look ahead at least a year to see what you could present together as a panel. Maybe there is a new controversy around dating dinosaur bones in Montana or Serbia. Who could argue the different positions around dating or categorization? How can you make the panel exciting for other people who want to be in on the latest information? Then submit a proposal to the planning committee. Once you have the basic but catchy title and colleagues lined up, you can continue to tweak it up to the time of presentation. You can advertise yourself and the session in an email tag (the line below your signature) as well: "Don't miss this exciting panel, 'Dino's Teeth' at the Paleontological Association meeting in December."

Get something from the conference published. Take a paper you presented as part of a panel and either publish it individually or get the people on your panel together to publish the session later as a group. If the panel is well received, the conference will be a good place for you to talk with the editor of the sponsoring organization about including the papers as part of a themed issue. Alternatively, we know people who have used the panel as the starting point for an edited book with chapters by various people.

Poster sessions. Poster sessions are a great way to meet and interact with all manner of people attending the conference. Make sure your poster is eye-catching in some way. Great titles help in the program, and great images can help at the poster session. Later you can publish your poster as a paper or make it available online as a slideshow to showcase your research presentation abilities.

Volunteer. Conferences always need people to help, so consider volunteering as a table captain/moderator. If you are an expert in a particular area, volunteering is a terrific way to interact with colleagues and potential colleagues at a deeper level and to get better known. Some conferences set up roundtables, similar to poster sessions, where a question of particular interest to those attendees can be discussed (for instance, the use of non-invasive techniques for archaeological excavations, and what the most current technology allows). They may even post a flag in the center of a table with the topic, so interested people can join in. You can also meet people when you volunteer to cover technical details for a presentation room (for example, interacting with hotel staff to make sure water pitchers are refilled, monitoring room temperature, answering questions from attendees).

At the conference, remember to present yourself as a professional colleague at all times. It can be helpful to go out for meals with people you do not know well, rather than only eating with other graduate students you know. This can be difficult for introverts, and sometimes difficult if other students are attaching themselves to you because they are nervous. Striking out on your own may lead to new opportunities for collaboration or further introductions.[146]

Only volunteer if you actually have time to do the work. There is nothing worse for a potential hire than getting a reputation as someone who cannot be relied on and will never do the necessary work. If you do the work competently, your name will be more likely passed on to

Part 2: Staying on Top of Your Academic Job Search

Conference Attendance Worksheet			
Conference Name And Place	**Date**	**What will I do?**	**How and when do I follow up?**
		Ask for introductions when appropriate; use advance research to know who I want to connect with.	
		Attend seminar sessions and ask questions to make myself known.	
		Exchange manuscripts and/or determine if there is an opportunity to create a publication from seminar; volunteer to coordinate or edit	
		Interview (informally or formally)	
		Moderate, organize or present panels	
		Moderate, organize or present posters	
		Socialize: Coffee, happy hours, meals	
		View job bulletin boards and connect with anyone I know at hiring institution	
		Visit book vendors and ask questions to make myself known	

others with a positive comment and help you get more well known in your field earlier than you might think.

Why Publishing Sooner Instead of Later Is a Good Idea

Publishing while you are in graduate school is a good idea and may even be necessary to get a tenure-track job. Sadly, some schools will not even consider interviewing you unless you already have a book or at least a book contract or have published several articles even before you leave graduate school. These days you have to prove yourself before you even go on the job market.

Once upon a time, finishing several articles or getting a book published was the requirement for getting tenure, not for getting hired. One of our clients recently said, "Today, getting an article out is not enough. I need a book contract to be really competitive."

You should start thinking about and submitting articles for publication while you are still in graduate school. Publications are concrete proof of your planning, conceptualization, research, and writing abilities. They indicate your awareness of foundational and recent literature in your field and your facility with theory. Publishing while you are a graduate student usually means that you will have one or more faculty mentors to give you advice on your research and feedback on your writing. Coauthoring with faculty or other graduate students will give you experience negotiating and working in partnership with someone else. Whether you plan an academic career or not, honing your written communication skills will benefit you for years to come.

Truthfully, publishing is a lot of pressure for a graduate student trying to finish a degree. While you may not really need a book contract for all available academic jobs, refereed publications do look good on a CV, and are pretty much a prerequisite for landing a tenure-track job. **The Pre-PhD Publishing Plan Worksheet** will help you determine which papers you can work on earlier rather than later. Think about articles from a conference presentation or from your dissertation, papers you presented at a conference that will not be part of your dissertation, papers you wrote for your dissertation comps, and other kinds of papers that you may write during or after your dissertation.

Articles you should not spend time on include basically anything in a non-refereed journal, such as a collection of edited papers from a conference (see Kelsky, 2015[147]) and your blog. If you have nothing else, though, you may have to start with a paper in a conference volume. Just don't spend a lot of time on it. Self-publishing on Academia.edu and ResearchGate (both are for-profit organizations) is generally not well regarded in the academic community for job hunting purposes.

Sometimes graduate students want to try out their writing skills by reviewing a book in their field, but such a publication does not count much, if at all, in a job search. The Association of American University Presses has created a *Best practices for peer review handbook*.[148] It may help more graduate students get published, since it includes an acknowledgment that "Institutions are relying more on non-tenured faculty, they are grappling with how best to diversify their faculty and provide support to interdisciplinary fields, and scholars are experimenting with digital publications that do not conform to the stability of a printed page."[149] The use of younger untenured scholars is also increasingly accepted as a change in the peer review process and may help graduate students or very recent PhDs get published as their work is more likely to be known to their younger peers.

If you expect to turn your dissertation into a book instead of several articles, ask your faculty mentors how that will be viewed on a job application in your field. Ideally, under this option, you would go into your job search with a book contract in hand, something that may be difficult to juggle with the timing of finishing your dissertation, applying for jobs, and your dissertation defense. Some academic presses want to see most, but not all, of your dissertation chapters. They may also ask for an additional chapter or two that will require additional research. Depending on your field, the peer review process may be different for a book than for journal articles, so even publishing a complete book may not be seen as quite as worthy as several peer-reviewed articles.

One caveat: if you are working for a university while finishing your dissertation, you may need to make certain no proprietary information is included in a proposed publication. Many universities have an office of intellectual property and policies related to that. You can find an example of a fairly typical policy by looking at Harvard's statement of policy in regard to intellectual property,[150] shorthanded as IP policy. Most authored work is protected by copyright, except in the case of software programs, database design, and actual technology including laboratory techniques for research. Remember the key word here is *most*. Make sure you know the policies at your institution before publishing. Some academic researchers have even left their institutions because of the proprietary contracts involved.[151]

If you have decided a book is the best way to go, a good article on what to include in a book proposal is available at the *Chronicle's Vitae* site [152] with the straightforward title, "Writing a Book Proposal." It includes questions to ask yourself about the content such as, "What important intellectual conversations are you engaging and influencing?" and "Does your work possess any crossover appeal or timeliness?" It also includes information about negotiating contract advice and notes on how to determine if you will be working with the right editor.

The best advice we can give you is to submit your work early and often. Celebrate if you get a request to "revise and resubmit"; if you get a rejection, move on to another possible journal to publish, revise the piece slightly to reflect the interests of the alternate publication, and send your work out the door again quickly.

We return to the subject of publishing in the next section, "What to do between your PhD and your new job," and follow that discussion with a series of worksheets to help you think about publishing both as a graduate student and a new PhD.

What To Do between Your PhD and Your New Job

Sometimes new PhDs wonder what they should be doing while they continue to search for an academic job. Our simple answer is to keep trying to publish, find work that pays (adjuncting is one option), and if you have decided to go for a teaching track position, get some specific training and/or experience teaching.

Publish

If you have defended your dissertation, but do not yet have an academic job, you still need to be working on getting publications to put on your CV. If you wish to publish part of your dissertation as an article or a book, it is important to (again) pay attention to what the publisher is looking for and follow all the guidelines for submission. You may want to put aside the dissertation for a little while and work on something new before returning to your graduate work document. A little distance can help you cut substantial portions that are not relative to a more general readership, or help you decide where fleshing out descriptions of why your work is important should be added. Guidelines for work published for a wider audience are very different from what is expected in a dissertation.

J. David Velleman, a philosophy professor at New York University, was quoted as writing that the emphasis on early publishing means the "volume of article submissions has 'exploded,' to the tune of 500 to 600 per year to a single journal and attention to each submission has declined proportionately."[153] Unfortunately, all this makes getting noticed and getting published more difficult. Don't let that stop you from submitting your work. You are unlikely to get hired without peer-reviewed work.

Here's some good advice around getting your work out to a large audience from Jonathan Rees:

> I've learned to think of my own writing as a reflection of a moment in time. Just the process of working out how to write something changes how you see what you wrote before. This kind of detachment has not only made reading my finished writing easier for me, it has helped me revise as I go because I don't get too attached to any particular phrasing.[154]

Thinking this way can help you let go of perfectionism and get the writing out. Being published increases your visibility and potential connections with people having similar research interests, bringing awareness to your work. It also helps establish your professional reputation and expertise, not to mention reducing anxiety by avoiding procrastination and getting your own writing actually done.

Once you have been published, you may want to see if your work is being cited anywhere. Getting your work known may take longer than getting your first professorial position. Here are some places to look for citations of your work: Google Scholar, Clarivate Analytics' Web of Science, Elsevier's Scopus, and CiteSeer[x]. Google Scholar probably has the largest database, roughly 160 million documents.

Pre-PhD publishing plan directions. As you begin to consider what you might work on to get published before you finish your PhD, consider papers that are not from a presentation at a conference or from your dissertation; e.g., your potential article may be material you wrote as part of a course requirement, for a comprehensive exam, or a short report on preliminary research. Think about how much work it will take you to get the paper into publishable form. The items you should consider are listed below and a worksheet to help you see this information at a glance is provided for your benefit.

- List any papers you have written for classes or comps prior to your dissertation proposal that you might be able to make into a journal article. Indicate the type of paper (e.g., review paper, pedagogical technique, research or lab technique, research data paper, theory paper, etc.).
- Next to the paper title, write A and indicate what journal you might submit it to. How prestigious is this journal? What is the journal's acceptance rate? When you think about Journal A, consider the theoretical aspect of your work: how might this research affect your field? How might it change the theory about how things work in your field? Why would this particular journal find your work of interest? How can you frame it for an inquiry letter matching their perspective?
- Next to the journal name, indicate the word limit for this type of article in the journal.
- Now write a couple lines about what it will take to make this paper into a publish-worthy article. Be realistic.
- Indicate your plan B journal with word limit for an article there.

Part 2: Staying on Top of Your Academic Job Search

Pre-PhD publishing plan directions from presentations and conference work. In considering pre-PhD publishing, look at papers you presented at a conference, or a presentation at a professional group not related to an actual conference, but which will not be part of your dissertation. A worksheet to help you see this information at a glance is provided for your benefit.

- List conference papers that are not part of your dissertation. If any of your presentations were requested as part of conference proceedings, make sure you still hold the copyright to it, so you can publish it in a journal of your choice. Journals often ask authors to verify that the paper has not been published elsewhere.
- Indicate the type of paper (e.g., review paper, pedagogical technique, research or lab technique, research data paper, theory paper, etc.). Will you be the first author?
- Next to the paper title, write A and indicate what journal you might submit it to. How prestigious is this journal? What is the journal's acceptance rate?
- Next to the journal name, indicate the word limit for this type of paper in the journal.
- Now write a couple lines about what it will take to make this paper into a publish-worthy article. Indicate your plan B journal and the word limit for an article there.

Publishing plan post-dissertation directions. After you have written and defended your dissertation proposal, continue following the same sort of guidelines suggested above, but now focused specifically on what pieces of your dissertation can be published separately to create a potential publication list for yourself. A worksheet to help you see this information at a glance is provided for your benefit.

Look at your statement of purpose, research question(s), and/or hypotheses and think about what kind(s) of data you plan to collect. Will your research data tell one story or more?

- Assign a working title to each story arc (e.g., quantitative data and qualitative data).
- Next to the working title, write A and indicate what journal you might submit it to. How prestigious is this journal? What is the journal's acceptance rate?
- Next to the journal name, indicate the word limit for this type of paper in the journal.
- Indicate your plan B journal and the word limit for an article there.

Continue your plan as you think about direction to take your research forward into the future using the **Publishing—Continued Plan Worksheet**.

We have also provided a **Sample Publication Plan Worksheet** below to show you how to very simply flesh out your ideas.

Publishing—Pre-PhD Plan Worksheet **Coursework, Comps, or Preliminary Research**							
Enter papers that are not from a conference or your dissertation. Be realistic about how much work you think it would take to get the paper into publishable form. Consider setting up this form as a landscaped document to give yourself more space.							
Paper & Title (Paper title and source: class papers, comprehensive exams, PhD proposal)	**Type** (review paper, pedagogical technique, research or lab technique, research data paper, theory paper, etc.)	**Journal A** (requirements, desired topics, prestige level, acceptance rate)	**Word Limit**	**Synopsis** or "what makes this interesting?"	**Journal B** (requirements, desired topics, prestige level, acceptance rate)	**Word Limit**	**Synopsis** or "what makes this interesting?"

Part 2: Staying on Top of Your Academic Job Search

Publishing—Pre-PhD Plan Worksheet
From Presentations and Conferences

Enter papers that are from a presentation or conference. Be realistic about how much work you think it would take to get the paper into publishable form. Consider setting up this form as a landscaped document to give yourself more space.

Paper & Title (Paper title and source: class papers, comprehensive exams, PhD proposal)	Type (review paper, pedagogical technique, research or lab technique, research data paper, theory paper, etc.)	Journal A (requirements, desired topics, prestige level, acceptance rate)	Word Limit	Synopsis or "what makes this interesting?"	Journal B (requirements, desired topics, prestige level, acceptance rate)	Word Limit	Synopsis or "what makes this interesting?"

Publishing—Dissertation and Post-PhD Publishing Plan Worksheet

List other articles that you want to write during or after your dissertation. These may be a review article, a methods paper, or a pedagogical article. In the chart that follows, we have also made space for you to propose (to yourself) articles that may result from next research steps. If your previous work has led you to a new direction, you are going to have to find some new journals and new publishers to approach. Find the best match for your ideas, and you will have a specific audience to write for as well. Consider setting up this form as a landscaped document to give yourself more space.

Working Title (New ideas for research areas, new theoretical approaches, anecdotal stories that would help tell your story)	**Type** (Trade journal versus academic journal? Popular magazine? Blog post? Web-only publication?)	**Journal A** (Requirements, desired topics, prestige level, acceptance rate)	**Word limit**	**Synopsis** or "what makes this interesting?" (Will you tell your story using quantitative or qualitative data?)	**Journal B** (Requirements, desired topics, prestige level, acceptance rate)	**Word limit**	**Synopsis** or "what makes this interesting?" (Will you tell your story using quantitative or qualitative data?)

Publishing—Continued Plan Worksheet

Now, consider where you want to take your publishing career. Assume you have already gotten a few articles or even a book out of your actual dissertation.

Journal A (Requirements, desired topics, prestige level, acceptance rate)	Word Limit	Synopsis or "what makes this interesting?" (Will you tell your story using quantitative or qualitative data?)	Journal B (Requirements, desired topics, prestige level, acceptance rate)	Word Limit	Synopsis or "what makes this interesting?" (Will you tell your story using quantitative or qualitative data?)

Sample Publishing—Publication Plan Worksheet

To begin, list papers that are not from a conference or your dissertation. Think about how much work you think it would take to get the paper into publishable form.

Paper & Title (class papers, comprehensive exams, PhD proposal)	Type (review paper, pedagogical technique, research or lab technique, research data paper, theory paper, etc.)	Journal A (requirements, desired topics, prestige level, acceptance rate)	Word limit	Synopsis or what makes this interesting? What will I have to do to make this into a publishable article?	Journal B (requirements, desired topics, prestige level, acceptance rate)	Word limit	Synopsis or what makes this interesting? What will I have to do to make this into a publishable article?
Possible title: How to get your article published	Technique	Topic: ABD survival guide Need to query ABDSG editor	500-1500	Needs outline, then writing..	No idea. Need to research.		

Part 2: Staying on Top of Your Academic Job Search

Find Work That Pays

Two major issues that arise when you are between graduate school and an ongoing faculty position are earning money and obtaining access to a good university library so that you can keep up to date on the literature. No matter what, you are going to have to find some form of paid work while you continue to look for that academic job. Adjuncting, or as the AAUP (American Association of University Professors, an advocacy group) defines it, "working as a part-time faculty teaching on a per-section basis,"[155] generally does not pay very well, though the data is extremely difficult to nail down. *The Chronicle of Higher Education* conducted a crowdsourced survey [156] finalized in 2015 that listed the average self-reported pay for adjuncts as $2,943 per three-credit course. The range can be as low as $1,000 or as high as $11,000 per course. In 2017, the AAUP's *Annual Report on the Economic Status of the Profession* reported an average per course of $7,066 "with serious limitations to [averaging] the data."[157] Part-time faculty in law and sciences, who are known experts in the community or their fields and come in to teach just one course partly account for the extreme disparity in the reported amounts paid to adjuncts.

If you want to do your own research for the particular amount paid to an adjunct in 2016-2017 at a particular institution, go to the *Chronicle Data* [158] and search the data set. Because course loads are so variable for part-time faculty, as are types of institution and geographic locations, what the average annual salary is across the United States is hard to say, but in 2013, NPR reported it was between $20,000 to $25,000.[159] In September 2015, *The Atlantic* published a comparison of college presidents' pay to adjunct pay with charts showing an average adjunct salary of $20,000 at both public and private institutions.[160]

Many adjuncts have to cobble together several courses at more than one institution of higher education to make ends meet, not to mention the stress and time involved in constantly commuting from one institution to another. And many adjuncts find that they must engage in some other form of paid work if they want to teach just one or two courses to keep their hands in academia.

If you are interested in learning more, two additional sources for salary data are salary.com or the US Department of Labor Statistics. [161] Salary.com will let you search by job title, and give you some "job title history" information such as, "The median annual Asst. Professor History salary in Irvine, CA is $61,221, as of February 22, 2017, with a range usually between $48,885-$85,337 not including bonus and benefit information and other factors that impact base pay." One author, Jason Brennan, sought to figure out what the average hourly pay would be for an adjunct earning $3000 per course and determined it was $22.71 in 2015. He argued that this was substantially better than minimum wage,[162] but he used the figure of 135 hours per course and stated that if someone spent more time than that on the class, that was bad time management. For example, he estimated that an instructor should only spend an hour a week on course prep *and* grading.

If you are considering adjuncting, and if you are fortunate enough to be offered a job with benefits, you still need to figure out if what you are being offered will constitute a livable wage in that geographic area. Www.payscale.com [163] can give you some specific information, but you have to give them a lot of personal data and create an account to get it. A 2014 congressional report, "The Just-In-Time Professor"[164] called adjuncting "low pay at a piece rate" with many people trying to piece together a full-time salary by working at multiple institutions. According to that report, 89 percent of adjuncts work at more than one institution and 13 percent work at four or more. Finally, only 36 percent offer benefits including health care [165] to adjuncts. In addition, contract workers have no job security: you may find yourself wondering from semester to semester if you are going to be rehired. One adjunct said, "The life of an adjunct is one of worry, stress, and tension because you never know what the future will bring."[166]

A project called "Adjunct Action" undertaken by the Service Employees International Union (SIEU) looked at costs and pay scales for adjuncts at various locations including Florida, New York, and Massachusetts. A special report, due to the high concentration of educational institutions in the geographic area, was *The High Cost of Adjunct Living: Boston* (2013)[167] and included these findings:

- The median pay per course in New England was $3,750 for master's level courses at private not-for-profit institutions and $5,225 for doctoral level courses at private not-for-profit institutions. This means an adjunct teaching 12 courses a year—an extraordinary course load—may have an annual income of just $45,000.
- An adjunct professor must teach between 17 and 24 classes a year to afford a home and utilities in Boston.
- An adjunct professor would need to teach up to four classes per year to cover the cost of groceries for a family.
- An adjunct professor would need to teach three to four classes to afford care for a heart attack at certain Boston hospitals.

In 2017, Flaherty of *Inside Higher Ed* reported that across the US part-time, adjunct faculty members make about $1,000 per credit hour.[168]

For adjuncts, ways to get university library privileges vary. Wherever you are considering an adjunct teaching position, whether or not you would be teaching full time, inquire about the library privileges that accompany your position at each institution. Depending on your field, being employed as a research assistant on someone's grant is another way to earn money and have library privileges. If you have a postdoctoral position, you may be expected to start a new research project, which may take time away from your job application process. If you take a job that is not in an academic setting, look into getting visiting scholar privileges or becoming a "community member" at a nearby university. You may have to pay an annual fee for library privileges in some circumstances. Regardless of your type of employment, you will still need to set aside some time every week (ideally several times a week) to work on your own publications.

Some former graduate students have had luck with finding a research or administrative position at the institution where they received their PhD, whether working as a postdoc, administrative assistant, academic advisor, or in an information technology position. Large institutions may have small institutes associated with them that need someone to coordinate all aspects of running them, from answering telephones to preparing grant applications. If you like variety in your work day, staying affiliated in some way with your graduating institution in one of these types of positions can provide you with the personal network to find unexpected opportunities for adjunct work either there or at nearby institutions, and may also allow you library access privileges. Your connections may even lead to a "heads up" when a new full-time job in your field comes on the market.

Part 2: Staying on Top of Your Academic Job Search

Prepare for a Teaching Career (If You Want To Go to a Teaching Institution)

While many applicants are looking for employment at an institution of higher learning where they will be expected to be engaged in research as well as teaching, some PhDs prefer to look for a job that emphasizes teaching instead of research. James Lang (2017) has made several suggestions about preparing for a higher education teaching career in a *The Chronicle of Higher Education* article.[169] His advice includes 1) find a way to get teaching experience, 2) get educated about teaching (start with your own faculty development center for resources, and 3) get outside your department to gain a wider perspective.

If you haven't taught as a graduate student, you should get some experience teaching at a community college or as an adjunct at a college or university. Notice what you are good at and what aspects of teaching you need to work on. Unless one's PhD is in education, graduate students usually don't learn a lot (or any) theory about teaching. Some starting points may be Bloom's taxonomy of learning, flipped classrooms, and active learning. You might also consider doing some reading about online teaching[170] since it is more commonly becoming part of a college professor's job. Getting outside your department means getting experience at service in the community or in the larger university setting.

After you have fully considered all the ways and places you might publish, found interim work that pays, and enhanced your teaching skills, you now need to consider exactly what you want from a job in academia.

Be Clear about What You Want from an Academic Job

In spite of prophecies of doom about job search outcomes, quite a few positions are being advertised in most fields. Whether you are a graduate student, adjunct or junior faculty, or administrator looking to change jobs, prior to your job search take time to assess your current progress toward degree completion, long-term career goals, and requirements for personal and career satisfaction. At least initially, take the perspective that you want to find a job in a department where you will be happy and remember that you are checking out opportunities as well as being checked out.

Keeping the job hunt in perspective by thinking about what else you want out of your life besides a job will actually make this process easier. You may even want to define what a great life looks like for you personally. Some people want a family or time to sail or the ability to still read for pleasure. Susan Robison suggested that a happy academic life involves doing "high-impact work in a timely fashion" that should lead to satisfaction over the course of your life.[171] Thinking about these issues not only helps you plan for the future, but also will make you a stronger job candidate by allowing you to more persuasively express your interests and convictions in your cover letter, CV, and interview. Use the **General Job Search Preparation Worksheet** to help you narrow down the positions you actually want to spend time applying for and give those enhanced attention.

Mark Tonelli (2017) interviewed Amy Gusick, a successful job applicant in 2015.[172] She reported really evaluating for herself what she wanted to do in an academic job and where she wanted to live for family support and other lifestyle issues enabled her to narrow down the jobs she actually

General Job Search Preparation Worksheet

Take some time to consider and write your answers below the questions here. If you are having problems answering the questions, an academic job search coach may be able to help.

What type of positions am I considering? [Adjuncting, non-teaching, research jobs or postdocs? Another way to look at this is, "What compromises am I willing to make?"]What specializations am I comfortable teaching?

What are my preferences for a specific type or size of institution?

What types of positions am I reasonably qualified for?

What are my geographic preferences? Are any particular locations deal breakers?

What personal issues and lifestyle requirements influence my search?

Are there networks [friends, family, mentors or other supporters] than can make a community under consideration more or less attractive?

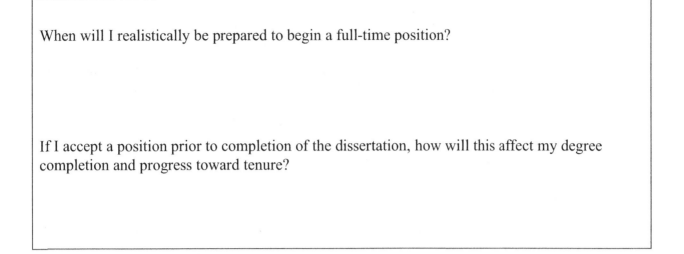

wanted to apply to, rather than trying the shotgun approach of applying to all manner of positions whether she was qualified or not. She was also willing to work in a private cultural resource management firm while continuing to pursue a tenure-track position in archaeology. Her advice to job applicants:

"Be open to a variety of opportunities. You never know what type of experience will set you apart from other job applicants. I never thought that my work outside of academia would be the reason I was able to get an academic position."

PART 3: ORGANIZING YOUR JOB SEARCH

Why would anyone take the time to get organized? For academics on the job hunt, the simple answer is to keep track of what they've done throughout the application process. Being organized simplifies the mundane so you can emphasize what's really important. It enables you to concentrate more easily. Not surprisingly, organizing allows big projects to get done more quickly and efficiently. All this can help you manage the challenge of a tough job market with greater equanimity, calm, and focus instead of scrabbling for answers in a pile of papers on your desk or floor. After all, many academics tend to "pile" rather than "file." If you are only applying to a few jobs, setting up a system to organize your job search may not initially appear to be the best use of your time, but starting organized is a lot easier than trying to put order to applications for 20 or more positions after you have applied. Consider organizing as laying the foundation of your house.

Getting organized also increases productivity, reduces stress, helps you gain more control over workload, feel less exhausted, and live a more enjoyable life. Having a **SYSTEM S**aves **Y**ou **S**tress **T**ime **E**nergy and **M**oney. With a system, you know what to do with any incoming item. Incoming items can include voice mail, email, regular mail, documents people hand to you, requests people make of you, or even things you think of for yourself to do, such as researching a paper, finding potential employers, or possible future colleagues. It also provides a way to recover from short or major (long-lasting) interruptions. Interruptions can be small, like a colleague who stops by while you are in the throes of writing, or large, like coping with cross-country moves, serious illness, or natural disasters.

Although you have to spend time and energy to get organized, once a system is in place, it should be easy to maintain, helping you prioritize your tasks and reduce feelings of overwhelm. Good habits are the key to driving the system and providing accountability for yourself and for others you may depend on. (For more detailed information on both psychological aspects of getting more organized, as well as how to do it to reduce feelings of overwhelm, see Appendix A.)

If you are applying for multiple positions, you may quickly lose track of the status of each application. Organizing your materials *from the very beginning* of your search is extremely important. A good organizing system will enable you to be sharp and prepared if you are unexpectedly contacted via telephone or video for an initial screening or pre-interview. Maintaining organized files of position announcements, materials submitted, and information about respective institutions is important. You will need a system to handle both hard copy materials and electronic materials.

Why Keep Paper Copies?

Though most job application materials, sometimes even including the actual offer of employment and the contract, are handled electronically these days, a wise person will keep some hard copies, especially documents that may not be easy to replicate. These might include documents with legal ramifications like the final contract offer or materials related to your research. Very rarely, a scholar is involved in a legal dispute involving research materials, and any papers associated with that should be kept as hard copies somewhere safe and accessible.

In this day of cloud-computing with Google docs, Dropbox, and other document-sharing sites, you might think keeping paper backup copies seems silly but technology can and does fail. Unfortunately, experience shows that technology can fail at the exact point when it matters most for accessing information. Weather patterns interrupt communications, brownouts can happen on overloaded energy grids, the laptop computer you planned to use for the presentation got left at the airport. We have also seen increased failures from breaches in cybersecurity when websites and servers are inaccessible for hours and sometimes days, as technicians scramble to fix the violations. Finally, there is the very real problem of rapid changes in technology making the way you have stored and accessed your material obsolete. All these possibilities make keeping your most valuable documents on paper as well as in electronic files important. Hard copies also mean you have a place to start rebuilding, without having to start from scratch, in the event of a catastrophic system failure. Even if you store all your application or presentation documents using a cloud service, it may prove inaccessible at a critical time, and a backup paper copy may become really important.

Our advice is to be duplicative, by having both paper and electronic copies of your final documents. You do not necessarily need to keep paper drafts of every iteration. However, paper copies have been around for centuries, and while production methods for documents have changed, you can still read material on paper. Computers are great for managing information, and keywords make finding items without digging through piles of paper easy, but when computers fail, you need a serviceable non-digital backup. Both of us have had clients calling in a panic because they were suddenly without digital access to a file that we may have worked on together and they wanted us to send them the latest version via email or Dropbox. We are always glad to help out, but sometimes we don't get the message in time to act on it or we do not have the most current document due to modifications clients made later.

Retaining hard copies of the application materials within each file helps you keep track of details and enables you to respond quickly and appropriately. Hard copies should include your job search materials, from CV to any articles in the press. Given the amount of material, you may well find yourself using the notebook as a cross-reference for a file drawer full of material. If you don't have an empty file drawer you can devote to this paperwork, you can use portable file storage boxes, often on sale at office supply stores, for under $10.00. Many academics use portable files for projects if they need to take documents for research away from their office.

We have known academics contacted for potential employment while they were conducting fieldwork, from archival work to zoology, so it may be useful to drag such a box around with you a while for easy access even in the field, especially if you are driving to your fieldwork site and can easily throw an extra box or job log notebook into your transportation. One paleontologist we know was working at a university in upstate New York and doing fieldwork in Wyoming when an offer came through during the summer field season for a university in Colorado. It was pretty clear he wanted the Colorado position, putting him much closer to his fieldwork site, but his fieldwork location was so remote that computers and cell phones were not operational. Only when he went to town to read email on his computer did he discover the school had been trying to reach him for about a week. And though he called back immediately, he had no materials available to help him negotiate the offer.

Pay special attention to retaining hard copies of materials you receive back from the institution, as not every document will come to you electronically, particularly job offers or contracts requiring your signature. If you are contacted by email for an interview or additional materials, you may want to consider printing out the email and including it in your hard copy notebook. If you do receive a contract, consider signing in blue ink to help keep originals separate from copies. You can also mark the documents "Original" or "Extra Copy" to help with this.

If you happen to be applying for non-academic and academic positions simultaneously, you may want to consider a way to differentiate the two searches, perhaps by color-coding the two types differently or dividing the notebook into two parts. Keeping two different notebooks is NOT recommended. The object is to have all the deadlines and notes relative to any job application accessible in one place in case a potential employer calls you.

Systems You Can Use to Organize Your Job Search

You can use one of several systems to organize your job search, whether for a traditional teaching/research position, a postdoctoral fellowship, a research appointment, or a post-ac position.

Here are a few options:

- A word file log, a spreadsheet log, or as we often recommend, a combination of the two, using the word log as an index with a binder notebook for materials behind it;
- An electronic file of your own creation;
- A hard copy daily tickler system using simple manila file folders;
- Variations of the "keep a running list," aka the grocery list style;
- The "one-stop bullet journal" method; or
- An electronic application (KanBanFlow, Dropbox, Evernote, Google Drive, GTD [Getting Things Done], or Text Expander)

Each allows for greater or lesser degrees of detail. Just remember, organizing is an art and not a science. Do not spend so much time organizing your tracking system to perfection that you procrastinate doing the actual application work. You may have to experiment to find which of the above methods work best for you.

Use a Log or Spreadsheet for the Big Picture Look at Your Job Search Efforts

A log or a spreadsheet can serve as your centralized overview record associated with each position. It can help you prioritize applications, meet crucial deadlines, and better manage the search process. Obviously, you can keep it as a paper copy or you can have it as an electronic document, whichever is easier and faster for you to use. We've given you a sample log, followed by a worksheet you can tweak to meet your needs. Since the log is for your personal use, you can consider adding a column such as "things I want to remember," such as the physical characteristics of a person you met at an on-site interview. For example, you might note: "Dr. Guthrie, middle-aged woman, short gray hair." You may be surprised at how quickly you lose track of such details when concentrating on the information you have to present, and such notes can be invaluable when following up, or when you are asked for a later interview.

A spreadsheet will look similar except that you will have lettered columns and numbered rows. Spreadsheets are generally easier to reorganize than word table documents because you can sort them whenever you need, using the data function to display by name in alphabetical order, or by due date. We have provided **Job Log for Academic Position Search Worksheet** with headers you can copy and paste into *either* Word or Excel formats for you. You can set these documents to "landscape" for more space as well.

Use the Notebook Method for Tracking Job Searches with Hard Copies

Using a spreadsheet or word log will help you keep track of what you have done in your job search process, but we like adding the notebook method for tracking hard copies of documents. Start by getting a large 3-ring binder notebook, then place your log at the front of the binder. Use the log sheet as a kind of table of contents for all the job applications you have done. Your notebook should have pockets to put materials in, so you don't have to three-hole punch everything. You can take relevant the part of the notebook with you when you go to an interview. Divide the notebook into sections by position and keep information in a pocket for each position. You will need some sort of dividers for each institution, whether you use tabs with the name of the school or just colored paper to separate the schools. Here is a list of the materials you will be collecting for each application in your organizing files:

- Position announcement, including where and when it was published, because sometimes positions are advertised slightly differently in different places
- A copy of all application materials submitted
- Acknowledgment letters received
- Notes about any conversations with members of the search committee
- Notes from interviews and relevant telephone conversations
- Additional research gathered about that institution, for instance, number of undergraduate student majors, background on members of the search committee, specialties of the department, internet information about the institution or department, and comments from friends or acquaintances about the institution or department

    A note about notes: These are for your benefit to help you remember things. It's ok to write next to a name "bald guy interested in Celts of the Siberian steppes." This is your private space to write.

- Rejection or offer letters
- A copy of your letter of acceptance or of your rejection of their offer, should you decide this job is not for you
- A list of dates and addresses for all correspondence

Inside your notebook, you may want to keep a separate face sheet for each search, to place in front of your materials.

Sample Job Log for Academic Position Search								
Institution	Contact	Area of expertise sought?	Deadline	Materials sent (what, when, and how)	Response	Interview schedule	Any other material	Thank-you letter sent
Illinois Wesleyan University	June Williams, Chair Dept. of History IWU PO Box 2900 Bloomington IL 61702-2900	Early European civilization	12/1/17	CV, cover letter emailed. Requested letters from Prof. Long, Prof. Chin, & Prof. Guthrie.	1/10/18	AHA- 1/8/2018 Interviewed with Prof. James Winn & Prof. June Williams	12/11/17 Emailed teaching video link, conf. paper, journal article.	1/13/18
University of Nebraska at Kearney	Dr. William Potter Chair of Search Committee, History Dept. UNK Kearney, NE 68849 (308) 865-8509	Not specified	11/24/17	CV, cover letter, journal article, statement of teaching philosophy syllabi from 113 & 114 sent by USPS. Requested letters from Prof. Long, Prof. Chin, & Guthrie.	11/12/17	AHA- 1/9/2018 Interviews w. Amy Potter, Steve Smith	N/A	1/14/18

Job Log for Academic Position Search Worksheet								
Institution	Contact	Area of expertise sought?	Deadline	Materials mailed (what, when, and how)	Responses	Interview schedule	Any other material	Thank-you letter sent

Part 3: Organizing Your Job Search

Job Log Face Sheet—Optional Worksheet
University of XYZ

Job Title:

Deadline for Application:

Job Location:

Paste in job listing here:

Materials submitted and when:

Correspondence (list by topic and date):

Phone calls, by date and type, including notes:

Interviews, by date and place, including notes:

Outcome:

Set Up Your Own Simple System for Electronic Files

If you choose to track your application status electronically, because many parts of the academic job search and applications are done over the internet, then setting up a folder for each job search in your email, on your desktop, or on a cloud-based service, may be the best way to file materials as soon as you receive them. We recommend that you set up an electronic folder for any position you are considering applying for as soon as you see or hear about a job opening. Since you will be tweaking your CV, cover letter, etc., for each application, and there is really no limit on space with this method, you can also store copies of the specific materials you sent and any electronic documents you receive in return in the same folder.

If you want to keep all email correspondence in the same file folder with your other application materials, you will have to create a word or spreadsheet document where you cut and paste the email and its contents. Don't forget to copy the header, including date and sender as part of this process. We know this process may seem a bit cumbersome, but you will value having everything in one place. Once again, documents with legal implications like an offer or an actual contract should still be printed and retained somewhere as hard copies.

How to Stay Organized if Spreadsheets Are Not Your Thing?

If spreadsheets or loose-leaf notebooks are not your thing, consider the grocery list method, the hard copy daily tickler file system, or the bullet journal methods as alternatives.

    Hard copy daily tickler file system. The hard copy daily tickler file system may be the oldest method for getting things done since the beginning of the industrial age. Many variations on it exist, but one of the best one in terms of available information about *how* to do it is David Allen's *Getting things done*.[173] What started as his book became a website and now also has an electronic app associated with it. The system is meant to help you keep track of everything you do in your life, so you would modify it to cover only your job search process. I have my own system called TAFFY, which is an acronym for the 5 questions you ask yourself as you decide what to do with any incoming item. (See the graphic and expanded description in Appendix A.) To create your tickler, you will set up physical file folders for each month of the year, and each day in the month. Use these four steps to create a simple ticker system to help you get and stay on track with all your tasks:

1. Get 43 hanging file folders.
2. Number the first set of file folders from 1-31. There will be 31 folders, each with a number on it in sequence: 1, 2, 3, until you reach 31 for the days in the month.
3. Label the remaining folders by month: January, February, until you reach December.
4. Place the (1-31) numbered folders together in a file cabinet. Place the monthly folders together, behind the numbered folders in a file drawer. This system works best if the drawer is within arm's reach. If a filing drawer is not available, use a portable and inexpensive plastic file box.

Once you have this system set up you will be rotating through the files as the month progresses, and you will always be working on both the current month and the next months in your "day folders." Start by putting the current day in front. For instance, if today is October 19th, the number

19 folder should be first. Put hardcopies for whatever you are going to be doing on October 19 in the number 19 folder in October. For instance, if you have a follow-up phone call to make on the 19th, and you kept notes on the first call, you would place those notes in the file for the 19th so you have those notes at the ready.

Each day, remove that day's folder and process the contents. At the end of the day, move the now empty file folder to the end of the day files so it becomes that date for the next month. Using our October 19th example, after you have either finished everything in the file for October 19th or moved the contents to another date, you then move the file to the back of number 18. Now the first file you see will be numbered 20. Eventually, day 31 will be reached and you rotate into the next month, in this case, starting with November 1st. You will now be filing things for the days of November and December. This filing system is a simple reminder (tickler) system to help you get things done when needed.

On the last day of each month or a few days before the end of the month, look at any items you placed in the monthly folder moving the contents of the monthly folder into the daily numbered folders. This beauty of this system is that you can start where you are and begin using it immediately. If you know dates projects are due, you count backward by estimating when you need to start a project and put a reminder in your file. You can even place a hard copy of whatever you are working on, perhaps an article that needs additional editing, inside the folder on the date you plan to work on it, so you don't have to search through the piles on your desk to find it and get started. You can quickly tame a pile of papers by breaking it down into smaller, more manageable pieces. For job hunters, you can place materials you plan to use to write a letter or research statement on a day of your choosing so you do not have to spend your actual writing time gathering up materials. If you cannot get a picture of how this works, take a look at this tickler file demonstration. [174]

Obviously, this is a paper-based method, designed to organize every part of your life not just your job search, and it is not for everyone. However, I know many people who, once they get used to the method, swear by it for staying on top of whatever needs to be done. They feel it is a great way to outsource their brains and stop worrying about when something will get done because they know it will come up at an appropriate time when they open the day file of the current month.

Grocery list method. The grocery list method is nothing more than keeping lists. We have all used this method, so it's familiar and easy to understand. Most people just write down the things they need to do on a notepad, sometimes adding a due date. For job preparation materials, the date can be of your own invention as you think about how long you need to prepare an application before submitting it or an actual hard and fast deadline. You can create lists electronically as well using a variety of apps from Apple's reminders to Asana or Todoist for Windows machines.[175]

Lists are generally very simple and easy to use, but the list method can be too simple. People like lists because you just scribble down things to do as they occur to you in no particular order. Many of us like to cross out the things that have been done to get a sense of accomplishment. Crossing out brings up one of the drawbacks—if you are using physical notepads, your material will not be particularly well-organized or accessible when you need it. On the other hand, having a list of the items you need to finish to prepare any given application can be quite useful.

Bullet journal. A better and slightly more complicated list system is using a bound journal that goes everywhere with you. One example of this style is the *bullet journal*, a method for non-consecutive tracking for a variety of items. The bullet journal is meant to help you keep track of everything you do in your life, but you can modify it to cover only your job search process. As described in a blog post at The Lazy Genius Collective,[176] the beauty of the system is that it resembles a potato: boring in and of itself, but exciting for what can be done with it. Because the bullet journal is very visual, we recommend that you read the illustrated instructions online,[177] watch the narrated video,[178] listen to the podcast,[179] or all of these things to get started.

Kendra of the Lazy Collective uses signifiers [180] to the left of her items to help her keep track of things. Her signifier system description is part of her blog post on how to bullet journal. Her bonus lessons [181] are ways to make using your bullet journal more fun.

A bullet journal is a great way to get rid of all those sticky notes reminding you to do something and has some of the advantages of a todo list if you like being able to celebrate progress by crossing off items you have finished. The upside of the bullet journal is you can take it wherever you go and add to it as necessary, but it will take some time to get used to it, especially remembering to update the index when you add new pages. Without the cross-reference from the index to the contents, it will quickly become useless to you.

The downside of a bullet journal is two-fold: you have to create it from scratch for yourself, and for some of us, this is a fun way to procrastinate (online supplemental materials even show how to use colors and stickers in bullet journal creation) when we should be actually writing application materials.

There's an App for That! Organizing Electronically

Like so many other things in life these days, apps are also available to make your job search easier. You may have used some of these already to organize your own academic research, but below are a few that seem particularly useful for the job search process. All these apps can be used to help you be ready for a phone, video, or in-person interview without scrambling to find the relevant material.

Dropbox:[182] You set up an account and a fairly small storage plan is free. You only pay after you have exceeded the storage amount. Sometimes described as a "cloud-based filing cabinet," Dropbox will allow you to store your material and only share it with others you have designated. It now allows for online collaboration when two or more people are looking at the same document, although you may have to actually discuss who is responsible for typing and saving the changes to avoid problems with "conflicted copies." Using Dropbox to store a variety of CVs or resumes so you can retrieve and edit them easily and quickly is a very good use of this app. If you have created some files that you want readily available should you be traveling to an interview, this is a good choice.

Evernote:[183] The array of ways you can organize material in Evernote is too vast to explain in detail here, but it is essentially a database you build to your own specifications. It is designed as a "note" labeling system and not for storing big documents. The app requires an account set up with a monthly fee and works across a wide variety of platforms. The big advantage of Evernote is the ability to "clip pages from the web" as you organize a job search. So for every school where you have applied, you may "clip and save" some website information about the department and faculty or even something about the surrounding community and the population the institution serves. Having this information at your fingertips, whether on a desktop computer, laptop, or other mobile device means information is readily available when you want to compose a cover letter, create a research or teaching statement, and tailor it to the interests of potential colleagues. You might use Evernote files to help address your own particular talents in a way that fits with the mission of the department or institution and you can store items as your professional headshot photos or photographs of your research, for example, lab micrographs to an archaeological sitemap.

Google Drive: [184] This file storage and synchronization service is a great tool for creating an on-the-go spreadsheet for every job you apply for (look at the information we include in the worksheet Job Search Log for Academic Positions in this workbook to see what you might want to include). The easiest way to create a job search log using this app is to generate a summary sheet, followed by another sheet for each job, following the model of a multi-sheet document in Excel by using the Microsoft® Office Compatibility Mode (OCM) or convert Microsoft® Office files to Google Docs, Sheets, and Slides. You can create some of the categories we have suggested, then color code them to your preference "all items in green must be submitted electronically; all items in red must be sent as a hard copy" reminding yourself that "red" documents may take longer to get the institution. You can create separate spreadsheets for any fellowships or postdoctoral positions you may be applying to, and keep them in the same Google document. The great advantage of the Google document is that it is easily shareable with someone else or you can keep it entirely private.

Text Expander: [185] This is one of several apps that allow you to store "snippets" of information you are constantly typing over and over again. If that's a feature you need, this app is for you. Phrases or data can be stored in a "snippet" with keyboard shortcuts to descriptions of your current contact information, educational status, courses you've taught, places you've taught, the title and abstract for your current research, referees, advisors or anything else you are entering repeatedly. Snippets generated by a text expander look a bit like web address codes and can also be used to fill out web forms more easily, once the snippet is set up. Several different paid versions, most of which are extremely inexpensive, are available. Your own computer also has some very simple snippet options: On a Mac, you can take abbreviations like "SMU" and tell your computer to replace that with "Southern Methodist University," by going to System Preferences > Keyboard > Text. Windows users have AutoHotkey (AHK),[186] a free, open-source macro-creation software that lets users automate repetitive items, again like creating shortcut abbreviations that will automatically be lengthened to the correct designation.

Remember, you should know *why* you want to do something using one of these apps or you could spend a lot of time figuring out how to use them only to find them personally useless. "People learn by doing, but they also learn by reflecting," said Steven Ovadia,[187] a professor and web services librarian at LaGuardia Community College (CUNY). In other words, get clear about your goals before you start looking at all the possible apps you want to use in conjunction with the applications you want to fill out.

Sites for Help with Your Academic Job Search

We have listed some helpful sites for your academic job search, along with some basic material to differentiate them for you. These links will take you to sites that can connect you to a community or that get you to general advice about looking for an academic job. Take a moment to explore a site that sounds useful to you. Use the **Website Evaluation Worksheet** to make any notes based on your first pass through concerning whether you find the site personally useful.

Academic Jobs Wiki. Academic Jobs Wiki [188] is a wiki for tracking academic jobs for the upcoming academic year by academic faculty, research, and post-doc positions, listed alphabetically by subject area, for example, anthropology, neuroscience, or Arabic language and literature. The plus side is many more international positions are covered than in the US-based sites; the downside is that as a Wiki, the site is built by participants, so available information can be a bit hit or miss. As the Brock Read (2016), a senior editor at *The Chronicle of Higher Education*, put it:

> Poke around the Academic Jobs Wiki, and you'll see an almost-intoxicating mix of rumors and cryptic updates. But the wiki, by design, only tells part of the story—a bunch of small stories, actually, that always end the same way: "Job offer has been accepted." What happens before, after, and between those stories affords a much realer [sic] portrait of academic labor.[189]

Try out this site by going to a job you are interested in, and click on the link. You may find information such as "more materials requested than originally anticipated; phone interview; job now deferred for fall search and next academic year." If a posting is closed, you may find it useful to know that before you spend time applying.

The Chronicle of Higher Education. Based in Washington, DC, *The Chronicle* [190] has more than 70 full-time writers and editors, as well as 17 foreign correspondents around the world. Online, *The Chronicle* is published every weekday and is the top destination for news, advice, and jobs for people in academe. If you go to this website and click on "Jobs,"[191] you will be redirected to a relatively new service, *Chronicle Vitae*. You can sign up for free. *Vitae* is "designed just for faculty and administrators [and] offers you access to free career management tools, including a dossier service." A search function allows you to enter keyword(s), position type, location and date posted (up to past 30 days). The job alerts allow you to save job search parameters to your account and to select emails to arrive daily, weekly, or monthly for newly advertised positions.

Vitae includes a "JobTracker"[192] section where individuals may post the jobs they have gotten in different fields outside the academy, or submit a profile with a header like "job seeker at XYZ University" including their current geographical location as a way of finding potential employers once they create a free account. Without an account, you can still look at the aggregate data for listings both geographically and by discipline. *The Chronicle Vitae* has also created a PDF entitled "Soup to nuts: An exclusive booklet on academic career development," which is a collection of articles the editors deemed useful to this topic.[193]

Website Evaluation Worksheet	
Use this table to note your thoughts about how you might use the website for your benefit.	
Academic Jobs Wiki	
Chronicle of Higher Education	
Inside Higher Ed	
Versatile PhD (VPhD)	
Other	

Inside Higher Ed. *Inside Higher Ed*,[194] founded in 2004, is a free online source for news, opinions, and jobs for all of higher education. Click on the "jobs tab" and you will find a list of how many jobs are available to browse, often more than 10,000, and the number of current positions in each category currently being advertised:

- Faculty Jobs
- Social Sciences / Education
- Humanities
- Fine And Performing Arts
- Professions
- Science / Engineering / Mathematics
- Administrative Jobs
- Executive Positions
- Alt-Ac or Post-Ac Careers
- Community Colleges
- Outside US

Administrative jobs tend to be the largest group advertised, often followed by "alt-ac" positions; while "Outside US" is the group that generally has the smallest number. This site also offers a search function with "job seeker tools" divided into Career Search, Dual Career Search, Career

Advice, My Job Alerts, and My Saved Jobs. Here you can search by keywords and location or sort by posted date or relevance.

Versatile PhD (VPhD). This site is most useful for those job seekers with a PhD and academic skills that are willing or interested in working outside higher education. Founded by Paula Chambers, VPhD also has an online community where humanities and social science PhDs can get excellent first-hand advice about nonacademic careers.[195] Membership is free, confidential, and open to anyone, provided they abide by the code of ethics. This section is divided into types of job (consulting, grant writing, and research) opportunities outside academia using high-level academic skills. However, much of this portion of the site is restricted to people who are affiliated with a subscribing institution, generally a university.

The jobs portion of the VPhD site [196] states, "All jobs listings are posted by volunteers from the Versatile PhD community. Anyone, including recruiters and company representatives, may post a job for free. VPhD registration is required, but that's free too." This site also includes monthly summaries of job postings, in case you might have missed one. And though it is oriented to those leaving the academy, there is a lot of useful advice for those seeking employment inside the academy, too.

PART 4: YOUR ACADEMIC JOB PORTFOLIO

Your job search began with reading job announcements posted by colleges and universities, in journals, and on other sites. You've networked, thought about what you want from your job, and organized the materials related to job postings. Next, you need to work on writing the pieces of your job search portfolio. Before we discuss the nine elements of your academic job portfolio and advice for each piece, you will need to think about your approach to submitting materials and how you will handle the written segments.

Timing of Submission

Although the job posting may give a deadline for you to get your application materials in, job search committee members may start to look over application materials as soon as they receive them. If you wait until the deadline to submit a complete application, the committee may already have found some applicants who look good to them and may even have conducted some preliminary phone or conference interviews. However, many applicants choose to submit all the materials at once exactly at the deadline in case they want to tweak materials before the final submission. If you do this, you will not be alone.

Whether to submit all the pieces of your application at the same time or piecemeal is debatable and dependent on the way the search committee is gathering applications. On the one hand, getting your cover letter and CV in quickly, then following up with other documents after you have fine-tuned them for a particular position, may give you time to better research the department you are applying to and to revise your materials accordingly. Be careful with this step. A good cover letter still counts, and it should directly address the particular position and not be a generic document.

Some people feel that piecemeal application materials keep your name in the minds of the search committee members. On the other hand, an administrative assistant who is keeping track of which applications are complete and which aren't may be annoyed by having to keep track of individual pieces, or could simply forget to enter a late document into a tracking spreadsheet. The search committee chair will scan the list early in the process and might view your incomplete application materials as a negative sign of things to come when working with you. Additionally, some online application-handling programs require a complete application before you can hit "submit."

Written Materials

Before you begin preparing the pieces of your application, make sure you have carefully read the instructions about *what* to submit to apply for any given job and follow these directions even if you feel that what they ask for is repetitive or too time-consuming. Remember some of what you submit may be seen by a search committee and other pieces may be evaluated by a computer program or a Human Resources office. Resist the temptation to refer readers to your CV as you fill out the online application. Failure to comply with the application requirements could eliminate you from the pool immediately.

Although most institutions will request a teaching philosophy and a research statement, some will also request a writing sample. Sometimes this is an actual piece of academic writing you have done and either published or submitted for publication. Try to pick something recent and directly related to your research or reflective of your research philosophy. It should be a stand-alone piece that does not require extensive background explanation for search committee members. It should exhibit your basic understanding of the literature and authors in your particular field. Even if a writing sample is not required as a part of the application, you can consider submitting it as supplemental information.

One service you might consider using to help organize your portfolio is Dossier from Interfolio, where you can certainly do everything being offered on your own computer, or in another cloud-based system. There is a free version and a moderately priced premium version. The service is designed to help both job seekers and employers manage all the elements of a job portfolio. Some large universities, such as the University of California and Princeton University use the service to "host" positions, so all materials are easily accessed by all members of a search committee. One big advantage is that you can use the service as a parking place for reusable confidential letters of recommendation and as an easy way to request updates to those letters.[197]

The Ten Elements of Your Academic Job Portfolio

The ten items listed below can be drafted initially to form the basis for all submissions, then modified to meet the requirements for each posting. We will consider each item in turn.

1. Cover letter
2. CV
3. Recommendations/Professional References
4. Teaching Philosophy Statement
5. Sample Syllabi
6. Research Statement
7. Research Presentation, aka 1st Job Talk
8. Sample Class, aka 2nd Job Talk
9. Equity and Diversity Statement
10. Teaching evaluations from your students

We are often asked for examples of the portfolio pieces. For the most part, we are not providing examples because we have found so much variation in the requirements from field to field. Our experience has been that people tend to copy the example, in order to get *it* right, when *it* can vary a great deal. Even for one person, a research statement could look surprisingly different for two different positions. Some teaching statements emphasize the use of current technology and online classes while others may be more traditional.

What we do provide in **Part 4** are many worksheets designed to help you assemble the information you need to include for any version of your CV, cover letter, teaching philosophy, research statement, and sample syllabi. We strongly suggest that you take some time early in your application process to research the expectations in your field for format and content of documents covered in Part 3. Ask faculty, your cohort, and other colleagues in your field for sample CVs, cover letters, teaching philosophy and research statements. For jobs that particularly interest you, look online for CVs of faculty in the department to which you are applying. Find out if your professional association, whether it is the National Association of Social Workers, the American Chemical Society, or some other, has standard formats for CVs. Write a draft of each document for yourself and then tailor it to fit each position you are applying to. This will serve you better than trying to shoehorn your skills and qualifications into a sample document that may not fit.

The Cover Letter

Yes, cover letters still matter. You might not think so in this age of texting and emojis, but the truth is that cover letters are an integral part of your job search strategy. Like your CV, the cover letter should be treated as a living document that you craft slightly differently for each position. It's actually somewhat surprising how few academics know how to craft a good cover letter. Unlike scholarly writing, a good cover letter can, and should, show your personality and passions. You will also discuss, in the first person, your qualifications. This gives the institution a sense of what they will get if they hire you, whether an excellent researcher in an R1 setting or an excellent teacher in a two-year college committed to helping students enter the paid workforce. A great exercise is to write the letter as if you are telling a good friend everything about what excites you in the advertised position.

A good cover letter is where you make your first good impression and is the first piece of writing the search committee will likely see from you. Decisions are made about interviewing candidates based on strong cover letters showing off the personality, originality, and the general likeability of an applicant. All are important components for those determining whether or not you are looking like a future colleague worth hiring. The academic cover letter is the introduction to all the other written materials you will submit to the search committee. One assistant professor who has served on various search committees wrote, "Fifty percent of applicants are removed from the [applicant] pool because of incomplete, poorly written, and/or badly formatted cover letters."[198]

Academic cover letters generally run anywhere from two to ten pages, unlike the industry standard of one to one and a half pages. The length may depend on what particular information the search committee has, or has not, asked for as part of the cover letter. For instance, if the committee asks for separate research and teaching philosophy statements, your cover letter will be far shorter than if you need to include this information in the cover letter itself.

The cover letter is the place where you can explain anomalies. For instance, if you need to explain the length of time to it took you to finish your degree, or your time out of academia, or any other item, and to find a way to say it with confidence. For example, if you followed your spouse who took who a job when you had small children, whether you are male or female, explain that you remained up to date with your field by reading the literature, teaching as an adjunct, serving as a classroom aide in your field at the local public school, or that you published two articles from your dissertation and have roughed out a grant proposal for the next step in your research path in that time. Write confidently about what you have done. Instead of "I was a trailing spouse," write, "I have remained active in my field by doing x."

Writing a cover letter is an intellectual pursuit. You will need to figure out how to best sell yourself in a few words. Before you start reading about what to include in each paragraph, take a few minutes to relax and imagine a conversation with a colleague based what you want to highlight in the cover letter about yourself and your unique talents. Imagining a friendly audience is a great way to get over the fear of saying the wrong thing.

Christopher Yates, an assistant professor of philosophy, aesthetics, and art theory at Institute for Doctoral Studies in the Visual Arts, has written an amusing essay for the *Chronicle Vitae* titled, "Prolegomena to My Cover Letter."[199] His letter is a critical or discursive introduction to himself as a philosophy professor seeking a better position. He makes self-deprecatory observations such as "Also, my languages are shoddy. When I say I have a 'reading knowledge of French and German,' I actually mean: I haven't spoken those things in years, and I rarely read in them (though I could if I had to). Truth be told my high-school Spanish is probably better. I'm not a European or anything."

Though Yates's letter is humorous, he actually buries some good advice in it. 1) Write from the position where you *already are* [a philosopher, an anthropologist, a neuroscientist, a zoologist...pick your discipline]. 2) Notice that you can say "I got into the field because I love" some specific aspect of what you do. That may be teaching students to think critically or conducting your own lab research. 3) Be willing to present yourself as a colleague, perhaps mentioning that you are willing to take on duties like curriculum committee work for the good of the greater whole.

Now let's go back to a more prosaic look at the elements you need to consider to write a dynamic academic cover letter:

1. Anticipate that the academic cover letter will run two to ten pages. Normally, it will be only two pages unless teaching, research, or other items are requested as part of the cover letter.
2. Use institutional letterhead if at all possible. Most graduate students are allowed to use the letterhead from the department where they are enrolled.
3. No spelling, grammar, punctuation, or typing errors are allowed.
4. Address your letter to the correct person, with the correct title.
5. Make sure the letter is dated with the current date.
6. Do not get fancy with font or margins: Use a standard typeface and one-inch margins.
7. Remember, this letter is about telling your story.
8. Be confident in explaining the length of time to degree or time out of academia.
9. Construct your letter using the following paragraph by paragraph guidelines we provide.

In preparing this letter, *make sure you address the person, usually the chair of the search committee, by the correct name and title*. Be certain the name is spelled correctly and the title is correct. If you don't know the name of the search chair, be proactive—call someone in the department and find out. A touch of formality is good: Address the person as "Dr." or "Professor." You are the petitioner, so do what you should to show respect. (Note: if you receive an answer, signed just "John," you may consider that an invitation to treat this person as a colleague and address him or her by their first name; however, if the letter you receive back is signed "John L. Rose," you should continue to address that person formally by title and surname.)

As you review your letter, *be sure you have no spelling or typing errors.* Not even one. You are applying for an academic job, and such errors will not reflect well on you. Do not trust spell checker or even your own brain to do this work for you. The brain sees what it thinks is there and not what is actually there at times. Have another person, who is a detail person, read it for you before you submit it. If you are in a pinch and have to do your own proofreading, read it out loud backward. You may be surprised at what you find.

Let's now look at the pieces of your cover letter. A little later in this section, we have provided a **Cover Letter Planning Worksheet** and a **Cover Letter Worksheet** to use to draft your cover letter. There are also some cover letter "builders" available on the web, which can help with formatting issues, though they are generally related to inquiries in the business world and not academia.[200]

The first paragraph. You want to make your letter dynamic and attention grabbing from the first sentence. Your charge is to create an opening line that draws the reader in. Think about unforgettable first lines of well-known novels: "It was the best of times, it was the worst of times" or "Call me Ishmael." Lead your reader into your own personal story.

This **story** is about who you are and why *anyone* should be interested in hiring to you. OK, so you can't be quite as creative as a fiction writer, but you can still build a case for your desired position. Try incorporating your passion into your first sentence, and letting the reader know why you are drawn to a particular area of study:

> *"I have a personal interest in archaeology that dates back to my youth. On a camping trip, my family stumbled upon the ruins of an old cabin only identifiable by the remaining chimney and stone stoop. My father charted the location and asked our local university for help finding information about this site. Imagine my surprise when, after many months of speculation, this cabin was recognized as the homestead of a freed slave, leading to its inclusion in the national registry of historically significant structures. I'd spent weeks imagining what the people who lived there were like, and find myself excited by the prospect of teaching others about our shared history."*

The cover letter is about getting your foot in the door and is only part of the total process. You want to pique their interest enough to get to the next stage, i.e., the interview. Maintain a confident, enthusiastic tone and state what you are bringing to benefit the school/department hiring you. What makes you the *best* candidate? If you are doing some unique research, why does it matter? Is your particular strength in teaching undergraduates, or getting research money for graduate laboratories? What makes *you* stand out from the crowd? For example: "I bring students into an active research laboratory."

Do not, repeat, do not, reiterate word for word the hiring advertisement and say, "I am writing today to apply for the position of Assistant Professor in History as advertised in *The Chronicle of Higher Education.*" They don't care how you found out…they just want to know if you should be put in the "trash immediately" or in the "further consideration" pile. If you created something exceptional at your last institution, this is where you put that information. Again, think, "How am I unique?" and put it up front. If you decide to say, "I saw the ad for the Assistant Professor in History at XYZ institution," make absolutely certain that the name of the institution you mention matches the institution in your address line. Using an incorrect institutional name is a silly mistake, but one that is easy to make in the world of cut and paste word software since all letters are expected to be tailored to specific positions.

The second paragraph. Focus on your accomplishments rather than specific duties and responsibilities. Here's where you provide more detail about your professional and/or academic qualifications. Did you design a web page for the last department you were in? Did you work with an architect to plan a laboratory? Say so.

Remember to refer the committee back to specific items on your CV that are relevant to the position you are seeking. Are they looking for an American history professor? Did you teach an Introduction to American History? If so, how often? Did you run a breakout group for this course as well? Use action words to keep the readers' attention. In fact, having a list of action words on hand as you write this section and others may be really helpful. We have provided a list of action words at the end of the CV section. Use them to help generate energy or enthusiasm in your cover letter, or just to brainstorm some ideas for presentation.

How will you relate your CV to the job advertisement? If you do not have a lot of solid experience, focus on your transferable skills, for example, the skills you used teaching a Biology 101 lab for which you also led discussions and graded tests. When responding to a job advertisement in a cover letter, you mirror the language of the ad to show that you both understand what the committee is looking for and that you are the best candidate, without parroting. As an example, you might indicate that you emphasize process rather than requiring a memorization of facts for an introduction to biological science. Consider using key competencies in bullet format to break up the text and hold the attention of the reader. White spaces work wonders to draw attention to what you've done. You can build a list of key competencies for yourself by using the **Key Competencies or Contributions to Research Worksheet**.

The third (possibly fourth, fifth or more) paragraph. Relate yourself to the school, by giving additional details about why you should be considered for the position. Continue expanding on your qualifications while showing knowledge of the school and, in particular, the department. *Explain:* "For over twenty years, I have worked at the interface of biology and evolutionary biology, which is a specialty area of x university." Show that you know something about the school and the community in which it is located by doing some research on it. A school located in a rural community will have very different resources and needs from a school located in a large urban area. Pay attention to the situation. You will write a better, more directed letter if you do.

In these paragraphs, you can briefly discuss your research plans for the near and far future, referring to colleagues you would be interested in working with at the institution you are applying to, and explaining why collaborating with them interests you. Your research plans can be separate paragraphs, or may be part of a separate document, depending on the requirements listed in the job ad.

The final paragraph. The final paragraph of your cover letter should be proactive. You can ask for an opportunity to interview and express confidence in your ability to do the job as the

Part 4: Your Academic Job Portfolio

Key Competencies or Contributions to Research Worksheet

Think about the best way for you to succinctly describe your abilities and contributions for someone that has never met you, for use in a cover letter, elevator speech or at a conference. What do you bring that is unique? Use this space to brainstorm your ideas.

1.

2.

3.

4.

5.

most qualified candidate. You can close with, "I look forward to hearing from you," or you can request that the committee contact you with an approximate time frame for the decision process on hiring. Make a note to yourself to call within a couple of weeks to make certain your application was received, to determine its current status, and to inquire about the decision timeline for your own peace of mind. You may follow up by email or telephone, but make sure you follow up! Since so few people bother with the follow-up step these days, the fact you did will likely end up noted in your file and possibly make a positive impression.

Use a formal closure, like "All the best," or "Best regards." Sign the letter and make sure you type your name underneath it. Even if you are submitting the letter electronically, use an image of your signature and place it in the correct location. If you are enclosing or attaching a CV or any other materials, be professional and include an enclosure line like this:

Enc.   Application Form
       CV, or written out "Curriculum Vitae"
       Letters of reference
       Article [title, and status if appropriate, such as "in press"]

Last but not least, celebrate! You are finished with this challenging task.

A few things to not do in your cover letter. Before you have written the cover letter, let's assume you have done a little web sleuthing to determine the classes taught in the department to which you are applying. If you have discovered a narrowly defined elective course that jumps off the page as something you would like to teach, look at who teaches it, how often she teaches it, and how closely it is linked to her particular expertise. You won't win any friends or influence people on the hiring committee if you boast that this is one of the courses you know you can teach. You might actually annoy the person already teaching in that bailiwick.

You also do not need to mention in your cover letter that you have two children, one of whom is special needs, and you want to be in that particular location because there is a good school to meet those needs. That kind of information can come informally in the on-campus interview process, should you get to that stage, and should you choose to share it. In the earlier stages, keep focused on the professional contributions you can make to the department and the school. However, if applying to a school that might be considered seen as in an unpopular location in a small Midwestern town, you may mention you have family in the area (if you do) as that could indicate to the hiring committee that you are a candidate likely to both accept the position and to stay with it.

If you are on the market because you do not want to continue at a particular institution for personal reasons such as departmental infighting (a lot more common than you might expect) or you experienced animosity from one person on your committee while working on your dissertation, do not mention, repeat, do not mention any of the negative reasons you might be leaving, even if they are true. Instead focus on what makes the current position attractive to you: the institution, the potential collaborators in the department, access to resources such as a specialized library, laboratory, or institute focusing on your area of research.

Part 4: Your Academic Job Portfolio

Cover Letter for Interdisciplinary Positions

As we discussed earlier, some positions are considered either "cluster hires" or you may actually be hired as part of an interdisciplinary team where the hiring line is split between only two departments. You will need to think carefully about and address in your cover letter how you fit the two departments or the cluster. You are not addressing the needs of one single department, but the needs of two or more separate or combined entities. Initially, you have to find out why the hire is for more than one department. For example, a neuropsychology position might require the person hired to teach in a psychology department as well as in a biology department or pre-med program. A Women's Studies and Gender Issues Program may be located in a sociology department. A biostatistician may need to know math and epidemiology and may be located in a School of Public Health.

How are you going to show that what you do serves the needs of the particular interweave of fields that the position requires? Is there a way to show that methodologies or theoretical questions are similar in both fields? Can you show you have a working knowledge of the major issues in each discipline? Be careful you are not just giving lip service to some disciplinary practices you actually do not have; for example, the terms ethnography, oral history, and archival work can be thrown around rather loosely but the people interviewing will know if you really do not have the in-depth understanding of the methodologies. Sometimes language and literature teachers are hired together; can you make a case for how your knowledge of Hebrew clearly enhances the study of Yiddish literature or theater? Your cover letter should show that you can integrate the knowledge or perceptions concerning the field for a wide reach to students or for collaborative with a team from various disciplines.

Postdoc Application Cover Letter

If you are applying for a post-doctoral position, consider tweaking your cover letter by creating a thread or train of thought linking your doctoral research to your current plans for research. Move on to describe your current research including the topic, methods you plan to use, underpinning theory, any preliminary findings you may have, and a final statement that ties this up together. This is usually one paragraph, up to six sentences long. Next, explain the contribution made by your doctoral research to your field in one to three sentences. This way you demonstrate an organic evolution from your previous research to your current interests. If you are writing to a specific advertisement or notification of availability for a postdoc position, note what the hiring institution is looking for, and write in greater detail about either your proposed research plans or how you can make a contribution to some ongoing research. To repeat, you should delineate what your work contributes to their mission and why it is important for you to be the person hired to pursue it. You can think in the broadest possible terms here, for example, "My work will contribute to more accurate ice cap measurements to validate the current thinking of the scientific majority on climate change.

    Sample academic cover letter. We have created a sample academic cover letter to help you get started. Additional academic cover letter examples can be found on the web at Harvard,[201] the Illinois Graduate College,[202] the Purdue Online Writing Lab (OWL), [203] the University of California, San Francisco,[204] and (surprisingly) at The Balance,[205] a personal finance website. The

Illinois Graduate College example offers the best example of telling a compelling story to draw the reader in; the Purdue example is fine for formatting a letter, but the actual style there is a bit outdated.

Curriculum Vitae (CV)

Your Curriculum Vitae (CV) format is particular to your professional field or university and is considerably different from a resume for non-academic jobs. In the US, the term Curriculum Vitae (or CV) is only used by a researcher, educator, or academic. Outside of the US, the term CV equates with what would be called a resume inside the US. When we use the term CV in this book, we are referring to an academic CV.

CV formatting basics. If you are used to writing 1-2 page resumes for the world of work, you may find that writing an academic CV requires some different skills. Academic CVs are often long and include so much information that you may feel that you are bragging; however, in your job search, judicious self-promotion is the name of the game.

Before crafting your CV, look at how professional experience is typically presented in your field, whether you are in physics or social work. An example of a particular format required by a field of study is that of the Council on Social Work Education (CSWE). CSWE has a template you should use to create your CV if you are applying for social work faculty jobs and the CSWE template differs from the format for nonacademic social work jobs and from what may be expected in other fields. Check to see whether there is a preferred format in your field or a template required by the institution to which you are applying. This information may well appear in the job advertisement. If you aren't sure how CVs in your field should be formatted and what they should contain, look at the CVs of other professionals in your field., faculty members you know in the field, and even checking in with your university's career services office for models. You can often find CVs for current faculty members online through the website of the department where they are employed.

You should start putting together your CV as early in your academic career as you can. You may feel like it doesn't look like much at first, but this is how everyone starts. You just keep adding information year after year, accomplishment after accomplishment. Information should be added from the most recent to the least recent, whether publications, fellowships, seminar presentations, etc. After the cover letter, CVs are often the first thing that search committees will review to determine if you should be included as an applicant for consideration. In our experience, between 10-30% of all applications will be rejected outright because committees are looking for a way to eliminate candidates given the overwhelming number of applications they receive.[206] If you do not follow the standards in your field, your CV will get tossed.

Tailor your CV to the place you are applying. For a research job, you might add a category about your research and/or consulting work. For a teaching job, you might add a list of courses taught or these things might go in a "Professional Experience" section.

Use the skill of *gapping*. Gapping means you provide a job title, use action verbs, make the objects of verbs describe what you did. Focus on *results* rather than on duties.

Sample Academic Cover Letter

[On university letterhead]

YOUR NAME

Best phone number to reach you: xxx-xxx-xxxx; video name if applicable

xxxxxxxxx@gmail.com   www.YourSiteName.com if applicable

Date

Dr. John Smith
Chair, Search Committee
XYZ University
Department
Address

Re: Position number if applicable

Dear Dr. Smith,

[The hook]
As a feminist geographer with a specialization in the social and spatial processes that constitute and shape cities, I am excited by the Lecturer in Human Geography teaching position at University XYZ. I have a personal interest in how geography shapes the human experience that dates back to my youth: I was involved in creating a soccer league for women and girls in Soweto a township of the city of Johannesburg in Gauteng, South Africa when my family was located there in connection with work being done by an international non-governmental organization (INGO). I know first-hand how the accidents of geography can shape the location and actions of social organizations.

[More on professional qualifications]
My research program links social, urban, and feminist geography with an empirically rich and community-engaged qualitative research practice. My scholarship has attended to the spatial logics of sport-centered urban policies and the social geographies and mobility of marginalized communities, with an emphasis on women. I completed my PhD at the University of XXX in 20xx and am currently hold the [XYZ] Fellowship in Gender & Urban Studies at ABC University. I have published in *Gender, Place and Culture*, *Social & Cultural Geography*, and the *Journal of Leisure Studies*, as well as contributed chapters to edited volumes such as *Planning for Marginalized Groups' Participation in City Recreational Facilities* (20xx, publisher name). My research agenda has been funded by the Social Science and Humanities Research Council and several internal research groups at the University of XXX. During my fellowship, I have focused on urban studies through research, writing, and teaching.

My recent research project, "[Insert idea here or name of actual study you may be working on]" involves the development of an oral history archive and an analysis of these and other stories of the city (such as social policies and participatory planning schemes) to tease apart the relationships between the lives of women and girls and the rapidly changing urban social geographies of a growing city. The project is an inquiry into the spatial and temporal factors make social difference visible, while paying heed to the material effects of social difference.

One of my strengths as a teacher is to bridge theory and practice in a classroom setting. Currently, I teach an advanced seminar that brings together diverse literatures and fieldwork assignments to generate a praxis for social inclusion in the city. The course is an opportunity to think broadly about how, and for whom, cities work, via academic scholarship (especially feminist geography, urban studies, and planning theory), policy briefs, INGO-centered research, artistic interventions, and students' own reflections on their experiences in urban spaces. Students use participatory methods to design and produce an outreach activity intended to investigate and address how people imagine and construct a relationship to their cities. With these strategies, I aim to demonstrate an integrated engagement with urban social inclusion while helping students develop tools for qualitative inquiry that they may draw upon in and beyond the classroom.

[Show you know something about their organization here; i.e., what you can do for them]
I have over ten years of university teaching experience at all levels, from introductory survey classes to small advanced seminars and independent studies. I have developed social geography, urban studies, qualitative methods, and population geography courses. These and other courses are readily adaptable to fit the course coverage required in this position, and I would be excited to develop other courses in political and historical geography to fit the needs of the Geography Department.

I am committed to developing links between research and teaching as a way to create an active pedagogy and mentorship opportunities for burgeoning student researchers. My planned project on [insert here] may allow the opportunity for a partnership and urban oral history projects for undergraduate students.

My experience with community-engaged research and university-community partnerships will directly contribute to the diverse academic and student communities of the University XYZ. For instance, my involvement in the [insert project] gives me immediate access to additional resources for studying urban geographies. I am actively involved with various professional organizations, where I have participated as an organizer of [panels, workshops, anything else]. In my presentation entitled [insert title here] to the Association of American Geographers conference, I set out an analysis of my research data showing how service location matters in urban planning.

[Wrap it up in a proactive way]
As requested, three reference letters are being sent to your attention. Please contact me if I can provide any additional materials in support of my application. Thank you for your time and consideration.

Best regards,

Signature
Your name typed
Enc.: CV

Part 4: Your Academic Job Portfolio

Cover Letter Planning Worksheet

What will be your lead sentence?

What makes you unique?
education degree?

What is your best strength?
determination
organization

How will you explain time to completion or time gaps?

What do you bring to the institution [what's in it for them]?

What are 2-3 reasons why you know you are capable of handling this job?
3 yrs University teaching
9 yrs teaching

What are 4-5 competencies you could present in a bullet form?

What evidence do you personally have proving you can do this job?

What can you point to as an accomplishment(s)?

How will you relate your CV to the job advertisement?

What have you discovered about the school or department that you want to remember to mention in your letter?

What research plans would you like to pursue? [Do not censor yourself. This exercise is for your benefit, so whatever pops into your mind, no matter how far-fetched, include it.]

How will you wordsmith your letter to demonstrate confidence in performing the advertised position?

How will you close your letter? Is that formal enough?

How will you close your letter? Is that formal enough?

When will you follow-up? (3 days, 1 week, etc.)

Whom will you ask to edit your letter?

Other information you think *must* be included? [Family in the area? Compelling reasons to move to the area?]

Cover Letter Worksheet

The First Paragraph:
Attention-getting opening sentence: What's my story? How did I get hooked on doing whatever I do?

Follow up with details about what makes me an outstanding candidate for the job. What makes me unique? Work the title of the job position advertised into this paragraph.

The Second Paragraph:
What are my accomplishments and professional and/or academic qualifications? (Degree, courses taught, grants secured any other specific accomplishments.) Refer to CV here.

The Third and Fourth Paragraph(s)
What can I do for you? (Demonstrate my knowledge of the institution, potential colleagues, students, research plans, and the local community, etc.)

Fifth Paragraph:
How will I politely wrap this up?

Cover Letter Checklist Worksheet

Make sure you have done these things:

- ☐ Created letterhead with contact information as part of document (not in header)
- ☐ Correct name and title of person in address
- ☐ Correct physical address
- ☐ Date
- ☐ Reference to job number or job title
- ☐ Correct salutation with title (Dr. So-and-So)
- ☐ Read, reread, and had someone else read for grammar and typos
- ☐ Crafted a compelling first sentence to hook the reader ("Why *this* job?")
- ☐ Told a story about who I am in relation to the position
- ☐ Provided detail about my accomplishments
- ☐ Showed knowledge of the institution and its particular issues and/or types of students
- ☐ Demonstrated familiarity with department and potential colleagues
- ☐ Discussed current and future research plans
- ☐ Referred back to CV at least twice in the body of the letter
- ☐ Explained any anomalies in time to degree or time out of academia
- ☐ Carefully read and specifically addressed issues mentioned in advertisement
- ☐ Formal closure
- ☐ Signed letter
- ☐ Listed enclosures
- ☐ Made sure enclosures are attached
- ☐ Made note to self about date to follow up

Be sure to consider *parallelism*. As you format your document, list all items about your professional experience in the same way. Use the same verb tense and use the same amount of white space for each entry in the same section. This rule applies to each section of the document.

Make the CV as easy to read as possible with use of headings, white space, and brief descriptions. Think *clarity* and *consistency*. Do *not* get creative with font type or size. Stick with the basics, such as Times New Roman, 12 point font, and black type. You want to be seen as serious.

Use *action words* to help make the CV feel live a dynamic living document (which it is). We have provided a list at the end of this section to help you find some words that will work for you.

Information to include and not include in your CV. Start by putting together the information that is bullet-pointed below. Later, you may have to adapt this list to meet the expectations of your field or for a specific job listing.

- **Your basic contact information**, including the heading—Curriculum Vitae—followed by your legal name, your current address if desired (either your institutional address or home address), a phone number where you can be reached during the day (check to make sure that the outgoing message sounds professional), and a current professional email address (i.e., yourname @gmail.com, not flybynight@gmail.com). Remember, you can have your professional email forwarded to your flybynight email, since you may not want your flybynight to be seen by potential employers, but still want to use that name for personal email correspondence. If you are between physical addresses, put an address on your CV where you know materials can reach you. Rent a Post Office box if you need to.

- **Consider adding media links** to your address information, or even deleting the physical address and replacing with your own website, your LinkedIn profile, or your Twitter name if you are active there. People are so much more mobile than they used to be, and new PhD graduates may find themselves spread across institutions or even across the country while finishing the dissertation, so this makes practical sense. It also indicates you are up to date with technology and social media.

- **No date**: You do not need to put a date on your CV as long as your CV is current.

- **Education**: You should list the most recent degree first. Information to include is institution, year (or anticipated date) of graduation, degree received, dissertation or thesis title, if applicable. Diplomas or certificates, professional license and license date may follow, but not license number unless specifically requested.

- **Professional experience**: Depending on the format for your field, you will list the institution or other employer where you worked, the start and end dates (which may just be years), and your job title. For instance, your job title may have been Assistant Professor of Anatomy, a position you held from Fall 2011 to Spring 2013. Beneath the title you provide brief information about your job duties. You should list the most recent work first, but this is not the place to list every class you have ever taught. You want this to convey the kind of work you've done, using action verbs to demonstrate the breadth of your skill set. For instance, in the Anatomy example, convert "taught intro to blood flow physiology" to "developed and taught physiology curriculum for first-year medical students," which is more specific and shows breadth of expertise. Include items like faculty teaching experience, research experience, editorial board experience, and consulting or administrative jobs in this professional experience section.

- **Specialized Skills**: If you have specialized skills, such other languages, include written and oral levels of fluency. You can also list other technical skills, such as how to do DNA sequencing, ability to run statistical packages, qualitative analysis skills, or computer skills like particular programming or modeling languages.

- **Post Graduate Training**: If you have held a postdoctorate position, list it in this section. Do not, however, list every continuing education class you've ever taken. If you have a certificate for a specialty area, such as geriatrics, you can include that here.

- **Publications**: Just as you did with your professional positions, put the most recent first, with the format appropriate to your field. Include live links to electronic versions, if they exist. Test the links to make sure they work. List the publications where you are the first author before publications where you are not the first author. Be prepared to explain your contribution to papers where you were not the first author in an interview. You can list book reviews and peer-reviewed contributions to volumes in this section as well, though you may want to set them off somehow with a separate heading denoting other types of written contributions. Put the publication section before the presentation section because publications generally garner more prestige.

- **Presentations**: In terms of presentations, all the same rules apply, with the most recent first, and formatting appropriate to your field including date and place of presentation. Include links to electronic versions like a PowerPoint online, if they exist. Again, test the links to make sure they work. Unlike publications, less importance is placed on who is first author so just list the presentation the way it appeared in the program. Be prepared to discuss your contribution to the presentation in an interview.

- **Grants Secured**: List the most recent first in the format appropriate to your field. If you were the principal author of the grant *and it was funded,* be sure to *state the amount*. Grants that paid you for doing certain work belong in professional experience. You can also list things like NSF grants and Fulbright applications that are currently under consideration.

- **Teaching Philosophy**: Usually, people are asked to address their teaching philosophy in a separate document. If not, make sure you follow the instructions for including this in your CV in terms of length and content.

- **Honors and Awards**: List the most prestigious in your field, with the most recent first. If you received an honor or award that might not be recognized by your reader, give a brief explanation of it. For instance, if you received a "Gabriel A. Almond Award," explain that this was an award given by the American Political Science Association for the best dissertation of that year in comparative politics.

- **Professional Associations or Memberships**: Again, list the most prestigious in your field first. Be sure to indicate if you were an officer, chair of a major committee, a conference organizer, or another type of major contributor. List years of membership.

- **Licenses**: Sometimes licenses are listed toward the end of the CV and sometimes in the education section. Determine what is common in your field and put your licensure there. Listing licenses received or in progress is most common in the medical arena.

- **Background**: Personal information that doesn't fit elsewhere, such as citizenship status, residence abroad, etc., is only included if it is applicable to your eligibility for the job. *Do not* list personal information like birth date, number of children, and marital status.

- **Service**: You can list academic service such as serving on a university or department curriculum committee, professional service as a reviewer on a recognized journal in your field, or community service such as serving on the board of a local organization. You may have to decide whether the community organization is something you want others to know about you. For instance, if you served as Finance Committee Chair at your local church, the skills you used might be pertinent, but you may not want to divulge your religion. Service is often a real consideration when it comes to advancement and tenure promotions, so this may be a section that is important to the hiring committee, depending on the position you are applying for. If you are applying for your first faculty position, think about what kinds of academic, professional, and community services you have been engaged in while enrolled as a graduate student and which might translate favorably into a job application. For example, if you chaired a committee like "Graduate Students of Color" or you were the graduate student representative for hiring a new faculty member in your department, you would want to list that here.

- **Volunteer work** is often either listed under service or as a separate category. If you did specific work for a specific organization (organized speakers for a monthly colloquium in biology department), treat it as work, listing the span of time you did it, and any special skills it entailed. If you feel so compelled, you can add "pro-bono" to the description, but the idea is to show off your capabilities and would be assumed for volunteer work.

- **References**: References are included last and on a separate page. Generally, you should only include the name, title, institution, and reference's contact information unless the place to which you are applying requires something different. You do not include details about your relationship to them. You may or may not be asked to provide references, especially early in the application process, but it is wise to have the list ready. Recommendations, which we will discuss shortly, are letters sent by your referees to the institution where you are applying. You may have a pool of referees, depending which jobs you are applying for, so be sure the References page is modified for each application as necessary.

Other CV details

- **Typos and spelling errors**: You must not make any typos or spelling errors because they become part of the impression you are making with your CV. Have someone else who is good at detail work review your CV after you have completed it. Find someone who knows the difference between a CV and a resume to take on this rather thankless task.

- **Feedback**: When you have completed a good draft CV, check with faculty members whom you trust for feedback on your CV. Ask them to comment on format, content, and readability.

- **Updates**: You may update your CV at any time, including after you have sent in your application, particularly if a major change has occurred. For instance, if you have now graduated, received a grant award, or gotten something published that was previously under consideration, use this as an opportunity to let the hiring committee know of your success. You can send the updated CV along with a brief cover letter noting the changes or additions so the hiring committee is not left wondering what has changed. Just tell them. Make the change easy for them to understand and you can both impress them with your news and keep your name in their minds.

- **Create a specific file name:** So that you can find the latest version of your CV quickly, create a file name and keep it consistent for yourself, such as "CV Jane Roe-May 2017" or by date of last revision, "2017-11-20 Jane Roe CV." This type of simple naming structure also helps the search committee to find your CV quickly when comparing candidates.

When to write your CV. Ideally, you will begin writing your CV during your first year of graduate school and update it on a yearly basis or more often. Get faculty advice from the start in terms of format, content, and readability. At the end of each year, review your CV not only for what you need to add, but also for what kinds of things you want to be able to add a year from now.

Aspirational CV. Amy Minto, PhD in Business Management (University of Oregon, 2016) recommends that graduate students and recent PhDs also write an *aspirational CV*, in which they note down items they want to add in the next 1-5 years. For instance, you might aspire to a co-authored article in the next year, an article for which you are the solo author in two years, two articles (one as a solo author) in three years, and a grant proposal in four years. If you have ideas of the journals you want to publish in, list those as well as the working titles of the articles or proposals. What conferences do you aspire to attend in the next few years and what role do you want to take at those conferences: present a paper, moderate a discussion, lead a workshop, etc.?

If your aspirational CV includes attending or presenting at a conference, think about how you can make your presentation interesting and engaging for an audience in your field. In other words, include notes in your aspirational CV about using an outline and not reading a paper word for word. Add notes about how you will interact with fellow panelists and the audience. Think about connections you can make between your work and that of someone else whose work you know—after all, you are probably all in the same field and you likely know of their work, even if you do not know them. If you feel that you need more professional teaching experience beyond a teaching fellowship, plan in a time to teach a summer or online course at a nearby academic institution and make that part of your aspirational CV. The aspirational CV serves as a roadmap of where you want to take your professional life.

Online CV. You may not be able to update a CV you included with a job application, but you can build a simple website, using WordPress or another program, that serves as an easily

Part 4: Your Academic Job Portfolio

CV Checklist Worksheet

- ☐ Correct contact and institution information
- ☐ Correct contact information for yourself
- ☐ Correct spelling and no typos
- ☐ All hyperlinks work
- ☐ Correct and consistent verb tense used
- ☐ Font and size are consistent
- ☐ No unnecessary jargon unless terms specific to your field are needed
- ☐ Document is formatted as requested, typically a PDF
- ☐ Included numbers and facts, where possible
- ☐ Checked for readability
- ☐ Checked for accuracy
- ☐ Listed all academic qualifications:
- ☐ Education
- ☐ Professional experience
- ☐ Publications and presentations
- ☐ Research
- ☐ Teaching
- ☐ Service, including grant writing
- ☐ Professional associations or memberships
- ☐ Honors and awards
- ☐ Licenses, if applicable
- ☐ References, if applicable
- ☐ Created a specific file name that identifies you and the date for yourself

updatable online CV. List the link to your online CV at the end of your actual application CV. You may have pages for basic information and education, professional experience, publications, presentations, special skills, and links to talks you have given. Make sure that any photo you include looks professional and current. Some people also feel the profiles on LinkedIn, academia.edu, or Google+ serve them as a general resume, but a true academic CV usually includes a lot more information than a resume. Whatever you choose, be sure to keep it updated, and make sure any links you include still work. You can go to most faculty pages on the website of any university and download a CV from someone in your field as a template for yourself. Or check out a LinkedIn profile for an academic where CVs are sometimes uploaded. Remember as you search these sites that in the rest of the industrial world, the term "CV" is used to describe what Americans would call a "resume," so what you download may not look very much like an American academic CV.

CV/resume builders. Many applications are available to help you build a resume using the web, and many of them are free. Most are designed for job hunters outside of the educational arena and none available to date seem to have the ability to build a true academic CV, since it is a much more complicated and specialized document than the typical resume.

If you want to experiment with building a CV using software for your desktop device, here are a few options: CVMaker,[207] YourCVBuilder,[208] or Resumonk.[209]

If you want to experiment with building a CV using software for mobile devices, here are a couple of options:

For Android:
Curriculum Vitae [210]
This free app is available through Google play, and creates a PDF for your CV after all the appropriate information is entered. However, like most apps that claim to build a CV, the end result looks far more like a resume than a CV. There are plenty of ways to customize fonts and templates, and once the document is created it can be mailed directly from a phone.

For Apple devices:
Pocket Resume [211]
Available for Apple devices for a small fee, currently $4.99, you can download this app which will allow you to craft a professionally formatted resume or CV right from your iPhone or iPad. This mobile app also includes the ability to write cover letters. The PDF rendering technology means you don't have to spend time on layout or design. You can then send your document directly from your mobile device and iCloud will store and sync it with all your other devices. It will also allow you to **publish a professional website with** your resume or CV without the cost of paying a domain host.

Shortening your CV. If you are told to shorten your CV for a particular committee, the headings above are still the headings you should use, though you may want to delete service, if you really can't point to any service in your graduate student career. The service category is usually used for building a tenure case anyway. If you have included anything like a summary of your dissertation research in the CV, move it to your research interests page. You may be able to delete teaching philosophy since it is usually a separate document. You may also want to delete professional associations or memberships unless you are an officer. Karen Kelsky has recommended adding "selected" to all content headings to make clear this is an abbreviated version of your CV.[212]

We have provided an **Action Words for Cover Letters and CVs Worksheet** to help you as you think about wordsmithing the various versions of your cover letters and CVs. We follow that with a **CV Worksheet**.

Action Words for Cover Letters and CVs Worksheet

We have provided several action words to stimulate your thinking. Feel free to add your own words to this list.

A- Accelerated, Accomplished, Accounted for, Accumulated, Achieved, Active in, Arbitrated, Articulated
    Your word(s) here:
B- Boosted, Briefed, Broadened, Budgeted
    Your word(s) here:
C- Campaigned, Chaired, Championed, Clarified, Coached, Collaborated, Coordinated, Corroborated, Cultivated, Customized
    Your word(s) here:
D- Decided, Decreased, Delegated, Demonstrated, Designated, Developed, Devised, Diagnosed, Documented, Doubled
    Your word(s) here:
E- Economized, Edited, Educated, Empowered, Enabled, Encouraged, Endorsed, Enhanced
    Your word(s) here:
F- Facilitated, Focused, Forecasted
    Your word(s) here:
G- Generated, Grew
    Your word(s) here:
H- Harmonized, Harnessed
    Your word(s) here:
I- Identified, Illustrated, Impressed, Improved, Increased
    Your word(s) here:
J- Justified
    Your word(s) here:
K- Kept, Knowledgeable
    Your word(s) here:
L- Launched, Led
    Your word(s) here:
M- Magnified, Managed, Marketed, Mastered
    Your word(s) here:
N- Navigated, Negotiated
    Your word(s) here:
O- Observed, Obtained, Orchestrated, Organized,
    Your word(s) here:
P- Participated, Pinpointed, Performed, Publicized, Published
    Your word(s) here:
Q- Qualified, Queried, Questioned, Quoted
    Your word(s) here:
R- Realigned, Recognized, Recommended
    Your word(s) here:

S- Selected, Separated, Spearheaded, Stimulated, Succeeded, Surpassed, Synchronized, Synergized
    Your word(s) here:
T- Tabulated, Targeted, Tested, Took over, Traded, Translated, Triggered, Triumphed, Troubleshot
    Your word(s) here:
U- Uncovered, Underwrote, Unearthed, Unified, Upgraded, Urged, Utilized
    Your word(s) here:
V- Validated, Verbalized, Verified, Vitalized
    Your word(s) here:
W- Won, Welcomed, Witnessed, Worked, Wrote
    Your word(s) here:
X- eXceeded, eXcelled, eXemplified, eXpanded, eXpedited
    Your word(s) here:
Y- Yielded
    Your word(s) here:
Z- Zeroed, Zoomed
    Your word(s) here:

Words you want to use are mainly verbs; these proscribed words are adjectives and smack of job search jargon.

Some words should not ever be used in your CV or in your cover letter. Below are just a few that will be a red flag to anyone reading your material and why. Feel free to add your own.

*Words **not** to use:*

    Unemployed. You have just said two things you don't want to say:

    1) You do not have a very high opinion of whatever you are doing now, whether you are finishing your dissertation or volunteering while you look for work; and

    2) You have now highlighted any "breaks in service" that may not otherwise have caused any comment at all. Academic work is often sporadic and intermittent.

    Expert. You have a doctoral degree. You are already considered an expert. No need to belabor it. Expect that you will be asked to demonstrate your expertise in an interview.

    Ambitious, hard-working, driven, accomplished, etc. OK, that's a series of words, but you get the idea.

    Synergy, wheelhouse, etc. This type of jargon has been used so often by job seekers that it is nearly meaningless.

    Responsible for, Results oriented. Start with what you did and skip these introductory words.

Part 4: Your Academic Job Portfolio

CV Worksheet

You can list details in the categories below or start with an online template.

Basic contact information
Legal name:
Address where mail will reach you:
Daytime phone number:
Professional email address:

Education

Most recent degree:
Institution:
Year of degree:
Dissertation or thesis title, if applicable:

Next most recent degree:
Institution:
Year of degree:
Dissertation or thesis title, if applicable:

Next most recent degree:
Institution:
Year of degree:
Dissertation or thesis title, if applicable

Diplomas or certificates, professional license and license date may follow, but not license number unless specifically requested.

Relevant Professional Experience

Where you worked, when, job title:
Brief description of duties using action verbs:

Where you worked, when, job title:
Brief description of duties using action verbs:

Where you worked, when, job title:
Brief description of duties using action verbs:

Specialized Skills:

Postdoctoral Training [If none, omit the heading]:

> **Publications** [Label as submitted, in press, or published]:
>
> **Presentations**
>
> **Grants Secured:**
>
> **Teaching Philosophy** [This may not be needed here]:
>
> **Honors and Awards:**
>
> **Professional Associations or Memberships:**
>
> **Languages** [Level read or spoken, and fluency]:
>
> **Other Skills** [Only if there is something pertinent to your field]:
>
> **Service:**
>
> **References:** Should be placed on a separate page, with names, titles, and current contact information [make certain it is correct]. That is sufficient.

Recommendations/Professional References

Some academics on search committees advocate for dropping this requirement until a candidate is in the later rounds of interviews, as recommendations are generally not read [213] until the candidate is truly under consideration. For both candidates and their referees, reference letters are a burdensome requirement. Nevertheless, if you are a new PhD, sooner or later you will need a letter from your advisor or dissertation chair. This is simply standard operating procedure for the newly minted PhD. Use the **Recommendations Worksheet** to brainstorm your possible references.

Make sure you know what your referees are going to say. Ask if they can give you a positive recommendation: You don't want to be surprised if what they write or say over the phone is not as flattering as you expect! Make sure your referees really do know something about you and the quality your work, so they do not write something vague and half-hearted about you. Sometimes reference writers find it helpful if you give them a list of areas to address and remind them of things like the dates of important events (graduation, conference presentations) since it may be many years after you worked most closely with them that you are asking for a recommendation. Consider getting references even from people outside your academic area and institution as well.

You've heard this before, but it is still true. The best way to get good recommendations is to use your network connections. Ask people directly if they are willing to give you a good recommendation. You never know when asking for a recommendation will lead to a conversation providing some inside information about what a school is really looking for in a candidate, which may or may not be in the advertisement for the academic position. The recommender may even be able to tell you something about the search committee members if she or he knows them. When a recommender provides a strong endorsement for you and your work, you are much more like to actually get an interview. It's human nature to interview a "known quantity" rather than to gamble on a candidate whom no one knows personally. You also need to have at least one referee who was not on your doctoral committee and who is not from your doctorate-granting institution.

Help your referees write the recommendation by telling them what to say or even by drafting the letter and make sure you offer any assistance they require. Try to write in the style you imagine for them, rather than in your own voice. If you are writing sample letters for your recommenders, write a different letter for each recommender, and make it easy on yourself by letting one letter speak to your research, another to your teaching, another to your collegiality…or whatever is your strongest area. For example, your dissertation chair may be the best person to write about your research; someone else you were a teaching assistant for may be the best person to write about your teaching; and someone else who employed you to help with his or her own research may be able to speak to your qualities as an employee or colleague. Your referees will thank you as will the search committee because they are not reading the same letter from your referees again and again.

Tell your referees all the places you are applying and provide a copy of the job announcement so they can calibrate *their* letters. Consider that when referees write letters for multiple people applying for the same position, they want to put each person in the best light. Do not blindside your referees with a short turnaround time for letters.

Delayed reference letters are the single biggest problem schools have with job applications; ask for yours early, and often if necessary, until you know they have been submitted. You may have to keep reminding your referees (without being a pest) until the reference is done, so your application is not held up waiting for it. Make sure all your references are in by the deadline.

When new jobs become available, and you require additional letters, encourage your referees to simply tweak the earlier version. You can offer to send them a copy of the earlier letter, but this means you need a copy for yourself of the reference letter they previously submitted. Some referees are willing to share their letters of recommendation, while some will not be comfortable doing so. Make sure your referees understand the deadlines and the method of submission (hard copy or electronic).

Some large institutions allow people to arrange for generic letters from referees to be put in their placement files at a career center. This practice can be useful for obtaining references when referees are on sabbatical or engaged in an off-campus, long research project and are difficult to contact.

Old placement letters can also be useful when you've decided after several years that you would like to move on to a better position. They allow you to jog the memory of the referees with, "Here's what you wrote about me five years ago. Could you refresh this letter and update this recommendation for this new job I am applying for?" Don't forget to send along the job announcement for them.

Finally, now is a good time for you to start looking for good sample letters of recommendation that you can use as templates. Ask your advisor or other faculty and your friends for good samples (with names omitted). If you have ever served as part of a search committee, notice what made good letters memorable and add those ideas to your own template. We have also provided a **Recommendations Letter Worksheet and a Sample Recommendation Letter**.

Reference letters may be used by the committee to help rank candidates according to how interested the committee is in interviewing them. An example of such ranking for use by committee members may look like this:

1=Not interested
2=Keep in the pool for the time being
3=Strong candidate but some concerns
4=Outstanding candidate, move to next stage
5=Excellent candidate, move quickly to next stage

Teaching Philosophy Statement

Many institutions require a teaching philosophy statement as part of the teaching application package. Before you start writing your statement, research the mission of the college/university and of the department. Does this institution have a religious mission? An environmental mission? An antiracist mission? Or something else?

You also need to research the kinds of students you will be teaching. You should write something different if you will be teaching working adults at a community college, undergraduates at a traditionally black college, or graduate seminars at an upper-level research institution. Do not iterate every course that you have taught. Stay away from abstract, vague statements. Back up your points with examples or details.

Most institutions want to know not only your philosophy but how exactly you will use tools at your disposal to reach the students. For instance, how do you use online teaching tools like Blackboard, Moodle, or others? How do you use social networking media to engage your students? How do you plan assignments to help students become better critical thinkers? Do you like to have students work individually or in groups or both, and why? How important is it for you to have students become aware of practical applications for what they are learning? Do you like to have students work on your research, and if so, how? Do you believe service-learning components are important, and why? If you have experience teaching in flipped classrooms or teaching online courses, be sure to mention these experiences, as they are the current hot trends in teaching methodologies.

Connect your experiences to your actual teaching philosophy and why you believe these methodologies are useful for students. Ground your teaching philosophy in your discipline. For example, if applying for a job as an ecologist, you might want to discuss how you gave students a first-hand experience of the effects of a sewage treatment plant on the environment or to write about taking students outdoors to look at the vegetation on the north versus south sides of a canyon.

Recommendations Worksheet

List 5 faculty members at your institution that you might ask for recommendations and add some notes about what you want each of them to address in their letters.

1.

2.

3.

4.

5.

Now list 5 more people who are not at your institution whom you might also ask for recommendations and what you want each of them to address in their letters. These may be people you worked with to organize a panel at a conference, peers in your profession, faculty at a previous institution, or other professionals who may be able to comment positively about you, your teaching, or your research.

1.

2.

3.

4.

5.

Ask each person directly if she or he will provide you with a positive reference.

1. Include the amount of turnaround time you anticipate each reference will need to write an initial draft or to tweak it for a specific job.

2. Note whether (and if so, where) you have a copy of the letters on file somewhere.

Recommendation Letter Worksheet

[On university letterhead]

Recommender department and direct phone number
Email xxxxxxxx@dept.edu, video name if applicable
Website www.ProfessionalWebsite.edu if applicable

Date

Dr. Janet Smith
Chair, Search Committee
Department Name
XYZ University
Street Address
City, State, Zip

Re: Position number if applicable or description of position

Dear Dr. Smith,

The first paragraph of the recommendation letter explains why the recommender is writing and shows the connection to the person being recommended, including how you know each other, in what capacity, and for how long.

The second paragraph of the recommendation letter gives some specific information about you to the person being addressed, including why you are qualified for the advertised position, and what you can contribute. Your recommender can include a lot of details about your research work here if it is known to them, and may actually go longer than one paragraph. It should include specific examples relating to your qualifications. For instance, a recommender might say: "Dr. So-and-So worked as a genetic researcher in my lab and discovered a previously unknown allele which bears further investigation. His exemplary research techniques were used as a model for other workers in this lab."

The third paragraph should actually include the statement, "I highly recommend Dr. So-and-So" or "I recommend Dr. So-and-So without reservation." Another possible phrase might be "I have no doubt that Dr. So-and-So will make a wonderful colleague and addition to your department's research mission." The positivity needs to be obvious.

The final paragraph should include an offer to provide more information if requested.

Best regards,

Signature
Printed Recommender Name
Position or Title

Sample Recommendation Letter

[*On university letterhead*]
Department and contact information of recommender

February 11, 20XX

Dr. Janet Smith
Chair, Search Committee
Department Name
XYZ University
Street Address
City, State, Zip

Re: Position number if applicable

Dear Dr. Smith,

I am writing to enthusiastically support the application of MacKenzie Brown, who is currently a senior graduate student in my laboratory, as an assistant professor. She joined my group five years ago and will defend her dissertation in about a month, March 20xx.

MacKenzie graduated from the University of Southern California where she received a BS degree in Astronomy in 20xx. In her specialty area, the formation of planets, MacKenzie has tackled all aspects of her work, whether technical or intellectual, with determination and has successfully presented it to her committee. She has been recognized with awards and scholarships. A manuscript on her main project will be submitted to PQR [journal] this coming month. She has already co-authored one study and I expect at least one more manuscript to come from her work in 20xx. She is an exceptional student, one of the best it has been my privilege to know. I am confident that she will excel as a scientist, teacher, and mentor at XYZ University.

While working on her dissertation, MacKenzie was also a teaching assistant for two undergraduate courses and participated in mentoring programs for high school students, arranging field trips to our local planetarium for them. She engaged the students, directed work and/or class, and had great insights into what worked well in teaching. She is a delight to work with, and I believe you will find her to be an excellent colleague. She is mature, independent, and resourceful, knowing when and where to seek advice and help. She is full of enthusiasm with a genuine interest in teaching and in science. I would expect her to continue developing ideas for her own research in planetary science.

In summary, I have no doubt that MacKenzie would be an excellent addition to your department. Please do not hesitate to call or email me if you have any further questions.

With best regards,

Dr. Sam Jones
Associate Professor

Your statement must be well written, and cannot contain typos, spelling, grammar, sentence structure, or word usage mistakes. You are applying for a college position after all. Keep your statement short. Stick to the page limits requested. Think about what you would emphasize differently if you had a limit of one page versus two pages because different institutions have different requirements. Make sure someone other than yourself edits this statement before you send it out. It's amazing what your own eyes will miss after you have reread a statement several times. Your brain will see what it thinks is there, and not necessarily what really is on the page.

Remember, a teaching philosophy statement is *really* about the students, and *not* about you!

You will also want to discuss the kind of work you normally assign to students and how you evaluate it. If you do not have a lot of teaching experience to draw on in framing your philosophy, think about your favorite professors and what they did that made you like their style. Or if you can't find an example from that realm of experience, think about what you wish you had seen in a teaching professor.

Sample Syllabi

We have provided a worksheet to help create a syllabus, rather than giving you a sample to copy. So much variation on what should be included depends on the type of institution you are applying to. You have probably seen numerous syllabi in your time as a student and may even have kept a few in your own field for reference. If you need a framework, look online for examples in your field. Think about what worked and didn't work in syllabi for courses you took or courses you taught yourself as you craft your own sample syllabi.

Sometimes institutions also request one to three sample syllabi as part of your application package. You might be tempted to just send off any old syllabi. You should give their request more thought than that. You may have to create a new syllabus or significantly revise some earlier version of one. Make sure your syllabus is interesting: Not, "Week 1, Chapter 1" but actual examples of the topics you will be covering, such as "The rise of the mammals" or "Why the brain is really a social organ." A syllabus is one of your teaching tools, a way to let potential colleagues and students know your expectations and your perspective on a topic.

Tailor at least one of your syllabi to the job you are applying for (even if you have not ever taught this course). Give some consideration to what you want to communicate to the hiring committee about yourself through your syllabus: for instance, how up to date your readings are, whether you are a big picture person or a detail person, and how interactive with students your classes will be. Include topics for each session, assigned readings, papers or other assignments that will be part of the grade, statements about when things are due, and other such logistical items.

Be clear about what people have to do to pass the class; if you require 15% class participation, know how you will measure that or how you will weight assignments or tests to show this. By being proactive, you prevent students' comments that "I didn't know I had to do that" for the grade at the end of the course. State your policies with regard to lateness, skipping class, late papers, your appointment availability, or issues around incivility or technology use in the classroom. If

Teaching Philosophy Statement Worksheet

Here are some additional questions to consider as you prepare your teaching philosophy statement. Take a moment and use the space under each question to give an honest answer to each one. It will help you write that teaching philosophy statement.

1. What do you believe about teaching?

2. What do you believe about learning?

3. How do those beliefs play out in your classroom?

4. How do student identity and background make a difference when you teach?

5. What do you struggle with in terms of teaching and student learning?

6. What don't you like in a teacher?

7. How do you assess your students' learning needs?

8. How do you see your identity as a teacher? (e.g., expert, learning coach, cheerleader, challenger of ideas, guide?)

9. What is your approach to subject matter? (e.g., key concepts, content organization, methods of presentation, learning activities, desired learning outcomes?)

10. How do you evaluate student progress?

> 11. What are your expectations about out of class interactions with students?
>
> 12. What have you learned from your students about teaching?
>
> 13. How do your research interests figure into your teaching?
>
> 14. How would you mentor both graduate and undergraduate students?

you have access to the departmental policies for the institution where you are applying, you can mirror these on your syllabus.

Your sample syllabus can show you are welcoming to students by inviting them to come to talk with you during office hours if they are having difficulty or are confused about an assignment. You can include whether you are open to email or text message contact between classes or how you feel about meeting by special appointment.

You may want to do some research on the variety of course syllabi. Some people write very detailed syllabi and others want to allow themselves more flexibility by writing sparser syllabi. We suggest that you look at several course syllabi written by department members of the institution where you are applying to get a sense of the conventions of that department or institution. Some course syllabi can be found online.

A good print resource for veteran and new syllabus authors is *The course syllabus: A learning-centered approach*, 2nd ed., by B. J. Mills, M. W. Cohen, and J. G. O'Brien (2009). Linda B. Nilson's (2007) book, *The graphic syllabus: Communicating your course,* offers additional creative ideas for teachers who want to use diagrams, flowcharts, or concept maps instead of the traditional syllabus approaches. She also has a newer book, *Teaching at its best: A research-based resource for college instructors* (4th edition, 2016) that includes information on designing a syllabus as well as information on pedagogical styles and approaches. You can also refer to some of the more recent books for online course design such as *Conquering the content: A blueprint for online course design and development* by Robin M. Smith (2014).[214] Finally, if you are completely stuck, try looking at The Open Syllabus Project [215] where course texts are generally included on the syllabi for 38 fields, and some actual syllabi are posted by teachers willing to share them. You might also check out Dr. Guy McHendry's interactive syllabus project for ideas.[216] The *ChronicleVitae* also has some available examples.[217]

Remember, neatness counts, and all the same rules apply here as they do for the teaching philosophy statement: Your syllabi must be well written, and cannot contain typos, spelling, grammar, sentence structure, or word usage mistakes. If you include the books you will use, make sure book or article citations are correct, and are appropriately formatted for your field. Have someone other than yourself edit the syllabi before you send them out.

Research Statement

For the research statement, you will have to write about what you are trying to achieve and summarize your research approach. We will begin with what to include in your content, and finish with a discussion of format. Take some time to answer the questions in the following worksheet to prepare this important part of your academic job search portfolio. If you absolutely don't know where to start, look at faculty web pages at the institution where you are applying and see how those people describe their research interests.

Begin by summarizing your research achievements to this point. If you have done three research projects on the nesting habits of arctic terns, what have you concluded? What knowledge did you gain; e.g., techniques or lab or field procedures, new equipment used, or additions to theory? Then present your proposal of upcoming research. If you are going to continue with your study of terns, what is your next step? If you plan to change your research emphasis to Ecuadorian finches, give reasons for this change and a brief explanation of your new area of emphasis. Indicate what resources you expect your job site to provide for your research in terms of space, equipment, access to other knowledge, etc. Specify what resources you will bring with you in terms of grant money or grant-writing experience. Consider and explain what your research will add to the department you are applying to. Mention how your proposed research will add to theory in your field. Indicate how your research will contribute to your teaching, if teaching will be a major expectation in your position. Suggest some ways you might involve undergrads or graduate students in your research.

As you craft your research statement, you must consider how to format the document. Begin by checking out the guidelines at the institution where you are applying to see what is generally accepted there. Aim for 1-2 pages, 3 pages at most, unless their guidelines indicate the statement should be shorter or longer. Use language appropriate to your field, remembering to be clear and concise. Other things to keep in mind:

- Avoid page long paragraphs because they are hard to read.
- Use headings and subheadings, and bullets where appropriate, to create some white space because these also make your statement easier to read.
- Proofread your statement aloud to yourself. You may be surprised by what you hear.
- Get someone else in your field to read your statement for both flow and content before you submit it, but edit carefully for grammar, spelling, and punctuation errors and make certain there are no typos before you give it to a trusted colleague for review. You want to make a good impression here, too.
- If you have to submit electronically, check the final formatting to ensure that it appears the way you think it will at the other end.

Syllabus Worksheet

Course title:

Course description:

Course purpose:

Instructor information:
    Name
    Office location
    Office hours
    Best way to communicate with me

Course topics (adapt to fit semester or quarter system) with required readings:

Course textbook(s):

Additional readings:

Course requirements:

Grading procedures:

Other expectations (often dictated by the institution):
    Attendance
    Late papers and missed exams
    Ethical behavior (includes warning about plagiarism)
    Professional behavior

Resources to help students succeed:

Other: (include policies if you have them, such as "cell phones will be left at the door.")

If you are currently early in the application process, you might want to consider drafting a long research statement and a short research statement now so that you will have basic documents to tweak for a particular job application.

Research Presentation, aka 1st Job Talk

Another item you are commonly asked to prepare is a research presentation, often known simply as the job talk. Perhaps the most challenging aspect of the job talk is that you are being evaluated on at least three criteria simultaneously. You are being judged as a scholar, as a colleague, and as a teacher. What do you need to consider when preparing your research presentation, aka 1st job talk? Being well-prepared is crucial. A number of people in the department who have a say in hiring you will only see you at your job talk, and will make their decision regarding your future based on that *one* performance. It's scary as the stakes are high. Start by finding out about your *audience*. Ask the search committee directly whether your research talk is open to anyone, or just faculty in the department. How familiar with your field is the audience likely to be? Your anticipated audience will determine your approach.

Be sure your *title* makes clear exactly what your talk is about. Should the department's members meet two or three weeks after your visit, you want the mention of your title to immediately bring its content and you to their minds. Something in the title must let the listener know what you are researching and needs to be memorable. An example of a forgettable title is: "Multi-scale systems for biology modeling with computer agents." Make it interesting by changing to: "Tortoises and Tumbleweeds: The role of multi-scale systems for biology modeling using computer agents." Now you've put in people's minds a picture that can be associated with you. Often departments put up flyers for your job talk, so you want a title that lends itself to memorable graphics and will create interest in your talk. You may not want to believe this is important in academia, but you have to sell yourself to your potential employer.

Be absolutely certain to *stay within the department's time limits*. In doing so, you demonstrate you respect your audience's time as well as showcase your ability to be organized and focused. Be sure to check in advance whether the time limit for the talk incorporates time for questions and answers, and modify your talk accordingly.

Make sure you provide a coherent and thoughtful picture that *tells a story* or *makes an argument* and, if possible, *demonstrates the originality of your analysis*. Young scholars too often make the mistake of presenting their research in chronological order, without explaining *why* the research is important. Discuss the methods you used, and why you chose a particular theoretical framework to explain your research, and make sure to **state your conclusions** at some point. End strong. Don't just fade away. Connect the end of your talk with the beginning and appear eager to answer questions.

Don't forget to include the direction you expect your research to take. This is your chance to show you have thought about the *future* beyond your dissertation project. If you know there is grant money for your type of project, make a short statement that you plan to pursue it.

Research Statement Worksheet

Think about what the search committee is looking for in hiring you as you answer the questions below.

What have been your accomplishments? If you have published your research, add citations.

What is your future direction? How will your research contribute to your field?

How do you approach research? In other words, how do you think?

Are you a linear or divergent, inductive or deductive thinker?

How are you an independent thinker?

Do you like to build on existing research or to start something brand new?

What are the major problems, theoretical or practical, you want to attack?

How does your research fit into or disrupt current theory in your field?

What is your potential for funding and where might you apply for funds?

How will your research be different, important, and innovative?

> How will your research fit with or expand the department or the program? For instance, how might you incorporate your research in the classroom or with graduate students?
>
> If you will be expected to have graduate students, what is your ability to manage and support them as part of your research agenda?
>
> What are your specific 3-5 year research goals?
>
> What resources do you think you will need to be successful in your job? For example: A chemist may need lab space, chemicals, equipment, and a fume hood; an English literature professor might want a new computer with two monitors and a bookcase.

Practice your job talk endlessly. Give it to your mirror, your dog, your cat, your hamster. Ask all your friends and family to listen and give you feedback as non-specialists, and to tell you what areas they find confusing so you can fix them. Then, if possible, give your talk to colleagues or your advisor to get their feedback. Practice, practice, practice until you can do it in your sleep. This will save you much grief when you are on the spot and nervous because your brain will already know what to do and say, and you won't be reading your talk. Reading your talk is a sure-fire way to kill your candidacy. You are engaged in a high stakes performance. Don't bore your audience—you should have done your research to know who is likely to be listening to you and be able to interact with them easily.

One of the ways you will be able to excel is to practice under stress, meaning approximating the situation as you will actually experience it as closely as possible. Make sure if you are using slides, you are practicing with slides so you will know where glitches may occur. One of the biggest malfunctions we hear about now is when embedded videos do not work. This could be due to a variety of factors, including a firewall put up by the institution. Know what you are going to do when the video fails to play. When you have practiced under stress, you will have learned to manage your anxiety better. Some departments allow doctoral students to give presentations of their work as part of a colloquia series, which is a great place to practice.

Keep in mind that you are auditioning for the role of colleague. 218 As much as possible, give your talk in a relaxed manner, without reading it from a script. While we emphasize the ability to discuss your research, it can help to acknowledge from the outset that the audience has varying

Research Talk Questions & Answers Worksheet

What story do I want to tell in my research presentation?

What's a good beginning that will get people's attention?

What graphics/slides or other show and tell can I bring that will keep my audience engaged?

What is the strong ending to my talk?

Your audience may ask you questions related to your past or proposed research as well as things directly related to your talk. Below are some sample questions. These questions could be asked at your presentation, in individual meetings, or in small group settings, but you need to know your short, concise answers in advance. Take a few minutes to think through these additional questions about your research and in the space below, provide one to three sentence answers for each one. These questions may overlap with some of the questions in the research statement worksheet.

What are your research accomplishments and their significance?

What is your 3-5 year plan for research (and why)?

What is your 10-year plan for research (and why)?

What type of research group do you envision forming (how many students, how broad, how interdisciplinary, experimental vs. theoretical or a mix, etc.)?

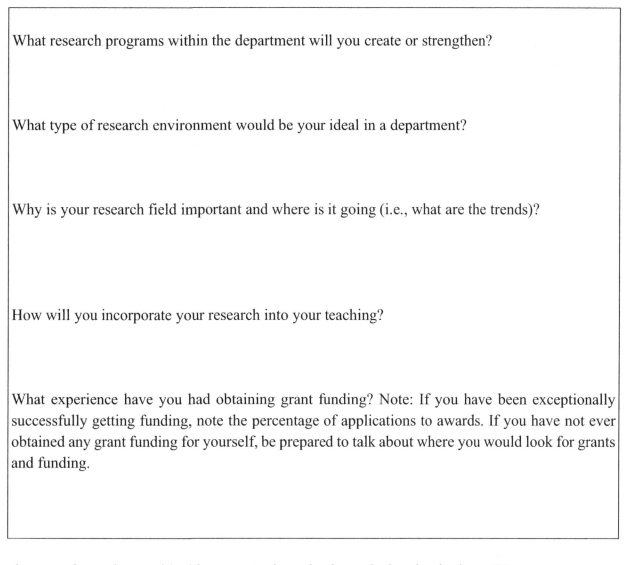

What research programs within the department will you create or strengthen?

What type of research environment would be your ideal in a department?

Why is your research field important and where is it going (i.e., what are the trends)?

How will you incorporate your research into your teaching?

What experience have you had obtaining grant funding? Note: If you have been exceptionally successfully getting funding, note the percentage of applications to awards. If you have not ever obtained any grant funding for yourself, be prepared to talk about where you would look for grants and funding.

degrees of experience with either your topic or the theoretical underpinnings. "How many are you familiar with current changes in the understanding of x?" 2 or 3 people raise their hands. "Well, just to clarify before I get into my talk, a new understanding of x that is now largely accepted has been offered by y." It doesn't matter if you are discussing frog anatomy or Jane Austen's *Emma*. This is about setting everyone in the room at ease and indirectly demonstrating your teaching abilities.

You should see questions from your audience as a positive way to impress them with how easy interacting with you is. It is imperative that you *take seriously every question from the audience*, no matter how uninformed or far-fetched or just plain stupid it seems to you. Maybe what someone asks is actually a question you had when starting the research. If so, acknowledge that you, too, had this issue, and that this was a good question.

Come prepared for technological hiccups. You may have great PowerPoint or Prezi slides, but what will you do if the power goes out? Be prepared to sketch your figures on the board or to ask audience members to visualize certain items. Remember, it's up to you to keep your audience engaged. Be a good sport about any problems, and your gracious humor will work in your favor.

Have backup copies of your slides available in several formats, a hard copy that may be reproduced as handouts in a pinch, and one that can easily access from the internet. We have personally experienced having a flash drive that did not work with the university-supplied computer, so we just downloaded our talk from the internet. Also, sometimes the format of your slides may not be compatible with the equipment the university supplies. Check out the format for slides in advance with the search committee or department administrative assistant. However, even with all these precautions, you may still end up in a different room with different equipment than even the search committee expected. Having a backup plan will keep you from getting flustered and will impress others with your equanimity and preparedness.

Sample Class, aka 2nd Job Talk

In addition to your research presentation, sometimes the department where you are applying to will ask you to conduct a sample class. Some applicants consider this their second job talk. Reminding yourself from the outset that everyone present recognizes this is an artificial set-up may help you. A teaching demonstration and actually teaching on a regular basis are not the same. The demo is akin to a sales pitch, designed to produce the excitement needed to move forward with an academic job offer. You do have to tailor your presentation to the audience, remembering that some in the room may be experts on your topic, while others (e.g., undergraduate students) may have no familiarity with it.

Unlike the research presentation which can be modeled to some degree on presentations you have done at conferences, this is going to be a lot more interactive and hands on. Parameters may vary: You may be asked to lecture on a specific topic to keep students on track in their current class syllabus or *sometimes* you will get to choose the topic. The class talk may be slightly less formal than your research presentation, but you may be able to discuss some issues that have come up in your own research. Whatever you decide to do, "start as you mean to go on." In other words, if you normally teach using a lecture format, do that in your demonstration; if you normally hold interactive classes with group problem-solving exercises, do that. You don't want the search committee to be surprised by your style when you do show up to teach at their school.

10 tips for planning and presenting your class talk. Some of the advice we present here, especially the technical issues, intentionally reiterates what we mentioned for preparing for your research talk.

First, determine the topic. If the institution tells you what to teach, find a syllabus for the course, and know what comes before and after the topic you have been given. Ideally, it will be a topic you already know a lot about because you have already been presenting it as a teaching assistant. If not, do a little background reading to see what other people recommend for presenting it. Textbooks often have a different version for the teacher that can be helpful here. If you get to choose the topic, get very, very clear on what you want to be the "big takeaway," and work

Second, find out exactly what the department wants you to demonstrate. Do they want to know how you handle a full 50-minute lecture or how you conduct an interactive seminar? Or do they want something else, for example, how you use technology in your teaching? The department will usually want you to teach as you would normally to get a sense of how you teach.

Third, find out who will be in your audience and how interactive your presentation should be. Are you going to lecture to a large group of students in a large lecture hall or will you be leading a small group discussion where you will be asking and responding to questions? Determine if anyone on the Search Committee will be attending your class, because this will change the delivery dynamic for your class presentation.

Fourth, try to engage the students but be conservative. Many times candidates are told, "The teaching demonstration is really important." Translated, this really means, "We want to see if you have the ability to interact with our kinds of students." It's likely you have already had some kind of teaching experience, whether leading a discussion section or giving a paper in a graduate seminar. (Yes, this counts, because you are engaging an audience and asking them to learn something from you.) Rely on your own experience to help you. If you have had good feedback about your teaching style, you might want to put it on a 3x5 card and read it right before you enter the classroom for a confidence boost.

If you have time, introduce yourself to the students and ask them to introduce themselves to you. Determine whether you will do this in a formal way once you have started teaching, or more informally, speaking to them as they enter the room. If you can, tie their interests to your talk as you teach the class. If you do not have time for introductions and know students will be sitting at desks or tables, pass out 5x7 index cards and ask them to fold the cards in half and write their first names on them for you to see. This strategy will allow you to call on students by name rather than pointing, "You…over there in the plaid shirt." Speakers use this trick all the time at workshops. This device also works when you want to promote student interaction with other students, allowing you to get Julia to ask Bill what he thinks about your topic, or even whether they agree with the conclusions you are positing for it.

Another technique to quickly engage the students is to take an informal poll on the topic. For a political science class, you could try something like, "How many of you think leaders are born? How many of you think leadership is learned?" Or for a sociology class, "How many of you think

living in poverty is a result of not trying hard enough to succeed? How many of you think it's simply 'luck of the draw'?" You can craft your own questions based on your topic. You can ask the students for their opinions before and after a PowerPoint presentation to engage them. Another idea is to stop in the middle of the PowerPoint presentation and pass out 3x5 index cards, asking students to answer a question related to the already presented material. If you are wondering about how to ask questions to engage students, check out David James Scott's blog [219] where he has written about his technique for engaging students with opinion questions.

If you break the class into groups as a way of interacting with them, make sure you have a system for getting them quickly into groups by counting off ("1…2…3…4), then aligning groups with the number they got ("all those who counted off as one, in that corner; all those who counted off as two in that corner," and so forth). Organizing the groups yourself is better than saying, "Get into groups," which is likely to result in a lot of milling around and leaving students feeling a bit directionless, not to mention reducing your precious teaching time in this crucial performance.

You can even have some exercises for students to do. If you are lecturing on stereotypes, you can provide a handout asking them to count the number of times men versus women appear. You can pass out a homework assignment to do at the end of the class as long as it is very short, or simply give it to them to do later. Make sure no activity takes more than 10 minutes to do, including set up time. In general, a person's focused attention span is roughly 7-10 minutes.

Allow yourself to move around the room instead of standing woodenly at the front. Staying in the front is tempting because you are likely nervous, but movement can help ease your own fears while giving you the chance to show you are in charge, the person in authority. You know your material, so strut your stuff. You're the star. Act the part. Envision yourself as a colleague at the institution and dispense with your picture of "lowly graduate student begging for a job."

Another trick to making an admittedly artificial class exercise work is to pretend that you are in the middle of the semester with students you know, and that there were classes before, and classes to come after, and talk as if that is real: "Next week we'll be discussing [topic] but for today, what has most intrigued you?" It's OK to treat the observing faculty as students for the purpose of the demonstration by asking them questions and responding to their answers. Only do this if you find doing so comfortable. Don't do it if it would just make you more anxious.

Fifth, remind yourself to breathe deeply before starting. Practice taking this breath when you test your sample class with friends before leaving for the interview city. It's a great habit to get into for whatever challenge you are facing.

Sixth, avoid reading from notes or memorizing your talk. It's better to have notes with you that are legible, with keywords or concepts highlighted. Your notes can be helpful to get you back on track, so they should not be too detailed. Outlines work well for this. Sometimes good speakers have their notes in a large, easy to read font on 3x5 cards, or even on a tablet. Other people prefer to speak using slides to keep them on track. You can also use the note section on a PowerPoint screen to remind you of what you want to say while keeping that invisible to your audience. You may even want to delay a PowerPoint portion of your talk by engaging the students from the beginning, and asking them what they already know about a topic. Be OK with using humor, and even telling a joke related to your topic, to loosen up the classroom.

Seventh, if you are using PowerPoint or another slide program, limit the number of words on your slides. You want your audience to be paying attention to your presentation, not reading your words. If the students are reading, they will not engage with you personally. We cannot stress enough that you do not want to read your slides. It's both distracting and boring. Pictures related to concepts work better than large amounts of text, especially if your pictures tell a story. Talking about logical fallacies? You could use a picture of Rodin's "The Thinker" or a small child looking puzzled. Don't overthink the pictures: you are going to speak the content. As we said earlier, if

Part 4: Your Academic Job Portfolio

Class Preparation Worksheet

Before you begin preparing your presentation, ask the Search Committee for the information below.

Course title:

Topic of class to be presented:

Length of class:

Modality of class (Lecture? Seminar discussion? Other?):

How many students in the class?

Are the attending students majors in the department?

Is this a beginning or upper-level class?

Who else will be attending the class?

What technology is available?

Will someone in the department make copies of my handouts or should I bring them with me?

Thinking through and planning your presentation:

How will you engage the students initially?

How will you introduce yourself?

> What will you do so that you can see the students as people you can interact with, people with names?
>
> What will you do to make your presentation interesting?
>
> What slides (PPT) will you bring?
>
> What handouts will you bring?
>
> What is your plan for engaging class members in discussion of the material you are presenting and for helping them tie it to what they already know?
>
> How do you want to end your class?
>
> What other classes might you want to teach or develop if you are hired at this institution?

plan to use slides, have a backup plan in case you experience technical problems. If you want to embed videos, make sure there is actually a web connection for your use, and ask permission to test it out before the class demonstration. If you are worried about forgetting what you plan to say, use the notes section for yourself, and present only the slides in the classroom. You know you have a good slide presentation when it doesn't make a whole lot of sense without your spoken words.

Eighth, in terms of technical details, be prepared for technical failure: make sure you have the PPT in different formats, email it to yourself, and be prepared to talk without slides. Take slide handouts with you, but do not pass them out unless the technology fails. All this matters, because you need to show that you can handle situations as they arise. One person we coached had to present his class during a power outage. He couldn't use any technology and had to depend on window light for illumination. With his handouts, he rose to the challenge.

Even if the technology works perfectly, other glitches can occur. Maybe a student or an administrator observer will come in late and disrupt your train of thought. Just invite them in, and carry on. Your ability to handle the situation will weigh into your evaluation. If you forget what you are going to say, you can take a moment to gather your thoughts and then say, "Now, where was I?" This is where those outline notes can really be of use while putting others at ease.

Ninth, remember, practice, practice, practice, especially the introductory portion so that it flows naturally into your content. Practice on your own and then with a friend or, even better, with a small group of colleagues. Tape or video yourself and review the video, so you can to see how you appear to others, then correct anything you think needs correcting. Research shows that practicing under pressure yields better performance results. Even though departments know that any teaching situation arranged for an interview is artificial, you still want to perform well.

Tenth, at some point after your class presentation, you may want to talk with Search Committee members about what classes you should expect to teach as part of your job. Have in mind the course numbering for the university and reflect back whether your courses would be undergraduate lower or upper level or graduate level. Also, have in mind 1-2 undergraduate and graduate courses you would like to *create* along with a brief description of the content. All this shows that you are thinking professionally beyond just getting through the teaching demonstration.

Equity and Diversity Statement

A request for an *equity and diversity* statement as part of your application materials is becoming more common, especially in the California state higher education system, but also in other parts of the US. The equity and diversity statement can be thought of as "the variety of personal experiences, values, and worldviews that arise from differences of culture and circumstance. Such differences include race, ethnicity, gender, age, religion, language, abilities/disabilities, sexual orientation, gender identity, socioeconomic status, and geographic region, and more."[220] If you are asked to write and submit an equity and diversity statement, check the website of the institution to which you are applying for their institutional equity and diversity statement and their directions for what information such a statement should contain. If you are not asked to submit an equity and diversity statement for a particular job, you don't have to submit one.

What information to include. The three parts of your statement will be a) your personal experiences around minority status and equity and diversity issues; b) a statement about how you will include ideas related to equity and diversity in your teaching; and c) a description of any non-classroom programs for equity and diversity that you have been involved in or want to take part in. On the whole, your statement should be about social justice *action*, not just about your philosophy. Think about your experiences, but tailor your statement to the institution you are applying to.

You can claim your minority status, if it exists, as part of telling your story. Race and gender are the top characteristics that come to mind for many people, but economic status, being a first-generation college student, disability, age, religion, and culture may also contribute to your experiences with diversity.

A social justice and diversity perspective can be applied when teaching, even if your classes are not in a social justice area. Think about who the authors of the articles or books you assign are and how they are diverse. Consider how your syllabi and assignments reflect your perspectives on equity and diversity. What do you do to make sure your classes are accessible to students with a variety of abilities and backgrounds?

Equity and Diversity Statement Worksheet

Before beginning your statement, check the website of the institution to which you are applying, and look for any reference to the kinds of diversity that are valued. You should also check to see if the institution has its own equity and diversity statement or its own instructions for the statement they want from you. Your statement may address personal or cultural worldviews including experience of race, ethnicity, gender, age, religion, language, abilities/disabilities, sexual orientation, gender identity, socioeconomic status, and geographic region. Below are some questions to get you started.

What past experiences helped shape your understandings of what diversity and inclusion mean? [Tell a story from your own life.]

How have you addressed issues of diversity in the past:

In the classroom?

In your research?

In your service, which may include volunteer work? [Here may be a place to discuss your involvement with the Native Americans library movement or advancing middle school girls in coding camp.]

How do you envision your work incorporating diversity and inclusion at this institution that is committed to [same sex education, historically black colleges and universities (HBCUs), military education for veterans, etc.]?

What, if any, initiatives you would like to pursue with any particular underrepresented constituency of the institution? [Helping first-generation college students integrate, dealing with immigration or language issues, recruiting new students from diverse populations in summer school program, etc.]?

In terms of involvement with social justice outside the classroom, what programs or projects at the college or university to which you are applying to work do you want to become involved in? How do you see yourself taking on a leadership role? How can you involve people with minority status in your research? What kinds of students would you like to mentor and how?

Tanya Golash-Boza has provided an excellent outline of the elements to include in an equity and diversity statement.[221] She advises you to write to the people on the committee who are most likely to care about this, and not to worry about those on the committee you feel will not be interested. If they are not interested in this issue, they won't read it, but if they are, they may read it very closely to see how well your values align with theirs.

Resources. You can find some excellent examples of statements online. Here we include links to samples and other resources.

- University of California at Berkeley [222] sample statement
- Guidelines for Writing a Diversity Statement [UC Davis] [223]
- University of Cincinnati's required diversity and inclusion statement for job applicants [224]
- The diversity question in an interview [225]

Teaching Evaluations

The final and often optional part of your portfolio may be teaching evaluations.[226] They may be required with your application, but even if they are not, you may want to include them with your

application materials or make reference to them in your cover letter or CV. The point of teaching evaluations is to make *you* look good. You can address negative comments by saying, "Based on what students have said, I need to change X," or even better, "After getting student input, I *did* change X the next time I taught this course." Use evaluations to your advantage and show that you are learning, too.

Sometimes departments or schools have a standard evaluation form, and the responses can be boring or be just numbers that are difficult to interpret without having an evaluation key. In such cases, you may want to just summarize or write a paragraph illustrating the high points of the evaluation for the search committee materials. Most evaluations will look at learning goals for the course, student's perceived results, perceptions of interactions between student and instructor, and sometimes, peer-reviewed class observations. If there are significant differences between evaluations, and not an overall pattern that can be discerned by reading them, you may want to have a ready explanation for that as well.

You can also create your own additional form, use it, and take *those* results with you. By customizing your evaluation, you will often get better feedback than by using a standard numerical form. You can sprinkle your evaluations throughout the semester. Sample questions for constructing your own evaluations are: "What worked best in today's class?" "What didn't work?" and "What are you taking away from today's discussion?" Unfortunately, evaluations done at the end of term at the last class won't get you your best feedback, as students are rushing away and do not want to be bothered, not to mention that generally, the people who want to complain will write

Teacher Evaluation Form (Your Own) Worksheet

1) Are you getting what you expected out of this course?

   -If you answered "yes," what do you see as your most important learning?

   -If you answered "no," What did you think should be different?

2) How do you see me as a teacher?

3) Do you feel comfortable approaching me either in class or privately with any concerns you have related to this class?

4) Are my expectations of you clear?

5) What would you like to see done differently or the same?

6) Add anything else you want to comment on.

the most and the most scathingly. Students who are satisfied or have no quarrel with you may still evaluate you in a neutral way because they don't like doing the evaluations any more than you like reading them. The sample form that follows asks for narrative answers from the students. I have used it about half-way through the term to get a sense of what changes, if any, I want to make based on student feedback. Try answering the questions from the point of view of a student you know to test it out.

Job Application Feedback

We often hear complaints from job applicants that, even though they have put together a complete CV, written teaching and research statements, prepared a research talk and a classroom lecture, constructed sample syllabi, gathered evaluations from their students, and asked faculty and colleagues for recommendations, when they get online to submit their job applications, they are still confronted with a form of several pages to fill in. This application form often asks for information that applicants have prepared in other documents and sometimes the forms are not easy to just copy and paste into, so applicants have to spend their precious time restating what they have already stated elsewhere. If you are tempted to skip this part of the application or just write something like "see attached documents," don't give in to the temptation. The documents you prepared may go to the search committee while the form goes to Human Resources, and an application will most likely not be considered complete without all the pieces, including the fill-

---

Sample Postcard/Email Application Follow-up

Tweak this form to suit your needs.

Name: [your put your name here]
Position applied for [you fill this in]

Dear [Hiring Committee Head]: I would be grateful if you could let me know how my application stands by checking off the items below, and returning this already-stamped postcard. Thank you.

Date: [you enter date you are sending request]

Is the application you received complete?   ____Y   ____N

If any documents are missing, please check below:
____ CV
____ Research statement
____ Teaching statement
____ Sample syllabi
____ Other, list:
____ Recommendation from Dr. _____
____ Recommendation from Dr. _____
____ Recommendation from Dr. _____

in-the-blanks application form. Annoying, yes, but do it anyway.

Sometimes the administrative assistant to the search committee has been told to pass only complete applications—all the documents requested and the application form—on to the committee.

Incomplete applications languish on a desk or in a file somewhere until the hiring process has been completed. If you are feeling overwhelmed with jobs to apply to and want to skip completing the form, consider prioritizing your search and send a complete application to places where you really want to be considered. You are not saving yourself any time by submitting incomplete applications. Consider using a text expander, discussed earlier, to help you clip and drop information you need to enter repeatedly.

Another complaint we often hear is that the applicant never hears back from the search committee about whether they have received any or all the pieces of the application. In this case, you might consider sending a self-addressed, stamped postcard to the search committee with blanks to check for the information you want from them. It's old-fashioned but it may get their attention. Of course, you could also try doing this by email. There is no guarantee that you will actually get an answer, but you have made it relatively easy for them to tell you if anything is missing in your file so that you can take steps to rectify the omissions.

PART 5: YOUR JOB SEARCH INTERVIEWS

Interviews are a necessary but scary part of the job search process. In this section, we will address the types of interviews you may get, background preparation for interviews, general interview preparation for yourself, and basic interview etiquette. This section includes an exercise to help you tell your story about why you are the best fit for the position. We offer some links to articles we think are particularly useful for people interviewing on the academic job market. We also provide some practical information about handling telephone and video interviews, in-person or on-campus interviews, and best practices for closing the interview and handling follow-ups. We'll give you a few tips on dressing and handling meals, as well as on graciously handling unwanted or illegal questions. Last but not least, we'll present some information on how to respond to an actual job offer and some tips on negotiation.

Types of Interviews for Academics

Different from interviews in other economic sectors, *the preliminary academic interview* is the first "in-person" interview you are likely to get. It may be by telephone or video conference (such as Skype or Zoom), depending on where people are located, or it may be a very brief meeting with prospective employers at a conference. The initial interview is sometimes referred to as "the airport interview" because it is typically very short and held in places other than the job location. Preliminary academic interviews come about mid-way through the entire process of looking for jobs and submitting applications. Just to remind you, the academic job search cycle is longer and more convoluted than any you are likely to encounter outside academia. Try not to get discouraged by the length of the process.

If you make it through the preliminary interviews, you may be asked for a longer interview. With the cost constraints facing many institutions, this may be another video interview or you may be asked to meet department or search committee members in person at a conference as a second step. How preliminary interviews are handled are at the discretion of the hiring institution. If the budget allows it, the institution will invite its top three candidates for on-campus in-person interviews. Many of the "do's" and "don'ts" we discuss apply to any type of interview, but there are some special considerations for each format.

At the end of this section, we have also provided several worksheets to help you figure out what you want to say about yourself and your work in an interview, as well as a preparation checklist for each type of interview.

General Interview Preparation

If you are having trouble figuring out what you want to say about yourself and your academic work in an interview, do some brainstorming. Write down five things you would like to share about your work or yourself, and why each is important to you. Now boil this down into the most important thing by asking yourself, "Why do I think this is important?" Your personal values will come into play as you decide how to share the passion underlying your work.

Research—Most Important Considerations to Me Worksheet

The five most important things about me and my research and *why* they are important:

1.

2.

3.

4.

5.

Now, think about how you will talk about your work to people who are not familiar with it. Think about your most important points, how you came to the topic, how you came to your conclusions, and what you brought to the table in terms of personal qualities or knowledge. Learning to tell your own story clearly will help you get prepared for the kinds of questions that may arise in any interview. Write down your one to two sentence explanation for non-experts here:

Part 5: Your Job Search Interviews

Telling My Story Worksheet

Use this worksheet to help you prepare more deeply for the academic interview and authentically tell your own story.

What are the major assertions I will make for the unique value contribution of my research?

What brought me to the point of believing this was the topic I wanted to investigate (context)? (4-5 sentences)

Why is it important?

What are the most likely questions people will ask about my research? (Most doctoral students have had to answer this in seminars or with an advisor already, so it should be easy to come up with 2 or 3 possibilities).

How will I describe the role of my major advisor in fashioning my research questions, and how did I make the research my own?

What are the best personal attributes I bring to the interviewing institution? (Examples include collegiality, leadership, or mediator.)

How will these qualities contribute to the interviewing institution? (Example of how you mediated disagreement among colleagues approaching a funding agency or how you worked with graduate students and faculty emeritus to create a survey instrument. Speak using "I" statements: "My most gratifying moment as a mediator occurred when I..." Be specific!)

What will I do to project a vision of myself teaching at this institution? What classes do I hope to teach, using what textbooks, incorporating my own research, with what pedagogical style?

What example will I use to reveal my flexibility and willingness to adjust to changing circumstances, from uncooperative students to a change in research direction?

How will I project myself as a colleague rather than a graduate student? What narrative shows me ready to step into a new role?

Once you actually have the interview scheduled, be sure to practice answering questions with a trusted colleague or a coach. Practice will increase your confidence, give you a sense of how to shorten or lengthen in your answers, reduce your anxiety, and keep your mind from going blank when you are asked a question about yourself or your work to date during the actual interview.

Remember to keep your audience in mind because your answers may differ depending on whether you are interviewing at a community college or a research institution. Talk about your research without giving the impression that your insights about your research are the most important thing in the world. Graduate students often get so caught up in defending their work as part of the dissertation process that they forget to modify this perspective for those outside their immediate academic community once they finish.

Above all, do not lie. Nicole Matos wrote about talking to a job candidate who lied about his prior experience as a student at the same community college where he was now interviewing. The candidate claimed to have been an exceptional student when, in fact, he had withdrawn from classes in his first semester. Although the listener was initially charmed by the candidate, the result when the truth was revealed "…sank his candidacy. There was no coming back from such a deliberate deception."[227]

It's great to use your own stories, but make sure they are your own. Practice telling them and realize that both your elevator speech and later, your job interview, are kinds of performances. If you are telling something humorous, just like a stand-up comedian, you must give the audience time to laugh rather than rushing on. You might have a funny story involving concrete examples of how you dealt with a challenge from uncooperative students or a serious surprise related to unexpected research impediments.

The interviewer or interviewing committee should have done their own homework to prepare to speak with you, including reading any information the committee chair deemed relevant, scheduling the appropriate amount of time for an interview, being able to provide simple logistical information like anticipated course load, coming with knowledge of the institutional timeline for hiring, and allowing time for the candidate to ask questions. If the committee seems completely disorganized, unprepared, or even hostile, take that into consideration when considering possible employment. This kind of situation may just be the result of one person's untrained approach or it may be a red flag about larger problems in that department or at that institution.

Background Preparation: Know Your Institution

Before you interview, make sure you understand whether the institution is a research-focused R01 with a lot of National Institute of Health (NIH) or other grant funding or one with less emphasis on research and mainly funded by state government, tuition, or endowments. Understand whether a religious affiliation reflects a current emphasis or a historical connection. It's unlikely an interviewer will ask about your own religious affiliation or practice (see "Unpleasant Surprises"), but you may want to think about whether your academic work fits an institution with a religious mission like "helping students understand and act on their Christian faith."

Private schools use many different funding mechanisms, but you might want to check into the institution's financial viability. You may also want to look in advance at how people at the institution are compensated for positions like the one you are interviewing for. Compensation is unlikely to emerge as a topic in any interview because it is generally discussed only when an offer is made, but occasionally someone will say, "You know, assistant professors around here only make about [$60,000]. How do you feel about that?" Try to have an answer based on comparable salary data to the extent that you can find it.

Take time to research your audience, including the work of potential colleagues at the institution, especially familiarizing yourself with the kinds of research being done where you are interviewing. Notice whether potential colleagues publish only in traditional venues or if they are doing more with digital scholarship. Although the jury is out on how well digital venues will ultimately fare, given the cost of physical journals and books, the push is on to use new formats. Be ready to answer directly how you feel about these online publishing venues, and why.

You may have realized as a new scholar you are perfectly comfortable with using the world of digital media for both research and connecting with far-flung colleagues. However, potential colleagues at the institutions where you are interviewing may not be quite as up to date with the newest technology. Explain why any digital material you have presented in your CV or cover letter is important, and how you have used it to reach both academic and non-academic audiences. Though creation and transference of knowledge production remains the foundation of modern scholarship, there are increasing expectations your work will move quickly into useful applications or understanding outside academia. Depending on your field, as part of your interview process, you may want to address the technology issue and how you have handled it.

Know the types of students who attend the institution and, whether the emphasis is on undergraduate research or more basic preparation for life outside the classroom with a focus on communication skills like writing, speaking, or mastery of media presentations. Ask yourself: Are the majority of their students on Pell grants? What percent of undergraduate students in the department are foreign students in the department? How many are first-generation college students? How many of them are working to support themselves or a family while attending college? Does the institution want to see more research projects or lab work for their students? How can you incorporate research experience for students (without making yourself crazy busy)? Will you be expected to prepare future scholars or help students enter the workforce? Crafting answers in advance to interview questions show you know and care about the types of students being served.

Expect that the teaching load will be as advertised. Do you have a course already prepared that meets their requirements? If not, what can you offer as a plan? What can you offer with regard to online course instruction? Most schools now expect this to be part of your portfolio, and if you don't already have experience, be prepared to learn how to teach such classes, and to say that you are willing to learn how in the interview. If you have experience using video to augment in-class teaching, be ready to talk about that.

Understand that your predecessors may have been able to negotiate class release times, moving expenses, or expensive laboratory equipment, but you shouldn't expect to do that as an entry-level academic now. Unrealistic demands at the interview level are seriously off-putting for the hiring committee. You may be able to ask for some of these items during contract negotiations after you have actually been offered a job, but expect only small modifications to the original offer. Budgets are seriously constrained for most institutions of higher education at this point in time.

Show you have thought about future possibilities by asking questions like: "Do you see the potential to expand this program of study in the future?" or "If I can bring in a grant (of estimated dollars), would the university be able to give me a course release at that time?" Craft a vision for yourself of how your work will fit into the department.

Remember, the kinds of questions you are likely to get in an interview are directly related to the institution. At an R01, you will be asked about research funding potential; at a community college, the interview will be focused on teaching.

Links to Particularly Useful Articles about Interviewing

We found these articles helpful in thinking about how to prepare for academic interviews, and though some are several years old, the basic advice is still sound:[228]

- Roseanne J. Foti, Ph.D. (2009). "Academic Job Interviews: Questions and Advice." https://vtechworks.lib.vt.edu/bitstream/handle/10919/72241/gsls_roseanne_foti_interviews.pdf?sequence=1 [PowerPoint slides]
- Four articles on interviewing grouped into one document, mostly from the *Chronicle of Higher Education, Manage Your Career*. Authors are Ruth Schemmer, Mary Corbin Sies, Steven M Cahn, and Mary Dillon Johnson. Available at https://my.vanderbilt.edu/gradcareer/files/2013/01/Academic_Interview_handout.pdf
- Allison M. Vaillancourt. (2013, January 2). What Search Committees Wish You Knew. *The Chronicle of Higher Education Advice*. Available at http://chronicle.com/article/What-Search-Committees Wish/136399/?cid=at&utm_source=at&utm_medium=en

Basic Interview Etiquette

We have included some basic and pragmatic advice about interviewing in this section, including how to handle issues that come up around the academic interview not related to the actual job search or the content of your job talk, research agenda, and teaching philosophy but are important to your successfully negotiating this process. You can expect to go through at least two and possibly three interviews, up to and possibly including a campus visit before you are actually offered a job. In addition, for your convenience, we have provided an **Interview Checklist** for each interview type at the end of this section.

Please remember that whether you are on the phone or interviewing in person, once you embark on this part of the job search path, there is never a time when you are not actually interviewing. As the song says, "Every move you make, every step you take," the interviewers will be watching you. This includes the very first call you get to set up the interview. You will need to start answering your phone in a professional manner if you don't already, generally "Hi, this is Joe Smith" and not "Joe's Pizza."

If you are offered a chance for an interview, you may feel like jumping up and down and shrieking with delight, but restrain yourself. A simple, "Thank you, yes, I'd love to meet with you. When and where?" will do. If they give you a choice of time, like 10:00 AM or 4:00 PM, think about when you are at your best. Hillary is a morning person and by 4:00 PM, she is dragging. Her husband is just coming to life at that time, and likes to stay up until 2:00 or 3:00 AM doing his research. Interviewing at 10:00 AM when he is just blearily coming to consciousness would be a very bad idea for him.

As you set up the interview, you may want to ask, "Is there anything I should bring with me?" but even if they do not say so, you should always have a CV and some business cards handy. Yes, you can share contacts on a wide variety of cell phones these days, but as already noted, technology can fail, or simply not be compatible. You don't have to be affiliated with any particular organization to create a "calling card" for yourself. It just has to have basic information about how to contact you, such as email, phone number, and your web or blog site, if you have one.

You may never need to pass out your CV, as most members of the hiring committee will have already reviewed it, but it's great to have handy in case a guest who would like a copy is present. You can demonstrate preparedness by handing it over immediately rather than saying, "Can I send it to you?" or "It's available for download at my institution." Besides, if you are traveling to an in-person interview, you may make some contacts on the plane or at the airport, and want to give those people your CV or business card.

Interviewing is a specific skill that takes practice and is not the same thing as the job you are applying for. Rehearing is necessary. Be prepared to present the credentials that make you the ideal candidate by practicing out loud. First impressions do matter, and the first few minutes of any interview are especially important to establishing credibility and presence.

As we mentioned earlier, the academic job market uses different types of interviews to narrow down the search field for a candidate. Typically, 3-10 candidates will be initially invited to phone or conference interviews, while only 3-4 will ever be invited to make an on-campus or face-to-face visit. Occasionally, depending on the expense of bringing in a candidate, an online video interview will be substituted for an on-campus visit, but the more likely situation is that a video interview will be a preliminary screening process. You can anticipate that you will be treated well no matter how or where you interview because they are also trying to put their best foot forward for you.

No matter what kind of interview you get—telephone, video, or in-person—a few tips apply. Interviewers are looking at you as a whole person, not just the intellectual pedigree represented on your CV. They want to know how you relate to and treat others. Are you courteous, respectful, and reliable? Do you seem friendly and approachable? Never underestimate the power of a smile to charm your interviewer, especially when you are nervous. Approaching the process with energy and enthusiasm will also help you quash your own nervousness. Once you begin to get more deeply into the interview, you may find you lose some of the anxious energy.

In person, begin the interview by making sure you give a good handshake. There is actually an etiquette to this, and it differs from culture to culture. In North American interviews, the handshake should be firm, but not painful, for the recipient, with hands connected "web-to-web," followed by a light pumping of roughly three times while standing approximately two feet apart.

Place any personal items on the floor rather than on a table or a desk to keep distractions at bay. If you are offered a beverage, your best bet is to politely turn it down, to avoid any accidental spillages, though some people place a bottle of sealed water on the floor for dry mouth caused by nervousness. The only item in front of you should be a notepad, and then only if you have asked permission to take notes.

If you do want to take notes or record the interview, ask in advance. "Is it OK if I scribble down a few notes to remind me of what we discussed?" or "I'd like to record this conversation to help me prepare for our future discussions." If they say no, don't do it; just write down what you can remember immediately following the discussion.

Turn off your cell phone or any other noise-making devices, such as a computer that pings when emails are sent or received. If something goes off while you are interviewing, both you and the interviewer can be sidetracked. If a cell phone does ring, do not answer it; just calmly turn the phone off. If you answer even to say, "I can't talk right now," you are doing a discourtesy to the person you are with. Better to turn it off, smile, and use the opportunity to say something like, "I was so excited to meet you, I forgot to turn off my phone."

Dress conservatively to show respect to the interviewer, even if you know that the person interviewing you always shows up in blue jeans. You know your field. "Dressing up" can mean khakis and a nice shirt, or it could mean a jacket and tie with slacks. Women do best to wear a dress or skirt with a jacket. These are all things you can dispense with once you have the job, but as long as you are an applicant, you should abide by the rule of dressing up. Hiring committee members respond to many nonverbal cues, some of which may be invisible even to the interviewer.

Positive body language can be communicated with good posture. You want to be relaxed but not sloppy. If you tend to slouch, sit comfortably, with feet flat on the floor to help you remember how to sit up straight. You can rest your arms on a table or chair, but don't try to hide them under a table or behind you because you don't want someone to see how nervous you are—hiding the hands tends to go against you more than a slightly nervous shaking. If you have asked for permission to take notes, you can glance down occasionally to write, but minimize this action as much as possible so that it does not become distracting or disrupt you or your interviewer from the questions at hand. Keep anxious hand movements to a minimum to avoid distraction as well, even if you have to push your hands into the table in front of you to do so. Some people use the notepad while holding onto a pen or pencil for security, even if they never write anything down. If a prop keeps you from nervous fidgeting, then use one.

Eye contact is encouraged in North America to establish trust, but again that varies from culture to culture, so know the norms of those interviewing you. By aligning your body with the interviewer, you foster a sense of conversational openness and trustworthiness.

If you are being interviewed by a committee, with two or more people asking you questions, staying calm is usually harder than a one-to-one conversation. Remind yourself to breathe deeply at least two times before answering any question, as that literally brings oxygen into your brain and can help you think more clearly. Breathing also gives you an extra bit of time to pull your answer together. Answer your interlocutor directly, then glance at the others present, indicating your willingness to elaborate for anyone else, should they want you to follow up. Listen carefully, and make sure you actually answer the question being asked. If you are unsure what you are being asked, paraphrase the question before you answer it.[229]

As people are introduced to you in a group setting, you may need to remember who is who. This may be an opportunity to use that notepad, by writing the last name and the order the committee is introduced, usually just from one side of the panel to the other. Memory experts say you need to repeat the name three times in the first encounter to commit the name and face to memory. You may not have that luxury in an interview, but if you keep track of the names, you can look at your seating diagram and say, "Thank you, Dr. Smith, for that question." Then stay on topic. Interviewers will often ask you to "give an example" of how you handled something—this is where having completed the worksheet for "telling your story" can really help you shine. Again, before answering, take a moment to review in your own mind whether your example fits with the other kinds of concerns that may have been discussed previously.

The most common interview closing is: "Do you have any questions for us?" Be prepared for it. Even if you just heard about the institution interviewing you for the first time that day, do your own research on them. Conference facilities have wi-fi connections and even computer terminals available in the business services area. At the very least, visit the institution's main web page and learn a little bit about the department and the institution and its primary focus before you interview. In an academic interview, you should know whether the emphasis is on teaching undergraduates or large research projects funded through grants and conducted using many graduate students and one principal investigator. Then you can ask intelligent questions about the programs offered, the kinds of students they typically enroll, or even the courses generally offered each semester. This basic gumshoe work can help you during the interview to relate what you are interested in to what they are interested in. You can even score points by using the correct titles for offered courses, for instance, stating your ability to teach "The History of the British Royal Family" rather than a more generic "British History," if you know the former is the actual title of an offered course.

After the interview is finished, thank the interviewers for their time, smile, and tell them again how interested you are in the position. In person, you might shake hands again before taking your leave. You can ask them about the time-frame for their decision, or when they expect the search committee to meet to discuss final candidates. This question is to ease your own mind, so you have some sense of how long you may have to wait for another contact from the hiring committee. Keep reminding yourself that the academic job interview process is incredibly slow compared to that in any other economic sector. After the time has passed when they indicated they would make a decision, and you still have heard nothing, you have an opportunity to call whoever is handling inquiries on the position to ask the current status of the search. This call allows you to be a bit proactive to determine if you are still in the running.

Once you have actually left the in-person interview, make sure to send a thank-you note. Many people do this by email, but a hand-written note can sometimes make a bigger impression because academics (and everyone else) are often overwhelmed by incoming electronic communications. If you feel like too much time has passed to write a thank you note, do it anyway. It will work in your favor when not writing might work against you.

Special note to women*:* Be aware women tend to downplay themselves in an interview when a man would not. When reporting concrete successes, do not use qualifiers, such as "I could use more experience [fundraising, writing grant proposals, etc.]," even if that is true. Do not apologize or discount your role in an institutional success: It may be true that many people worked on a project or initiative to make it successful, but this is *your* job interview. You have to promote yourself. This is not a denial of others who worked with you. If you are asked a question about your ability to do something you have not done before, state assertively, "Yes, I can do that." Women need to claim the space in the room as men do, rather than being afraid to speak expansively. Use gestures when appropriate to express confidence and project command of the issues and your ability to handle them. Just don't go overboard and gesticulate wildly with every sentence.

General Considerations before an Actual Academic Interview

First and most important, know how to contact the search committee chair in the event of an emergency of any type whether personal, weather, or transportation related. The chair of the search committee will likely give you his or her cell phone number so that you can call in the event of any serious problem or delay. Having with you the name and telephone number of the administrative staff member handling the details also does not hurt. In the event of a problem, time is of the essence, and you don't want to waste it scrambling for a name or number. Better to remain unperturbed and professional.

You may also want to forward your telephone while traveling so you do not miss any important phone call from the hiring committee, like "We've had to change to a different room" or the dreadful pronouncement, "We need to reschedule your interview."

If you need any sort of special accommodation, such as TTY for the hearing impaired, or prefer to use voice setting on a video call because you are blind or nearly blind, or need access help such as an elevator or a ramp for the wheelchair users, be sure to ask for it early on in the arrangements. No one on either side of the conversation wants to find out at the last minute that conversation is impossible because no accommodations have been made. You are legally within your rights to ask, and the interviewer is proscribed from denying consideration of your candidacy on this basis.

We coached one candidate who was seriously visually impaired and had spent most of his life proving he could do whatever any other scholar could do in the library or the classroom. He never included this information in a cover letter or asked for accommodation when interviewing. Eventually he learned two things: 1) preparing the interviewers for his needs in advance reduced their concerns about his vision and gave them more opportunity to talk to him about the content of his scholarship, and 2) once the committee knew about his disability, that knowledge could even act in his favor if the institution was trying to fill certain kinds of diversity quotas. He never wanted his disability to be a reason he was offered employment, and went to great lengths to be the best scholar possible, but in these days of very limited available positions, candidates need to use any advantage they may have.

For any interview that is not in person, whether on a phone or on the computer, make sure you have a secure and reliable connection. If you know you have "dead zones" in your home, you clearly don't want to speak from there, even if it is near your workspace. For video conferencing, you must have a reliable internet connection. If the connection from your home or office base is not dependable, use someone else's base that is reliable. For video interviewing, make sure the background is not messy or distracting.

Spend some time crafting and practicing your answer to the inquiry, "Tell me about yourself" and for academics, the related, "Tell me a little bit about your research." Both of these open-ended statements are designed to set you at ease, not panic you into speechlessness. Practice your one sentence answer aloud with anyone willing to listen. If you have to practice by talking to a pet, so be it. As you most likely know from your own teaching experience, saying things out loud is vastly different from rehearsing them in your head, and you may be surprised to discover where, exactly, you trip over your own tongue. You might even be able to combine both inquiries into one answer, such as "I've been studying the Neolithic period in Italy for the past nine years, and I am excited to join this archaeology department with a yearly overseas field school as well as an excellent laboratory."

You will no doubt be asked to discuss some aspect of your teaching, usually what you see yourself teaching as opposed to what you currently teach. Remember to include the basics: course title and topic, themes or main takeaway points, anticipated textbooks or readings, and kinds of assignments you will give. What you include here will vary depending on whether the class is an undergraduate course or a graduate seminar.

We have provided more detailed sample questions for different types of interviews later in this chapter. Before you get to the detailed interview questions on the **Research, Teaching, Writing and Other Duties Worksheets,** take a moment to look over the **Basic Interview Questions Worksheet** and the **Videoconference (Skype, Zoom, or Other Service) and Telephone Job Interview Worksheet** to think about how technology may impact the interview.

It doesn't hurt to set up a mock interview as well. The best hour my now-deceased English husband said he ever spent in preparing for an interview was a dry run with his advisor. In a surprise to him, Americans think differently in terms of how they represent themselves in an interview. They make far more declarations of confidence in their work and have a willingness to "toot their own horn." Both are culturally abhorrent to an Englishman. Learning how to answer questions for an American hiring committee without being overly deferential was a completely new skill for him. He felt that practicing the interview with a trusted advisor helped alleviate his initial awkwardness and ultimately land his first academic job.

Be aware of the confidentiality in the search process. The job description may be posted, but most search committees do not want people outside to know who is being interviewed. This may even include the members of their own department to keep the search as fair as possible for the candidates. Some currently employed interviewees may not want to let others know they are looking. Additionally, we also do not recommend a candidate's contacting anybody in the department prior to the interview, as it may be seen as a breach of confidentiality.

In this day and age of over-sharing the personal details of your life, think hard about how much you want to share about your interview process with others, both before and after you go. If you use social media (Twitter, Facebook, Instagram), be careful about posting too much information. Many people don't even want to mention that they are interviewing for a position for fear of jinxing the outcome or for having to later admit they did not get the job. Before you post, think seriously about how you will feel if you have to keep answering questions about what happened and you were either denied the job or do not have an answer yet.

Sometimes a friend or colleague of yours will be interviewing for the same job, a not uncommon situation when you are part of a cohort or working in highly specialized areas. After all, how many jobs per year are going to be offered to linguists of medieval English or those who use JAX® Mice to study age-related hearing loss? Be mature in handling your disappointment if your friend or colleague gets the offer. Offer your personal congratulations. Take the high road if anyone asks you about it by saying something like, "The department has gotten an accomplished researcher." Sour grapes do not make anyone look good.

Make sure you never burn any bridges, even if you turn down a job offer, which may seem unlikely now, but it does happen. You may have discovered in the interview process that you are not at all interested in moving to a small town in the middle of Canada to get your academic career off the ground. Maybe you dread the winter, the remote location, or the isolation from research colleagues. You don't need to elaborate on the disadvantages of the place or institution, or speak at length about what you don't like. Just politely say, "I appreciate the offer, but I regret I cannot accept it." Speak positively to the search committee and keep the lines of communication open. You never know who might have a connection with someone else you know at a place you *do* want to work.

Things You Might Need To Do During an Academic Job Interview

If you have not been given a written agenda for the interview, get clear about the length of time allotted and the process before you start. You can say, "I understand we have about 30 minutes. Will just one or all of you be asking the questions?" If you have a written agenda with that information, don't waste everyone's time by asking this question.

Whether for a preliminary or later interview, you will want to assess the interviewers as they are evaluating you. That's fine. This is your life, and you want to get a sense of whether you could be comfortable working with these people. Notice who seems particularly interested or disinterested in you or your research topic. For an on-campus interview, you will likely see several members of the search committee more than once, and you may be able to tell if someone is distracted because they have a class to teach coming up or if they simply are not interested in the type of work you do. Try not to take it personally.

It's rare in academia, but occasionally the interviewer will suggest you are over-qualified for either the school or the position. Perhaps you have a research agenda that is more ambitious than what is typical of a teaching school; perhaps you want to be at a less demanding institution than the one where you did your graduate work. Whatever the reason, you are the person to redirect the conversation. Have an answer in mind to meet those types of objections. "Because you are the only people who gave me an interview" is not a good reason for considering the position.

It's helpful to know the anticipated salary range for the institution where you are interviewing, because that may be at the root of the "overqualified" comment. If you get the sense that a comment about your being overqualified is about pay scale, a simple response may be, "I realize the cost of living is lower here." If you want a comparison, a great resource is Payscale,[230] which has a built-in calculator. If you are currently a graduate assistant, you may want to put in the institution's current average salary for assistant professors to get a good idea. But don't tell your interviewers what you expect to be paid. Save the salary for negotiations after you are hired.

Try to see the interview from the committee's point of view: committees do not want to make an offer to someone they think will turn it down, and they are trying to ascertain whether or not you are serious about taking the position. Be positive, and focus on what you will bring to the position, reassuring the people asking the questions that you are a serious candidate and you want the position. Show them how your accomplishments to date, and what you anticipate doing there, meshes with their hopes for the future of their department.

Whatever you say, don't apologize for your abilities or your preferences. Instead, have some good, positive answers prepared in advance, such as, "I have always really enjoyed the interactions with undergraduate students who are truly open to considering new ways of thinking about x." If you are comfortable with it, you can bring in personal reasons such as, "My wife and I believe that the stability and intimacy of a small community will be good for our children as they grow up." I know of one person who intentionally left a high prestige academic university for a much smaller teaching college because of the opportunity to work with undergraduates organizing a small natural history museum for the campus.

You may need a bathroom break. It's OK, ask for one. No need to be uncomfortable and every human being has bodily functions. No one will begrudge you the few private minutes you need for this.

Pay attention to the rules of the road. If several people are riding to dinner in the same car, do not automatically assume you will be given the place of honor in the passenger seat next to the driver. Wait a moment as people sort themselves out. If they want you to ride there, someone will tell you to sit down in the front seat.

Stay vigilant. Be careful not to let your guard down and slip into a relaxed mode of conversation in restrooms or cars. While it may seem informal, you are still under the microscope. And since there are so many questions interviewers know to be off-limits, some of the normal casual conversational topics like, "Do you have kids? How many?" or "What does your spouse do?" may not be asked; in all likelihood, talk with you is going to circle back to your current research, graduate student status ("How close are you to graduating, anyway?") or your impressions of the place where you are interviewing. Know the lack of personal questions is not because the interviewers don't want to get to know you: they are just being careful. And you should be, too. You can relax up to a point, but always, always be ready to talk about your work.

Traits You Want To Project During the Actual Interview

You may experience a slight amount of stage fright at the beginning of the interview but remember a bit of adrenaline is fine to give you a cutting performance edge as long as you are not frozen with anxiety. If you are feeling agitated during the interview process, notice which people present are calm, and use your mirror neurons to quiet yourself down by mimicking them. Model your behavior after the most serene person in the room, not the one so hopped up on caffeine that their words spill over themselves. Breathe slowly and deeply to allow oxygen into your brain and to let you think more clearly.

Confidence. Confidence is the single most important attribute to project during the actual interview. No matter how uncertain, insecure, or scared you feel, you have to fake it till you make it by acting sure of yourself even if you do not feel 100% that way. The best antidote for insecurity is preparation. Now is the time to believe in yourself. You got this interview based on all the work you have done to this point.

Though it may feel unnatural at first, allow yourself to practice feeling confident. You can do this even with simple interactions like saying hello with a smile to people you do not know well. It's infectious and will make both of you more upbeat. If you are introverted and fearful, using a low-stakes interaction and getting positive responses to a greeting at a check-out counter can be a great way to inure yourself to anxiety. Various studies have shown confidence has an effect on better performance. If this is an issue for you, revisit our earlier section on "Building Confidence."

Most academics suffer from "the imposter syndrome," meaning they think that at some point others will discover they really don't know what they are talking about and they will be revealed as "imposters." There is a lot of literature out there about why this happens and what to do about it if imposter syndrome is an issue for you. You may want to go back to the earlier section on the "Imposter Syndrome" to address this issue in greater depth. For the purposes of an interview, here are three simple things you can do to reduce the feeling of being an imposter:

1) Remind yourself that you did, in fact, finish a doctorate, an accomplishment that puts you in an elite category of 1-2% of the entire population;

2) Know that it's normal as you move up the educational ranks to be surrounded by more and more people as accomplished as you are, even if it makes you feel like you are getting less intelligent. Being with equally accomplished people is actually a good thing because you will find people with compatible interests and abilities as potential partners or researchers; and

3) Though many people won't admit it, and you probably don't want to voice it during an interview, just like everyone else, academics go through periods when they are unproductive or highly productive. You're not an imposter because you happen to be at a low point in the productivity cycle.

Collegiality. The next most important trait to project is collegiality. Never, ever badmouth anyone: not anyone on your committee or in another department. It may come back to bite you. These interviewers are the people you eventually want to work with, and they want to know, like, and trust you before making an offer. Give them a sense of who you are and why you would be a good fit, speaking graciously of all those who have made it possible to get to this point. Bad advisor? Turn it around: "I learned from my advisor the importance of staying in communication with researchers working at a distance." Difficult editor? Try: "I am working with my publisher to polish my final submission."

Authenticity. Finally, we know it sounds trite, but be yourself. As Rebecca Schuman has said, "No amount of overpreparation will make interviewers like you if they don't."[231] People want to get to know who *you* really are, and learn about you as a whole person. If you like to go to science fiction movies and the topic comes up, it's OK to admit it. Don't hide who you are by creating different answers to please different interviewers. The committee members will be comparing notes, so saying "my favorite activity is x" to one person and "my favorite activity is y" to another can lead to questioning you at other levels. On the other hand, be careful about giving too much personal information—they don't need to know about your contentious relationship with your mother-in-law.

How To Handle a Variety of Types of Interviews

Telephone interviews have become increasingly common as a way to screen job candidates both inside and outside academia because they are significantly less costly than bringing in each candidate in a small pool to interview for a position. A phone interview is a way for a hiring institution to determine how interested you are in the position and how interested they are in hiring you for it. It is also a chance for you to determine if you actually want to work for them.

If you are called for a telephone interview, celebrate! The pool has already been narrowed down to 10, or typically even fewer, candidates. You will be assessed for your ability to speak and communicate clearly and concisely, as well as your ability to answer questions directly. These preliminary interviews rarely last longer than 20-minutes and will determine whether you are invited for a second longer interview either by video or on campus.

Most of the telephone interview questions will be scripted, since many Human Resources departments of larger organizations require that all candidates be asked to answer the same questions with a view toward fairness and leveling the playing field. If a question seems relatively unrelated to who you are, or what they are hiring you to do, most likely it is a scripted question. Just answer the question and stop worrying about why they asked it.

As you prepare for a telephone interview, make sure you know in advance exactly when the call will be made, and determine whether they are calling you or you are calling them at the appointed time. It is extremely rare these days for a committee chair to call you without warning. Use a landline if at all possible, because a dropped call is going to upset your momentum; cell phones are notorious for this issue. Landlines are also slightly less likely to have static and other noise issues. We do recognize that many people no longer have landlines, or even access to one, so at the very least make sure you are in a place with good cell phone reception.

Disable call waiting if you have it. Any interruption can disturb your train of thought. On average, your brain takes 15 minutes to get back on track, too long to recover while interviewing. You can imagine what happens if your long-lost brother's number pops up, making you wonder what awful thing is happening in your family. Or as actually happened to me once, a doctor's phone number popped up making me wonder if one of my kids was in the emergency ward at the hospital, when it was nothing more than an appointment reminder.

You should be in a quiet place with no potential distractions or interruptions like barking dogs or crying kids. Whether working from home or from an office, post a "Do not disturb" sign for the duration. You should not be in a coffee shop during your interview, with all the noise and possible commotion, not to mention the possibility of someone you know trying to get your attention and see what you are doing. Coffee shops are places to work while being among other people, but this is not the time for it. And neither is coffee, if you are sensitive to caffeine and it makes you nervous.

Once you find a secluded, quiet, comfortable spot to chat, perhaps in your own home, get a glass of water and keep it handy. Water can soothe your throat after speaking for a while. During what is bound to be a stressful conversation, no matter how well it goes, keeping yourself hydrated can help reduce anxiety and help your brain work better. You may even want to tank up 3-4 hours before the interview since symptoms like being forgetful, confused, or even feeling mentally lethargic can all be traced to mild dehydration. Caffeine is a known dehydrator, so that's another reason to limit its intake prior to an interview.

Make sure you have all your application materials near you in case you need to refer to them. You may want to print out things like your teaching philosophy or research objectives so that you do not have to search your computer while you are talking to the interviewer(s). You may want copies of any correspondence depending on how detailed it has been, or if you were asked to address something specific to your area. You probably don't need copies of logistical emails setting up the interview. If you are a visual learner, you may need to take notes while being interviewed. Allow notes and printed documents to be an aid and not a crutch. My own notes are so cryptic that no one besides me can ever decipher them because I tend to write just one word at a time on a notepad I keep to the right side of my computer to help jog my memory on possible replies.

Other items you may want to have in front of you can include words that help you focus or remind yourself of how you want to be perceived, like "calm, cool and collected." Breathing slowly while looking at these words before the interview can help you mentally prepare yourself to be at your best. If you know that a red shirt, or any other special piece of clothing will help you feel confident, go ahead and wear that.

Be sure you know in advance to whom you will be speaking and address them by name or title as appropriate. If necessary, be prepared to politely request the names of all people on the call, and write them down. Most committees understand that you can't always see who is speaking, and that you want to be respectful. This can also help calm you down since you are unlikely to recognize anyone's voice in the early stages of the interview game.

Just a few more pointers for a telephone interview:

- Speak slowly and enunciate. Breath between sentences. If you race through your answer, you can lose your audience because they literally could not understand you.
- Expect moments of silence as what you say is processed. If the call is not scripted, this may be when the committee will ask a specific follow-up question.
- Don't feel compelled to talk all the time. Pauses are natural. As the candidate, you may be hypersensitive to pauses. Try counting to 10, and if you feel at that point that the silence has gone on too long, ask a question of your own about the department, the campus, or the location.
- Smile and act confident as if they can see you even though they can't; interviewers can tell if you are happy and enthusiastic even when you aren't visible.
- Dress professionally to help you play the part of a potential colleague, even if they can't see you. It is amazing how well this works to train your brain to behave competently.

Video interviews are in a special category. The most commonly used service is Skype, although others, like Zoom, are becoming increasingly popular. There are a few unique items to consider when preparing for a video interview [232] that differ from preparing for a telephone interview. Unlike industry video interviews, it is extremely unlikely you will be asked to submit a pre-recorded answer to a pre-determined set of questions.

The first thing to ask when setting up the interview is what version of video conferencing you will be using. Incompatible software can make you crazy. You may have more lag time, issues with the screen freezing unexpectedly, or the call dropping. Many of these issues will disappear if both sides are using the same version of the software.

As with any other interview, make sure you know who is placing the call and who is answering it. Usually, the interviewer calls the candidate, which should alleviate some anxiety around making sure you are connecting properly.

Make sure you know how to talk to the camera instead of to one side. You may also have to practice looking at the camera, rather than the inset of your own face. You can generally set up the screen so that you and the interviewer appear side by side, or you get a big view of the interviewer with a small inset of yourself. Most people choose to use the insert because it is easier to ignore than the larger picture and finding yourself wondering why you chose to wear that outfit. Remember the nuances of body language and facial expressions are not so clear on video and don't be surprised if you find it much more difficult to read the room.

Make sure you test your camera and know where the camera and mike are placed for best viewing by your audience. A tilt that cuts off your head or leaves off your shoulders makes for disturbing viewing at the receiving end. Experiment with where you place the video picture on your computer screen. If it is down toward the bottom, rather than at the top, you may be looking down more than you would like.

If you have not used a video service much, find a friend or colleague to help you test the technology. Sometimes simple things trip people up unnecessarily. When I first started using

Skype, I sometimes hung up on people calling me because I hit the red telephone (which means "hang up") instead of the green telephone (which means "answer phone"). Another thing that tripped me up, in the beginning, was the small icon that looks like a document, usually appearing in the bottom left hand of your screen, for "conversations." It operates much like a chat feature, allowing you to type questions and responses. It is also where you can drop a document for someone else to see. Just knowing how the software works can reduce a huge amount of anxiety. You might want to practice it with a friend so any little glitches while you are interviewing (e.g., you touched something accidently and the picture became huge) can be dealt with easily and won't panic you.

Test to ensure the lighting is good: too many times I have worked with clients who have a window in the background, leaving them as merely a darkly outlined profile. Think about what a professional photographer would do to light you using a reflector overhead. Since you probably don't have professional equipment, test out your lamps. You may be able to position two of them above and off to either side to stop the silhouette effect.

Skype will let you test out the lighting without actually making a phone call: go to your profile and click on the camera icon below your picture and you can see what you will look like on the other end. Simple. In connection with this, you may discover that the glare of your computer is adding unwanted lighting. Just tone down your computer brightness to reduce the chance of reflected light turning into a distraction. If you wear make-up, make sure it does not reflect the light too much, making your face look like a mask. If you wear earrings, they should be smallish and not attention grabbing like enormous dangles. If you wear glasses, make sure the glare does not give you blue bottle fly eyes. Any of these things can be distracting for the viewer.

Make sure your interview clothing looks good on camera. Cameras can change colors of clothing and since you are only a talking head, you may need to lose that scarf that looks so good in person. Or you may need to spark up the colors since videos can wash out neutral tones, and make you look wan rather than robust. Also, check out your hairstyle: my hair tends to go its own way, and for me, tying it back is generally a good idea for talking to people over video. Finally, do not assume you can just dress the top half of your body appropriately and ignore the bottom half. You may have to stand up momentarily or you accidentally tilt the computer camera too far down, and oops, your PJs are there for the world to see.

Be careful of what shows up in your camera lens as background for others to see. A very messy work area or humorous posters or any other item that could be potentially misinterpreted should be left out of the frame. I knew someone who got in trouble because he liked science fiction movies and had a classic poster from *Forbidden Planet* of a woman being carted off by a robot on the wall behind him. The interviewers interpreted this as sexist. Remember, you do not know what biases your audience is bringing to the table. A simple clean background is best.

As always, make sure you have a backup plan in place with interviewers in case the technology fails or the call gets dropped. Video conferences have come a long way from the days of the start-stop animation that often cut out in the middle of a sentence, but the technology is still in flux. I'm sure you have already had the experience of talking to someone and wondering why you are getting no feedback, only to discover that you have been talking to yourself because the call was disconnected and you had not realized it.

If the video conference connection fails for whatever reason, having the telephone number of the head of the search committee nearby is usually a good option. Call the committee directly and you may be able to immediately get on with the actual interview rather than spending time trying to fix something that might not even be fixable, even if the interviewers have to put you on a speaker so everyone can hear you.

It does not hurt to practice interviewing by recording yourself as well. You can do this on your phone, via free conference software like Zoom, or signing up for a free Interview4.ME account. Or simply use the voice memo feature of your phone to hear yourself speaking. Professional musicians and actors always record themselves and dissect their own performances in order to improve. Don't hesitate to ask a close friend or colleague to rehearse with you to help you know how you come across or tell you what items in the field of vision they find distracting.

If you notice any personal quirks when viewing the recording, like always looking up before you answer a question, you can practice lessening that action before the actual interview. Here's a piece of trivia on why you might do that: Looking up and eye movement are often associated with how the mind processes information, and you may be a visual learner who literally looks for information in your mind's eye. Personal tics are easy to catch in a recording, but otherwise generally invisible to yourself.

A recording is also a chance to practice speaking slowly and concisely answering anticipated questions. I am notorious for speaking too quickly, leaving the person at the other end asking me to repeat myself. Remember that elevator speech? Be prepared to use it in this context, and to speak about your work in an unhurried manner.

Special note for users of mobile phones. If you know the interview is going to be conducted over a mobile phone, make sure your phone is fully charged or plugged into a power source. For any video interview conducted on a mobile device, you may want to consider investing in a very small mobile tripod that allows you to attach the phone securely. You can then place it on a flat surface, stabilizing the view others see from the phone's camera. All the other rules apply, of course, but speaking on the phone and trying to hold it at the same time is far more likely to cause your picture to accidentally move, be jerked around, or even flipped so that all you see is yourself speaking. Using a tripod avoids all those pitfalls.

Conference interviews may or may not be a prerequisite for an on-campus interview, or they may be the first in-person interview after a telephone or video interview. These interviews tend to last from 30-45 minutes. Most of the time, the committee will try to space the candidate interviews out so candidates do not see or encounter each other. If you are talking to more than one interviewing group, make sure you allow enough time in a large conference center to get from one to another comfortably. You may want to have some energy bars and water with you, too, in case you do not have time to eat.

Interview—Videoconference (Skype, Zoom, or Other Service) and Telephone Considerations Worksheet

What will I wear (for building confidence and visual impact)?

How will I test the set-up (connection, lighting, etc.)?

What is my plan in the event of technology failure (alternate phone number, etc.)?

What else do I need to do to prepare (restroom break, get water)?

How will I know who the interviewers are and who is speaking?

How long am I willing to tolerate silence?

How will I handle illegal questions or microaggressions? (We explain these later in the chapter).

How will I keep track of the people I meet (notes on appearance, etc.)

How will I track the important dates (application materials, letters, etc.)

How will I be clear about the next steps for me in this process?

What is my plan for reconnecting with the interviewers?

How will I decompress after the interview (e.g., trusted confidante)?

Anything else I want to do to prepare (breathe, meditate, affirmations) ?

Part 5: Your Job Search Interviews

We recommend an hour between interviews to clear your head and get to the next place. It's not fun to arrive stressed out from running through the lobby to make your appointment, breathing hard with your hair askew. You don't want to undermine your professional appearance, nor will your brain function at its best.

It doesn't hurt to participate in interviews even if you know up front that you are not interested in the position. Accept any you are invited to. Practice may help you when the job you really, really want is on the line.

Since large academic conferences are frequently held in large meeting spaces that the organizers use for presentations, it is likely you will be invited up into a hotel room to meet your interviewers. Awkward. With any luck, the interviewer will offer you the only chair in the room and sit on the bed rather than making you sit there. The first time this happened to me, I kept wondering if the interview was a scam…but it turns out this is quite common at conferences.

Just know it's normal to feel like a fish out of water in this type of interview situation, and do what works best for you to calm down your system. Taking a few minutes in a bathroom stall using Amy Cuddy's "power postures"[233] discussed earlier can help. Breathing deeply and counting to ten before you enter a hotel room is often useful, too.

Some people find reading an affirmation like "I am already an accomplished and competent academic," or reciting a mantra like "I've got this," or simply repeating positive words like "confident, competent, and calm" to themselves can help. Some candidates find envisioning a calm natural setting like a placid lake can aid in offsetting the jitters. Or maybe remembering a humorous piece on the academic job search, like the "The Academic Beastiary for the Intrepid Job Seeker,"[234] may provide some relief. Use whatever works for you to calm yourself down.

The conference interview is very much about first impressions. You want to be the consummate professional, not the perpetual graduate student. Project yourself as a colleague, and establish yourself as a good match for the position in the first five minutes. The person(s) you are meeting may or may not be the person(s) ultimately in charge of hiring you, but you still need to put your best self forward.

The fact that you were even asked in for an interview means the committee has already decided you have the qualifications for the job and that at least one person on the committee is interested enough in you and your work to get you invited. As a reminder, it's important to begin with a firm handshake, discussed in detail earlier in the section "Basic Interview Etiquette." It's part of making that initial good impression, and you don't get a second chance for that. Follow the lead of the interviewer(s) in answering questions.

There may be only one interviewer, or as many as ten. The usual number is 3-4 people with one person taking the lead in asking questions. Most small schools cannot afford to send more than one or two people to a conference, so the conversation will naturally be more intimate and informal. Large research schools, especially medical teaching facilities, may send a larger group. A large group of interviewers will still likely have a lead questioner. It may be that half of the people there are simply observing the interview process. Unless they tell you, you may never know the exact role of the individual participants.

Interview—Basic Questions Worksheet

Focus on your answers, and be prepared to answer these questions at a bare minimum.

What makes you unique?

Why are you a good fit for this position?

Tell us about your dissertation project. [Keep your answer to two sentences at most, and present it confidently. You really do know this stuff; now you have to make sure other people understand what you have been doing.]

What is your teaching philosophy? [Expect about 10 minutes for this.]

What is your research plan? This could include anticipated books or articles, grant proposals, new directions to take your research. [Expect about 10 minutes for this.]

Part 5: Your Job Search Interviews

As you answer the questions, even if only one person is asking them, make eye contact with the other people present. You don't want them to feel ignored or that you don't care about their opinion as well, because you do. One client reported how upsetting it was to have a "baleful basilisk" on the interviewing panel, so she focused on the friendliest face in the room as she answered questions.

The **Interview—Basic Questions Worksheet** will help you anticipate some of the questions you may be asked in a conference interview or preliminary interview.

Whatever the interviewer actually asks, answer it. Don't dodge it. Interviewers notice direct and Be prepared to pay your own way for dinner or drinks, even if it means you have to take more money out of an ATM than you first anticipated. It's not a dating situation where the inviting party generally pays. Conference attendees may be on a limited budget themselves, and cannot be seen to show favoritism by paying for a more social interaction with a particular candidate. We've known some women (admittedly this was years ago) who assumed payment would be made by the inviting colleague, only to literally come up short when it was time to pay the bill. "Can I borrow $20.00 and pay you back later?" is not the act of a consummate professional.

On-campus interviews/site visits. On-campus visits are usually the last phase in a search process. If you get offered one, celebrate again! With many positions receiving over 300 applicants, you really are special and probably really nervous. Build your confidence by realizing you just made it to the true short list. Remind yourself as you travel to campus, breathing deeply, that you made this very select list. This will both calm you down and increase your confidence. To get through the interview, preparation is key, and that's what this workbook is designed to help you with.

Manya Whitaker, Assistant Professor of Education at Colorado College, has served on 5 search committees where candidates were invited to campus for two-day visits. She wrote: "Each of those searches resulted in one of two clear outcomes: an obvious front-runner or a failed search. How the candidates came across in person was the determining factor."[235]

Typically, a maximum of 3-4 candidates are brought in for on-campus interviews, usually for 1 to 2 days. Expect to be asked to present a "job talk" about your research, possibly conduct a class, engage in a variety of interviews with various stakeholders from students to provosts, and eat meals with search committee members or other members of the hiring department. In the face-to-face situation, you are being vetted for your intellectual abilities *and* your potential fit with department colleagues.

Behave as though you are being carefully examined in all aspects of yourself, because you are. There are plenty of funny stories about the interview process for academics, partly because academics do not do a lot of interviewing and are unskilled in conducting them. Mark W. Pleiss, now at the University of Colorado at Boulder, related how he was "treated" to dinner with faculty who were so bored with the process, or who had already made their hiring decision, that they literally spent the time photographing the food for social media instead of talking to him.[236] No matter what happens, breathe deeply and remain professional. You'll then be able to leave with your dignity intact.

Expect mistakes to happen and take them in stride. As mentioned above, you will not be the only candidate interviewing for the position. Sometimes emails are mistakenly sent to the wrong person and you will discover the name(s) of your competition. You may be unable to resist looking them up if you don't already know them, but the polite thing to do is send the email back to the sender with a note, "I don't think this was meant for me." Sometimes the slip-ups will relate to scheduling. Be gracious.

There may not be time to meet each member of the search committee separately as schedules are tight. Tight schedules and multiple candidates can also result in peculiar questions because those people meeting you aren't well informed about your research or have confused your particular specialty with another candidate. You can redirect befuddled questions with a polite, "That's not my area of expertise; my work is related to [invertebrate animals]."

Sometimes, the interviewer will unintentionally undermine your confidence, noting as you begin a classroom presentation that you are "Dr. So-and-So, our third candidate for this position." Most likely it is a completely unintentional gaffe. In this case, you may need to call on your mental allies, whether real or imaginary, to boost your confidence. Stride to the front of the classroom with a positive attitude like "third time's the charm," and expect the teaching demonstration will go well for you.

Community college interviews. Quite a few articles have been written about how interviews for positions at community colleges differ from those at research institutions or 4-year colleges. Rob Jenkins (2018) has provided a good summary of "What to expect at a community-college interview."[237] Although Jenkins points out that no standard interview format exists for community college jobs, he adds that community college interviews are not conducted at conferences, as is the case for various levels of interviews for 4-year colleges or research institutions. The community college generally does not pay your travel expenses for the interview and most community colleges are looking for candidates already in their geographical area. The interview for a long-term job may last only part of a day and probably will not include a presentation on your doctoral research. A teaching demonstration may be required and may be an important part of the interview process, but your audience could be either actual students or only search committee members. Many community colleges hire contract workers for a term at a time at the last minute, so you may not even be asked to demonstrate teaching skills.

Preparation before an On-site Interview

As you begin the exciting process of preparing for an on-campus interview, the first thing you want to know is who is paying for your trip and who is making the reservations for transportation and, with luck, an overnight stay. It may be the department's administrative assistant, so you will want to get all the contact information for that person. But making all these arrangements should not fall on you, other than to express your preference for a time.

Be sure to wear your professional clothes while traveling. You never know who may be traveling alongside you to the same institution, especially if you end up on a commuter flight as the last leg of your journey. Dressing for success is part of making a good impression from the outset, and it's amazing what a difference sitting in your professional clothing can make to projecting a professional attitude as you wait in an airport lounge.

Your style should be fashionable but not trendy. What people normally wear to conferences is a big clue as to what you will be expected to wear. As the petitioner for a job, you need to dress a bit more formally than you will have to once you have secured the position. There is often an informal dress code for particular communities of scholars, and you know what it is for your specialty area. For example, archeologists interviewing you may be wearing jeans to work, but you'll need to dress more formally, in skirts or slacks, unless you are going out into the field with them as part of the process. Classicists who often incorporate archaeologists into their department tend to dress in jackets and khaki pants. If you can add something distinctively "you" to the outfit, such as an interesting tie or a beautiful scarf without violating such conventions, it may help the interviewers remember you. For example, if I were applying for a job in a biology department, I would wear my scarf with dragonflies on it. For a physics department, a blue necktie featuring mathematical formulas might get you noticed and also be a conversation starter.

Before you travel, many schools will send you an itinerary or list of activities. If they haven't and time is getting short, contact them. You need this! As you are looking the schedule over, make sure you know when you will have breaks for resting and practicing, as well as freshening up. A typical two-day schedule will look something like this:

Sample On-campus Interview Schedule

Day 1
- Arrive night before (airline, date and time); pick up and drop off at hotel by administrative assistant
- 8:00 AM Breakfast alone or scheduled with search committee member
- 9:00 AM Meet with Provost
- 10:00 AM Informal meeting with faculty and graduate students in lounge area
- 11:30 AM to 1:00 PM Lunch with Department Chair or Dean or both
- 1:30 PM Time alone to prepare for presentation (1st job talk) on your research
- 2:00 PM Presentation (1st job talk) in Conference Room A
- 5:30 PM Dinner with search committee member(s)

Day 2
- 8:00 AM Breakfast alone or scheduled with search committee member
- 9:00 AM Tour of campus
- 10:30 AM Time alone to prepare for demo class (2nd job talk)
- 11:00 AM Presentation (2nd job talk) in Classroom 202
- 1:00 PM Lunch with school President or Dean or both (whoever you have not yet met)
- 3:00 PM Meet with full committee in Room 312
- Depart (airline, date and time); drop off by Search Committee chair.

In a seriously compressed one-day visit, you may find you are expected to do a morning teaching demonstration and an afternoon presentation on your research, or vice versa. However, you are more likely to be asked for a teaching demonstration (in effect, the second job talk) when the visit spans more than one day. For visits of more than one day, expect that more items related to the vicinity and institution will be introduced to you. These might include a campus tour, a town tour, meetings with librarians or directors of special institutes related to your topic, or a writing center for undergraduates. Treat all groups you meet with equal respect. Students may have more influence than you realize: one may just happen to have a close relationship with an advisor who asks them, "What did you think of so-and-so?" You do not want the answer to be, "She ignored me when I asked a question."

The general "boilerplate" items included in a job itinerary will differ from school to school as will the times people are available to meet. You are more likely to meet the provost (chief academic officer) and the president at smaller institutions. Sometimes, meeting the provost and the president may actually be a requirement of the school prior to offering a position. Who else you meet will vary from institution to institution. Large public schools will almost always state that the offer of a position is contingent on a background criminal check. Don't freak out. It's become standard practice, and that DUI you got as a freshman in college is unlikely to stop you from getting a job.

As you review the itinerary, make sure you know exactly where and when interviews with the various participants will be held. There may be times when you are expected to get yourself to the next event on the agenda, perhaps because you have been returned to your hotel to rest or organize yourself. You need all the details of where you are expected next, including the building, room, and time of day you are supposed to be there. Hopefully, the person(s) preparing your schedule will build "travel time" into the timetable. Knowing this information is especially important for physically large campuses.

Make sure you are on time for every appointment. While you may be shepherded through the majority of the process, when you are on your own, be sure to get back early to wherever you are supposed to be according to the itinerary. Being early allows you to gather yourself together before plunging into the next conversation. Being respectful of the time potential future colleagues have set aside to meet you helps set the right tone for current and future interactions.

Next, you want to make sure you know how long the interview segments will last. With the exception of your job talks and meals, which are likely to be an hour to an hour and a half, most of the time you will be scheduled for 30-minute segments to meet with the various people, from student leaders to the provost or president of the school. If you have an agenda, the anticipated meeting will likely be on it, but if not, be prepared to ask when a particular meeting will occur.

To reiterate the advice about cell phones, turn them off while you are actually meeting with people. Obviously, it is OK to have them on and take calls while you are between meetings, on your own or in your hotel room taking a break. But if you take calls, text, or play videos while meeting with people, you are sending a clear, concrete message that "you people are so unimportant to me, I would rather engage with someone/something else." Ouch. Not the message you want to send. The no cell phone rule even holds for difficult situations. Perhaps your elderly father is having an operation for a knee replacement and you are worried about how he will do under anesthesia. You are far away from the operating room, and even if you were there, you could do nothing about what is happening. Even though you are anxious, wait to call or have someone call you rather than taking a call. It's OK to let people know you may be a little distracted for this particular reason but do this informally outside of the actual interview. Silence your cell phone even during meals you are sharing with potential colleagues.

If you have the names of the people you will be meeting with in advance, investigate their interests, research, and accomplishments so that know your audience. Most of this research can easily be done on the university or department website, especially if the school expects faculty to maintain a website of their own tied to the school's. This includes researching the graduate students. It won't hurt to know the name of a particular researcher in a lab, or the leader of a graduate studies association. Graduate students are potential future colleagues, and while their voices may not count for as much as faculty's during this hiring process, you can believe that if you make a seriously bad impression with these people, the information will reach the ears of the search committee. For good or ill, they may even remember you later, after they have their own positions, and you are looking to advance by moving laterally to a new institution. Graduate students are checking out how you dress, how you answer questions, and what you present in your job talks because they know they will be on the job market soon and they will pick-up dos and don'ts from watching you.

Our last bit of simple advice before any on-campus interview is to get a good night's sleep, drink lots of water, and stay away from coffee or anything else that might make you agitated during the actual interview. Both lack of sleep and lack of water can fog your brain, making you incoherent at a time when you want to be at your most focused and articulate. If you are used to taking in a certain amount of caffeine in the morning, now is not the time to quit and give yourself a withdrawal headache. But you don't want to overdo the intake either, causing your hands to shake and making your nervous energy apparent. Appearing calm and confident and taking time to answer any question will reflect well on you.

Prior to traveling, you will no doubt have been asked to send the title and any publicity you have available for your job talk. Remember the earlier discussion about interesting conference paper titles? This holds double for job talk titles. You want to make the title interesting enough that even people with no interest whatsoever in linguistics will be intrigued enough to drop in on *"Without our language we have no culture: Arabic in the Mahgreb."* For a job talk on the mental health of veterans, you could use something like, *"War and Peace: Symptoms of PTSD in returning veterans and what to do about it."*

If you have a great graphic you can attach, even if it's just a publicly available picture of something related, like a picture of a sea turtle when discussing climate change, use it. It's just another way to make your topic memorable. Or maybe you use Matura MT Script Capitals for the title *Mysteries of the Ottoman Harem,* which suggests a talk about the Middle East and will attract attention. If you don't provide some specific guidance for publicity, you are at the mercy of whatever the department manages to send out. Even if they have some set blueprint for advertising job talks, you will get points for preparedness.

Sometimes you will be asked to send the entire job talk, but that should be negotiable. Responding "I would rather have people listen to what I have to say" is a legitimate reason for not providing the full text. You can always offer to send your slides or the text of your talk after your presentation, in case someone interested in you and your topic cannot make it to your session due to scheduling commitments of their own for teaching or advising.

What To Keep in Mind during the Campus Interview

Establish rapport. The *most important thing* to remember during the on-campus interview is to establish rapport with the interviewer(s). Start from a positive place of imagining yourself as a colleague. From your advance research on the department, know what you might be able to contribute to the work of other colleagues. Show enthusiasm for your own work, and let them know that you believe *your* work matters. Even though the term "good fit" can get interviewers into trouble if used to explain why a candidate did not get a job offer, whether a candidate is a good fit is actually what most interviewers want to know. Don't worry that you can't answer every question perfectly, or occasionally stumble when presented with a new idea you haven't had time to process; interviewers know you are nervous and will give you some latitude for that. Their job is to select the best possible candidate, whether or not you charm the socks off them. But you do have to be relatable.

Stay on point. Know how to present your research and plans in a succinct manner even to people with no training in your field. This is especially important if you have an interview scheduled with someone in an administrative position, because a dean or a provost may be the one holding the purse strings on the job and the amount you may be offered. These people are most likely not to be experts in your field, so speak concisely and assuredly about what you do. Show how your research would help others at the institution or add to the reputation of the school. Without braggadocio, jargon, or going too deeply into how your research agenda will be pursued, express how your current skills and knowledge will make you an asset to the institution.

Relax. As you begin the interview, imagine the dialogue taking place over coffee with a good colleague who is genuinely interested in what you are doing. This image allows you to relax into the conversation and may lighten the weight of an interview. Remind yourself that committee members *want* to like you, and are generally quite welcoming and friendly as they start to get to know you.

Be concrete. In considering how to answer the teaching questions, be clear with yourself about the way you would describe your teaching style. Concrete examples of activities in the classroom or lab are the best way to get that across. If you are interviewing at a community college, the teaching demonstration is the most critical thing you will do, along with answering questions about your teaching style in relation to their particular kind of typical student.

Stay engaged (even if you are tired). On-campus interviews are exhausting for the candidates, the search committee members, and the support staff. Be aware that you will likely get to a point where you feel you have said the same thing to different people a hundred times. This can make you look a lot less enthusiastic than you may actually feel about the job opportunity. Try varying your answers to mesh with what you know about the questioner. For instance, if the person asking the question has pioneered a particular research program, tailor your response about how your research could complement that area of study. "I understand you started a program focused on the role of financial organizations in prolonging/curtailing international conflicts. Would my research on the economic issues behind World War II be of interest to you?"

Be prepared for in-depth questions. In preparing for the actual interview with the search committee, expect the questions to go deeper than on the previous telephone, video, or conference interviews. Nevertheless, be ready to answer the basic questions discussed during that preliminary interview because not everyone on the search committee will have heard your answers before. Repetition may also help to consolidate your expertise in the minds of those who have spoken with you earlier.

In the next worksheet are some additional questions that may come up with regard to teaching, research, writing, and other duties, which we have broken into four separate worksheets for you. These questions are neither a comprehensive list nor will all of these questions be asked. We provide it to help you practice the answers you would like to give. Thinking about, and literally answering these questions aloud, particularly to someone without expertise in your field, is an excellent way to prepare for an in-depth interview. You may be surprised to discover the places where your answers are unclear to the listener precisely because they are unfamiliar with your field. Finding ways to clarify your answers for the non-expert is a great exercise.

As you answer the standard questions about your research, teaching philosophy, and connections for future research possibilities, give enough information to be clear, but don't ramble. By this point, you should have a thumbnail sketch of exactly what your work is about and why you think it matters even to people outside of your field. As we said, you will be repeating it many times in the course of two days during the on-campus interview because you will be meeting a lot of different stakeholders. Be succinct and stay away from the details unless specifically asked.

You should be ready to ask questions of the interviewer's line of research or the type of work they do at the university; for example, a professor's role is substantially different from that of the director of an institute like the Center for Democracy. Know the difference and be able to tailor your own questions accordingly. Your questions should indicate some basic familiarity with your potential colleagues and demonstrate you are capable of thinking about someone other than yourself. After all, search committee members for tenure-track jobs usually expect the relationship with a new faculty member to be long-term. They want to be assured of your congeniality.

Your interview is a good time to ask about anticipated teaching loads, class size, number of majors, courses you would likely teach, and availability of library resources for both you and your students, if this has not already been discussed. While you may be able to get some of this information online as you prepare for the campus visit, hearing a current faculty member's perspective can be very helpful. You can even say something like, "I read about x in the online information about this department, but I'm wondering how this works for you in reality."

Occasionally, departments will narrow the search down to just two candidates and still be undecided as to the best fit. In this instance, you may be asked to conduct some sort of follow-up interview, most likely by telephone or video. Be prepared to offer some *new* information about why you think you are the best fit for the job on offer.

Try to relate whatever new information you offer to the interviewer(s) or the department with comments to show how you can actually fit in as a new colleague. Suppose during an interview

Interview—In-depth Questions Related to Teaching Worksheet

What do you consider your strengths/weaknesses as a teacher? [Be careful here. Emphasize your strengths (connecting with students from diverse backgrounds, classroom engagement, promoting critical thinking) and downplay weaknesses. Speaking negatively about yourself, even if you see it as humility, is not useful in an interview context.]

What best describes your teaching style? [Committee is generally looking for an answer related to a mix of approaches, from lecturing, to in-class writing assignments, to small group discussions, to lab participation; answers may depend on your field.]

Tell us how you would teach our students for undergraduate introductory courses or methods/core theory course for graduates. [This requires you know something about the kinds of students who are generally attending the school, for instance, a high percentage of first-generation college entrants, or high percentage of community college transfers, or likely number of graduate students in a particular program.]

Do you modify your teaching style based on class size? How?

How does your teaching philosophy play out in the classroom?

How would you teach [a big name in your field like Darwin, Marx, Shakespeare] or how would you teach the history of your field?

How do you get students excited about your topic?

Part 5: Your Job Search Interviews

In your experience, where are the areas students have the most difficulty learning with your topic? How do you address this? [Could be anything from lab work to creative writing.]

How do you deal with [controversial term, like feminism, creationism, polygamy, cultural appropriation, etc.] in the classroom?

Tell us about an experience of classroom controversy and how you handled it.

How would you teach an introductory survey course versus a capstone course?

Tell us which of the courses we usually offer are of most interest to you.

What is your favorite course to teach? Why?

The teaching load here is [4-4, 3-2, or any other permutation]. What are your personal strategies for handling this?

How do you use technology in the classroom? How familiar are you with teacher-student interactive software [Blackboard, Moodle, Canvas]?

What on-line teaching experience have you had? Are you willing to teach/design online courses?

Describe your experience with handling diversity [code for race, ethnicity, religion, socioeconomic status, gender, sexuality, and/or disability] in and out of the classroom. [Best strategy: be aware of what is most likely to come up in the institutional context where you are interviewing, and address that directly.]

Interview—In-depth Questions Related to Research Worksheet

How you can bring your research interests into an undergraduate classroom or graduate seminar?

Why is this work important? Or, how does your work contribute to this field?

What changes do you anticipate for your field in the next five years?

How does your research align with [theory or theorist]?

What is your research agenda or next anticipated project?

How do you see yourself mentoring graduate students?

Where do you see yourself/your research in the next five years?

Remember, if you are actually in a tenure-track position, you generally have 6 years to the point where the tenure decision is made, and 3 years to a review of your progress toward tenure. You may want to prepare a 5-year research plan in order to answer this question easily, while knowing all the while that it could change drastically depending on the answers to research conducted in the first year. That's OK. Scholars are not held to research agendas when the work takes them in new directions. You just want to have an idea of where your work might be headed.

Interview—In-depth Questions Related to Writing Worksheet

Tell us more about the context for the writing sample you submitted. [Some search committees will have actually read whatever you provided to them and ask about why you included one theory/researcher and not another. You don't have to defend your choices, just explain them.]

What are your next writing projects [turning dissertation into a book; revising chapters for journal articles; new article, new book, new digital archive]? Be prepared to discuss at least two upcoming projects.

What helps you get a writing project finished? [You can discuss everything from daily habits to the rhythm of the academic year, for instance, "I write best over the summer" or, if the summer is spent in the field, "I generally write up my summer research during school break periods."]

Where do you plan to submit your material [traditional publishing houses, online journals]?

What grants have you successfully applied for in the past? What grants do you expect to help fund your work here?

Interview—In-depth Questions Related to Other Duties Worksheet

How do you understand the mission of our school?

What does "service" mean to you, in this educational context? [Most universities say that promotions are based on teaching, research, and service. Service may include work advising students, restructuring curricula, serving on a faculty Senate; is there something you have done before or that appeals more to you than others?]

How do you feel about administering [particular program]?

How would you recruit new students to our major?

How do you see yourself fitting into this department? [An answer to this question is a good place to show you have some knowledge of who else is in the department, and if there are ways you might want to collaborate with them.]

Are you aware our institution offers [certificate program, accelerated degree, remedial classes]? How can you contribute to that?

you found out the department wanted you to teach a particular course that was only tangential to your research and experience. For this kind of follow-up interview you might say: "You brought up such-and-such course, and I've been thinking about it, and have started a syllabus for it. Would you like me to send it to you?" Or, "I think I would be really good at teaching the course you mentioned when we spoke before because..." This proves to them that you listened and are responsive to their needs.

Meals. As part of some interviews, you will be asked to share meals with potential colleagues. Do not underestimate the importance of "the lunch test." [238] Many careers are made or broken at this juncture.

Be on time. Your hosts have likely made a reservation at a place they can afford but will still impress you. Dress suitably. If you are all arriving at the same time, you may want to shake hands before you sit down. If you need to introduce yourself, do so. Make sure your phone is both turned off and not on the table. Research shows that even having a phone on the table is distracting enough to influence the flow of conversation.[239] Speaking of conversation, if you have not been told who your mealtime companions are going to be, and you do not know anything about them, ask them to: "Tell me a little bit about [your background, your research or teaching, what you do in your position]." People love to talk about themselves, and the more you listen attentively, the more you will be remembered kindly. Stay away from speaking too personally about the big taboo topics: sex, politics, and religion, unless one of those is your field of study. The conversation may include discussions of departmental issues; don't worry about it or ask for clarification. Just listen.

Know basic mealtime etiquette. Put your napkin in your lap, chew with your mouth closed, use your silverware and china appropriately. If you need a crash course in etiquette, take one. Mealtime etiquette is a skill that is not always taught but is easily learned. We personally know of at least two candidates that failed to close their mouths when eating, and this became a negative topic of discussion for members of the hiring committee. Scary, but true.

Stay away from pasta, soup, or other messy food that you might be expected to hold in your hands, like burritos; you have enough to worry about without spots on your travel clothes. In addition, pasta or other heavy food can make you feel lethargic when you want to be on your toes. It's probably best to go with tried and true dishes for yourself, rather than experimenting with outré ethnic dishes and unfamiliar spices.

Hydration is necessary for handling stress, but you may not always have time to relieve yourself. Take advantage of any opportunity to use the facilities. Meals are an obvious time to take these breaks. A fundamental rule for anyone traveling anywhere anytime is to use the facilities whenever you have an opportunity, because even if you don't think you need to relieve yourself at that moment, you may not get the opportunity later. I always remember one of my graduate school peers talking about how she failed to take advantage of a restroom stop when her escort came to take her to campus, and because of a traffic tie-up, she was desperate with no opportunity for relief because they barely made it in time for the first appointment. Talk about distracting.

Energy pickups are great if you know your own tolerance for them. A campus visit is not the time to experiment with power drinks that primarily jazz you up with caffeine and sugar and a few other ingredients such as guarana, taurine, ginseng, and various vitamins. Know how these things affect you personally and act accordingly. Too much caffeine can leave you with shaking hands while giving your talk or cause an energy slump when the effect wears off in the middle of your class demonstration.

Unless others are ordering alcohol, stay away from it. In general, alcohol will only be offered after 5:00 PM or at dinner. Know your own limits, and consume appropriately. If the bottle is left on the table for you to pour your own wine, moderate your intake by never pouring more than 1/3 of a glass for yourself. And if you don't drink alcohol or any other beverage that is offered such as tea, coffee, or cola because of the caffeine, just politely decline without making a big deal of it. It's surprising how many candidates spoil their hiring chances because they used alcohol to calm their nerves.

Be good to your servers, thanking them when they deliver your food. Wait until everyone has received their food before digging in. At the end of the meal, try to gauge whether people want coffee or can't wait to get done and go home. Guests are asked for their preference for the sake of politeness. If you a preference, say so, but you can also say something like, "I wouldn't mind having a coffee and/or dessert, but I can go either way." That gives the host a chance to extend the meal with, "Oh, great, I'd really like a cappuccino," or end the meal with "I'd really rather skip dessert since it is not on my diet." If the host says, "I still need to prepare for my morning lecture," everyone, including you, should understand the time to break up the meal has come.

A few additional things you *don't* want to do during the interview. It is never appropriate to badger the interviewers for information, particularly around practical matters like insurance and salary. These discussions come later in the process, during negotiations, once you have been offered the position. Even then, you don't want to harass anyone involved in the negotiations. In the short run, impress your hiring committee with your admirable restraint around these issues.

Don't make excuses for anything, whether it's getting lost on-campus, or why you did not meet your last publication deadline. If you did get lost, just apologize for being late. Don't blame the department assistant who tried to tell you where to go, but accidentally forgot to give you some crucial landmark. If you did not meet your publication deadline, just say so. This happens all the time, for a variety of reasons. Even tenured professors miss deadlines as they get caught up in teaching or research. Explaining without being defensive is an art.

You do not want to appear evasive regarding your qualifications or experience: If you don't know the answer to a question, it is OK to say that. Depending on the question, you could say, "I don't know but I could look into that," or, "I don't know, but that is an excellent question for future consideration." You do not need to be evasive about funding prospects, either. If your future research depends on receiving the next grant, then anticipate the question by stating "the grant is currently under review and funding should commence [on such and such a date]." You look much better just stating the facts than trying to sidestep the issue.

Don't argue with the interviewer or anyone else about anything, whether it's related to theoretical perspective, best practices, or anything else. To do so will make you look arrogant or belligerent.

One search committee member confided to me after speaking with a combative candidate that the person was no longer under consideration because he was perceived as lacking the necessary collegiality. Sometimes the person trying to argue with you about research methods or data interpretation is just trying to show off how much they know. Or she is the newest member of the department and you make her feel insecure. Let it go.

Stay away from anything that would make you appear "high maintenance" to a potential colleague or interviewer. One candidate who was enormously qualified made a bad impression with the hiring committee by focusing on university amenities and whether she would have privileges at a faculty gym or be able to take time to go off campus to swim during the day. This is for you to determine, not the hiring committee, and it does not focus on what you do as an academic. Another candidate demanded to know what office he would be given, and whether bookcases would be furnished. Really? The hiring committee is getting strong signals that you would be a royal pain to deal with in the future.

Never, ever say negative things about your previous position, employer, peers, or supervisor. Even if you absolutely hated every minute you spent with bluebloods getting your Ivy League degree, keep it to yourself. You never know who this might get back to and torpedo an otherwise promising career. Besides, it only reflects badly on you, and that's not who you want to be in the world, is it?

Finally, when the interview appears to be over, leave graciously. Don't keep trying to prolong contact thinking that will somehow help your cause. Actually, the opposite is true. Search committees are under a great deal of pressure to stay on schedule while maximizing the number of candidates they see. Delaying your leave can do more harm than good, even it feels like the whole process is over too soon for you.

Unpleasant surprises. Sometimes people make comments, also called microaggressions, that are not intentionally hurtful, but nevertheless, give you pause. Miriam-Webster only added the word microaggression [240] to its online dictionary in 2017, so recognition of these types of interactions has been relatively slow, though the term was coined in the 1970s by psychologist Chester Pierce. These kinds of comments are often related to the "isms": physical ability, gender, race, sexual orientation, age, and others. Sometimes the other person is projecting his or her feelings onto you. It may not be intentional but negative comments can reveal some underlying assumptions.

Years ago, I was applying for an academic job, and one member of the search committee did not want to hire me. I wasn't sure why but the antipathy was clear. The job was at a large state university where many of the students where I would be teaching botany were from farm families. The interviewer made the assumption that I was a city girl, and said something like, "You know, we're a big ag school and our faculty need to be able to relate to farm kids. This probably isn't a good fit for you." I said, "On the contrary, I grew up on a farm and was very active in 4-H. I have lots of experience getting along with, and teaching, kids from farms." In this case, I had a good answer to the stereotype. But that isn't always the case.

What can you do if faced with such a small unpleasant surprise?

First, be aware. Notice what happened and wonder why to yourself. It may be obvious or it may be subtle, depending on what was said. It never hurts to notice when you get that "sinking feeling" in your gut. You get nine times more information from your body in the form of unconscious clues than you do from your strategic prefrontal cortex (Clancy, 2015).[241] Pay attention to what your body is telling you. Your body will not lie.

Second, choose your battles. Breathe before responding. Decide whether or not you want to make an issue of the comment. You are still in the petitioner position. Do you really want to take this on right now? Is it morally imperative for you to address this at this time? Or can you let it go, knowing that you may have to deal with it later once you are offered (or in) the position? Assuming the microaggression is verbal, and you are not in danger of immediate harm, it may not be worth your time and effort to address right now.

Third, watch your own language. Take the high road and don't sink to the level of the commenter. No snide remarks. Women often hear from men, "You are so smart…and pretty, too," which can be very demeaning to an academically accomplished woman. Try just saying, "Thank you." If you are asked about being married or have children, John Cawley recommends this response: "Perhaps you're wondering about my ability to accept the position and give it the dedication it requires; I can assure you that the answer is yes."[242]

Or, another example: "So, you're Jewish, right? Does that mean you will want to take different holidays from the ones offered at our school?" This is clearly an assumption about background. You want to model good behavior. A bad answer would be to sarcastically say, "What gave it away? My big nose?" A good answer would be a simple, "Yes, I am Jewish." If the interviewer pursues this line of questioning about your holiday schedule, you may want to add, "Well, that's a question for Human Resources." The same need for a polite non-defensive answer would apply to a comment like, "You're not really [White-Black-Asian-Latino], are you?" Here's a possible response: "Being Latina is about a shared cultural heritage for me."

Fourth, decide if you really want to work there. This can be a particularly hard call if this is the only in-person interview you have gotten, and you really, really want an academic job. However, it can be a signal of things to come, and you are going to have a hard enough time adjusting to a new place to live and work, without dealing with a hostile environment as well. That can wrench a huge amount of energy away from getting your work done. If you decide it's not big enough to stop you from working there, that's fine, too. Awareness of your reasons for your decision is key.

Fifth, know your legal rights. Obviously, if you are interviewing in person or by video, many of the things an interviewer cannot ask can still be seen or inferred, such as race, age, and sex. Amazingly, a 2017 AP-CNBC [243] poll showed that 51% of all Americans had been asked illegal or inappropriate questions in job interviews. Here is a list of 10 areas that employers are specifically prohibited from asking you about directly, because they can be used to discriminate against you:

- Race
- Color

- Ethnic origin
- Sex
- Religion
- National origin
- Birthplace
- Age
- Disability
- Marital/family status

If you are asked questions in any of these areas, you have essentially two choices: answer the question or refuse to answer. You may choose to answer assuming that either the interviewer doesn't know the question was inappropriate or illegal or because you understand the intent behind the question to be an item that could weigh on the hiring decision. Perhaps they are trying to find out if you have a green card or whether the institution would have to sponsor you; maybe they have an idea for a job for your partner, but they don't know if the partner is involved in the decision. Tact, and your own discernment, is required here. You are under no obligation to provide personal information if you choose not to do so.

We know that, in situations where the hierarchical power structure leaves you in a subordinate position, restraining yourself from answering even illegal questions is particularly difficult. Just having a sense of what might be asked inappropriately can lessen your anxiety. Reminding yourself that you are not employed there yet can also help reduce your tension.

Be graceful and professional in your answer unless you feel that there is a deliberate attempt to discriminate. If so, you can choose legal action and file a claim, though we don't recommend this way of handling the issue. Better would be to simply point out that the question is inappropriate and you choose not to answer it. Or keep your peace by redirecting the conversation, politely telling the interviewer(s) that you are able and willing to handle the position. Recognize that the question reveals something about the culture of the organization interviewing you. Larger institutions are generally very careful to adhere to HR guidelines; smaller ones sometimes do not even consult HR until the point of hire.

If you feel that something of this nature has occurred during the interview and you deliberately choose not to address it, remember you may have to deal with it again once you are hired. Dealing with stereotypes or being grouped in some negative way will need to be addressed as quickly as possible for both your own peace of mind as well as handling any credibility issues. Your prior knowledge of those federal discrimination laws can come in handy at that point. After being hired, if necessary, you will also have the option of using any available HR resources.

Special note to women: Unfortunately, women should pay particular attention to discussing their relationship status in the interview. There is a confirmed bias against hiring women with high-status partners, whether those partners work in academia or elsewhere. Hiring committees frequently assume those women cannot move, and often exclude them from academic offers, especially when a "viable" male or single woman is available. Typically, a man's relationship status will not even be discussed, and this issue will not enter into discussions around hiring.[244]

If you are pregnant, but not obviously so, you may not want to mention this. It is technically against the law for pregnancy to be used as a reason to avoid hiring you.[245] However, a huge amount of anecdotal evidence, and even a few lawsuits, exist demonstrating that both being pregnant or recently giving birth taps into underlying assumptions (sadly, still prevalent in the 21st century paid work world) that you will not be as dedicated, focused, or productive as a male counterpart or a non-parent would be. Considering the length of time for expected employment in the academic world, even if you are unfocussed for the first few months after birth due to "baby brain," there is plenty of time to make up your productivity. Some schools even allow a stopping of the tenure clock for childbirth. Unfortunately, neither this, nor maternity leave, is remotely uniform in the United States. If you are applying for academic jobs in other parts of the developed world, you will have much better support for pregnancy and childbirth.

If your conscience or a late stage pregnancy dictates a different response and you want to disclose your pregnancy, that's fine.

Use the **Interview—On-campus Worksheet** to help you prepare.

As the Interview Is Ending

When the process or interview is finished, make sure you are clear about the next steps in the interview process. Here are a few clarification questions you might want to ask the search committee: Will they be interviewing more candidates? If so, when will the process finish at their end? When can you expect to hear about either another interview or a job offer? What are the steps you should take to stay in touch with them? Is the search committee chair OK with a follow-up telephone call if you want to clarify something or have some news to share?

Always be courteous. Use sound judgment to avoid pushing too hard for a firm answer, but still have a good sense for yourself of how long the post-interview process is going to be. Interviewers know you are anxious about the outcome and they are generally very happy to tell you an anticipated timeline. Frequently, they will even let you know that "a decision must be made by such-and-such a date, in order to be included in next year's budget." If you are nervous about following up, ask a trusted colleague for advice. You can also rehearse this portion when you practice the interview so it feels more natural to you to ask these questions.

After the Interview

Send a letter directed to the person heading the search committee, thanking that person and the committee for their time. Tell them truthfully how much you enjoyed meeting them and what you think you can contribute. Ask if they need any further information and say you will call them to find out if they need anything. This communication gives you a chance to be proactive by finding out where the search process stands instead of just waiting around for the next contact. Send a hard copy card that can be added to your file; these days, hard copies of anything are unusual enough to draw positive attention to you.

Part 5: Your Job Search Interviews

Interview—On-campus Worksheet

What will I wear (professional and idiosyncratic)?

    Traveling to and from interview?

    At the interview?

How will I know what to expect at interview (get agenda, schedules, etc.)?

What is my plan for redundancy with presentation materials, in case of a technology glitch?

What is my short research explanation for non-academic staff?

For academics outside my primary research area?

How will I project confidence and collegiality asking about others (Remember WIFT rule—"What's In It For Them")?

Whom do I want to talk to besides the interviewers?

What do I need to know about meal etiquette?

Are there other problems I need to address like allergies or the messiness of the food?

How will I stay refressed and take necessary breaks during the interview?

How will I let interviewers know me at a personal level (what am I willing to reveal)?

How will I handle illegal questions or microaggressions?

How will I keep track of the people I meet (notes on appearance, etc.)

How will I track the important dates (application materials, letters, etc.)

How will I obtain clarity about the next steps for me in this process?

What is my plan for reconnecting with people I met?

How will I decompress after the interview (trusted confidante)?

Part 5: Your Job Search Interviews

Interview Checklist Worksheet

Telephone

- ☐ Know when call will be made
- ☐ Know who will be on the call
- ☐ Have quiet secluded place
- ☐ Have secure telephone connection
- ☐ Disable call waiting
- ☐ Glass of water handy
- ☐ Application materials nearby
- ☐ Comfortable, professional clothing

Video (e.g, Skype, Zoom)—Special considerations

- ☐ Camera and microphone tested and functioning
- ☐ Decluttered area within camera view
- ☐ Comfortable, professional clothing, tested for on-camera appearance
- ☐ Backup plan for failed technology
- ☐ For mobile phone (i.e., Facetime), small tripod or other means to keep phone steady

In person

- ☐ Know who is paying for trip and handling the reservations
- ☐ Have an emergency contact number in case of any uncontrollable problem
- ☐ Know when and where interviews with the various participants will be held
- ☐ Know the anticipated length of each on-campus interview
- ☐ Do research on the interviewers (all of them) in advance
- ☐ Look at schedule and plan for breaks
- ☐ Prepare for what is expected of you: research talk, class demonstration, graduate student meeting
- ☐ Have a technology backup plan
- ☐ Dress for success while traveling and while on site
- ☐ Respect your body and mind by sleeping, drinking water, and staying calm

---

If you prefer to use email for the speed of delivery, be sure to attach the thank-you note as a PDF document. The ability to craft a letter, whether formal or informal, is less common among professionals than is frequently assumed. Use that to your advantage.

Whichever form of thank-you communication you choose, remember this is simply an acknowledgment of the time people spent with you. This is not the place to say, "I forgot to mention in my talk..." and then add three more paragraphs with new information. You also do not have to be entertaining or cute. It may actually count against you if you try it. How many email jokes have you seen fall flat due to lack of context?

If you decide to follow up with a telephone call whether you contact the search committee chair or the department administrator, be sure you ask only about a timeline for their decision, assuming you were not told in the interview. You are not going to get an answer to "So, what has been decided?" But asking whether a decision has been made may set your mind at rest that the process has not yet been concluded. You may even get another tidbit you really wanted, such as, "The committee has one more meeting scheduled for next Tuesday, and after that, we expect an offer to go out." True, you do not yet know if the offer will be made to you, but it may help you stop thinking about it…until after Tuesday has come and gone. Do not call or email the committee once a week. Manya Whitaker offered the following explanation: "Be patient and know that the search committee wants a decision just as quickly as you do. Frequent inquiries do nothing to speed the process, and may irritate the very people you are trying to impress with your collegiality."[246]

The next bit of advice may seem inane, but you'd be surprised at the number of people who haven't thought about it: If you leave a follow-up voicemail message, speak slowly and clearly with extra enunciation. State your name and phone number clearly at the beginning *and* end of the message. On your end, the voice mail message someone hears when leaving a message should be simple and clear: "This is ____. Please leave a message after the tone and I will call you back as soon as possible." Do not create a cute outgoing message, have someone other than yourself record it, or add extraneous information. People, including those on search committees, have limited time and patience, so don't test it with an unprofessional voicemail response. We know of a theological seminary candidate who was rejected for a job because the committee members were annoyed by waiting through a long religious quote before they could leave a message.

Sometimes, especially with deep preparation, an interview goes exceptionally well, but no job offer is forthcoming. To put this in perspective, it helps to know that other factors may be at play within the hiring institution. There are sometimes "fake searches" for available positions, designed to placate Human Resource departments trying to abide by federal hiring regulations. A job advertisement's seeming too specific or the time frame seeming exceptionally rushed may indicate that an inside candidate is favored for the position and, unless someone with a remarkable reputation and credentials unexpectedly applies, the inside candidate will prevail. Other factors could include prejudice against your graduating department, university, or advisor that is not specifically about you and will never come to light but nevertheless influences the outcome. If one member of the committee happens to have vociferous objections, it may be bothersome for committee members to overcome one minority voice, and they may go with a candidate whom all can more easily support. Other reasons could include budget cuts that eliminated the position after it was advertised or even after interviews had taken place. A hiring line may have been moved to a different department due to a reorganization or may be split between two departments for budgetary reasons, and the position must be advertised anew.

Daniel Perlmutter mentioned a "nuclear error" resulting in rejection when "[…the candidates] said or did something objectionable or even offensive that someone in the department took as evidence they were unqualified or unfit to be hired. The gaffe was objectively small but the consequences were fatal."[247] Some of his examples included telling a real estate agent that your spouse does not really want to move to the institution's locale because it's a backwater, accidentally offending someone with a joke during a job talk, dressing counter to prevailing norms in the organization, not dressing formally enough when interviewing, or showing a lack of understanding of the general surrounding culture such as whether faculty are expected to know fine food or spend time in outdoor recreation. The point is, even if you are spectacularly prepared, and in your opinion, you aced the interview, reasons completely unknown to you may determine why you were not hired.

Don't waste your time worrying about whether or not the position is still open or who has gotten an offer. Many sites purport to track this information, but honestly, until an offer has been made and accepted, this information is of no use to you. If you are a candidate still in the running, you will hear something official soon enough. Obsessively trying to find out is just going to make you anxious. To paraphrase Whitaker, the best strategy is to "submit and forget."[248]

In general, hiring committees will be kind and compassionate with you. Most of their members have been on the other side of the interview, some fairly recently, and know how hard it can be. Even if they ask tough questions, know they are trying to figure out who you are and what perspectives you can bring to their department or discipline.

When the Hiring Process Does Not Include a Final On-campus Interview

Sometimes interviews are conducted and hiring is finalized without your ever being invited to an on-campus interview due to cost constraints for travel. If you do not go to the campus, but are seriously interviewed for a position, you will want to know all you can about the department and its people, as well as information on the locale. Figure out how you are going to get the kind of information that would otherwise naturally flow from an on-campus visit. You need to understand what your life will be like if you accept the job offer. One useful source of information about the campus and department may be the head administrative assistant. They are often willing to chat with candidates about their town and nearby amenities. However, do not expect them to give you the inside scoop on the search process.

The local Chamber of Commerce is also a good source of information about the community (schools, hospital, recreational opportunities, etc.). Sometimes understanding how the institution fits together with other employers in the area is useful. For instance, the university or college may be a huge piece of the local economy or just one section. Web searches can yield a tremendous amount of information about both the community and the institution. Google Earth can even give you a sense of the actual campus and its surroundings, from both aerial and street views.

A realtor is another good source of information about the area, including housing prices and schools, especially if you have children. Realtors are hoping to persuade you to become a client, so be cautious regarding their enthusiasm. Also, be aware that there are many things a realtor will not comment on because it could potentially violate the Fair Housing Act, such as rates of crime or the demographics of a particular neighborhood. You may have to go back to the web or find someone already living in the area to get particular information. One client we worked with wanted to know if there was an active Jewish community before accepting a position; he was able to contact the local synagogue for that information. Another client wanted to know if there were any colleagues with children enrolled in a Waldorf School for the purposes of carpooling, since she was a new professor and the family only had one car; the school could not provide that information directly, but they were willing to pass along the information to the appropriate parties to allow them to call her back, if they wished.

If You Receive a Job Offer

If you receive a job offer, consider it carefully. Even if you have decided to accept the employment offer, the process is not finished. You will most likely have to embark on negotiations concerning your salary, your equipment, space (office, lab, or studio), whether or not your moving costs will be covered, and what money you can anticipate receiving from the department for items such as travel expenses for conferences or other professional development. Most institutions of higher education can give you up to two weeks to negotiate and make a decision.

Be aware of the salary issues. In the United States as reported in a 2015-2016 *Higher Ed Jobs* survey [249] for all types of institutions whether research, doctoral, masters, or baccalaureate sector, the average in all disciplines combined for new assistant professors was $65,372. While this may sound like a lot of money to someone living on $20,000 a year as a graduate assistant, it is barely over the poverty line in many metropolitan areas of the country, especially after deducting taxes, health care, living expenses, daycare, and commuting costs. For instance, if you happened to land a tenure-track job at a small college in New York City, you would need $130,000 to cover basic expenses like housing, food, and transportation. And that's not taking into account the wear and tear on your psyche if you end up with teaching load as high as 5-4.

As you enter these negotiations, you need to be absolutely clear on your bottom line: what is the absolute least you can accept and still actually survive the move and transition? How willing are you to live with the absolute least? You should check to see *when* that first paycheck will be arriving as well, since you may not get anything for a full month and a half after you start, depending on how salary payments are made by the institution. Frequently, payment is made at the end of the period for which service is rendered.

Take time to look at the financial implications of accepting any position. If you haven't already thought this through, the AAUW (American Association of University Women) offers some advice to determine what base salary is the minimum you should accept, based on knowledge of peers and cost-of-living in the area you plan to locate. This information applies to men as well as women.

Here is the basic AAUW formula for calculating a livable income:
Base salary – taxes and other expenses = take home pay – budgeted items + benefits.

Plug in all the numbers in the formula, and see if the offer makes financial sense. Many new faculty members have been hurt by the apparent luster of a salary higher than they have ever made before, only to be blindsided when faced with the realities of living costs in the locale of the new position. Be clear about what business people call the BATNA (Best Alternative to a Negotiated Agreement) for determining the lowest salary at which you can afford to accept the offer. The school is trying to hire you for the least amount of money possible and you are trying to get hired at the highest level of pay possible. The difference between these two is sometimes referred to as *the bargaining zone*, where some flexibility in the offer is possible.

Determining the appropriate salary requires that you have a strong grasp of your current budget. The simple 50/20/30 proportion is 50% to essential expenses (including housing, food, transportation, and utilities), 20% toward other financial goals (savings, retirement plans, student debt reduction, or children's college fund), 30% flexible spending (hobbies, travel, and entertainment). Many, many students forgo the second item while in graduate school but now is the time to begin such savings. And depending on where you will be living, housing costs may far overshadow all other expenses. You need to be realistically aware of what resources you will need to live in a particular area. If you need help on preparing a budget, many instruments such as Mint.com [250] or LearnVest.com [251] are available on the web. Steps up for more complicated accounting, should you need it, are AceMoney Lite [252] or GnuCash. [253] Your bank may even have an electronic budgeting system you can use. Though we have mentioned it earlier, a very handy cost-of-living calculator at PayScale [254] can help you with comparisons.

Find out about and consider other monetary benefits, like health insurance, disability or long-term illness insurance, retirement, and faculty development money, which may come with the job. What are the health insurance choices? How much of the cost of health insurance will you be expected to contribute? If you have a family, what will you have to pay to have your family members included on your health insurance? If you have a domestic partner, but are not married, will your health insurance cover that person? What is the sick leave policy and how does the institution handle long-term illness or disability? What retirement plan, if any, comes with the job? Is there money for a new faculty member to set up or equip a lab, studio, or any other physical space you need? What kind of annual faculty development money is available for conferences or other ways you may want to keep current in your field? All of these non-monetary benefits will impact the value of the offer in real terms.

If your partner is an academic and would like to negotiate a job, bring that up early in the negotiation process. If this is the case, your partner has to be as prepared as you are for an interview: up to date CV, research, teaching statements, etc. Even if you cannot negotiate another tenure-track offer, the hiring institution may be able to offer an administrative position of some sort such as accountant, office manager, event planner, or development officer, to name a few.

If your partner is not an academic, ask if the hiring institution has any resources available to help with finding employment in the geographic area. Depending on what your partner does, and the location of your new institution, arranging some introductions to local employers may be fairly easy. Having an entrée is always better than going in cold.

You may be at the institution for years to come, and you are in your strongest negotiating position when the institution is invested in bringing you on. Given the likelihood of salary compression issues that frequently go unaddressed at universities, you may be fighting in a few years to "level the playing field" for your salary in comparison to younger, newer colleagues hired with a larger salary because of changing cost-of-living situations in your area of the world. Get the best possible offer now without appearing greedy.

Negotiating

Keep in mind that faculty salaries and other compensation fall on the business side of the university equation. Operating on a business model, the institution offering you a job will pay you as little as they can. Negotiation is mainly about salary, but you may need to take into account other things as well. You must get the university's offer in writing as part of your contract negotiations. Again, be very clear about when you will actually receive that first paycheck. If you end your previous employment in June, move in July, and start in August, especially if your institution pays at the end of the first month, and not at the beginning, you may not actually get a paycheck until September 30th. You may need to arrange for an advance on that first paycheck, rather than be caught short. More details for negotiating are offered below.

Start strong. We have coached faculty members, candidates for administrative offices, and directors of centers on how to start strong, given the specific situation. In every case where the job was not accepted on the spot, a counter-offer on the part of the candidate resulted in a higher base salary than originally offered. The salary you accept may not come up to the ideal level you hoped for, but it's important to start at the highest level you can. Given issues of salary compression over time (nearly every increase in salary will be a percentage of the original offer), negotiating for a decent salary is especially important.

State universities typically only offer 3% increases a year, and we know plenty of them that offer only 1% or nothing, especially in states where the legislature determines faculty salaries as part of the overall budgetary process. Do not sell yourself short or underestimate what you are worth. Do not start too low. An offer has been made, so you can assume the institution is excited to hire you. Be willing, but careful about reading the tenor of the discussions, to ask for $10,000 more than offered. Depending on the situation, requesting $10,000 more can make you appear greedy. Generally, all the latitude available when salaries are offered in a range is $2,000-$5,000.

Investigate. What have other people done to negotiate when offered this type of position? Do you know anyone at the institution who was recently hired who might be willing to talk to you about the process there? What are the typical salaries at this institution? Public university salaries are easy to find with a little digging; AAUP surveys of faculty income can be another source for this information. Find positions that align with your position level and type of hiring institution to get an idea of what might come up for you. You also need to know what the likely resources of the institution are.

There are many articles in *Inside Higher Ed* and *The Chronicle of Higher Education* on negotiating salary in academic jobs. Your professional organization may have some tips for your specialty area. You may have cohorts that recently went through this same negotiation process; ask if they are willing to share their list of negotiated items. Once you know some of the basics about what others have received in a position like yours, you are more likely to ask for what is reasonable. The key to successful negotiation is to neither undersell yourself nor ask for exorbitant amounts of money.

Below are some items specifics to academia that you need to consider when negotiating:

- *What is the anticipated teaching load, class size, and amount of new preps?* In general, a 4-4 teaching load (5-5 for community colleges) is the expectation for a full-time employee who only teaches and for whom no research or service expectations exist.[255] Even in jobs with some research and service expectations, a 3-3 teaching load with 30

Part 5: Your Job Search Interviews

Considering a Job Offer Worksheet

Take the time to look at the position in depth. Ask yourself:

What is the absolute least amount I can accept and still actually survive the move and transition?

How willing am I to live with the absolute minimum?

When will the first paycheck arrive?

Will I be doing something new? Or things I already do? What do I anticipate the preparation time for the job duties to be?

What are the resources I will have?

Who will my colleagues be, and will there be an opportunity to collaborate if desired?

Will this job put me on the path toward a leadership role? Is that important to me?

What are the commute times and will that have an impact on my work?

What benefits like health insurance and faculty development money does this job offer include?

What are the benefits and drawbacks for me? [Location, cost of living, community, research facilities, etc.]

If applicable, what are the opportunities for my partner?

students per class is vastly different from a teaching load with larger classes (60 students or even larger lecture sections). If you are in the sciences, how much credit will you get for teaching labs or organizing several lab sections for a large lecture class? Similar concerns apply for large classes with additional studio sections in the arts. Finally, find out how many preps (and associated grading) you will be doing per term. Three sections of the same class can take quite a bit less prep time than prep for 3 completely different classes. Will you be preparing all the class material yourself or does the institution have existing syllabi you will be expected to follow? Will you get to choose your own textbooks? What is the institution's policy on the number of papers a student must write to pass the course?

- *What are the tenure expectations?* You need to have information about tenure expectations in writing at the outset. Perhaps the college or university has a faculty handbook spelling them out. If not, or if you want to amend the expectations to meet your needs as well as those of the university, get the agreement to the amendments in writing. Issues to consider include when tenure will be decided and what intermediate evaluations you will have before the tenure decision, publication expectations for the award of tenure (how many research papers in what tiers of journals, how books will count). What are the expectations with regard to quantitative versus qualitative research? Some institutions do not view qualitative research as being as valid as quantitative research (see note about gender bias that follows). How much credit will you get for papers or a book based on your doctoral research versus research you have done since starting the job? How much credit will you get for co-authored papers?

- *For cluster hires, or for cross-listed positions, who will be evaluating you for tenure?* Often cluster hires are housed with their interdepartmental cluster but individual positions are attached to a specific academic department housed elsewhere, for the purposes of tenure. How will the college or university take this into consideration at tenure time?

Special note to women: Women in all cultures typically find negotiating more difficult than men to do, often resulting in their asking for a lesser starting salary than men. If you are a female person of color, you may have additional cultural overlays to overcome, such as standing up to male authority or not wanting a superior to be put into a position of saying "no" to a request. Some men find negotiating exhilarating and get hormonally revved up to engage in conflict. Women are generally expected and trained to avoid conflict, and may find the prospect of negotiation so stressful that they choose not to engage in the process. Don't give up!

Starting at a lower salary means you have more to make up late. Get practice asking for what you want; it will make a huge difference in what you earn over the years, since almost every increase in salary will be a percentage of your current salary. If a woman's starting salary is $60,000 and her male counterpart starts at $70,000, even with a measly 1% increase in salary per year, over 30 years the man will earn $3,479 more per year; at 3% per year, the difference will be $14,269 more.[256] Even in the short run, after 5 years, the person who started at $60,000 with 1% per year increase will be making $63,060 per year while the person who started at $70,000 will be making $73,570 per year. The actual difference in compensation may not seem like a lot, but it can make a difference in attitude to know you are being compensated equally.

Another aspect of academic job negotiation that hinders higher starting salaries for women is that qualitative research by a woman is not valued as much as that same research done by a man. The unconscious anti-female bias (sometimes referred to "implicit bias") is particularly strong in the sciences, even when the research is more quantitative. Given all the research on gender bias, it should no longer be an issue, but it is. We personally know of one case where a man and a woman did essentially the same type of research, but during the tenure process, her articles were submitted to additional outside reviewers while the man's were not. She found out only because a person on the tenure committee told her. The tenure committee member had even protested that the process was discriminatory, so the gender bias was not even unconscious in this case. During the hiring process, be sure that you get in writing the institution's or department's expectations for you in attaining tenure.

There are some special accommodations you may want to ask about, such as on-campus daycare (which is not to say a male candidate should not be asking about this!) or whether the tenure clock can be stopped due to pregnancy. Many male and female early career academics are also starting families given their age, but clearly, the actual pregnancy happens to the woman. When women were expected to stay home and be a helpmate to a spouse, accommodation for pregnancy was not such a big issue in the academic arena. Unfortunately, academia changes more slowly than the rest of the world, and is often still structured as though the faculty member has a wife at home handling the children and all other aspects of life outside of work. Some academic institutions are still learning how to handle the biological demands of pregnancy for female employees. Know in advance what to expect if you are pregnant or if you plan to get pregnant.

Be cautious about being hired as "an experiment." If anything is unusual about your position (expected fundraising responsibilities, mentoring a set number of students in addition to class time, outreach to community), know what has happened to other people in that situation, even at other institutions. Get your job description in writing, including some information about how these unusual duties will be considered when you come up for tenure. Experiments tend to fail, and it should not be all on you if it does.

Rehearse. Just as is true for interviewing, preparation and practice can help make you a better negotiator. Rehearsing possible directions for the conversation can be a great help. Get someone you trust to take on the role of the hiring official. Start by acknowledging your gratitude and desire to work there. You may want to add something related to shared educational goals before getting into the nitty-gritty. Be clear on your priorities before you begin the process. You may even want to create an itemized list for yourself to keep front and center during negotiations.

Expect iterations. The process will likely go through three rounds or more: their offer, your counter offer, their counter offer, your counter to their counter. You will arrive at something mutually agreeable at some point. Just be sure you are being realistic about what is available and negotiable. Be realistic. Have good concrete reasons to explain why you are seeking additional money, not just "because I'm worth it." Reasons might include cost-of-living in the area, pay at comparable institutions, etc.

Record. Make sure you keep track of what is happening and know when you need to follow up. Refer to the information about job search logs and the sample job search log in **Part 3** to help

Negotiating Your Job Offer Worksheet

Below are some negotiation enquiries, depending on your issues.

According to my research, a fair salary range for people in this position, taking into account the cost-of-living here is $_____. Can we come to an agreement that reflects this?

Comparable public salaries indicate _____ for starting assistant professors here.

You advertised for someone with _____ years of experience and _____ qualifications. In my time at _____, in addition to finishing my degree, I was responsible for _____ [teaching classes, running labs, writing program curriculum, organizing colloquia, conferences]. I also earned these professional credentials [license to practice, teaching certificate, honor society officer]. Based on my background, and the extent of my anticipated responsibilities, I would like to see a base salary closer to _____.

What is your flexibility in the salary offered? Or: Could you share with me what the range in the budget for this position is?

Is this a nine or twelve-month offer?

If nine, is a summer stipend offered?

If nine, what benefits continue through the summer [health insurance, office, access to library].

What is the anticipated teaching load for my first year? Going forward?

Are there any research, travel, professional development, office, lab or studio equipment funds as part of this offer?

Are there any restrictions on outside [consulting, expert witness] income.

What are the benefits associated with this position [health care; time off; faculty housing; office, lab, or studio space; sabbatical clock; cross-listings with other departments].

Are there any opportunities for my partner here?

What is the allowance for moving expenses?

How is the salary payment structured [monthly, twice a month]?

When will I get my first salary payment?

Is it possible to get an advance if necessary?

Part 5: Your Job Search Interviews

Negotiation Checklist Worksheet

- ☐ Salary: Base [determine if 9-month or 12-month period] + benefits [health, retirement]
- ☐ Summer salary if applicable [1, 2, or 3 months]
- ☐ Any restrictions on outside income
- ☐ Moving expenses
- ☐ Orientation dates [may be earlier than official start date]
- ☐ Start date
- ☐ First paycheck date
- ☐ Email activation date
- ☐ Title [especially if you are cross-listed between department and/or academic centers]
- ☐ Housing
- ☐ Resources/employment for spouse
- ☐ Equipment and start-up funds [bookcases, computer, desk, telephone, laboratory materials or field equipment, renovations; indicate if these items are to be used solely by you or shared with others]
- ☐ Office space [your own or shared]
- ☐ Parking
- ☐ Course load and service assignments [check for pre-tenure release and family leave]
- ☐ Tenure clock/time to sabbaticals
- ☐ Assistants [graduate, research, technician]
- ☐ Funding for assistants
- ☐ Grant writing assistance [big universities often have offices for this]
- ☐ Research monies
- ☐ Professional development funds
- ☐ Travel monies
- ☐ Written, signed [by you and all necessary parties] dated agreement; email does *not* count as final contract, though it may be fine for negotiating purposes

you track dates for conversations. We highly recommend creating a paper trail, since negotiations are sometimes conducted over the phone, and what you thought was being offered was not actually on the table. If the interviewer does not send you an email detailing the offer, then send a "memorializing memo" via email outlining your understanding of each item mentioned. These details should be reflected in the final offer letter before you sign it as well.

To sum up, be serious and gracious as you consider each offer. Your offer can disappear if you seem disinterested or arrogant. Negotiate thoughtfully for what you want and need in order to accept the position. Don't ask for the moon because you won't get it. You might, however, get a satellite station.

Sign (and make sure they do, too). Make sure you get the final offer in writing, once you think all the items have been agreed to. It's difficult to negotiate after you have already moved and taken a job. We know of people who were offered an academic tenure-track job at a particular salary, with the promise that the contract would follow. One new hire did not get the contract until she had moved across the country and the contract was written for several thousand dollars less than the amount offered and accepted over the phone. She wasn't going to quit or move back, but it stung. Both sides benefit when the terms are spelled out clearly from the beginning of employment. It's amazing what you will forget after three years on the job, or the person who hired you and with whom you did all the negotiation regarding your position has moved on.

Celebrate. When you have completely finished the job search process and accepted a position, you may want to gather up all the rejection letters and ritually burn them as a form of self-care. I know one assistant professor who decorated his bathroom with rejection letters for jobs and continued doing this for publication rejection letters. It never failed to cheer up graduate students visiting his lavatory.

Complications

Although it may seem unlikely now, another reason to take your time with the decision is occasionally a person receives more than one job offer. For example, an assistant professor candidate we know received a job offer that involved only online distance teaching. About a week later, after he had already accepted the first offer, he was offered a tenure-track job on a physical campus. If you were he, what would you do? How would you do it?

Most likely, you would simply inform the first institution a better offer had come through and you were regretfully turning down their very much appreciated offer of employment. Do this only after you have a signed a written contract with the second institution. An email offer does not count; while it may provide a paper trail, email offers are not necessarily binding. A contract signed by the Dean, Provost, President, or even institution's legal office is what you need before moving forward.

Recent PhD graduates new to the world of negotiating employment sometimes think they have to stick with the agreement and accept the first offer, sort of like your mother once told you once you accept a prom date, you were not allowed to accept a better offer later because it was bad manners.

Mom's rule does not hold true for job offers. Universities are littered with job offers that failed to go forward for a whole variety of reasons, which is one reason why adjuncts are so frequently called in at the very last minute to teach the following semester. Don't feel bad. Do what is right for you. Just do it politely.

PART 6: ADDITIONAL CONSIDERATIONS

Next we look at some of the available information affecting new PhDs seeking work in higher education, including the very limited data tracking career outcomes for those recently completing their doctorates, the number of candidates competing for any given job, the probabilities of being offered a tenure-track job, the role of contract workers and adjuncts, and the sense that tenure and higher education as we have known them are in decline. It is, unfortunately, not a pretty picture. We also suggest alternatives to seeking a tenure-track job and offer a worksheet to help you assess your transferable skills.

Failure to Track PhDs' Career Outcomes [257]

"The future of the American economy—and the jobs that will drive it—is inextricably tied to higher education," declared Scott Carlson in *The future of work: How colleges can prepare students for the jobs ahead*, a 2017 report by the *Chronicle of Higher Education*.[258] The report predicted a labor market needing people with at least 6,190,000 graduate and 13,510,000 undergraduate degrees by 2024.[259] Unfortunately, the report did not tackle the issue of how many advanced degree holders will be needed in higher education to train that workforce or where they will get their degrees.

A real question exists of whether too many PhDs are being produced for the number of available jobs. At present, universities find themselves strapped for cash, fighting for students, and under fire for not producing practical outcomes leading to job placement for new PhDs. Schillebeeckx, Marique, and Lewis[260] have documented this problem and suggested a solution, at least for graduate scholars in biotechnology. They feel that collaboration of graduate students and postdocs with biotech companies will lead to a more complete education and to job opportunities after the researcher leaves the university. Fernanda Zamudio-Suaréz wrote an excellent essay on why one academic gave up the job search and went to work at BuzzFeed, noting that getting a professorship is a serious longshot,[261] while Lenny Teyrelman's piece provides statistics to bolster the argument that too many PhDs are being produced.[262] *Inside Higher Ed* has also reported on the decline in job postings in the humanities for English, language other than English, history, philosophy, religion and classical studies from 2000-2016[263] based on the Humanities Indicator Project.[264]

The best source of information in the US for the actual numbers of PhDs produced remains the National Center for Education Statistics (NCES) at the Department of Education. Data broken down by whether the recipient is male or female through the academic year 2014-15 (the most recent year for which data are available) show a total of 178,547 PhD degrees awarded, with 84,921 conferred to men, and 93,626 conferred to women in that time frame.[265] The number of doctorates awarded in all major fields of study is also tracked by the National Science Foundation. The numbers of doctorates-granted increased roughly 2% per year between 2011 (48,911 PhDs awarded) and 2015 (54,909 PhDs awarded) only dropping for the first time in 2016 (54,904 PhDs awarded) by 432 doctoral granting institutions.[266] Regrettably, no national database in the United States exists that shows the number of PhDs by year and where those people end up employed.

Part 6: Additional Considerations

While discussions about possible ways to limit the number of doctorates produced are ongoing, such a change is unlikely any time soon. The underlying philosophy of education in the United States is that you should not winnow people out of the system too soon because you don't know who is most likely to go on to a highly productive academic career, a model distinctly at odds with that of the rest of the world, where students are winnowed out from higher education at very early ages. The US model is *let them come, let them try, and let them fail* as the way to sort out students.

Precious little data exist on what happens to PhDs once they graduate. Efforts to track the employment of new graduates have been sporadic and incomplete. A 2014 report by the Council of Graduate Schools (CGS) indicated a real need to get more (and more accurate) information, as opposed to anecdotal accounts, about what happens to PhDs after graduation.[267] The report called for an initiative to standardize the statistics gathered about PhD career pathways after noting that the vast majority (53%) of the information collected had been done informally. The usefulness of most material is limited, given the variability in PhD programs, the way data are collected, the difficulty of collecting the information, and the cost associated with tracking graduates of a PhD program.[268] Following its own advice, in 2016 the CGS launched a new initiative to figure out where PhDs in the humanities actually end up working, the first attempt to do so in 20 years.[269] Their plan was to work with 15 partner universities to compile data. According to Suzanne Ortega, Council president, the ultimate purpose is to "enable current and prospective students to make more informed decisions when selecting degree programs and planning their careers."[270] In 2017, the American Historical Association's Career Diversity initiative released a field-specific interactive database on where historians work.[271]

Below, we provide some of the findings released in the last five years by various institutions including Stanford University, the Council of Graduate Schools, the American Institutes for Research, the American Historical Association and others, that have made the effort to track PhD post-graduate careers.

The Stanford [University] PhD Alumni Employment Project, which launched in 2013, tracked PhDs granted by the school in any field. The project located 2,420 PhD graduates of 10,000 PhDs granted by Stanford since 2003, slightly over 24% of these graduates. The interactive website created by the Stanford Office of Institutional Research and Decision Support allows you to see the collected data in 20 different ways, including by the economic sector currently employing Stanford graduates, and whether those in academia are in faculty jobs or not.[272] Participating alumni were either 5 or 10 years post-PhD, so the trajectories were long-term. The responding Stanford graduates, in order of most to least number of graduates, were from the following disciplines: engineering, biosciences, natural sciences, humanities, social sciences, education, earth sciences, business, and law. The results Stanford obtained from scouring available online information (such as LinkedIn) about its own graduates indicated:

> 44% of PhD alumni combining cohorts were *initially employed* in the academic sector (including faculty, postdocs, & academic staff) and 31% in the business, government, and non-profit sectors. For 25% of graduates, no employment information was publicly available online.[273]

Stanford also conducted a separate study of STEM PhDs graduating between 2002 and 2004, or graduating between 2007 and 2009, and found that only 50% stayed in academia (many stayed on at Stanford where they had graduate training) while 18% were employed by industry, 4% in government, and 9% in nonprofit organizations. The remaining 23% did not make their information public.[274]

Maren Wood worked with the American Historical Association (AHA) to track 2,500 PhDs in the US and Canada who graduated with history degrees over a 12-year period from 1998-2009, then published her results in 2013.[275] She cited a combination of lack of resources, survey fatigue, and the laborious nature of assembling the data as obstacles for obtaining good information around PhD employment:

> Unless administrators across the university believe that there are many viable and valuable career outcomes for Ph.D.'s [sic] beyond the professoriate, and unless that message is clearly communicated to academic departments, faculty members won't want to participate in these placement studies or make their data public.[276]

Wood's own feeling was that the information gathered was bound to show many fewer PhD graduates in tenure-track positions than their degree-granting institutions might like to admit.

In 2014, the American Institutes for Research (AIR) reported that, as of 2010, 61% of science, technology, engineering, and math (STEM) PhDs were working in nonacademic careers, mainly in private companies. Roughly 50% of those were in development or applied research. Approximately 13% of STEM PhDs had left these disciplines altogether. Black, Hispanic and white female STEM PhDs were more likely than others to work outside the STEM field or in government, while Asian females and males of all ethnic groups were more likely to work in private, for-profit organizations using their STEM training.[277]

The Humanities Indicator Project at the American Academy of Arts and Sciences (AAAS) released data in October 2017 clearly indicating that many new PhDs struggle to find tenure-track positions, and often only find employment in non-tenure-track positions, such as adjuncting.[278] According to the National Science Foundation, PhD graduates in the life sciences with tenure or tenure-track positions numbered 10.6% in 2013.[279] Where the other 89.4% of the natural sciences graduates were employed is unclear. One blogger, Sven Hendrix, posted his own findings for PhDs in science: "…you have a 30% chance to become a postdoc and a 3% chance to become a professor. In other words: there is a 97% chance that you are going to work in a non-academic environment."[280]

Life cycle events may play a part in finding an academic job. In a piece of good news, three scholars (Main, Prevnovitz, & Ehrenberg, 2017) released a working paper through the ILR [formerly the Industrial and Labor Relations] School of Cornell University using a life course perspective to look at the career paths of more than 5,000 humanities and social science doctoral graduates.[281] The authors looked at the role life cycles played in academic employment to discern long-term career patterns; surprisingly, PhDs that went to work in academia actually had "multiple pathways to the professoriate." By tracking all positions held 6 months, 36 months, and 96 months after earning a PhD, the authors reported that more "permeability," or movement, between academic and non-academic jobs existed than has often been assumed. It is often claimed having children causes problems with pursuing an academic career, but this did not ultimately hold women back from long-term academic success.[282] The authors also noted, "While the majority of PhDs intended academic careers, PhDs in the non-profit (non-academic) sector report a higher rate of job satisfaction compared to PhDs in tenure-track faculty positions."[283]

Individual departments rarely track the careers of their own graduates in or out of academia. As one commentator on departmental tracking humorously put it:

> Most programs opt for showcase alumni profiles rather than providing full data on the graduates. Of course, the selections for the profiles to be put on the departmental webpage tend to be biased towards Associate Professor of Widget Studies at Prestigious Widgets University; and rarely includes Project Manager at Company Having Nothing Whatever to Do with Widgets. (J. Khanova Personal email communication, March 14, 2018).

Interdisciplinary degrees, such as women's and gender studies or ethnic studies, are often not included in departmentally-based tenure-track lines, making hires in those areas harder to track and quantify than traditional lines. Working against the hiring of new faculty in these fields is an often-unacknowledged issue that these areas of study are again being marginalized.[284] Those fields are easy targets for ridicule and legislative funding cuts in public education institutions.

Very little data are available about the number of graduates who have left the academic milieu altogether or about what work they actually do after leaving. Since leaving academia is often stigmatized by those remaining in academia,[285] not surprisingly the numbers of those who leave it behind are rarely measured. Most of the available information is anecdotal, supplied by individuals telling their own stories to a variety of audiences via web blogs, at "alt-ac" panels at conferences, on Twitter at hashtags like #alt-academy, or even at conferences entirely dedicated to life outside the academy, like the annual "Beyond the Professoriate: Online Career Conference for PhDs." Contributing to the difficulty in tracking graduates, PhDs leaving the academic track may find themselves moving from one position to another as they try to land a permanent position in another economic sector. No reliable mechanism exists for tracking the PhDs who opt out by choice or necessity.

Getting current professors and departments to acknowledge the realities of the academic job market and the slim number of available full-time positions is difficult. No real incentives exist for departments to pursue data on all their graduates or to acknowledge all their PhD graduates who did *not* land an academic job. From the institution's point of view, producing a PhD takes precedence over tracking where a PhD goes after graduation.

Number of Academic Job Applicants

We are frequently asked, "How many people do you think are applying for this job?" Unfortunately, the answer is "an awful lot." You may have to send out many, many applications just to get an initial interview. Between 2010 and 2016 the number of applications averaged 100 per position in the social sciences at Boston University (personal communication, J. White, December 2, 2016). In 2017, a position advertised for a Visiting Professor at the College of Charleston elicited 100 qualified applicants (personal communication, A. Sterrett-Krause, February 8, 2018). Across the country in 2017, 400 people applied for an open sociology tenure-track job at a community college in the Seattle area (personal communication, J.S. Capps, April 19, 2018). Potential candidates may have to resign themselves to applying for anywhere between

35 and 50 positions to get one interview given the number of PhDs in any particular field often outpacing the number of jobs available. In 2017, Karen Kelsky wrote, "Escalating numbers of applications (anywhere from 200 to 1,000 for an opening) fall into the hands of an ever-shrinking tenure-line professoriate..."[286] Whether tenure-track or adjunct, academic job seekers are finding more competition than ever for fewer higher education positions.

Some of the more successful job search candidates publish their experiences: One example of this comes from Jeremy Yoder, a post-doctorate in biology. He spent two years applying for tenure-track positions in the US and Canada, and reported "...112 applications resulted in 17 interviews by phone or video conference, 11 campus visits and, ultimately, three job offers."[287] As a result of this experience, he concluded that it was impossible to really know what a hiring committee seeks, and "Probability works."[288] His advice was to apply for as many jobs as you can. Yoder wrote a follow up after conducting a non-scientific Twitter Hashtag survey with roughly 100 participants and found:

- Eight people (including Yoder) reported submitting 100 or more applications.
- Ten participants said they had landed a job with a single application.
- The median respondent reported sending in 19 applications.[289]

It's possible that unsuccessful applicants did not participate in Yoder's straw poll, and that they submitted even more applications without the same results.

Another example is the job search experience of Brian Goedde, MFA, after "adjuncting for years." Take what he says with a grain of salt, as he was specifically looking for community college positions without a doctoral degree:

> When I was looking for a job I found it comforting to learn other job-seekers' stats, so here are mine: In my first year on the market, I sent out 16 applications, got one interview, and one temporary full-time job. In my second year, I sent out 20 applications, and my search ended with two offers. After accepting my current position, I turned down four other interview requests.[290]

The general sentiments of most candidates can be summed up with this quote from the anonymous Lego Graduate Student. He graduated in the social sciences at a large university on the West Coast, then spent two years looking for academic work. After going on the job market twice and finally getting hired as an Assistant Professor, he said, "I've also come to realize that the process is so arduous and uncertain that my words of support can only do so much to help endure the market season. It's the toughest experience I've had in recent memory."[291]

If you are willing to forego the traditional path of tenured professor, other opportunities with fewer applicants may be available.[292] The instructional designer who develops course materials for others to teach within traditional university settings may offer new employment opportunities for newly graduated PhDs, especially those with knowledge of "learning management systems" or experience converting a face-to-face classroom proficiency into either an online or hybrid course. Private for-profit entities like Phoenix or Strayer universities now offer both "online" and "on ground" teaching positions. In addition, several freshly minted PhDs we worked with in the recent past landed jobs in "digital libraries" in areas ranging from classical literature to civil rights archives.

Other areas where you might be able to send fewer applications because professors are still needed are:
- Architecture, with emphasis on design and design implementation;
- Computer and information science, both programming and understanding data;
- Economics, given the constant fluctuations in policy;
- Engineering, especially biomedical;
- Finance, including accounting, business administration, and economics;
- Medical professions, including nursing, geriatric care, hospital administration; and
- Psychology, all areas (because, so far, people are better than bots for interaction).[293]

Lamentably, this is not a great list for arts, basic science, humanities, and social science graduates, reflecting as it does the concerns of dealing with information technology and an aging population. Expect to send large numbers of applications for employment in traditional areas of study.

What Are the Chances of Being Offered a Tenure-track Job?

Fewer and fewer schools of any size are offering tenure-track jobs. If you are currently on the job market, you may have heard some the statistics like these:

> No more than one-third of all college and university faculty members are tenured. The reason? More and more colleges are relying on part-time or temporary nontenure-track faculty to teach undergraduates—part-timers constituted about 38 percent of the professoriate in 1987 and grew to 43 percent in 1992.[294]

By 2011, the number of non-tenured teaching instructors had grown to roughly 70%, or three adjuncts for every four full-timers.[295] In the fall of 2015, only a third of faculty members at all colleges were tenured or on the tenure track.[296] In an effort to establish some statistical information on the number of tenure-track jobs offered in 2016-17 in the US and Canada, Maren Woods began a crowd-sourced survey in 2018 to "figure out who was hired." The results are not yet available.[297] Regardless, fewer and fewer job applicants are getting tenure-track jobs.

A 2014 report by the National Science Foundation said "first-generation"[298] doctoral students were about evenly split between careers in the education sector (including all positions in higher education, primary and secondary schools, and school systems) and careers in industry.[299] No data were provided on which were recipients of tenure-track positions. However, this NSF study also confirmed Wood's surprising research result that new tenure-track hires in the humanities and social sciences actually go to those who have had their degree in hand for two years or less.[300] According to Wood, the largest cohort hired were ABDs, graduate students in their final year. Data from CUPA-HR finds that in the 2016-17 academic year, new tenure-track hires in nursing, psychology, English, math, and music were mostly given to new PhDs, possibly because starting salaries are lower for these hires.[301]

In a now-classic study done nearly two decades ago, data suggested that over 50% of those actually finishing a PhD would not get a job in academia and that only 25% who were offered an academic job would be on a tenure track in any field. The percentage remains fairly consistent for reporting fields: Recent statistics from the American Political Science Association (APSA) shows roughly 25% of new doctorates getting tenure-track positions in 2016-17.[302] However, 75% of recent PhDs in humanities are not on the tenure track because they tend to end up in jobs outside the academy. This is problematic since "the primary motivation for seeking a Ph.D. in the humanities continues to be an academic career."[303]

The availability of tenure-track jobs continues to dwindle in the sciences. One report on biological sciences suggested the placement after receiving a doctorate in tenure-track jobs was 16.5%.[304] Other STEM PhDs may have as little as a 15% chance of getting a tenure-track job.[305] In biological sciences, where 55% of PhDs obtained tenure-track jobs in 1973, that number had fallen to 15% in 2013.[306] Since 1982, roughly 800,000 doctorates have been awarded in STEM fields, but only about 100,000 academic faculty jobs were available during that same time period.[307] Meanwhile, according to Maximiliaan Schillebeeckx et al., only 3,000 or so positions are created each year for faculty in scientific fields.[308]

Bruce Alberts, a professor of biochemistry at the University of California, San Francisco (UCSF), and co-founder of the nonprofit organization Rescuing Biomedical Research (RBR) said, "The real world for [biomedical PhD students] is that maybe a fifth [20%] will ever get [tenured] academic jobs." And it's not just academia that's overpopulated. He added: "There aren't even enough jobs currently in the private sector to make it possible for all of them to get research jobs."[309] As reported by Scott Jaschik and Doug Lederman in their webinar on *Evolving Faculty Careers* held April 12, 2018, statistics from *Word, Journal of International Linguistics*, tracked advertised jobs in the field from 1,515 in 1975-76, with the highest spike in 1997-98 with 2,075 advertised, and 2016-17 showing the lowest number ever at 851 total advertised positions.[310]

In short, the chances of getting tenure are continuing to decrease. In his posting on June 29, 2016, Jacques Berlinerblau, Director of the Center for Jewish Civilization at Georgetown University, wrote that on average getting a doctorate in the humanities takes 10 years. His prediction:

> The likeliest future for tenure in the liberal arts is that everything will stay the same — and somehow gradually get worse. In 25 years, 10 percent or so of our Ph.D.s in the liberal arts will ride the tenure line. Thirty percent will hold full-time non-tenure-track positions — a category that has experienced a conspicuous growth spurt in recent years. The remainder will be adjuncts, exploited and expendable.

His shorthand for this situation is "10/30/60 (tenured/non-tenured/adjuncts)" as compared with a current breakdown of roughly "30/15/55." He suggests the current numbers will be looked upon with nostalgia for the "Good Old Days" in the very near future.[311]

Hiring on tenure-track lines also varies by discipline. A 2016-17 survey by CUPA-HR (College and University Professional Association-Human Resources) in a total respondent group of 708 indicated new tenure-track hires in math and English to be roughly even. Rosemary Feal, executive director of the Modern Language Association, noted that if tenure-track hiring patterns held for all

2,481 federally tracked institutions as for the CUPA-HR respondents, "...that extrapolates to 634 new tenure-track hires" or roughly half the 1,200 English PhDs awarded each year.[312] Feal felt the report was overly optimistic. In 2014, *The Atlantic* had already reported 45.7% of doctoral graduates in the humanities had no definite commitment for employment or postdoctoral study upon graduation.[313]

The advertising of a job in more than one subfield has also contributed to a false impression of the number of tenure-track positions available. In the humanities, one subfield showed the serious disconnect between PhD holders and jobs available: sociolinguistics. Between 2009 and 2012, roughly 165 degrees were granted for a total of 65 possible tenure-track jobs in both US and UK, as reported by blogger Chris Potts. He noted, "One caveat here is that there is probably still overinflation in the job numbers," because the same job may be advertised in more than one subfield noting "...a 'Syntax and Semantics' job was counted once for syntax and once for semantics, too."[314]

People who have not graduated from an Ivy League school have even slimmer chances of getting tenured academic employment compared to those with Ivy League degrees. Robert Oprisko graduated with a PhD in political science in 2011 from Purdue University. Despite numerous awards and publications, the best job he could get was a one-year visiting professorship at Butler University. He conducted a review of the 3,709 political science professors who were then employed by PhD-granting universities and found that just 11 schools had produced 50 percent of the total.[315] Harvard, at the top of the list, was responsible for 239 of the professors. Purdue, on the other hand, produced only 10 placed professors.[316]

Slate magazine reported the results of a study in *Science Advances* (2015) led by Aaron Clauset:

> [Examining more than] 16,000 faculty members in the fields of business, computer science, and history at 242 schools. The data revealed that just a quarter of all universities account for 71 to 86 percent of all tenure-track faculty in the US and Canada in these three fields. Just 18 elite universities produce half of all computer science professors, 16 schools produce half of all business professors, and eight schools account for half of all history professors.[317]

Not very good odds for getting a tenure-track position if you got your PhD at a "lower-tier" school.

According to an article in *Inside Higher Ed,* in December 2017, 10 institutions[318] in the Coalition for Next Generation Life Science announced a plan to track doctoral student career outcomes for life sciences programs and release data beginning in 2018. "Most students aren't going to end up in faculty jobs, and the founding members of the Coalition for Next Generation Life Science want potential trainees to know that up front."[319] An article by the presidents involved in this initiative suggested only 10% of life science students will get a faculty position within five years of graduation, partly due to a decrease of at least 22% in federal funding since 2003.[320] The coalition aims to let students know that opportunities exist outside academia and a tenure-track appointment.

Should faculty warn their graduate students about the slim job prospects post-PhD?[321] Blaine Greteman, associate professor of English at the University of Iowa, saw a dereliction of moral duty if graduate students were not clearly informed about job prospects for PhD students. He put it succinctly:

> I believe we commit professional malpractice if we don't frankly and frequently discuss the placement of our students and the sorts of salaries they make two, three, and four years after they complete their degrees. And I believe we are complicit in exploitation if we don't adjust the size and structure of our graduate programs to improve the placement of our students in decent, satisfying jobs, inside or outside academe.[322]

The search for a full-time permanent position, whether in sciences or the humanities, can drag on for five years or more while one is employed in a contingent position.[323] Kevin Gannon, a professor of history and director of the Center for Excellence in Teaching and Learning (CETL) at Grand View University in Des Moines, Iowa wrote, "For doctoral students, the path to traditional — i.e., tenure-track — positions is narrower and strewn with more obstacles than ever...The thing doctoral programs are really good at — producing Ph.D.s — is, in fact, exacerbating the problem as more qualified candidates compete for fewer tenure-track openings."[324] He suggested that one thing new PhDs can do to get work is to focus on teaching institutions rather than research institutions for employment.

For graduates, recognizing the real psychological toll that seeking tenure-track employment takes on applicants is important.[325] Consider this from Karen's Kelsy's blog:

> JMPTSD [Job Market PTSD] includes the survivor's guilt that you feel toward the comrades-in-arms you left behind as you boarded what seems like the last helicopter out of The Search. It includes classic trauma symptoms in that the sustained terror of potential joblessness/insolvency, combined with the psychological warfare of hope offered and then snatched away (particularly in the new phenomenon of searches and offers canceled at the last minute), steals away your sense of security in the world. It includes a large component of Imposter Syndrome, in that you wonder "Why me? Why did I get this position?" And it includes an element of Stockholm Syndrome, in that your gratitude for the offer is so abject that your normal emotional boundaries evaporate in a frantic attempt to please your new employer.[326]

Katie Fitzpatrick, a visiting assistant professor of English at Muhlenberg College, wrote about the toll of competing with peers for an academic job and concluded: "In the face of an economic system that atomizes us and an academic job market that pits us directly against one another, [cultivating] friendship is a powerful ethical and political practice," to maintain sanity and a sense of self outside of the job search arena."[327]

Tenure and tenure-track positions are now the aberration. Because the number of applicants far outweighs the number of recipients for tenure-track jobs, various people participating in social media sites have begun to joke that seeking a tenure-track position is actually the new "alt-ac" pathway.[328] The competition for new jobs is increased by the many people who have been on the job market for several years, treading water as adjuncts or working on as a post-doc, but who are still seeking the elusive tenure-track job. This is true whether they are graduates in the humanities or in science and technology.

Part 6: Additional Considerations

The shrinking professoriate and "contingent labor." Unfortunately, no discussion of what is currently taking place in higher education would be complete without a discussion of the ever-shrinking professoriate.[329] "From 1975 to 2011, the number of tenure-track and tenured professors increased by only 35.6 percent nationwide, while the number of part-time professors increased by 305.3 percent"[330] or approximately 70% of the total faculty providing instruction at nonprofit institutions in the United States.[331] Though the size of college faculties has grown over the past four decades, the AAUP reported the total number of tenure or tenure-track professors has declined.[332]

Keith Hoeller quoted Gwen Bradley, communications director for the American Association of University Professors (AAUP) as follows: "There has been a wide-scale transformation of the faculty workforce…It's reflecting what's happening in the economy in general. Some call it the Wal-Martization of higher education. It's much cheaper in the short term to hire part-time faculty."[333] The analogy refers to the Wal-Mart model of hiring many part-time workers without benefits and at a lower pay scale, rather than full-time employees with benefits, to keep employee costs down.

Provisional part-time labor is now the norm with adjuncts hired on a contract basis from academic year to academic year. We would argue that academia has always relied on the *contingent* or *casual*[334] labor model, but many people caught up in the system of graduate student labor have only recently begun to see it. One client described academia as the "ultimate pyramid scheme" because academia holds out the carrot of a permanent job "if only" you hang in there for years as an adjunct, with these attendant sticks: publishing and teaching for minimal compensation, dealing with high workloads, coping with poor work-life balance, and stressing over complicated schedules due to working at more than one institution simultaneously. The sad truth is that adjuncts are usually distanced and excluded from actual faculty decision making where they are employed yet considered too familiar to hire.

"The academic obsession with meritocracy places blame firmly upon the job seeker for not 'earning' a tenure-track job," wrote Kelly Baker.[335] The truth is that fewer and fewer tenure-track jobs are available, and many people remaining inside academia, or seeking to enter it, may *never* have anything other than contingent employment. Without any benefits, contingent laborers need a spouse or partner who earns enough to support a family or whose benefits provide health insurance for the contingent worker. In a *Chronicle of Higher Education Special Report* released February 2017, Katherine Morgan quoted Rudy H. Fichtenbaum, Professor Emeritus of Economics at Wright State University, as saying, "Nearly three-quarters of faculty members are contingent, most being part-timers earning little more than they would make serving fast food."[336]

Another issue for new PhDs seeking academic employment is that the greying of the professoriate has not translated into jobs for the newly graduated. According to a 2015 *Faculty Career and Retirement Survey* by the TIAA-CREF Institute, 49% of retirement-age faculty did not want to retire, only one-third are expected to retire by the age of 67, and many stay on past the age of 70.[337] But the large cohort of professors hired through the 1970s to teach baby-boomers are finally retiring. Unfortunately, as they retire, many institutions simply eliminate those tenure-track and tenured positions in response to budgetary constraints.

Is tenure facing extinction? Probably. While faculty members and college administrators generally express confidence in the central role tenure and academic freedom have had in establishing the United States as the global leader in higher education, many policymakers and governing boards do not. Recently, John Behling, the vice president of the University of Wisconsin System's Board of Regents, said, "Tenure may be the standard in higher education, but it is out of step with reality."[338] As colleges and universities seek to become more nimble in the marketplace by redefining their missions to reflect specialty areas rather than the widest possible swath of majors, more and more university administrations will likely reduce tenured positions to keep expenses down. These reductions will continue to significantly impact those seeking tenure-track jobs. The percent of tenured to non-tenured faculty has been steadily dropping. As noted in the section "What are the chances of being offered a tenure-track job?" roughly 70% of *all* positions are now "provisional."

Part-time contract faculty are less costly than full-time faculty roughly averaging $3-4,000 per three-credit course.[339] compared to hiring one full-time professor in the US, which averages $58,000 per year in the humanities. Part-time instructors have no institutional voice, since they are not integrated into the workplace, and may be offered very few resources, such as office space, to do their jobs, and may increase the demands on those full-time employees remaining in the system to handle administrative tasks like curriculum revisions. The *Chronicle of Higher Education Almanac,* reflecting the realities of contract labor, now includes non-tenure-track faculty positions and, at colleges with no tenure system, by sector and length of contract. While many acknowledge that the current situation of older tenured professors and younger non-tenured or contract teaching employees is not desirable, what will replace the current system is not clear.

You may be slightly more likely to be offered a tenure-track job if you are helping to fulfill an institution's quest for a more diverse faculty, whether you are black, Hispanic, female, disabled, or LGBT. If you can enhance a university's diversity initiative in some way, you may be in a smaller competitive pool. At present, of 400,000 tenured and tenure-track professors (not adjuncts) employed in the US, 75% for all institutions are white, and the percentage at smaller colleges is even greater.[340] Addressing hidden hiring criteria, Brian Leider, professor of jurisprudence and director of the Center for Law, Philosophy and Human Values at the University of Chicago, wrote:

> Any seasoned academic who has been involved with job searches knows there are two sets of criteria for some positions: the ones in the published ad and the "hidden" ones.
> "The dean says we must hire a woman this time," reports the chair. Or the dean says: "The department's lack of racial diversity is becoming a problem, you've got to fix that with this year's search." Or the department's star faculty member tells the chair, "If you don't hire my spouse into a permanent line finally, we will take jobs elsewhere next year." All of those fall into the hidden-criteria column.
> The published job ads connected to such searches reveal nothing of the underlying reality. For legal reasons, no job ad can say, "Only women should apply," or "This job is open only to spouses of very famous members of our department."[341]

Even if you get that elusive tenure-track job, most institutions are now requiring a "third-year review" before going forward in the process, and even if you receive tenure after a six-year process, you are likely to be required to do a post-tenure review three to six years later. A point may come when competing for a tenured position is no longer worthwhile.[342] If you are looking to work at a particular institution, you might want to look at how the school markets itself, what they are telling prospective students about the educational experience, and then take a close look at the school's financial health. As an up-and-coming professor, survival as an academic means being the very best you can be in your own field of study and flexibility in the types of employment you are willing to accept.

Alternatives to the Professoriate

Although this workbook is designed to help you land an academic job, given some of the statistics presented above, we acknowledge that many people will never get an academic job teaching and/or doing research, and certainly not that "ideal academic job," despite preparing for many years and possibly foregoing significant income during graduate school years. As Elizabeth Rodwell, anthropology lecturer at University of Houston noted, "What other line of work encourages you to train for as much as a decade, and leaves you potentially without an opportunity for local work?"[343] In this section, we set forth alternatives to the traditional tenure-track employment, listing opportunities both in and outside of institutions of higher education.

Inside Academia

If you still want to stay in the academic environment, look beyond adjuncting for alternatives to the professoriate. These alternatives include administrative positions, program director positions, technology management positions, editor positions (both in-house and virtual), to name a few of the non-faculty careers that may be associated with an institution of higher education. Since a few idiosyncratic issues may be present if you're interested in particular types of positions, you may want to research what those positions are and resources available to learn about those positions. For instance, if you want to become an academic advisor in order to stay in the university world, knowing that candidates who did their graduate work at same institution and have insider working knowledge of the place are more likely to be hired (Personal communication, Vahey, K., 2016, June 28) than candidates from outside is useful.[344] The National Association of Academic Advisors (NACADA) lists a variety of resources, including conceptual papers about advising, that may help you get positioned with current thinking and policies in the field.[345]

Administrative jobs. What kind of work does someone in an administrative job do?[346] The answer depends on the kind of position. The job search details for administrative jobs vary according to the job. You will probably be answerable to a dean or a provost (another administrator) instead of to a department chair. You may be working on your own with a student assistant or you may be supervising a few faculty members.

If you already know what kind of administrative position you would like to pursue, consider conducting some short (30 minute or less) informational interviews with people who already have a similar position. Ask about their pathways to that job, about any special skills or experience needed beyond the degree you already have, what they like best and least about the job, what professional organization(s) they belong to, their job titles, relationships to their colleagues, and whatever else you want to know. Most people are happy to talk about their jobs if they are happy in their work.

Hiring for administrative jobs goes on throughout the year. The hiring cycle and job requirements are not as predictable as for tenure-track jobs. The institution may want someone right now or the search may go on for a long time. Usually, you will need to provide a one-page resume rather than a CV as well as a cover letter. Recommendations will most likely be requested if you make it to a second-round interview. You may also need to complete HR paperwork. Even if you submit a resume electronically, the same rules apply that we mentioned in the academic interview process: just go ahead and submit the same information again if need be since the information may be going to different people. Read the job description or listing carefully and, as much as you can, tailor your cover letter and resume to the details of the job description. Beware, however, that "Administrative hiring is rife with class and name prejudice. Generally, everybody wants to hire from 'peer or better' institutions."[347]

Below are the types of administrative jobs that may be available depending on the size of the institution and the need for staff, with a brief description of typical responsibilities.

Admissions officer: Generally, a person in this position will be involved in both recruiting new students and reviewing applications of prospective students. You may be responsible for conducting interviews with those potential students. You could be involved in creating campaigns to promote the university or debates around how to construct the admissions process to increase diversity of all kinds at your institution.

Adult continuing education: As previously mentioned, a movement exists toward emphasizing life-long learning and continually upgrading work skills. Universities and community colleges often offer non-credit courses for community members. With an aging population, the desire for more leisure content, like music appreciation, may also be in bigger demand. For those with highly specialized areas, such as the history of European Jews, one growing area is university-sponsored, expert-led tours and cruises are targeted for adult education. Though well-paying, the competition is fierce.

Agricultural/farm administration: In addition to state university agricultural extension offices to train future farmers, niches also exist for specialty farms such as honey production and community–supported agriculture (CSAs). In affluent cosmopolitan areas, as the farm-to-table market grows, the combination of business savvy with agrarian knowledge is quite useful. In addition, genetic engineers are designing things from heat-resistant broccoli to fast-growing trees for construction timber. Some of these programs are directly associated with universities.

Art/museum administration: More opportunities for this type of work exist in large cosmopolitan areas but collections can physically reside anywhere. If you want to be a curator using your doctorate in art history at a major university, you will find gaining employment there highly competitive. Some large museums include conservation staff in addition to administrators. However, if you are more interested in maintaining a good collection, writing catalogs, and supplying information of service to a community, you may be surprised at what is available off the beaten track at smaller colleges. Many universities and small colleges house special collections, especially from well-known authors, politicians, artists, or scientists who may have been alums or otherwise associated with the institution.

Assistant dean: Depending on your background, the organizational chart and the size of the institution, you may become an assistant dean for things like community field placements, an internship requirement, or international programs. These types of "deanships" generally fall under the heading of Student Affairs. Academic deans will generally have assistants drawn from the ranks of faculty that fall under them.

Consultant: Depending on the type of degree you have received and perhaps your own work experience outside academia as you worked toward a degree, you may end up working in a consulting capacity with some division in your institution. Business schools sometimes hire their own graduates to streamline activities and evaluation processes.

Counselor: This is a title that can mean anything from academic advisor to mental health consultant. Academic advisors are usually employed by particular departments and responsibilities vary from helping undergraduates determine a major to the minutiae of counting credit hours toward a degree. Colleges and universities usually have an Accessibility or Disability Services office headed by an administrator and employing education but non-academic staff. Or you could be employed as a counselor through the Human Resources department. Many larger universities have Employee Assistance Programs (EAPs) that cover everything from alcoholism to sexual harassment to workplace violence. You do not necessarily need an advanced degree to perform this work, but again, the prestige factor of an advanced degree may help in gaining employment.

Cybersecurity/Information Technology: For academia, as in all industries, cybersecurity will continue to be an area of growth. If you have a degree in computer science or know something about international affairs, this could be a place for your knowledge. Cybersecurity is a bit like closing the door after the horse got out, as institutions of all sorts try to undo the damage already done. For instance, administrators at Cornell University discovered a security breach two years after it occurred when launching a new website for the school. IT professionals determined the source as "a foreign government possible seeking 'revenge' against the United States" by primarily pursuing research data.[348]

Development officer: Universities and colleges are constantly recruiting private donors as public monies dry up. Development offices love the cachet of staff members with the title of Dr. in front of their names on a signature line. It honestly does not matter what your degree is in, from anthropology to zoology. Most of the time, your discussion with potential donors will not be about your research, but about the prospect's desire to fund some particular program. Your work is to connect over time in a personal way so that your institution eventually benefits from planned giving. In this case, one of your best assets will be the ability to have a good conversation.

Diversity offices (Title IX): Many institutions have addressed the issue of discrimination for a variety of issues like racism and gender-based bias. Some universities house complaints about sexual harassment and assault in this office. Large universities may even have a dedicated

Diversity Office at the level of a Vice President, which requires staffing. How these offices will fair in the face of continually decreasing funding and uncertain public support remains to be seen.

Finance: If you are interested in finance, it's clear that student loan issues will continue to grow, as will the mechanisms for dealing with debt. ISAs (Income Share Agreements) that require the borrowers to pay back a percentage of their income for a set number of years are becoming more popular and may become an employment specialty area for financial aid university employees.

Government relations specialist: You may be assisting the president or someone on the board of directors as the institution's state governmental liaison, writing testimony for legislative committees, working with a particular state's Higher Education Coordinating Board, or reporting on educational developments to the officers of the institution during legislative sessions.

Grant writer (statistician/writer/editor): This is an area likely to grow as funds get tighter. The ability to write a coherent grant proposal meeting all the requirements of a granting entity and submit it on time requires organization, time management, and people skills to pull together disparate data streams into a seamless document. Your experience writing a dissertation is a clear asset here. If you have experience with software like SPSS or STATA for analyzing large data sets, your experience will be in even greater demand.

Institutional researcher: Many universities and colleges have offices of institutional research that can encompass reviewing grant proposals before submission or other decision-making and planning areas such as enrollment, financial aid, curriculum assessment, ethics of subject research, or other statistical analyses. Statisticians are especially in demand here. Other assets for employment include strong written and oral communication skills, attention to detail, and knowledge about how institutions of higher education operate. Graduate school certainly provides such training.

Legal office personnel: Universities, just like private industry, must abide by environment and health and safety regulations, whether from running on-site energy plants to handling small quantities of hazardous chemicals for laboratory use. Policies for handling or providing the appropriate legal information may be handled by attorneys but may also be provided through work done by a research staff. The campus police department may need advice or instruction for handling issues like domestic violence in on-campus housing. President's offices may need to craft compelling arguments for presenting their proposals to a legislative body. Research-oriented universities have legal staff that assist faculty with patents and intellectual property issues.

Medical school administration: As the name implies, this is a highly specialized type of administrator, and scientific training may be of particular use. Medical teaching schools are often located on, or immediately adjacent to, the educational institution of the same name. This kind of position can include recruiting medical students, assisting them with residency or visa issues, or guiding doctors-in-training with regard to publication.

On-line or for-profit school administration: As already noted, the demand for online training at for-profit schools has been increasing for some time. Online education is a non-traditional pathway that many students find more compatible with either lifestyle or availability of materials when in areas far away from physical campuses. Working students juggling demands of a full-time job with family as well as military people moving from place to place who want to continue their education will continue to push growth in this area. In addition, a rising market in Global South countries with growing populations desirous of increasing their skills exists. Doctoral-level knowledge of how higher education works can be an asset for those building such programs.

Policy analyst/speechwriter: There may also be new opportunities for analyzing and writing about state and federal education policy at the level of the Provost's or President's offices. In the US and elsewhere in the world, it is hard to fathom the new directions originating from various Departments of Education as governments at all levels grapple with the structural and financial issues that continue to plague the sector. In the past these kinds of jobs traditionally went to people already inside the institution. But perhaps you have some special knowledge or experience regarding the legislative agenda resulting from your dissertation research that could be of use.

Professional development: In the context of universities, professional development usually refers to helping professors teach or write better, sometimes through organizing "camps" over school break periods. It can also mean making sure that professional credentials, such as a license in social work, are maintained by faculty, or it could be providing resources to new employees. Depending on the organization, there may be roles in leadership training through assessments, workshops, coaching, and other offerings.

Program coordinator or administrator at academic centers/institutes: Schools of any size may have specialized centers based on particular faculty or donor endowments, such as the Humanities Institute or Institute for Classical Archaeology at the University of Texas at Austin. If you have a degree or outside experience in a particular field such as paleoanthropology or geology, you may find you are a candidate for running a center based on your specialized knowledge. Perhaps you have the expertise to act as an administrator of the university's Institutional Review Board (IRB). Or you may be a candidate at a lower level than the executive director as a program coordinator tracking grant money and assisting with the day-to-day operations.

Public relations/student recruiting: Alumni of particular institutions are often sought out for these positions, with the assumption that they will be able to speak with authority on a presumably good educational experience. Many schools look for PhDs in local areas where the school would not otherwise have a presence; however, these jobs tend to be seasonal and frequently are staffed by volunteers. Being a recruiter for a large educational institution can also keep you on the road much of the year.

Publications and university presses: Publications written within a college or university vary from school and department alumni magazines to institutional annual reports. As the old ways of publishing are in the midst of major change, the traditional jobs of university press acquisitions and editing may now be done outside the university. But for those university presses that remain, a person holding a doctorate is desirable for the organization in terms of ability to analyze the proposals and to discuss existing publications at book booths at academic conferences as well as to seek out new proposals for a press.

Research associate/lab manager: There are so many types of research associate positions that it is impossible to list them all here. If you have a doctorate in science and enjoy working in the lab, many research scientists would love to have you on their team handling anything from lab animals to gene sequencing to operating specialized spectrometry equipment. Some research associates provide statistical consultation or write research papers or grant proposals as well. We know a PhD who works as a lab researcher year-round and also teaches herpetology at the university in the summer.

Safety officer: Some universities are large enough to have their own police force. While you may not want to be an officer patrolling the campus, these offices also need staff that can liaise with a wide variety of campus officials, coordinating everything from public speakers on campus to handling investigations of all sorts. Some colleges consider officers professional staff under the authority of Student Services.

Student affairs professional: A wide variety of positions fall into the broad category of Student Affairs, but one of the major drawbacks in getting these positions is that they tend to go to people who have degrees in higher education administration. If you have one of those degrees, great. If not, consider attending some NASPA [349] conferences on mid-level administrators.

Leaving Academia

Although leaving academia could truly be a topic for another entire book, here we give you some basic information about feelings you may have about leaving the academy and about finding a job outside the academy. A Cornell University research study by Michael Roach and Henry Sauerman, released in September 2017,[350] found that when students started PhD programs, 80% were interested in academic careers, but as they came closer to graduation, fully one-third of those students had completely lost interest in academic careers. It is hard to tell whether this stemmed from lack of jobs or burnout with research and writing. [351] In an interview with *Inside Higher Ed,* Roach noted that non-academic careers "have long been the more common pathway and not the alternative" for natural science and engineering. He added that the "essential role of universities in training industrial scientists and applying scientific knowledge and research skills to the development of new medical devices or autonomous vehicles or alternative energy should not be seen as a failure."[352] Despite such comments, it is frequently frightening for graduate students to actually admit to advisors that they want to leave academia.[353]

"The future belongs to nerds, geeks, makers, dreamers, and knowmads," said John Moravec.[354] For those of you who are interested, see the electronic book, written by nine collaborating authors coining the term *Knowmad Society* (first released in 2013).[355] "Knowmads" as defined by Dr. John Moravec, a scholar on the future of work and education, are "creative, imaginative, and innovative people who can work with almost anybody, anytime, and anywhere."[356] He sees knowmadding as an emergent form of employment in the 21st century. Millennials are especially drawn to this lifestyle.[357] New PhDs are potentially ideally suited to this type of work though obviously not necessarily in the context of a traditional institution of higher learning.

Grieving Your Losses

After all the time, energy, and money you have spent on graduate school and the hopes you may have nurtured for a tenured academic job when you finished your doctoral program, you have the right to grieve if you take an alternative route or feel that it has been foisted on you. Some people get their doctorates with the idea of being employed outside of the academy, but if you weren't one of them, allow yourself to acknowledge your feelings about your change of plans. Remember that you can grieve the loss of your dreams and be excited about other possibilities concurrently.

A genre called "quit-lit" has emerged recently recounting the journeys or feelings of people who expected to be academics but either left the academy or stopped searching for a tenure-track job.[358] Erin Bartram, a Visiting Assistant Professor at Hartford University, now off the tenure track, wrote an essay "Why everybody loses when someone leaves academe."[359] The *Chronicle of Higher Education* also published Sarah Brown's interview [360] with Bartram, titled "She wrote a farewell letter to colleagues. Then 80,000 people read it." Leonard Cassuto wrote an essay responding to Bartram's entitled "The Grief of the Ex-Academic," saying, "How can we change graduate education so that it doesn't set people up to feel like failures in the face of a likely outcome?" which acknowledges just how difficult it is for new PhDs to find employment as a professor.[361]

We quote from Bartram's comments at length because she has so eloquently expressed her feelings on a rarely discussed issue. Her poignant perspective on leaving the academy begins with her own inability to allow herself the comfort of time to grieve, then moves on to the reactions of her colleagues still employed in higher education:[362]

> Despite the abundance of "quit lit" out there, we're still not, as a community of scholars, doing a great job dealing with this thing that happens to us all the time. The genre is almost universally written by those leaving, providing them with an outlet for their sorrow or rage, or allowing them to make an argument about what needs to change. Those left behind, or, as we usually think of them, those who "succeeded," don't often write about what it means to lose friends and colleagues. To do so would be to acknowledge not only the magnitude of the loss but also that it was a loss at all.
>
> If we don't see the loss of all of these scholars as an actual loss to the field, is it any wonder I felt I had no right to grieve? Why should I be sad about what has happened when the field itself won't be?

Bartram explained her own situation as follows: [363]

> I got a Ph.D. in history because I wanted to be a historian. I didn't write a dissertation on 19th-century Catholic women to learn the critical-thinking skills of history and then go

> work in insurance. I didn't spend my 20s earning so little I ended up helping unionize my co-workers because I wanted to be in nonprofit work.
>
> I've lost a huge part of my identity, and all of my book-learning on identity construction can't help me now. What hurts the most, in a way, is that my loss has been replicated a thousand times over, and will be replicated a thousand times more, and rather than face what that means, we have, as a profession and as people, found ways of dealing with it that largely erase the people we lose, erase their pain and grief, and erase our own.

In her interview with Sarah Brown, Bartram gave counsel to those engaged in their own academic job searches:[364]

> You're the one who has to decide. You're the one who would have to live with the consequences of adjuncting for another year.
>
> You had this life of the mind, and you imagined a future in it, and that's great. But if it didn't turn out to be a healthy and stable life for you, you're not obligated to stay in it.
>
> But one of the issues for historians — and I think for a lot of fields — is that the amount of scholarship you have to produce is just through the roof. And to put it bluntly, I have plenty of colleagues who I know have been turned down for jobs when their CVs as candidates already had more publications on them than senior members of that committee. That hurts.
>
> I was thinking this morning: I was the same writer and thinker a week ago. I was the same person. It's just like how the tenure-track job is the thing that validates you as a scholar. Had I not written this, I would have been nobody. And the essay didn't matter until other people said that it was worth something. That's pretty much the problem we're dealing with in academia.
>
> There are so many other people like me. Every one of my friends who have left as I did could have written, and has written, really great stuff. But until we're validated, we don't exist.

Much like the advice given to dating partners after breaking up, actually naming your feelings and allowing yourself to deal with all the conflicting emotions before moving on is important. As Bartram wrote, there are actually multiple losses: financial, intellectual, and social. Reminding yourself that you still have a future, even if it is not what you had hoped, planned, and dreamed about for many years, may be helpful.

Post Academia

In early 2017, Andy Thomason, Breaking News editor for the *Chronicle of Higher Education*, wrote in Your Daily Briefing "It's not unusual for humanities doctoral students to be unaware of the poor state of the academic job market," and the slim chances of employment as a professor.[365] I know from personal experience in graduate school, and in working with academic clients who recently finished their degrees, that a couple of explanations other than being unaware of the statistics exist. Fellow students may be discussing dim job prospects, but a kind of selective hearing can occur: "Oh, that's *them*, I won't be like that, my prospects are brighter." Some doctoral students tell me they deliberately ignore the reality of job prospects in their field in order to finish. They explain, "If I start thinking about this, I will freak out, and I will never get done."

Remarkably, the number of individuals *already* employed in academia that now want to leave continues to rise. Deciding to leave before even gaining employment may simply be a rational choice. In the US, Melanie Sinche wrote "Nonfaculty careers [for science PhDs] once considered Plan B are now preferred by the majority of degree holders."[366] Others leave because after years of adjuncting and pursuing the elusive full-time job, they are sick of the whole profession, from snobbish colleagues to overly entitled students. Rani Neutill wrote in a *Salon* post that she felt waitressing was better for her mental health than continuing in academia.[367] Lee Hall wrote that, as an adjunct professor with a five-class load, she earned "less than a pet-sitter."[368] Overseas, 42% of lecturers and professors in the United Kingdom are considering leaving as a result of Brexit vote, in part because they expected to lose research funding.[369]

This leads us to the term *alt-ac* first coined by Jason Rhody, then in the Office of Digital Humanities at National Endowment for the Humanities in 2009, during a Twitter Exchange with Bethany Nowviskie.[370] A lot has now been written about the alt-ac track. We prefer the term *post-ac* because it is more accurate for people who have consciously chosen to leave academia behind for whatever reason and pursue other lines of work. Leaving consciously can take away the huge stigma that many still feel of "not making it," despite the reality of the academic marketplace. Making a deliberate decision to depart can also help with grieving the loss of an academic career. For many of my clients, once the choice to leave the academy is made, a huge weight is lifted, and they begin to see the nonacademic possibilities as both exciting and, frequently, more remunerative. In addition, the US Bureau of Labor Statistics has projected the number of all jobs requiring doctoral degrees to be 4.6 million between 2012 and 2022, a roughly 16% increase in the total number of jobs requiring this degree.[371]

If you browse the term alt-ac or Altac, you will get about 1,500,000 results in 0.45 seconds. The first results will heavily favor publications like *Inside Higher Ed, The Chronicle of Higher Education,* and *Vitae,* all mentioned in this workbook previously. Many universities include some information on their websites using these search terms, an acknowledgment that not everyone who gets a PhD is destined to teach at the university level. You may want to check out some of the outsider articles on this topic, as found Slate magazine [372] or the Council on Library and Information Resources, [373] suggesting alt-ac should become a normalized post-PhD pathway.

As we noted post-ac is an emerging expression and some writers distinguish the terms this way: "…alt-ac (referring to non–tenure-track careers in academia) and post-ac (referring to careers outside of higher education altogether).[374] The majority of the careers discussed on forums, in blogs, and various publications about this topic focus on where PhDs might find work in industry: anthropologists in marketing, STEM scientists in the pharmaceutical industry, social scientists in policy, computer programmers in the film industry, health care service, and so on. Most of the time, however, newly minted PhDs want to exhaust all possible chances for a professorship before considering life outside the academy. Once they have concluded leaving academia is a viable career option, they often need to consider how to repackage their skills and story in order to be attractive to the world outside the academy.

Skills acquired in a graduate program are transferrable to jobs outside the academy. Stephen Aron, head of the University of California at Los Angeles's History Department, conducted his own in-house survey and determined in 2017 that 50% of his doctoral recipients got jobs for which they were trained in academia. These were not jobs in academia but were jobs using academic skills.[375] He created a graduate seminar titled "The many professions of history" to discuss the likely disappointing outcomes for an academic job search as well as to give graduate student ideas for using a history doctorate outside of academia.

James Grossman, head of the American Historical Association (AHA), created a list of five basic skills history PhDs can acquire in graduate school and offer to employers outside academia.[376] The list, published by the AHA in 2016, grew out of a 2014 Andrew W. Mellon Foundation grant of $1.6-million, split between four universities "to broaden the career paths of history doctoral students."[377] The skills are:

- Communication, in a variety of media to a variety of audiences;
- Collaboration, especially with those with different perspectives;
- Quantitative literacy, or the basic ability to understand and communicate information presented in numbers;
- Intellectual self-confidence, or the ability to work beyond one's subject matter expertise, and be "nimble and imaginative" in projects and plans; and
- Digital literacy, or a basic familiarity with digital tools and platforms.

Grossman's list applies to those acquiring PhDs in other fields as well. At the AHA annual meeting in 2017, Edward R. Dickinson, Chair of History at the University of California, Davis, led a panel titled "Collaboration for career diversity: Locating expertise at the institutional and national levels." His message to graduate students was "…be fearless—that when you leave this program you will have a more powerful, more well-trained, more flexible mind than 99 percent of the labor force, literally."[378]

Use the worksheet on **Transferable Skills** to begin your own assessment of skills you have acquired or sharpened in graduate school. Rate your competence in each area with 0 meaning not competent, and 5 meaning that you are quite confident of your skill in this area. For each skill that you rated yourself at a 2 or less, indicate what steps you can take, starting right now, to build your skill in that area, whether it is reading a book, talking to someone, or getting some training. Below the skills that Grossman suggested, we have listed a few more to get you thinking about what other skills you have developed that may serve you in a job outside the academy. You can also add your own ideas for skills here.

Not everyone agrees that the skills learned in graduate school are transferrable outside the academy. Lewis Solomon, education professor at UCLA and director of a five-year study on the job market for PhDs, has been quoted as saying:

> Maybe some people can afford the avocation of a degree in the humanities. But really most [PhD] programs don't prepare anybody to be anything except clones of the professor …

Part 6: Additional Considerations

> Anyone who says the PhD is a good way to prepare for the business world is self-serving or dishonest or simply wants cannon fodder for his own graduate courses.[379]

Being on the job market longer than 2-3 years for a tenure-track position probably means you should start looking elsewhere. Some of the areas to investigate, depending on your own interests, are business, government, the non-profit sector, and international opportunities. You may even find that your expertise in academia can lend itself to working to create university partnerships for innovative technology, outreach to community organizations by higher education entities, or cultivating programs to help students move from high school through graduate school. Another approach may be to look for alternative work to stay in, or move to, a particular geographic location.

Some former academics leave to create their own businesses. Many who have finished a PhD are remarkably suited to the role of entrepreneur. They have worked toward a long-term goal, frequently found a variety of funding sources in order to finish, juggled multiple responsibilities simultaneously from coursework to writing requiring "project management" skills, and are suited to working long hours alone to achieve their dreams. In discussing a very small 30 participant study based on Boise State faculty workloads and work habits, John Ziker, Chair of the Anthropology Department, noted faculty members have an "entrepreneurial spirit, [and]a willingness to exploit their free time for [their own research] work."[380] Some universities even provide mentorship and education on starting and running a business for people outside of a business school program. Exploring the funding mechanisms available to help launch a new business grounded in academia, including venture capitalists or technology transfer offices, can be worthwhile.

We've known faculty uncertain of receiving tenure who began the process of setting up their own business while still in the academy. Often, the chosen business showcased their academic specialty, like contract excavation for an archaeologist or music lessons for kindergarteners for a piano performance professor. The PhD can be used to establish credibility for a product or service based on academic research. "I'm going this way because it's something that I'm passionate about. It allows me to take the skills that I've learned in [kinesiology] research and have a larger impact," said Harrison Brown, creator of HeadCheck Health, a tool for athletic trainers to determine the existence of on-field concussions.[381]

Many more schools are beginning to deal with the reality that many PhDs do not stay in academia. Schools like University of Chicago and Stanford University are now offering career fairs targeted at PhDs who want to move on. Brooke Noonan, executive director of one such program, UChicagoGRAD, commented on a profound shift over the last 8-10 years in how PhDs think about the job market. He said, "We want to make sure that the pursuit of getting a Ph.D. remains worthwhile, and to make sure that there's a fulfilling professional life at the other end of this path."[382] So, if you have decided in the course of pursuing your PhD that academia is not the life for you, check into whether or not your particular institution offers any service like this. A few more places to look if you decide to go this route are:

- National Endowment for the Humanities Next Generation Ph.D. initiative.[383]
- American Council of Graduate Schools Understanding Career Pathways.[384]

Transferable Skills Acquired or Sharpened in Graduate School Worksheet

Skill

Rating
0 (none) →5 (high)

Steps I am
willing to take

Communication:

Collaboration:

Quantitative literacy:

Intellectual self-confidence:

Digital literacy:

Planning:

Writing:

Research:

Other (list):

Part 6: Additional Considerations

- Modern Language Association's Connected Academics.[385]
- American Historical Association's Career Diversity for Historians initiative.[386]

Many blogs, listserves, and websites are devoted to the topic of the rewards of life outside academia including the likelihood of better remuneration. Versatile PhD provides access without institution affiliation to PhD Career Finder to help people figure out what kinds of job opportunities are available for transitioning out of academia.[387] Jobs listed on the site in the past included:

- Data analyst at Disney Corporation (Burbank, CA);
- Consultant at The Education Advisory Board (Washington, DC); and
- Technical Publications Lead at National Cybersecurity Center of Excellence (DC or MD).

If you are currently enrolled at a school that has an institutional membership at Versatile PhD, then you will be able to access paid premium content with examples of "Real-Life Resumes" used for successful transitions by former academics to get particular jobs, such as "Ethnic Studies PhD hired as Digital Media Director at Parallax Press" or "Astronomer hired as Data Scientist in Finance."

There are now many sites available for investigating life and careers after finishing a PhD for alternatives to academia. Chris Humphrey, founder of Jobs on Toast, published a *Free resource guide: 10 career websites every PhD should visit* (2014), though we have noticed that some of the links he listed are now defunct. The unbroken links that are worth looking at include PhDs At Work — Insight and Advice on Life Beyond Academia[388], PhDeli, From PhD to Life, and Beyond the PhD. A Facebook group, Wildcards,[389] provides inspirational stories about leaving academia. One former academic wrote the following on VPhD about her transition to fiction writer:

> Since leaving academia for government contracting, my writing career has started to take off. Part of this is the greater openness to people occasionally going home from their jobs—and a lot of it has been the freedom from worrying that someone will stand up at a conference to warn my audience that I *write science fiction*. (An actual thing that happened to a friend of mine a while back.) (Personal email communication, R. Gordon, April 5, 2018).

For those of you who simply cannot let the idea of working in academia go completely, a compromise might be a double track: adjuncting and consulting. In certain disciplines, such as computer science and business, academia may be, or may become, part-time employment as universities are more and more willing to allow dual tracks for both budgeting reasons and the desire to provide "real world" information to their students. Because it will never pay well, adjuncting is much easier to justify if it is not your sole source of income. Universities may become even more receptive to allowing certain faculty members to do more fee-based consulting, too, in order to stop the intellectual "poaching" of university faculty by companies like Apple, Microsoft or Google.[390]

Finally, just because you leave academia, you do not have to leave behind the role of scholar. Michael Wing, PhD in earth sciences, has maintained an independent scholarly career outside of the role of professor. He wrote, "As a high-school teacher, I have tenure, I earn a secure six-figure income, and I've published as many peer-reviewed papers and books as some professors, and more than others."[391] He has won grant proposals from corporations and scholarly organizations like the National Geographic Society, attended conferences, traveled for field work on five different continents, and collaborated with scientists from NASA and the US Park Service. Basically, to be a scholar outside of the academy, he says to 1) find a way to stabilize your income for the sake of your sanity and the well-being of your family, and 2) follow your passion. He feels it is actually much easier to do this outside of academia than inside it with all of the attendant pressures of the academy. Other resources such as The National Coalition of Independent Scholars (NCIS) might help you make connections and find additional support for continuing scholarly work.[392]

Summary

To recap, looking for work outside the academy may be worthwhile, especially for those who finished graduate school without publications or anything in the publication pipeline. Without publications, your best bet is to learn how to talk about your work to those who might not understand the nuances by emphasizing the skills you learned in graduate school, like how to present engaging material to a live audience, how to research and organize a project from conception to finalization (that's a dissertation, if you're wondering), or run conferences, seminars, or anything else requiring the collaboration of multiple parties from inception through invitations to completed event. Life does exist beyond academia and it may even be less stressful, more lucrative, and more meaningful to you.

Ultimately, it is your choice whether you want to continue looking for work as a tenured professor, alter your expectations for the kind of work you are willing to pursue inside academia, or choose to leave academia altogether. We hope the information provided in this section will help you determine your own next best step.

PART 7: CONCLUSION

We've tried to include every aspect of the academic job search process with which we are familiar in this workbook. We hope you understand the difficulty of landing an academic job and know what to expect in applying for one. Being completely prepared for what needs to be done, beginning with reading the job listings through final interviews, can certainly give you an advantage compared to others seeking academic jobs.

At this point, we want to emphasize what we feel are the most important pieces of your job search process.

Passion: To continue in the process of an incredibly difficult job search process, find ways to stoke the passion that brought you to a particular academic field in the first place. Passion will shed some guiding light when your search feels dark; passion will allow you to focus on the outcome rather than the dreary day-to-day tasks of seeking work; passion will push you to seek excellence in all you do; passion will fuel your work and energize your days when they look particularly rough; passion will enable your creativity in all areas of your life, including the job hunt; and finally, and perhaps most important, passion will make you happy. Without a passion for your chosen field of work, you will find staying dedicated to looking for a position in academia incredibly difficult

Networking, aka connecting: Never underestimate the power of personal connections. All other things being equal, people generally prefer to hire someone they know than someone they do not know. There are several ways to network; quite possibly you are already doing them. Engage in social media (with care). Create a professional profile, whether on LinkedIn or your own web page or both. Attend conferences to give papers and connect with the people you want to know or whose work you truly want to know more about and to understand. Get to know people both as scholars and as individuals with personal lives and interests outside of academia. If you find that you feel a relationship should stay firmly in the realm of the professional, honor that rather than chatting up someone because you think that person might be of use in your job search. Think about how you can offer your skills in a professional setting, like being a table captain at a conference or offering to informally edit a colleague's paper when the opportunity is present. Finally, be kind to those who want to get to know you because, as the quote attributed to Maya Angelou says, "I've learned that people will forget what you said, people will forget what you did, but people will never forget how you made them feel."

Authenticity: While the truth is that you are looking to convince someone to hire you, a difference exists between being authentic and taking on a selling role. You do have real skills. It's important that the people you speak with understand your skills. You have already demonstrated your intellect and perseverance by finishing your PhD. You may have taught or assisted in a number of courses. You may have spoken at conferences or published an article. You may have obtained grant funding for your research. You do not need to brag nor hide your light.

You need to let potential employers know what they will get when they hire you. Search committees, and the folks the committee introduces you to, must have a reasonable idea of both your skills and knowledge. They are all looking at you as a potential colleague and wondering whether you will fit in. You can speak positively about the institution without pandering. If you have an idiosyncratic sense of humor, you can let that out (as long as you are not using sarcasm or making jokes at someone else's expense). Search committee members want to know the real you.

Confidence: You may have to act a lot more confident than you feel. That's OK. Try using some of the tricks for reducing the saboteur's voice we discussed in the section on the imposter syndrome. Thoughts like "I'm not good enough" or "I am a failure" are endemic to the human condition. Academics who have achieved a lot may still suffer more from these feelings than other people precisely because they are competing with the best and the brightest. You are worthy. All your previous academic work proves that. To get the chance you deserve, you need to let others know you can do the work you propose. Own your abilities. Let your body and voice reflect your confidence. You may need some practice in safe spaces, since rehearsal for cultivating a positive presence is just as important as rehearsing the actual words you plan to say.

Persistence versus "How long to look:" You need to honestly ask yourself, "How long am I willing to look for an academic job?" The job application cycle is long; you may need to take a lot of time and energy to apply to even one academic position. Given some of the statistics we mentioned above, those tenure-track dream jobs are few and far between. If you have been on the market for three years after finishing your PhD and have not found your dream position, indeed any position, are you willing to change your vision of the kind of academic job you want? Or are you ready to take your degree and use it someplace outside of the academy? Moving around from adjunct job to adjunct job can be emotionally wearing, not to mention that the workload may leave you too tired to do your best work on an application for a full-time tenure-track position. If you have not done so already, think about the time you have already invested, and have a frank discussion with your family about the merits of pursuing this particular career. Derrick Attig, Director of Career Service at the Graduate College of the University of Illinois at Urbana-Champaign, recommends "building an endpoint" into your plans for the faculty job search. Make a contract with yourself now regarding how many years you will spend on the academic job market before you stop applying and shift your efforts to new possibilities."[393] There is a time for being persistent and a time for letting go.

For those of you wishing to move laterally from one academic job to another at a different institution, all the constraints around applying for your first job still apply. The promotion timeline is generally finite, and every institution has a set number of requirements that generally take years to accomplish. For instance, the average time to tenure once you have actually landed an academic job is six years, and frequently there is now a three-year review that can determine whether you will be allowed to continue your job on the tenure track. Expectations must be met around teaching, research, administrative duties or other service, AND a set number of publications, whether articles in peer-reviewed journals or books. In no other economic sector is the time to promotion so defined and so lengthy. So, if you are interested in moving out and on, you may want to begin your job search following the same timeline we have suggested for those just entering the market.

To sum up, fully understand the academic job search process, be realistic about your chances of success while doing everything you can to be successful, cultivating the traits and skills most likely to help you in this pursuit. We wish you good fortune. We would love to hear how this workbook

Part 7: Conclusion

How Long To Look for a Faculty Job Worksheet

Should I quit looking after two or three years? What is my gut feeling about this?

What is a realistic timeframe to continue looking, considering my own financial resources?

Have I talked to all the other people that will be affected by this decision [spouse/partner, children if old enough to be a concern, advisor, other people involved in my research program]?

How much do I have my heart set on a faculty job and how much am I open to other possibilities? [Revisit this question after each year of job searching.]

How can I live true to my values outside the academy?

What other life goals do I want to fulfill outside the academy?

    List three goals here:

    1.

    2.

    3.

What are some places outside the academy where I can still use my PhD and be happy?

    List 5 possibilities to investigate:

    1.

    2.

    3.

    4.

    5.

What other resources do I want to investigate to help me with this decision [career services at alma mater, books, articles, websites, blogs or other online tools about leaving the academy]?

What am I willing to do in terms of retraining?

What am I willing to learn: new systems, techniques, languages (including computer programming)?

Conduct informational interviews to understand what jobs outside academy entail?

helped you when you do land a tenure-track job or how we can improve this workbook in the future.

Epilogue

After you have gotten your academic job, you may want to look at Robert J. Sternberg's "Career Advice From an Oldish Not-Quite Geezer"[394] on working in academia. Below is a paraphrased synopsis of what he says:

- Put family and close friends first.
- Make your health a close second and treat your body well.
- Save as much money as you can for retirement and invest wisely. Plan for retirement emotionally, socially, and spiritually, not just financially.
- Be kind and "stay away from jerks;" people will always remember how you treated them.
- If you are really unhappy in your job and not having fun, move on or go into therapy to see what you can change about yourself.
- Be true to yourself and be willing to take some risks. Your academic life cannot be about pleasing other people; you can't count on your publications and awards to take care of you.
- Respect yourself and your work: do not let the judgment of others destroy your self-esteem. Academic work, by its nature, invites intense criticism.
- Take stock periodically: e.g., have 5 and 10-year plans; be willing to change your goals.
- Have a hobby that will provide you with some continuity in retirement. Travel for new perspectives and let yourself become refreshed.
- Help others: Think about giving instead of getting.
- Be conscious about what legacy you want to leave; ideas may matter more than the names of the people who first discovered them.

We also recommend Susan Robison's book, *The peak performing professor: A practical guide to productivity and happiness*.[395] Robison believes that faculty should concern themselves with life management rather than time management and her book includes information and exercises on how to do that.

APPENDIX A: TIPS FOR ORGANIZING TO DEAL WITH OVERLOAD

This section includes a brief description of how to set up a basic tickler file system, using one calendaring system, and the five steps for handling any incoming item: **T**oss, **A**ssign, **F**ast Action, **F**ile for Reference, and **Y**ou Must Now Act (TAFFY). When it comes to action item **Y**ou, a system must be in place for determining *when* you will next act on the task, and *how much time* you expect to allot to the task.

Information

A big part of learning to be a professor is dealing with information overload. Research used to mean scouring the archives, spending hours in the laboratory, and ponderously gathering data. With the internet, all manner of information can be at our fingertips instantaneously. Some of it is quite useful, but a large amount of information is unhelpful.

The general causes of information overload include:

- A rapidly increasing rate of new information being produced;
- The ease of duplication and transmission of data across the internet;
- An increase in the available channels of incoming information (e.g., telephone, e-mail, instant messaging, rss feeds, etc.);
- Large amounts of historical information to dig through;
- Contradictions and inaccuracies in available information;
- A low signal-to-noise ratio (corruption of data during processing);
- A lack of a method for comparing and processing different kinds of information; and
- Pieces of information that are unrelated or do not have any overall structure to reveal their relationships.

Interruptions

We live in the "age of interruption," wrote Thomas Friedman, columnist in the *New York Times*.[396] Neurologically, here's what happens: You are interrupted, by an unexpected telephone call, email, or a colleague sticking her head in the door with unwelcome information. This elicits a startle response, prompting your body to produce some tiny amount of stress hormones, like cortisol and adrenaline. Your respiratory rate increases a little bit. Your heart rate goes up and your blood pressure follows suit.

This moment of stress will lead to a momentary elevation in glucose, giving the brain a bit of energy. That, in turn, will stimulate the production of insulin, leading to a blood glucose drop. Stress can hamper focus and cause a drop in mental energy, such that you may become angry or confused. You may find that your musculoskeletal system has tightened up or your digestion has been affected in some small way.

Once you have actually dealt with the interruption, you now have to get back on track with your previous task. Getting back on track is a non-trivial matter. You may find you are still distracted

Appendix A: Tips for Organizing To Deal with Overload

and not able to truly concentrate. The average amount of time *per interruption* to get back on track is 15-20 minutes (according to Edward M. Hallowell, a psychiatrist and author of *Crazybusy: Overstretched, overbooked, and about to snap!*[397]) The more complex the task, the longer you take to get back on track. Some people try to cope with constant interruptions by multitasking, but from an evolutionary perspective, the brain is not designed to multitask. What we speak of as multi-tasking is actually multi-switching from one context to another to another. Multi-switching can increase the amount of time you take to finish a task by four times what you would take to simply concentrate on the task fully.

In 2008, a PhD candidate at Chapel Hill wrote one of the first software programs enabling people to shut off their access to the internet for up to eight hours called Freedom. Now many programs including Freedom, Anti-Social, Cold Turkey and others for all types of systems can accomplish the same thing, so find the one that works for you.

OHIO Rule

Know that the OHIO rule, or "Only Handle It Once," doesn't actually work in all situations. What works better is knowing what to do with your incoming item, because papers and email arrive, the telephone rings, and people drop by all day long. Practice instead the two-minute rule: handle the easy interruptions right away and get rid of them to unclutter your brain for more important tasks. Professors especially need to let go of the idea that once handled appropriately, an item will not need to be revisited. Academia runs on multiple iterations.

Email

Once touted as a way to simplify asynchronous communication, email is now a major source of information overload. Cleaning out your mailboxes can be well worth the time. Remember that what you say when responding to an email is far more important than the email coming in, so feel free to delete incoming mail once you have answered. You can delete big chunks by simply going back and saying, "I am getting rid of all emails more than three years old." Chances are, nothing is worth keeping further back as all manner of things will have changed since those emails were sent. If you can get your inbox down to 25 to 100 messages, you can keep 10,000 in sent mail. What you see when you log in is what overloads the brain.

As a professor, you may want to consider including a policy about when and how students may contact you in any syllabus. Creating a standard signature line with contact information, and including a note that, "Emails will be answered in the order received within 48 hours," or whatever time period feels most comfortable to you, can also be worthwhile. Just because someone wants an immediate answer does not mean you have to provide it. Returning telephone calls and answering texts immediately are unnecessary as well. Remember the old saying, "Lack of planning on your part does not constitute an emergency on my part."

Calendar

Keep only one calendar. You can always print out your electronic calendars for your records, but make sure you have a calendar with you at all times. Use the same calendar to schedule personal appointments like the doctor as well as professional appointments like department meetings. That way you will not overbook yourself. Make sure you include estimated travel time when scheduling your appointments. Some departments share calendars of faculty with staff, so if you do not want items to be shared, just mark the time as "busy." Many families with multiple schedules to juggle now use Google calendar. Consider what information you are willing to share with staff and family and make sure you know who has the authority to edit appointments.

Backups

Remember the "3-2-1 rule": Backup on your computer, on your external hard drive, and somewhere externally in the cloud. In other words, you should have at least three copies of your data, storing the copies on two different media, and keeping one backup copy offsite. If you are lucky enough to work for a large institution, the information technology people may do this for you with an overnight backup process. Some people also keep separate files on flash drives as another form of backup for items they are currently working on like articles or books, in case the place they happen to be working does not have good cloud access.

Tickler file

Here are four steps system for creating a simple hard copy file tickler system that will help you get and stay on track with all your tasks:

1. Get 43 *hanging* files.
2. Number the first set of regular file folders from 1-31, representing each day of the month.
3. Label each remaining handing file by month, January through December.
4. Place the (1-31) numbered folders together in the filing system (cabinet, drawer, portable box). An easy way to do this is to place dates 1-3 in first hanging file, place 3-5 in second hanging file folder. You may want to place days 28-31 in one hanging file folder, so you don't have just one file in a hanging folder by itself. Next, place the monthly folders together, behind the folders numbered 1-31 in the same file.

Add additional files such as "Next Year," "Waiting on Response," "Someday/Maybe," or any other time category useful to you after the individual months. "Next Year" is a great place to put those flyers for a conference when you haven't decided whether or not to attend. "Waiting on Response" is a wonderful way to get pieces of paper that are literally waiting for someone else to do something or get back to you off your desk. Instead of rifling through your desk to find the note you wrote to yourself on a post-it or an inquiry letter, you have just one place to look for that kind of stuff and you can quickly respond when someone calls you back with needed information. Make sure you look periodically at the "Waiting" file so things you are waiting on do not fall through the cracks. "Someday/Maybe" is a great place to put your dreams such as articles on a vacation hiking in Scotland or radio equipment you think you might want to buy eventually.

This tickler file system is a simple reminder scheme to get things done when needed. You will always be rotating through the days, though the months will remain in the same order in the file. To get started, if today is the 19th day of the month, the number 19 folder should be the first folder

Appendix A: Tips for Organizing To Deal with Overload

in the file. At the beginning of each day pull out the day file, remove them and process the contents (you may have things like agendas or meeting notes for follow up in the folder; it doesn't matter what—this is your system, so use the reminders that work for you). When you are finished with the day, move the folder to the back of the day files. Now, the first file folder you see when you open it up should be 20. And so on. The day files will always be two months at a time on rotation. In this example, if you start your file rotation on day 19 in the month of April, days numbered 1-18 will now be used for May.

On the last day of each month, pull out the monthly folder for the next month and place the contents of that folder into the daily numbered folders. This system can be used immediately to quickly tame a pile of papers. Remember, you do not have to put anything in the tickler file if there is nothing special you need to remember to do that particular day. You can adapt this system to electronic calendars if you like, but the object is to keep things as simple as possible.

Incoming items

Next, you need to know what to do with every incoming item. My acronym for the five decisions you must make with every incoming item, whether voicemail, email, snail mail, things that people ask you to do, or things you ask yourself to do, is **TAFFY**. **TAFFY** stands for the following steps, which you do in exactly the order listed:

> **T** - Throw away. Rid yourself first of whatever you can, whether you tossing it in the trash, shred it, or recycle it. Purging whatever you don't need immediately leaves less for you to deal with.
>
> **A** – Assign tasks. Whatever you can, to whomever you can. Do you have an assistant who can do something when your time is better used elsewhere? Can you hire someone to do what you would be better served not doing, like data entry of basic information? Ask yourself, "What is my time worth?"
>
> **F** - Fast action. If it's possible to take care of something within two minutes, that constitutes fast action. Fast action could mean acting quickly to respond to a request like responding "yes" or "no" to an email about whether or not you can attend a meeting. Get it out of your inbox and delete the incoming message. Another example can be calling back someone who has requested a phone number. This requires some discernment on your part: you need to decide if the person you are calling is likely to want to talk or will be happy just to get the requested information. For many such requests, you can simply text a reply.
>
> **F** - File for reference. Move whatever you can farther away from you so that it is not cluttering up your space and mind. Professors get a lot of books that they may want to review at a later time, and those can easily be placed on a bookshelf. Other examples include notebooks from mandatory institutional trainings or seminar notebooks.
>
> **Y** - *You* must act now. You have now tossed, assigned, taken fast action, or filed the incoming items. You are now "it." You must ask yourself, "*What* do I need to do and *when* do I need to do it?" If an external deadline exists, make your personal deadline far enough

in advance of the due date to allow the time to get it finished; if no external deadline exists, figure out a realistic deadline for yourself that will motivate you to get whatever action needs to be done in a timely fashion. Get that action onto your calendar or into your tickler file for the appropriate start date.

See the graphic below to more easily understand the cycle of decisions for incoming items, tools you want to keep nearby your "command central" space, and rules for tossing items into the trash.

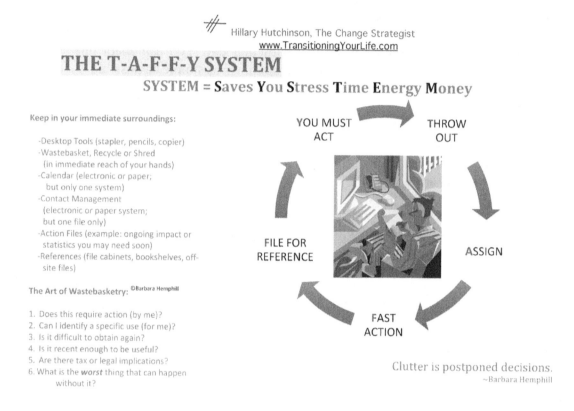

The real challenge of using a tickler file system of any kind is figuring out what is truly important to do, and setting your priorities, without getting sucked into questions of existential angst. Always ask yourself:

- Should I really be doing this activity?
- If I should, how can I do it more efficiently?

I worked with an academic librarian once. Talk about overloaded with information. She couldn't even see her desk when she called me. I am not kidding about this: she sometimes could not locate her cell phone under the piles of paper. She contacted me because she was up for promotion from

Appendix A: Tips for Organizing To Deal with Overload

Assistant Professor to Associate Professor and she needed to start preparing her promotion package.

Those of you who have gone through this process know how much you have to do: you need to gather up the evidence that you have been a good teacher, show published articles in peer-reviewed journals in your field, show you have provided some sort of community service, show evidence of collegiality by serving on departmental committees when needed, and in her case, staff the reference desk where any kind of interesting request from "How do I cite 'real' newspapers?" to "Do you have a copy of a treaty with a local Native American tribe?" can land in your lap. In other words, you can't count on time at the reference desk to get any of your own work done, which in her case included reviewing and ordering books based on both recommendations of faculty and reviews of those books in academic journals.

Her very first step? Clear the clutter, set up a 1-31 tickler file, and begin the process of scheduling appointments with herself to get her work done. This led to beginning the process of learning new habits so that she could create an actual physical notebook of her accomplishments for her promotion package with 100% less stress. Sometimes she even printed out email requests and responses to show how she had served the institution and her profession while on the reference desk. The end result was an easily presented case that won her promotion.

Procrastination Issues Related to Organizing

Think you are the only one with procrastination problems? Surprise, it turns out you are merely human. But as an academic, you may have higher and more unrealistic expectations of yourself than other people have of themselves. The truth is that *everyone procrastinates*, and sometimes the act of procrastination means a problem solves itself. This result can reinforce our tendency to procrastinate, though sometimes the opposite is true: the problem becomes larger and we have now set ourselves up for failure. Think about waiting until the last minute to start writing a big paper. Doing it in small chunks all along the way to the deadline makes it manageable. Not so true when facing a deadline only 24 hours away.

George Akerlof, an economist, tells a story on himself about how he could not get a box mailed to a friend in the United States when he was in India. Every day he would promise himself that he would do it, but then would find a host of reasons why not: the mail was slow, the lines would be long, the box could get damaged. Eventually, another friend literally hand carried the box for him across the ocean, so that he never did have to deal with mailing it.[398]

This experience led Akerlof to speculate about the nature of procrastination in a now classic paper he called "Procrastination and Obedience."[399] He argued that it revealed something important about the limits of rational thinking and that it could teach useful lessons about phenomena as diverse as substance abuse and savings habits. Since his essay was published, the study of procrastination has become a significant field in academia, with philosophers, psychologists, and economists all weighing in. Academics, who work for long periods in a self-directed fashion, may be especially prone to putting things off. Surveys have suggested that the vast majority of college students procrastinate,[400] and articles in the literature of procrastination often allude to the author's own problems with finishing any given piece. In *Procrastination: Why you do it, what to do about it*, psychologists Jane B. Burka and Lenora M. Yuen discussed procrastination in two ways: understanding why we procrastinate and outlining how to overcome it.[401] Although the book was published in 2008, it's still a quick but useful read; the writing is clear and the descriptions, precise.

Fear is the basis of all procrastination including fear of failure, of success, and of "losing the battle." Some of us procrastinate to show that *we're* in control of the situation. "You can't MAKE me do this!" we silently say, as we refuse to comply with a demanding colleague, an unappreciative boss or department chair, a nagging spouse, or even, somewhat ridiculously, an empty gas tank. The cures in the second half of Burka and Yuen's book are realistic. You didn't start procrastinating overnight, and you're not going to quit overnight either. The authors recommend starting a 2-week program using these key techniques:

- *Make goals that are observable.* Use a mental movie camera to truly "picture yourself" doing something specific. Instead of setting the goal to be "less overwhelmed," picture yourself mailing out 10 resumes to prospective employers.
- *Be specific.* Not "organize my life," but "go through one file drawer and discard unneeded papers."
- *Take small steps.* Writing down a goal can help you get a more realistic timeline - sometimes longer than you guessed, other times shorter than you had feared.
- *Beware of choice points.* These serve as a crossroads between success and sabotage. You finally call that client, but she's away on vacation. Take the next step, instead of giving up (and falling into the old habit which you're trying to break).
- *Reward yourself.* Many people procrastinate because they feel they deserve to suffer, to struggle, to stagnate. See yourself as the success you are trying to become.
- *Remember.* "*It doesn't have to be perfect; it just has to be done!*" It's better to get the holiday cards sent, rather than to delay them until you can personalize each one. One I like to use with clients is, "A good dissertation is a finished dissertation."

Summary

In summary, organizing helps you prioritize your tasks, lessen your stress, and enhance the probability that you will procrastinate less. Recognize that overload is now a natural state. With awareness, you can begin organizing by anticipating some of the major obstructions you may encounter, like resistance to throwing anything away or wanting to procrastinate because maybe the problem will go away. You can set some simple systems into place to help yourself: email purges, one calendar only, a tickler file system, and basic backups for your file materials.

APPENDIX B: LIST OF WORKSHEETS AND SAMPLE DOCUMENTS

Here are the links where you may download the worksheets and sample documents found in the previous pages:

Worksheets and Sample Documents PDF Version [https://www.transitioningyourlife.com/wp-content/uploads/2019/02/WORKSHEETS-AND-SAMPLE-DOCUMENTS-PDF-Version-2019-1-30.pdf]

1. Action Words for Cover Letters and CVs Worksheet
2. Application Tracking for Job Sources Worksheet
3. Class Preparation Worksheet
4. Conference Attendance Worksheet
5. Confidence Worksheet
6. Considerations in Applying for a Full-time Academic Job Worksheet
7. Considering a Job Offer worksheet
8. Considering an Adjunct Job Worksheet
9. Cover Letter Checklist Worksheet
10. Cover Letter Planning Worksheet
11. Cover Letter Worksheet
12. CV Checklist Worksheet
13. CV Worksheet
14. Elevator Speech Worksheet, Part 1
15. Elevator Speech Worksheet, Part 2
16. Equity and Diversity Statement Worksheet
17. General Job Search Preparation Worksheet
18. How Long To Look for a Faculty Job Worksheet
19. Imposter Syndrome Worksheet
20. Interview Checklist
21. Interview—Basic Questions Worksheet
22. Interview—In-depth Questions Related to Other Duties
23. Interview—In-depth Questions Related to Research
24. Interview—In-depth Questions Related to Teaching
25. Interview—In-depth Questions Related to Writing
26. Interview—On-campus Worksheet
27. Interview—Videoconference (Skype, Zoom, or Other Service) and Telephone Considerations Worksheet
28. Job Log Face Sheet-Optional
29. Job Log for Academic Position Search—Worksheet
30. Job Search Timeline Worksheet
31. Key Competencies or Contributions to Research Worksheet

32. Month by Month "To Do" List Worksheet
33. Negotiating Your Job Offer Worksheet
34. Negotiation Checklist Worksheet
35. Networking/Connecting Worksheet
36. Postdoctoral Position Worksheet
37. Publishing—Continued Publishing Plan Worksheet
38. Publishing—Dissertation and Post-PhD Publishing Plan Worksheet
39. Publishing—Pre-PhD Plan Worksheet Coursework, Comps, or Preliminary Research
40. Publishing—Pre-PhD Plan Worksheet from Presentations and Conferences
41. Recommendation Letter Worksheet
42. Recommendations Worksheet
43. Research Statement Worksheet
44. Research Talk Questions & Answers Worksheet
45. Research—Most Important Considerations to Me Worksheet
46. Sample Academic Cover Letter
47. Sample Job Log for Academic Position Search
48. Sample On-campus Interview Schedule
49. Sample Postcard/Email Application Follow-up Worksheet
50. Sample Publishing—Publication Plan Worksheet
51. Sample Recommendation Letter
52. Self-care Worksheets
53. Syllabus Worksheet
54. Teacher Evaluation Form (Your Own) Worksheet
55. Teaching Philosophy Statement Worksheet
56. Telling My Story Worksheet
57. Transferable Skills Acquired or Sharpened in Graduate School Worksheet
58. Website Evaluation Worksheet

ENDNOTES

All URLs are current as of September 1, 2018

Part 1: Job Search Overview

[1] Woolston, C. (2017, October 25). Graduate survey: A love-hurt relationship. *Nature, 550,* 549-552. doi:10.1038/nj7677-549a Available online at https://www.nature.com/naturejobs/science/articles/10.1038/nj7677-549a?WT.mc_id=FBK_NJOBS_1709_2017GRADSURVEY_PORTFOLIO This article gives a lot more information than we have cited here. It's well worth reading in its entirety.

[2] The Commission on the Future of Graduate Education. (2010). *The path forward: The future of graduate education in the United States* [PDF], p. 2. Princeton, NJ: The Commission on the Future of Graduate Education. Find this report at http://www.fgereport.org/ Data cited are from Figure 2. Doctoral completion rate, by field and number of years.

[3] American Association of University Professors. (n.d.). *Background facts on contingent faculty.* Available at https://www.aaup.org/issues/contingency/background-facts

[4] For more about brutality in higher education, see Prescod-Weinstein, C. (2017, September 7). The truth about colleges and universities. *Medium* [Blog]. Available at https://medium.com/@chanda/the-truth-about-colleges-and-universities-3d774bf5a36f

[5] Cited in Flaherty, C. (2017, November 16). Paying for the job search. *Inside Higher Ed, #News.* Available at https://www.insidehighered.com/news/2017/11/16/fordhams-english-department-adds-grants-job-search-expenses-those-finishing?utm_source=Inside+Higher+Ed&utm_campaign=73294cf63e-DNU20171116&utm_medium=email&utm_term=0_1fcbc04421-73294cf63e-197426605&mc_cid=73294cf63e&mc_eid=9ab110d608

[6] See more on the advantages of working at teaching colleges in Lang, J. M. (2016, October 30). Why you might love working at a teaching college. *The Chronicle of Higher Education, Advice.* Available at http://www.chronicle.com/article/Why-You-Might-Love-Working-at/238204

[7] For more on search committees, see Smith, Z. A. (2016, October 31). The best search committee. *The Chronicle of Higher Education, Advice.* Available at http://www.chronicle.com/article/The-Best-Search-Committees/238207?cid=trend_au&elqTrackId=7affd7b19c2f43ab8eec9765911143ed&elq=9b5a7ce250ab49e9b01e394863d9c4f8&elqaid=11322&elqat=1&elqCampaignId=4399

[8] For more on factors, such as publications, that influence your chances of getting an interview, see Flaherty, C. (2017, September 11). Inside a search committee. *Inside Higher Ed, #News.* Available at https://www.insidehighered.com/news/2017/09/11/study-offers-window-what-search-committee-members-value-assessing-faculty-

candidates?utm_source=Inside+Higher+Ed&utm_campaign=552ba5b809-DNU20170911&utm_medium=email&utm_term=0_1fcbc04421-552ba5b809-197426605&mc_cid=552ba5b809&mc_eid=9ab110d608

[9] Jenkins, R. (2016, August 30). The community-college FAQ: The hiring cycle. *The Chronicle of Higher Education, Vitae* Available at https://chroniclevitae.com/news/1527-the-community-college-job-search-the-hiring-cycle?cid=at&utm_source=at&utm_medium=en&elqTrackId=3f0b162d45e84739bb3a3aff0446ddab&elq=97d4717ca235471caa38294c19c8668b&elqaid=10492&elqat=1&elqCampaignId=3942

[10] Jenkins, R. (2016, August 30). The community-college FAQ: The hiring cycle. *The Chronicle of Higher Education, Vitae* available at https://chroniclevitae.com/news/1527-the-community-college-job-search-the-hiring-cycle?cid=at&utm_source=at&utm_medium=en&elqTrackId=3f0b162d45e84739bb3a3aff0446ddab&elq=97d4717ca235471caa38294c19c8668b&elqaid=10492&elqat=1&elqCampaignId=3942

[11] Will teaching at a community college be a good fit for you? See Jenkins, R. (2015, October 26). Community colleges might not be for you. *The Chronicle of Higher Education, Advice* available at http://www.chronicle.com/article/Community-Colleges-Might-Not/233914

[12] See comment from Dr. Klotz. (2015, September 10). From R1 to CC: 3 things I wish I had known about community college careers. *Tenure, she wrote* [Blog]. Available at https://tenureshewrote.wordpress.com/2015/09/10/from-r1-to-cc-3-things-i-wish-i-had-known-about-community-college-careers/

[13] Jenkins, R. (2016, November 29). Community-college FAQ: How long before I get tenure? *The Chronicle of Higher Education, Vitae*. Available at https://chroniclevitae.com/news/1626-community-college-faq-how-long-before-i-get-tenure

[14] Dennihy, M. (2018, March 13). How to land a community college job. *Inside Higher Ed, #Career Advice*. Available at https://www.insidehighered.com/advice/2018/03/13/applying-community-college-faculty-position-opinion?utm_source=Inside+Higher+Ed&utm_campaign=23e6059cf7-CI20180104&utm_medium=email&utm_term=0_1fcbc04421-23e6059cf7-228329673&mc_cid=23e6059cf7&mc_eid=b84a633c3a
This article provides information about what community colleges are looking for.

[15] The numbers were constructed using the *Chronicle Vitae* job site in October 2017; numbers will vary depending on the date you construct your results. See *Chronicle Vitae*. (2018). Faculty & Research Jobs. *Chronicle Vitae*. Available at https://chroniclevitae.com/job_search?utf8=%E2%9C%93&job_search%5Bkeywords%5D=+&job_search%5Bposition_type%5D=1&job_search%5Blocation%5D=&job_search%5Bstart_date%5D=&job_search%5Binstitution_type%5D=&job_search%5Bemployment_type%5D=&job_search%5Bdistance_from_zip%5D=10&job_search%5Bzip_code%5D=

[16] Collins, G. (2017, October 23). No profit in Betty DeVos. *The New York Times, Opinion.* Available at https://www.nytimes.com/2017/10/27/opinion/betsy-devos-for-profit-colleges.html?emc=edit_th_20171028&nl=todaysheadlines&nlid=38011780

[17] Three key takeaways from the Government Accountability Office report released in 2017 detailing the characteristics of adjunct faculty members, were:

- New PhDs and academics under 40 are most likely to get non-tenure track jobs.
- Women hold 53 percent of positions off the tenure track.
- The GAO labeled many contract positions as "pseudo tenure track."

See June, A.W. (2017, November 21). 3 insights about the professoriate from a new federal report. *The Chronicle of Higher Education, Labor & Work-Life.* Available at https://www.chronicle.com/article/3-Insights-About-the/241841/?cid=db&elqTrackId=98b7858f2b5441c1a518aa019262667d&elq=629db2ce1dec4c5c866c6e9489bad663&elqaid=16817&elqat=1&elqCampaignId=7280

[18] Schuman, R. (2014, October 27). What's in a name? If it's 'Assistant Professor,' then beats me. *The Chronicle of Higher Education, Vitae.* Available at https://chroniclevitae.com/news/771-what-s-in-a-name-if-it-s-assistant-professor-then-beats-me This article includes some examples of the misleading ads.

[19] Cham J. (2017, March 1). A fake promotion? *PhD Comics* [Cartoon]. Available at http://www.phdcomics.com/comics.php?f=1927

[20] In this book, we use the terms *adjunct faculty* or a*djuncts* to refer to all these positions. An interesting article about the Australian term for these kinds of job, see Hare, J. (2016, 7-6). The explosion of 'casual' labor. *Inside Higher Ed, #News, #Teaching and Learning.* Available at https://www.insidehighered.com/news/2016/07/06/use-casual-adjunct-instructors-spreads-australia?utm_source=Inside+Higher+Ed&utm_campaign=d5cb16d025-DNU20160706&utm_medium=email&utm_term=0_1fcbc04421-d5cb16d025-197426605

[21] Gee, A. (2017, September 28). Facing poverty, academics turn to sex, work and sleeping in cars, ¶ 9. *The Guardian, Outside in America.* Available at https://www.theguardian.com/us-news/2017/sep/28/adjunct-professors-homeless-sex-work-academia-poverty

[22] Looser, D. (2017, March 20). Why I teach online. *The Chronicle of Higher Education, Advice.* Available at http://www.chronicle.com/article/Why-I-Teach-Online/239509

[23] Fredericksen, E. E. (2018). Why your college needs a VP for online learning. *The Chronicle of Higher Education.* Available at https://www.chronicle.com/article/Why-Your-College-Needs-a-VP/243021?cid=at&utm_source=at&utm_medium=en&elqTrackId=6c9969577ba44447b63bad9e8a71d7a1&elq=245a340a47e5425996e4c5ab5f32b366&elqaid=18708&elqat=1&elqCampaignId=8433

[24] Patton, C. (2015, July 27). Cluster hiring: Fad or best practice? *University Business.* Available at https://www.universitybusiness.com/article/cluster-hiring-fad-or-best-practice See also Attis,

D. (2016). Cluster hiring: One answer to the 'grand challenge' in university research. *EAB*, https://www.eab.com/research-and-insights/academic-affairs-forum/expert-insights/2016/cluster-hires

For sample clusters at Dartmouth, See Office of the Provost, Darmouth. (2017, March 15). Academic cluster initiative. *Dartmouth*. Available at http://www.dartmouth.edu/~provost/clusters.html

[25] Reis, R. (n.d.). Becoming a job candidate: The timetable for your search. *Tomorrow's Professor* [Blog]. Available at https://tomprof.stanford.edu/posting/1523

[26] For the seminal work, see Bridges, W. (2001). *The way of transition: Embracing life's most difficult moments.* New York, NY: Perseus Publishing.

[27] Cuddy, A. (2012, June). Your body language may shape who you are. *TED Global* [Video]. Available at https://www.ted.com/talks/amy_cuddy_your_body_language_shapes_who_you_are

[28] Access our meditative visualization on Creating Confidence at https://youtu.be/ilL_G7W2C-I.

[29] For a brief explanation of imposter phenomenon and the "Imposter Syndrome" with a list of print resources, see Clance, P. R. (2013). *Imposter phenomenon.* [Website] Available at http://paulineroseclance.com/impostor_phenomenon.html

[30] Young, V. (n.d.) 10 Steps to overcome the imposter syndrome. *Talent Development Resources* [Blog]. Available at http://talentdevelop.com/articles/10STOTIS.html

[31] Young, V. (2018). *Imposter Syndrome* home page. Available at http://impostorsyndrome.com/valerie-young/

[32] Young, V. (2011). *The secret thoughts of successful women: Why capable people suffer from the imposter syndrome and how to thrive in spite of it.* New York, NY: Crown Business. The "seven perfectly good reasons" are section titles between pages 28 to 43.

[33] Wong, K. (2018, June 12). Dealing with imposter syndrome when you're treated as an imposter. *New York Times, Smarter Living.* Available at https://www.nytimes.com/2018/06/12/smarter-living/dealing-with-impostor-syndrome-when-youre-treated-as-an-impostor.html

[34] Woolston, C. (2017, October 25). Graduate survey: A love-hurt relationship. *Nature, 550,* 549-552. doi:10.1038/nj7677-549a. Available online at https://www.nature.com/naturejobs/science/articles/10.1038/nj7677-549a?WT.mc_id=FBK_NJOBS_1709_2017GRADSURVEY_PORTFOLIO

[35] Gluckman, N. (2017, November 26). How a dean got over imposter syndrome—and thinks you can, too. *The Chronicle of Higher Education, The Chronicle Interview.* Available at https://www.chronicle.com/article/How-a-Dean-Got-Over-Impostor/241863

Endnotes

[36] Srivastava, S., Tullett, A., & Vazire, S. (hosts). (2017, June 10). Episode 3: No, you're the impostor. *The Black Goat* [Podcast]. Available at http://www.theblackgoatpodcast.com/posts/episode-3-no-youre-the-impostor/

[37] For more on this topic, see Katie, B. (n.d.). Who would you be without your story? *The Work of Byron Katie.* Available at http://thework.com/en. Her four questions to turn around your thinking on any given topic are available at http://thework.com/en/do-work#questions
The questions are:
1. Is it true?
2. Can you absolutely know that it's true?
3. How do you react, what happens, when you believe that thought?
4. Who would you be without the thought?
   Her instructions are to turn the statement around, and find at least three genuine, specific examples of how [the flip side] is true in your life.

[38] For PhD comics on imposter voices, see Cham, J. (2017, October 1). You're not an imposter. *PhD Comics* [Cartoon]. Available at http://phdcomics.com/comics.php?f=1975
and Cham, J. (2017, October 2). It's perfectly normal to feel like an impostor. *PhD Comics* [Cartoon]. Available at http://phdcomics.com/comics.php?f=1976

[39] Gilliland, M. (2015, February 9). Brilliant forecasting article from 1957!!! *SAS Institute* [Blog]. Available at https://blogs.sas.com/content/forecasting/2015/02/09/brilliant-forecasting-article-from-1957/

[40] *Academia Obscura.* (n.d.). Academia Obscura. *Academia Obscura* [Blog]. Available at http://www.academiaobscura.com/

[41] @Lego Academics. (n.d.). Lego Academics@Lego Academics. *Twitter.com.* Available at https://twitter.com/LegoAcademics

[42] Young, V. (2011). *The secret thoughts of successful women: Why capable people suffer from the imposter syndrome and how to thrive in spite of it,* p. 22. New York, NY: Crown Business.

[43] Hutchinson, H. (2017, October 16). Overcoming imposter syndrome (a visualization). *YouTube* [Video]. Available at https://youtu.be/Wb7jvXZQvRs.

[44] Leary M. R., Tate E. B., Adams, C. E., Allen, A. B., & Hancock J. (2007). Self-compassion and reactions to unpleasant self-relevant events: The implications of treating oneself kindly. *Journal of Personality and Social Psychology*, *92*(5), 887-904. Available at https://www.ncbi.nlm.nih.gov/pubmed/17484611 The "grandmother of compassion research," Kristin Neff, now has a website http://self-compassion.org/ with exercises based on her work. You can find a list of compassion resources there, too: http://self-compassion.org/the-research/ A workbook release is planned for August 2018 for Neff, K., & Germer, C. (2018). *The mindful self-compassion workbook: A proven way to accept yourself, build inner strength, and thrive.* New York, NY: The Guilford Press.

[45] You can see a list of Kristin Neff's research publications at http://self-compassion.org/the-research/

[46] Wong, K. (2017, December 28). Why self-compassion beats self-confidence. *The New York Times, Smarter Living*. Available at https://mobile.nytimes.com/2017/12/28/smarter-living/why-self-compassion-beats-self-confidence.html?smid=fb-nytimes&smtyp=cur&referer=http://m.facebook.com

Part 2: Staying on Top of Your Academic Job Search

[47] See *Academia Stack Exchange*, a question and answer website for academics; answers are voted up or down by users. Available at https://academia.stackexchange.com/

[48] Find the home page for *The Chronicle of Higher Education* at https://www.chronicle.com/

[49] The main page for creating a profile for academic job hunting is available at https://chroniclevitae.com/job_search/new?cid=UCHETOPNAV

[50] ChronicleVitae. Advertisement for *Academic Year Kickoff* September 2018 issue at http://results.chronicle.com/ayk18?elqTrackId=6D4A5B9359C5B991BF582119208CDCBF&elq=c069232a2f4d43eb8631bb7c4ff31f04&elqaid=19920&elqat=1&elqCampaignId=9281

[51] Find the home page for the *Higher Education Recruitment Consortium* at http://main.hercjobs.org/

[52] Find the home page for *Inside Higher Ed* at https://www.insidehighered.com/

[53] Find the home page for the *National Center for Faculty Development and Diversity* at https://www.facultydiversity.org/join
To access additional resources, you will have to join at http://www.facultydiversity.org/?page=resources

[54] Find the NCGDD Resources page at https://www.facultydiversity.org/resources

[55] Find the home page for *Times Higher Education (THE)* at www.timeshighereducation.com

[56] Find the jobs resource page for *THE Unijobs* at https://www.timeshighereducation.com/unijobs/en-us/

[57] Find the jobs resource page for the Modern Language Association (MLA) at https://www.mla.org/Resources/Career/Job-Information-List

[58] Find the jobs resource page for the American Anthropological Association (AAA) at http://careercenter.aaanet.org/jobs

[59] Find the jobs resource page for The Honor Society of Phi Kappa Phi at https://careers.phikappaphi.org/

[60] Find the jobs resource page for *ChronicleVitae* at https://chroniclevitae.com/job_search/new

[61] Find the jobs resource page for *Inside Higher Ed* at www.higheredjobs.com

Endnotes

[62] Find the jobs resource page for the *Academic Jobs Wiki* at http://academicjobs.wikia.com/wiki/Academic_Jobs_Wiki

[63] Find the jobs resource page for the *Academic Careers Online* at http://www.academiccareers.com/

[64] Find the information about Research Calls at https://www.researchcalls.com/

[65] For some articles and resources about working abroad and overseas teaching jobs, see University of Michigan. (n.d.). Certified and experience teachers: University level teaching abroad. Available at http://internationalcenter.umich.edu/swt/work/teach/certified-experienced-teachers/teaching-at-university-level.html

Yip, B. (2014, June 26). Working abroad: Is the grass greener? Six academics share their experiences of university life overseas. *THE, World University Rankings.* Available at https://www.timeshighereducation.com/features/working-abroad-is-the-grass-greener/2014086.article

English teaching jobs may be hard to come by in the US, but many can be found elsewhere. See:
Faktorovich, A. (2012, December 21). English faculty jobs abroad. *Inside Higher Education, #Career Advice, #Global.* Available at https://www.insidehighered.com/advice/2012/12/21/how-find-college-teaching-jobs-english-abroad-essay

Gibson, Scott T. (2016, May 19). Why new humanities Ph.D.s should leave the country. *The Chronicle of Higher Education, Advice.* Available at http://chronicle.com/article/Why-New-Humanities-PhDs/236528?cid=rclink

Hodapp, J. (2016, June 08). Why I started my faculty career in the Middle East. *The Chronicle of Higher Education, Advice.* Available at http://chronicle.com/article/Why-I-Started-My-Faculty/236724?cid=trend_au&elqTrackId=345041ebc1954b0c83c9e2713e03a81a&elq=d7d0a5f55dd441a2abc8b456b054f6ed&elqaid=9393&elqat=1&elqCampaignId=3313

[66] For guidance on how to determine whether you would qualify for this exclusion, see IRS. (n.d). Foreign earned income exclusion. *IRS.* Available at https://www.irs.gov/individuals/international-taxpayers/foreign-earned-income-exclusion

[67] Dowdall, J., & Pike, K. M. (2011). *Focus: Teaching abroad* [PDF]. Washington, DC: The Chronicle of Higher Education. Available at http://www.chronicle.com/items/biz/resource/ChronFocus_TeachingAbroad_i_v3.pdf

[68] Cathey, G. (n.d.). Recruiters account for 1 in 20 U.S. LinkedIn profiles [Blog]. *Boolean Black Belt-Sourcing/Recruiting.* Available at http://booleanblackbelt.com/2009/06/recruiters-account-for-1-in-20-us-linkedin-profiles/

[69] Sundberg, J. (n.d.). Top 10 linkedin groups job seekers must join. *The Undercover Recruiter* [Blog]. Available at http://theundercoverrecruiter.com/top-10-linkedin-groups-job-seekers-must-join/

[70] Surolia, M. (group owner). (n.d.). E-Recruitment Network. *LinkedIn*. Available at https://www.linkedin.com/groups/1774369/profile

[71] Shapiro, D. (2016, October 6). Now you can privately signal to recruiters you're open to new job opportunities. *LinkedIn* [Blog]. Available at https://blog.linkedin.com/2016/10/06/now-you-can-privately-signal-to-recruiters-youre-open-to-new-job

[72] A list of search firms provided by HigherEdJobs is available at https://www.higheredjobs.com/career/sitelistings.cfm

[73] The home page of The Babb Group is available at https://www.thebabbgroup.com/

[74] The home page Higher Education Jobs and Career Resources is available at https://jobs.diversejobs.net/

[75] The hiring page of The Hudson Group is available at http://www.hudsongrp.com/about-us.html

[76] The home page of Isaacson, Miller is available at https://www.imsearch.com/

[77] The home page of Opus Partners is available at http://www.opuspartners.net/about/introduction

[78] The "What We Do" page of Parker Executive Search is available at https://www.parkersearch.com/what-we-do

[79] The Higher Education page of Russell Reynolds Associates is available at http://www.russellreynolds.com/industries/higher-education

[80] The recruiting page of Shefrin & Associates is available at https://www.careerschoolconsulting.com/recruiting.html

[81] The "Who We Are" page for Vector Careers, explaining focus on educational recruiting, is available at http://www.vector-careers.com/about/

[82] The "Experience and Expertise in Education Recruitment" page for Witt/Kieffer is available at http://www.wittkieffer.com/practice-areas/higher-education/

[83] The search firm listing page for Academic 360 is available at http://www.academic360.com/resources/listings.cfm?DiscID=125

[84] GetFive Blog, The. (2017, May 9). How social media contacts can aid your job hunt. The GetFive Blog. Available at https://fiveoclockclub.com/blog/how-social-media-contacts-can-aid-your-job-

Endnotes

hunt/?inf_contact_key=9846214688b194bb7ffd6f44bd9db114d3dab04c79cd11d4a3bb591936a2badf

[85] Rosenberg, J. M. (2017, May 17). With many social media options, small businesses need focus. *USA Today, Money.* Available at https://www.usatoday.com/story/money/small-business/2017/05/17/many-social-media-options-small-businesses-need-focus/101804946/

[86] Barnes, N. G., & Lescault, A. M. (2013). College presidents out-blog and out-tweet corporate CEO's as higher ed delves deeper into social media to recruit students. *University of Massachusetts Dartmouth.* Available at http://www.umassd.edu/cmr/socialmediaresearch/collegepresidentsoutblog/

[87] Seamean, J., & Kane, H. T. (2013, October 21; updated December 6, 2017). How professors are using social media (INFOGRAPHIC). *Huffington Post, College.* Available at http://www.huffingtonpost.com/2013/10/21/professors-social-media_n_4137697.html

[88] Any habit-forming behavior engaged in to excess (overconsumption, obsession, use to the point of withdrawal from other activities) can be a sign of addiction.

[89] Augenbraun, E. (2014, August 22). How real a risk is social media addiction? *CBS News.* Available at http://www.cbsnews.com/news/how-real-a-risk-is-social-media-addiction/

[90] Jaschik, S., & Lederman, D., (Eds.). (2016, November 29). Editors' discussion of "The 2016 Inside Higher Ed Survey of Faculty Attitudes on Technology" [PDF], p. 48. Washington, DC: Inside Higher Ed. Previously available at https://www.insidehighered.com/audio/2016/11/29/2016-survey-faculty-attitudes-technology

[91] Cottom, T. M. (2017, July 7). Academic outrage: When the culture wars go digital. *Tressiemc*[Blog]. Available at https://tressiemc.com/essays-2/academic-outrage-when-the-culture-wars-go-digital/

[92] Roll, N. (2017, August 7). Adjuncts under fire? *Inside Higher Ed, #News.* Available at https://www.insidehighered.com/news/2017/08/07/after-anti-trump-tweets-fresno-state-removes-adjunct-professor-teaching-position?utm_source=Inside+Higher+Ed&utm_campaign=99be5c637d-DNU20170807&utm_medium=email&utm_term=0_1fcbc04421-99be5c637d-197426605&mc_cid=99be5c637d&mc_eid=9ab110d608

[93] Quintana, C. (2017, August 18). A professor says she was penalized for an instructor's tweet. *The Chronicle of Higher Education, Administration.* Available at http://www.chronicle.com/article/A-Professor-Says-She-Was/240960?cid=at&utm_source=at&utm_medium=en&elqTrackId=bd07c8faf8644020930aa04a9c1b8723&elq=6bfcf766e09b45a0a5c3aa6289768fe7&elqaid=15223&elqat=1&elqCampaignId=6489
For more examples, see Bateman, O. (2017, May 10). The young academic's Twitter conundrum. *The Atlantic.* Available at https://www.theatlantic.com/education/archive/2017/05/the-young-academics-twitter-

conundrum/525924/?elqTrackId=fb72e01b1a0049818ffb4749f3d750d1&elq=f6a183c4a6774622962ca99ab1cbc7c9&elqaid=13876&elqat=1&elqCampaignId=5789

[94] Quintana, C. (2017, June 28). Under fire, these professors were criticized by their colleges. *The Chronicle of Higher Education, Academic Freedom*. Available at http://www.chronicle.com/article/Under-Fire-These-Professors/240457?cid=db&elqTrackId=644d5122769f4c3da16cfc9e233b1cc3&elq=0c3533b9235f4ec2931b7ffa46540cb6&elqaid=15395&elqat=1&elqCampaignId=6577

[95] Cottom, T. M. (2017, July 7). Academic outrage: When the culture wars go digital, ¶ 18. *Goodreads* [Blog]. Available at https://www.goodreads.com/author_blog_posts/15394733-academic-outrage-when-the-culture-wars-go-digital

[96] Flaherty, C. (2016, January 28). Academics get real. *Inside Higher Ed, #News*, ¶ 1. Available at https://www.insidehighered.com/news/2016/01/28/hashtag-unites-adjuncts-and-tenure-line-professors-over-work-life-balance-and-other?utm_source=Inside+Higher+Ed&utm_campaign=06e63f4631-DNU20160128&utm_medium=email&utm_term=0_1fcbc04421-06e63f4631-197426605

[97] Carrigan, M. (2016). *Social media for academics*. London: SAGE Publications.

See also Rasmussen, D.N. (2012) *Social media for academics: A practical guide*. Oxford, England: Chandos Publishing.

[98] Altmetric. (n.d.) Who's saying what about your published work? *Altmetric for Researchers*. Available at https://www.altmetric.com/audience/researchers/.

Bookmarklet for Researchers available at https://www.altmetric.com/products/free-tools/bookmarklet/

[99] Else, H. (2017, September 7). The unbearable emptiness of Tweeting. *Inside Higher Ed, #News*. Available at https://www.insidehighered.com/news/2017/09/07/study-blasts-twitter-discussions-academic-journal-articles?utm_source=Inside+Higher+Ed&utm_campaign=b64cd21f52-DNU20170907&utm_medium=email&utm_term=0_1fcbc04421-b64cd21f52-197426605&mc_cid=b64cd21f52&mc_eid=9ab110d608 .

[100] Zephoria Digital Marketing. (2018). The Top 20 valuable Facebook statistics—updated May 2018). *Zephoria Digital Marketing*. Available at
https://zephoria.com/top-15-valuable-facebook-statistics/

Also, as most users know by now, Facebook has at least as many as 60 million accounts of which 3% are fake. See Nicas, J. (2018, April 25). How fake Mark Zuckerbergs scam Facebook users out of their cash. *NewYork Times, Technology* Available at https://www.nytimes.com/2018/04/25/technology/fake-mark-zuckerberg-facebook.html?nl=top-stories&nlid=38011780ries&ref=cta
Data mining is also a very real issue. See Granville, K. (2018, March 19). Facebook and Cambridge Analytica: What you need to know as fallout widens. *New York Times, Technology*.

Available at https://www.nytimes.com/2018/03/19/technology/facebook-cambridge-analytica-explained.html

[101] Jenkins, B. (2012, December 18). How are colleges using social media to attract students? *Social Media Week.* Available at http://socialmediaweek.org/blog/2012/12/how-are-colleges-using-social-media-to-attract-students/

[102] Bailey, J. (2015, May 13). Does Facebook really own your photos? *Plagiarism Today.* Available at https://www.plagiarismtoday.com/2015/05/13/does-facebook-really-own-your-photos/

[103] Omnicore. (2018). Total number of LinkedIn users (last updated 12/6/18). *Omnicore.* Available at https://www.omnicoreagency.com/linkedin-statistics/ See also Numbers of LinkedIn members from 1st quarter 2009 to 3rd quarter 2016 (in millions). *Statista.* Available at https://www.omnicoreagency.com/linkedin-statistics/

[104] For using linked in for an "alt-ac" search, see Polk, J. & Wood, L. M. (2018, May 30). Answers to questions about using LinkedIn for alt-ac job searches [Opinion]. *Inside Higher Ed, #Career Advice.* Available at http://insidehighered.com/advice/2018/05/30/answers-questions-about-using-linkedin-alt-ac-job-searches-opinion

[105] Statista. (2017). Number of monthly active Twitter users worldwide from 1st quarter 2010 to 4th quarter 2017 (in millions). *Statista.* Available at http://www.statista.com/statistics/282087/number-of-monthly-active-twitter-users/
See also Isaac, M. (2016, October 27). Twitter to cut jobs as it aims for a turnaround. *The New York Times, Technology.* Available at http://www.nytimes.com/2016/10/28/technology/twitter-job-cuts-q3-earnings.html?emc=edit_th_20161028&nl=todaysheadlines&nlid=38011780

[106] Rolling number constantly updated using Worldometers RTS algorithm. See Internet Live Stats. (Last accessed 2018, April 26). Twitter usage statistics, *Internet Live Stats* [Webpage]. Available at http://www.internetlivestats.com/twitter-statistics/

[107] Berlatsky, N. (2017, November 15). The dangers of tweeting live at conferences. *The Chronicle of Higher Education, Advice.* Available at https://www.chronicle.com/article/The-Dangers-of-Tweeting-at/241767?cid=db&elq=629db2ce1dec4c5c866c6e9489bad663&elqCampaignId=7280&elqTrackId=1bb882f595de4235b324cb894cc1e807&elqaid=16817&elqat=1

[108] McCall, L., et al. (2016, August). "What counts? Evaluating public communication in tenure and promotion." *Final report of The ASA Subcommittee on the evaluation of social media and public communication in sociology* [PDF]. Washington: DC American Sociological Association. Available at http://www.asanet.org/sites/default/files/tf_report_what_counts_evaluating_public_communication_in_tenure_and_promotion_final_august_2016.pdf

See also Flaherty, C. (2016, September 8). Tweeting your way to tenure. *Inside Higher Ed, #News.* Available at https://www.insidehighered.com/news/2016/09/08/sociologists-discuss-how-departments-should-consider-social-media-activity-and-other?utm_source=Inside+Higher+Ed&utm_campaign=2a3591a4bf-DNU20160908&utm_medium=email&utm_term=0_1fcbc04421-2a3591a4bf-197426605&mc_cid=2a3591a4bf&mc_eid=9ab110d608

[109] Priem, J. (2011, November 30). Study: How many scholars use Twitter, and how do they use it? *GitHub*. Available at https://github.com/jasonPriem/5uni-twitter-study This study looked at Twitter use habits, if any, of 8,826 scholars from five diverse universities in the early days of the service to determine if Twitter use was just a fad. The 2011 poster can be found here: http://jasonpriem.com/self-archived/5uni-poster.png

[110] Wright, G. (2015, September 2). The weird and wonderful world of academic Twitter. *Times Higher Education (THE)*. Available at https://www.timeshighereducation.com/blog/weird-and-wonderful-world-academic-twitter

[111] Scoble, J. (n.d.). Twitter for academics [Blog]. *The Online Academic*. https://onlineacademic.wordpress.com/social-media-for-academics/twitter-for-academics/

[112] Gulliver, K. (2012, May 9). 10 commandments of Twitter for academics. *Chronicle of Higher Education, Advice*. Available at http://chronicle.com/article/10-Commandments-of-Twitter-for/131813/

[113] The home page for *Academic Jobs Wiki* is available at http://academicjobs.wikia.com/wiki/Category:AcademicJobSearch

[114] The home page for *Glassdoor* is available at https://www.glassdoor.com/index.htm

[115] The home page for *Idealist* is available at http://www.idealist.org/

[116] Chronicle Data. (n.d.). Search and explore faculty, staff, and adjunct salary data at thousands of colleges, updated 2016-17. *Chronicle Data*. Available at https://data.chronicle.com/?cid=db&elqTrackId=47479980173849dc8ecf2cd1e398f78e&elq=2785b54cb0af4a0ba7428ed876c19833&elqaid=18566&elqat=1&elqCampaignId=8341

[117] AAUP. (2018, March-April). *The annual report on the economic status of the profession, 2017-18* [PDF]. Washington, DC: American Association of University Professors. Available at https://www.aaup.org/report/annual-report-economic-status-profession-2017-18

[118] NCES. (2016). Digest of education statistics. *National Center for Education Statistics, US Department of Education*. Available at https://nces.ed.gov/programs/digest/d16/tables/dt16_316.50.asp. Please note that this site has changed its emphasis since 2016 to ElHi, and you may need to work harder to locate information on higher education in this database.

[119] O'Donnell, M., Bayer, J.B., Cascio, C. N., & Falk, E. B. (2017, January). Neural bases of recommendations differ according to social network structure. *Social Cognitive and Affective Neuroscience*. doi: 10.1093/scan/nsw158. Available at https://www.ncbi.nlm.nih.gov/pmc/articles/PMC5390723/

[120] Statista. (2016). *Average number of Facebook friends of users in the United States in 2016. Statista.* Available at http://www.statista.com/statistics/232499/americans-who-use-social-networking-sites-several-times-per-day/

[121] Agre, P. (2003, June 11). *Networking on the network: A guide to professional skills for PhD students.* Department of Information Studies, University of California, Los Angeles. Available at http://web.archive.org/web/20050310011804/http:/polaris.gseis.ucla.edu/pagre/network.html#section3

[122] Kwok, R. (2013, February 6). Communication: Two minutes to impress. *Nature, 494,* 137-138. doi:10.1038/nj7435-137a. Available at http://www.nature.com/naturejobs/science/articles/10.1038/nj7435-137a

[123] Kwok, R. (2013, February 6). Communication: Two minutes to impress, ¶ 2. *Nature, 494,* 137-138. doi:10.1038/nj7435-137a. Cecilia Seixas's speech as quoted in Kwok's article.

Archives from the previous ASCB Elevator Speech Contest with more examples are available at http://www.ascb.org/tag/elevator-speech/

[124] Fleischman, J. (2016, January 7). Clever metaphor tops ASCB elevator speech contest. *The American Society for Cell Biology* [Blog]. Available at http://www.ascb.org/blog/clever-metaphor-lands-the-prize-at-ascbs-2015-elevator-speech-contest/ This page also has links to some of the most recent contestants' elevator speech videos explaining research.

[125] Work It Daily. (n.d.) Turn frustration into careers. *Work It Daily.* Available at https://www.workitdaily.com/ An index on networking for *Work It Daily* is available at https://www.workitdaily.com/?s=networking

[126] LinkedIn. (2013). *How to network on LinkedIn* [PDF]. Sunnyvale, CA: LinkedIn. Available at https://university.linkedin.com/content/dam/university/global/en_US/site/pdf/TipSheet_NetworkingonLinkedIn.pdf

[127] Hankel, I. (2016). 8 networking tips for PhDs to advance their careers. *Cheeky Scientist* [Blog]. Available at http://cheekyscientist.com/8-networking-tips-for-phds-to-advance-their-careers/

[128] Ryan, Liz. (2013, October 16). Frustrating job search? Try a pain letter. *LinkedIn.* Available at https://www.linkedin.com/pulse/20131016170330-52594-frustrating-job-search-try-a-pain-letter/

[129] Human Workplace. (n.d.) Ready to get your career and/or your job search moving? *Human Workplace.* The membership page is available at https://humanworkplace.com/premium-membership/

[130] Lynch, L. (2008). *Smart networking: Attracting a following in person and online.* New York, NY: McGraw-Hill Education.

[131] Ferrazzi, K. (2014). *Never eat alone: And other secrets to success, one relationship at a time* (expanded and updated). New York, NY: Crown Publishing.

[132] Weir, M. (2009). *Confessions of an introvert: The shy girl's guide to career, networking and getting the most out of life.* Naperville, IL: Sphinx Publishing.

[133] Cain, S. (2013). *Quiet: The power of introverts in a world that can't stop talking.* New York, NY: Broadway Books.

[134] Carnegie, D. (1936; reissued 1998). *How to win friends & influence people.* New York, NY: Pocket Books, Simon and Schuster.

[135] Buzan, T. (n.d.). Mind mapping. *Tony Buzon* [Website]. Available at http://www.tonybuzan.com/about/mind-mapping/

[136] Ter Hoeve, A. (n. d.). Learn to create a mind map in word? Here's how! *Mind Maps Unleashed.* Available at https://mindmapsunleashed.com/learn-to-create-a-mind-map-in-word-heres-how Arjen ter Hoeve provides a free version of his uncluttered mind map template on this site.

[137] For a variety of mind map images, check out the following site: https://www.google.com/search?q=mind+map+images&oq=mind+map+image&aqs=chrome.0.0j69i57j0l4.2665j0j7&sourceid=chrome&ie=UTF-8&se_es_tkn=JqoJ4wG

[138] Mindjet home page is available at https://www.mindjet.com/

[139] XMind home page is available at http://www.xmind.net/

[140] Coggle home page is available at https://coggle.it/

[141] Whitaker, M. (2018, March 27). How to get the most out of a conference. *The Chronicle of Higher Education, Vitae.* Available at https://chroniclevitae.com/news/2025-how-to-get-the-most-out-of-a-conference?cid=VTEVPMSED1

[142] Martin, B. (2016, October 30). A title for your article. *Brian's Comments* [Blog]. Available at http://comments.bmartin.cc/2016/10/30/a-title-for-your-article/ Useful article for help to come up with a good title; title mentioned here is a real one.

[143] Burke, C. (1991). "Tulips, tinfoil and teaching: Journal of a freshman teacher." In C. Christensen, D. Garvin, & A. Sweet (Eds.). *Education for judgment: The artistry of discussion leadership* (pp. 38-49). Boston, MA: Harvard Business School Press.

[144] Poorman, M. (2017, April 11). Conferences: 'Adulting' for grad students. *Inside Higher Ed, #Blog.* Available at https://www.insidehighered.com/blogs/gradhacker/conferences-adulting-grad-students?utm_source=Inside+Higher+Ed&utm_campaign=5bea54615f-

DNU20170412&utm_medium=email&utm_term=0_1fcbc04421-5bea54615f-197624989&mc_cid=5bea54615f&mc_eid=6081602244

[145] Polk, J. (2018, June 4). Networking and staying in touch. *Beyond the professoriate* [Blog]. Available at https://mailchi.mp/beyondprof/advice-on-networking-at-conferences-and-keeping-in-touch?e=d7b5522a0c

[146] Hartshorn, J. (2017, November 14). Making conferences work for you. *University Affairs*. Available at https://www.universityaffairs.ca/career-advice/beyond-the-professoriate/making-conferences-work-career/?utm_source=Beyond+the+Professoriate&utm_campaign=336153b95c-EMAIL_CAMPAIGN_2018_06_04_04_49&utm_medium=email&utm_term=0_2768d8e051-336153b95c-216102081&mc_cid=336153b95c&mc_eid=d7b5522a0c

[147] Kelsky, K. (2015). *The professor is in: The essential guide to turning your Ph.D. into a job.* New York, NY: Three Rivers Press.

[148] AAUP. (2016, April). *AAUP handbook: Best practices for peer review* [PDF]. Washington, DC: American Association of University Professors. Available at http://www.aaupnet.org/resources/for-members/handbooks-and-toolkits/peer-review-best-practices

[149] Halley, B. (2017, February 5). The changing landscape of peer review. *Chronicle of Higher Education, Commentary.* Available at http://www.chronicle.com/article/The-Changing-Landscape-of-Peer/239111?cid=at&utm_source=at&utm_medium=en&elqTrackId=1717dc0c510949888a0254ec31a2d668&elq=87ac588a2c594e9eb0a4fa9f436786da&elqaid=12515&elqat=1&elqCampaignId=5103

[150] Harvard University. (2018). *Statement of policy in regard to intellectual property* (IP) (1975, updated through 2013) [PDF]. Boston, MA: Harvard Office of Technology Development. Available at http://otd.harvard.edu/faculty-inventors/resources/policies-and-procedures/statement-of-policy-in-regard-to-intellectual-property/

[151] Zandonella, C. (2001, April 1). Is it all just a pipe dream? *Nature, 410* (6830), 734-735. Zandonella quoted an anonymous scientist: "The project is going extremely well but we cannot publish our work because we have contracts that are proprietary. This is one of the reasons we are leaving academia." Article only available via subscription at https://www.nature.com/articles/35071183

[152] Flores, L. (2017, January 24). Writing a book proposal. *The Chronicle of Higher Education, Vitae.* Available at https://chroniclevitae.com/news/1677-writing-a-book-proposal?cid=pm&utm_source=pm&utm_medium=en&elqTrackId=af82c4612e524ce1a413273bde732645&elq=14005b01df20427ca61764b9af7a9adf&elqaid=12274&elqat=1&elqCampaignId=4982 Lori Flores is an assistant professor of history at Stony Brook University.

[153] Flaherty, C. (2017, August 23). Should grad students publish? *Inside Higher Ed, #News.* Available at https://www.insidehighered.com/news/2017/08/23/renewed-debate-over-whether-

graduate-students-should-publish This article was reproduced at Rick Reis's Stanford University blog, *Tomorrow's Professor*, Message Number 1598, https://tomprof.stanford.edu/posting/1598

A more recent article asserts publication is now required for graduate students to be taken seriously on the job market. See Kafka, A.C. (2018, May 30). Another sign of a tough job market: Grad students feel bigger push to publish. *The Chronicle of Higher Education, Graduate Students*. Available at https://www.chronicle.com/article/Another-Sign-of-a-Tough-Job/243536?cid=db&elqTrackId=8379adbf5a9542b2936b6d679c33fbc2&elq=80cda77f377f486d8f8dba5b1a465808

See also Velleman, J. D. (2017, July 31). The publication emergency (a guest post by J. David Velleman). *Daily Nous* [Blog]. Available at http://dailynous.com/2017/07/31/publication-emergency-guest-post-j-david-velleman/

[154] Rees, J. (2016, July 21). Get your manuscript out! ¶ 9 *The Chronicle of Higher Education, Vitae*. Available at https://chroniclevitae.com/news/1492-get-your-manuscript-out

[155] AAUP. (2017, March-April). *Visualizing change: The annual report on the economic status of the profession, 2016-17* [PDF]. Washington, DC: Academe. Available at https://www.aaup.org/report/visualizing-change-annual-report-economic-status-profession-2016-17 The definition given in the text is the definition used in this report.

See also AAUP. (2018, March-April). *The annual report on the economic status of the profession, 2017-18* [PDF]. Washington, DC: Academe. Available at https://www.aaup.org/sites/default/files/ARES_2017-18.pdf

[156] June, A. W., & Newman, J. (2013, January 4). Adjunct project reveals wide range in pay. *The Chronicle of Higher Education, Faculty*. Available at https://www.chronicle.com/article/Adjunct-Project-Shows-Wide/136439 This project was created by Joshua A. Boldt, a writing instructor in Georgia, who posted an on-line editable spreadsheet in February 2012.

[157] Flaherty, C. (2017, April 11). The more things change. *Inside Higher Ed, #News*. Available at https://www.insidehighered.com/news/2017/04/11/aaup-faculty-salaries-slightly-budgets-are-balanced-backs-adjuncts-and-out-state . Flaherty cited the AAUP report, Visualizing change: The annual report on the economic status of the profession, 2016-17.

[158] *Chronicle Data* is a searchable database for *The Chronicle of Higher Education* available at https://data.chronicle.com/

[159] Sanchez, C. (2013, September 22). The sad death of an adjunct professor sparks a labor debate. *NPR Education*. Available at https://www.npr.org/2013/09/22/224946206/adjunct-professor-dies-destitute-then-sparks-debate

[160] McKenna, L. (2015, September 24). The college president-to-adjunct pay ratio. *The Atlantic, Education*. Available at https://www.theatlantic.com/education/archive/2015/09/income-inequality-in-higher-education-the-college-president-to-adjunct-pay-ratio/407029/

Endnotes

[161] For salary information see Salary.com. (n.d.) Salary comparison: Unlock potential with the power of pay. *Salary.com*. Available at https://www.salary.com/ and

US Department of Labor, Bureau of Labor Statistics. (Last modified 2017, February 28). *US Department of Labor*. Available at https://www.bls.gov/bls/blswage.htm

[162] Brennan, J. (2015, April 30). Adjuncts: Highly paid per hour. *Bleeding Heart Libertarian* [Blog]. Available at http://bleedingheartlibertarians.com/2015/04/adjuncts-highly-paid-per-hour/ The writer, Jason Brennan, is a self-confessed Libertarian, and does not seem to take into account that the $3000 total earned for what he states is an average of 135 hours per course for class time, preparation time, and office hours does not even come close to the normal 2,000 hours worked by a 9-5 employee in the course of a year, so it's bit disingenuous to claim this is a livable wage.

[163] To search payale.com, see https://www.payscale.com/

[164] House Committee on Education and the Workforce Democratic Staff. (2014, January). *The just-in-time professor: A staff report summarizing eforum responses on the working conditions of contingent faculty in higher education*. [PDF]. Washington, DC: US House of Representatives. Available at http://democrats-edworkforce.house.gov/imo/media/doc/1.24.14-AdjunctEforumReport.pdf

[165] Kline, M. (2017, August 9). 5 Findings from CUPA-HR's 2017 healthcare benefits higher ed survey. *The Higher Ed Workplace Blog. CUPA-HR*. Available at https://www.cupahr.org/benefits-survey-findings/

[166] Adjunct Action, SEIU. (2013). *The high cost of adjunct living: Boston* [PDF]. Washington, DC: Service Employees International Union (SEIU). Available at http://campaign-media.seiumedia.net.s3.amazonaws.com/wp-content/uploads/2013/11/17694-White-paper-FINAL.pdf Unfortunately, most of the references are from 2013 or earlier.

[167] Adjunct Action, SEIU. (2013). *The high cost of adjunct living: Boston* [PDF]. Washington, DC: Service Employees International Union (SEIU). Available at http://campaign-media.seiumedia.net.s3.amazonaws.com/wp-content/uploads/2013/11/17694-White-paper-FINAL.pdf Unfortunately, most of the references are from 2013 or earlier.

[168] Flaherty, C. (2017, April 6). Where the faculty jobs are. *Inside Higher Ed, #News*. Available at https://www.insidehighered.com/news/2017/04/06/new-cupa-hr-study-looks-faculty-hiring-pay-chairs-and-adjuncts-and-more?utm_source=Inside+Higher+Ed&utm_campaign=002af6c135-DNU20170406&utm_medium=email&utm_term=0_1fcbc04421-002af6c135-197426605&mc_cid=002af6c135&mc_eid=9ab110d608

[169] Lang, J. M. (2017, January 8). How to prepare for a teaching career. *Chronicle of Higher Education, Advice*. Available at http://www.chronicle.com/article/How-to-Prepare-for-a-Teaching/238817?cid=wb&utm_source=wb&utm_medium=en&elqTrackId=0bd930f04e924e7a

99057170b057aec8&elq=d32926f3067a433c9c8791b3182515c9&elqaid=12052&elqat=1&elqCampaignId=4862

[170] A good resource for learning about online teaching is Boettcher, J. V., & Conrad, R. (2016). *The online teaching survival guide: Simple and practical pedagogical tips*, 2nd ed. San Francisco, CA: Jossey-Bass.

[171] Robison, S. (2013). *The peak performing professor*, p. 5. San Francisco, CA: Jossey-Bass.

[172] Tonelli, M. (2017, February 8). Job-market diaries: An archeology professor. *Chronicle of Higher Education, Vitae*. See more at: https://chroniclevitae.com/news/1710-job-market-diaries-an-archaeology-professor?cid=pm&utm_source=pm&utm_medium=en&elqTrackId=8bc8c737670b4193a9a0c2463c724593&elq=633a32c1e4784b0f9ad78dbb971b6b19&elqaid=12666&elqat=1&elqCampaignId=5179#sthash.TsYE3M6u.dpuf

Part 3: Organizing Your Job Search

[173] Allen, D. (2001). *Getting things done: The art of stress-free productivity*, New York, NY: Penguin Books. David Allen's well-known approach to organizing with online help. Available at http://gettingthingsdone.com/

[174] Conrad, N. (2011, February 7. Tickler file demonstration. *YouTube* [Video]. Available at https://www.youtube.com/watch?v=e-_Hl_Xaduc

[175] To find Asana software, go to https://asana.com/?utm_expid=.O7ONgeBRQr65MgeeutQ_6g.0&utm_referrer=https%3A%2F%2Fwww.google.com%2F To find Todolist software, go to https://en.todoist.com/ For a side by side comparison of the two, go to https://comparisons.financesonline.com/todoist-vs-asana

[176] Kendra and The Lazy Genius Collective. (2015-2018). How to bullet journal: The absolute ultimate guide. *The Lazy Genius Collective* [Blog]. Available at http://www.thelazygeniuscollective.com/blog/how-to-bullet-journal

[177] Kendra and The Lazy Genius Collective. (2015-2018). How to bullet journal: The absolute ultimate guide. *The Lazy Genius Collective* [Blog]. Available at http://www.thelazygeniuscollective.com/blog/how-to-bullet-journal

[178] Carroll, R. (Copyright 2013-2018) *How to bullet journal*. YouTube [Video]. Available at https://www.youtube.com/watch?v=fm15cmYU0IM&feature=youtu.be

[179] Kendra and The Lazy Genius Collective. (2015-2018). *#30: The Lazy Genius bullet journals* [Podcast]. Available at http://www.thelazygeniuscollective.com/lazy/bulletjournal?rq=bullet%20journal

[180] Kendra and The Lazy Genius Collective. (Copyright 2015-2018). How to bullet journal: The absolute ultimate guide. *The Lazy Genius Collective* [Blog].

Endnotes

http://www.thelazygeniuscollective.com/blog/how-to-bullet-journal?rq=bullet%20journal%20signifiers

[181] Kendra and The Lazy Genius Collective. (Copyright 2015-2018). 7 Bonus bullet journal lessons. *The Lazy Genius Collective* [Blog]. Available at http://www.thelazygeniuscollective.com/blog/bulletjournalessons

[182] Dropbox installation link is available at https://www.dropbox.com/install

[183] Evernote sign-up page to create an account is available at https://evernote.com/

[184] Google Drive page to begin setting up cloud-based storage is available at https://www.google.com/drive/

[185] The page to try out Text Expander for free, or to purchase access, is available at https://textexpander.com/?utm_source=bing&utm_medium=cpc&utm_campaign=keyword&utm_term=expander

[186] The home page for AutoHotKey is available at https://www.autohotkey.com/

[187] As quoted in Jones, J. A. (2016, May 13). The importance of reflection when learning technical skills, ¶ 4. *The Chronicle of Higher Education, ProfHacker*, available at http://chronicle.com/blogs/profhacker/the-importance-of-reflection-when-learning-technical-skills/62125?cid=pm&utm_source=pm&utm_medium=en&elqTrackId=b900f58b0d6144c89a3c6d8b5f4ba3f9&elq=316c51000f654925963c01ada36dbff0&elqaid=9057&elqat=1&elqCampaignId=3123

[188] The home page for Academic Jobs Wiki is available at http://academicjobs.wikia.com/wiki/Category:AcademicJobSearch

[189] Read, B. (2014, August 26). Who's getting tenure-track jobs? It's time to find out. *The Chronicle of Higher Education, Vitae*. Available at https://chroniclevitae.com/news/679-who-s-getting-tenure-track-jobs-it-s-time-to-find-out#sthash.tPZ3xLk0.dpuf

[190] The home page for *The Chronicle of Higher Education* is available at https://www.chronicle.com/

[191] *The Chronicle of Higher Education* job search website, now called *ChronicleVitae*, is available at https://chroniclevitae.com/job_search/new?cid=chenav

[192] ChronicleVitae. (2015). *Welcome to Vitae's jobTracker*. Available at https://jobtracker.chroniclevitae.com/ Accessing this page will redirect you to the *ChronicleVitae* Jobs site.

[193] Read, B. (ed.). (2015) *Higher ed soup to nuts: An exclusive booklet on academic career development*. [PDF]. Washington, DC: ChronicleVitae. Available for free at http://results.chronicle.com/advicebooklet?advicebooklet=AAA2014 This is a collection of previously published articles.

[194] The home page for *Inside Higher Ed* is available at https://www.insidehighered.com/

[195] The Virsatile PhD Career Finder page is available at http://versatilephd.com/phd-career-finder/ You may have to create a free account to access this information.

[196] The job listings are constantly updated and are loaded by either advertising institutions or by individuals thinking they may be of interest to the Versatile PhD community. Available at https://versatilephd.com/jobs/

Part 4: Your Academic Job Portfolio

[197] The home page for Interfolio's Dossier service is available at https://www.interfolio.com/dossier/

[198] Whitaker, M. (2017, October 11). The job market: Picking apart your application. *The Chronicle of Higher Education, Vitae*. Available at https://chroniclevitae.com/news/1920-the-job-market-picking-apart-your-application?cid=VTEVPMSED1

[199] The definition of prolegonmenon is available at https://www.google.com/search?q=Prolegomena&oq=Prolegomena&aqs=chrome..69i57j0j69i60j0l3.2292j0j7&sourceid=chrome&ie=UTF-8

[200] An example of cover letter builder software can be found at https://www.livecareer.com/cover-letter-builder

[201] Harvard University. (2017). *CVs and cover letters* [PDF]. Cambridge, MA: Harvard University, Office of Career Services. Available at https://ocs.fas.harvard.edu/files/ocs/files/gsas-cvs-and-cover-letters.pdf

[202] The Graduate College. (2014, June). *Cover letters for academic positions* [PDF]. Champaign, IL: The Graduate College: Career Development Office. Available at http://www.grad.illinois.edu/sites/default/files/pdfs/academiccoverletters.pdf

[203] Purdue University. (2011, September 21). *Academic cover letter sample*. West Lafayette, IN: Purdue University, OWL (Online Writing Lab). Available at https://owl.english.purdue.edu/owl/resource/639/02/

[204] University of California, San Francisco. (2105). Samples for academic positions [PDF]. San Francisco, CA: University of California, San Francisco, Office of Career and Professional Development. Available at https://career.ucsf.edu/grad-students-postdocs/career-planning/academic-jobs/applying/academic-samples

[205] Doyle, A. (2017, July 19). How to write an academic cover letter with examples. *The Balance Career, Job Searching*. Available at https://www.thebalance.com/how-to-write-an-academic-cover-letter-2060155

[206] In her article, Whitaker says 10-15% but we know of higher numbers from watching search committees. See Whitaker, M. (2017, October 11). The job market: Picking apart your application. *The Chronicle of Higher Education.* Available at https://chroniclevitae.com/news/1920-the-job-market-picking-apart-your-application?cid=VTEVPMSED1

[207] The home page for CV Maker is available at https://cvmkr.com/

[208] The home page for Your CV Builder is available at https://www.yourcvbuilder.com/

[209] The home page for Resumonk is available at https://www.resumonk.com/

[210] The free Android app is available through the Google Play [store website] at https://play.google.com/store/apps/details?id=fi.dntech.curriculumvitae

[211] The Pocket Resume App is available at www.pocketresume.net

[212] Kelsky, K. (2017, January 10). How to shorten your CV. *The Chronicle of Higher Education, Vitae.* Available at https://chroniclevitae.com/news/1662-how-to-shorten-a-cv?cid=pm&utm_source=pm&utm_medium=en&elqTrackId=dba01e31ff8044cbafe1cf4a56a479a1&elq=ad228f8f78134a2992b6bcc997ef3145&elqaid=12074&elqat=1&elqCampaignId=4873

[213] Thayler, A. (2017, February 9). No one is reading those reference letters. *The Chronicle of Higher Education, Vitae. Available* at https://chroniclevitae.com/news/1693-no-one-is-reading-those-reference-letters?cid=pm&utm_source=pm&utm_medium=en&elqTrackId=59c1995036fd495d87ada2aff219663c&elq=0c960d44f15548cda6109ccd6738579d&elqaid=12510&elqat=1&elqCampaignId=5101

[214] Some good books about constructing a syllabus are:
- Mills, B. J., Cohen, M. W., & O'Brien, J. G. (2009). *The course syllabus: A learning-centered approach*, 2nd ed. San Francisco, CA: Jossey-Bass
- Nilson, L. B. (2007). *The graphic syllabus and outcomes map: Communicating your course.* San Francisco, CA: Jossey-Bass
- Nilson, L. B. (2016). *Teaching at its best: A research-based resource for college instructors*, 4th ed. San Francisco, CA: Jossey-Bass
- Smith, R. M. (2014). *Conquering the content: A blueprint for online course design and development.* San Francisco, CA: Jossey-Bass
-

[215] The Open Syllabus Project. (n. d.). *The American Assembly, Columbia University.* Available at http://opensyllabusproject.org/

[216] McHendry, G. (2016, October 2). *Building an interactive syllabus version 2.0* [Blog]. George F. (Guy) McHendry, Jr. Available at http://www.georgefmchendry.com/single-post/2016/10/02/Building-an-Interactive-Syllabus-Version-20. Interactive Syllabus project available at https://interactivesyllabus.000webhostapp.com/index.html

[217] Currently 435 sample syllabi have been uploaded by participants. *Chronicle Vitae, Resources: Syllabi.* Available at https://chroniclevitae.com/resources/2-syllabi

[218] Lacy, K. (2016, November 14). Auditioning for the role of colleague: Why the content of your job talk matters less than how you handle the Q & A. *The Chronicle of Higher Education, Advice.* Available at http://www.chronicle.com/article/Auditioning-for-the-Role-of/238327?cid=gs&utm_source=gs&utm_medium=en&elqTrackId=afecadad6c3c41f698eadb06d5c6cca0&elq=81d778910b64443a88d2f2515ce1843f&elqaid=11432&elqat=1&elqCampaignId=4459

[219] For ideas about asking a class opinion questions to engage them, see Scott, D. J. (2011, May 29). Student opinions, class poll on leadership [Blog]. *The Man in China.* Available at http://www.themaninchina.com/Archive%20informal%20student%20opinion%20polls.htm

[220] This explanation of the equity and diversity statement is quoted from the University of California diversity statement and can be found on the UC San Diego website at http://facultydiversity.ucsd.edu/recruitment/index.html in the Recruitment section, ¶ 2.

[221] Golash-Boza, T. (2016, June 10). The effective diversity statement. *Inside Higher Ed, Career Advice.* Available at: https://www.insidehighered.com/advice/2016/06/10/how-write-effective-diversity-statement-essay

[222] Simmer, E. (2015, May 25). Example Statements Contributions to Diversity [PDF]. *University of California, Berkey, Human Resources.* Available at: https://ofew.berkeley.edu/sites/default/files/example_statements_contributions_to_diversity.pdf

[223] The Regents of the University of California, Davis campus. (2016, December 20). *Guidelines for writing a diversity statement.* Available at http://academicaffairs.ucdavis.edu/diversity/equity_inclusion/diversity_statements_writing.html

[224] Reilly, M. B. (2016, June 22). UC to request 'diversity and inclusion' statements of new faculty, staff job applicants. *University of Cincinnati, News* [Website]. Available at https://www.uc.edu/news/NR.aspx?id=23526

[225] Utz, R. (2017, January 18). The diversity question and the administrative-job interview. *The Chronicle of Higher Education, Advice.* Available at https://www.chronicle.com/article/The-Diversity-Questionthe/238914

[226] Teaching evaluations may become even more optional. Many institutions are beginning to recognize how inherently biased the answers are, particularly related to gender and field of study. See Flaherty, C. (2018, May 22). Teaching eval shake-up. *Inside Higher Ed, #News.* Available at https://www.insidehighered.com/news/2018/05/22/most-institutions-say-they-value-teaching-how-they-assess-it-tells-different-story?utm_source=Inside+Higher+Ed&utm_campaign=92984764da-DNU&utm_medium=email&utm_term=0_1fcbc04421-92984764da-197426605&mc_cid=92984764da&mc_eid=9ab110d608

Endnotes

[227] Matos, N. (2017, January 17). Authenticity and the job interview, ¶ 6. *The Chronicle of Higher Education, Vitae*. Available at https://chroniclevitae.com/news/1668-authenticity-and-the-job-interview?cid=at&utm_source=at&utm_medium=en&elqTrackId=1d2a35c90b6c43f9a30dbf85326f2938&elq=1c1b68f5c50a42f7b7eb31ff275d621f&elqaid=12177&elqat=1&elqCampaignId=4934#sthash.zLYLhuf7.dpuf

Part 5: Your Job Search Interviews

[228] Good articles on interviewing for academic job are:

Foti, R. J. (2009, March 19). Academic job interviews: Questions and advice [PPT]. *Roseanne J. Foti, Ph.D*. Available at https://vtechworks.lib.vt.edu/bitstream/handle/10919/72241/gsls_roseanne_foti_interviews.pdf?sequence=1 The slides on "Interviewing and Gender Differences" are especially interesting.

Vaillancourt, A. M. (2013, January 2). What search committees wish you knew. *The Chronicle of Higher Education, Advice*. Available at http://chronicle.com/article/What-Search-Committees-Wish/136399/?cid=at&utm_source=at&utm_medium=en

Schemmer, R., Seis, M., Cahn, S., & Johnson, M. D. (2012). Academic job interview [PDF]. *The Chronicle of Higher Education*. Available at https://my.vanderbilt.edu/gradcareer/files/2013/01/Academic_Interview_handout.pdf

Although the four articles linked here on the same PDF document are old, the basic advice and the sample questions remain relevant. At the time we assembled this list, the authors listed were all career development specialists in academia: Ruth Schemmer, Assistant Dean for Career Development; Mary Corbin Sies, Department of American Studies, University of Maryland, College Park; Steven M. Cahn, Professor of Philosophy, Graduate Center of the City of New York; and Mary Dillon Johnson, Director of Graduate-Career Services, Yale University.

[229] Dennihy, M. (2017, December 6). Strategies for a successful interview. *Inside Higher Ed, #Career Advice*. Available at https://www.insidehighered.com/advice/2017/12/06/eight-tips-strong-job-interview-opinion?utm_source=Inside+Higher+Ed&utm_campaign=fd7e3de187-DNU20171206&utm_medium=email&utm_term=0_1fcbc04421-fd7e3de187-197624989&mc_cid=fd7e3de187&mc_eid=6081602244

[230] The home page for Payscale is available at http://www.payscale.com/research/US/Country=United_States/Salary

[231] For an interesting essay on whether to be yourself in an interview or not, see Shuman, R. (2018, January 11). The academic apostate's guide to interviewing. *The Chronicle of Higher Education, Vitae*. Available at https://chroniclevitae.com/news/1978-the-academic-apostate-s-guide-to-interviewing?cid=VTEVPMSED1

[232] Brady, A., & Duncan, D. (2018, March 12). Smile, you're on camera. *Inside Higher Ed, #Career Advice*. Available at https://www.insidehighered.com/advice/2018/03/12/advice-

academics-preparing-video-interviews?utm_source=Inside+Higher+Ed&utm_campaign=23e6059cf7-CI20180104&utm_medium=email&utm_term=0_1fcbc04421-23e6059cf7-228329673&mc_cid=23e6059cf7&mc_eid=b84a633c3a

[233] Cuddy, A. (2012, June). Your body language may shape who you are. TED Global [Video]. Available at https://www.ted.com/talks/amy_cuddy_your_body_language_shapes_who_you_are

[234] McAllister, K. S., & Ruggill, J. S. (2010, January 15). The academic bestiary for the intrepid job seeker. *The Chronicle of Higher Education, Advice.* Available at http://www.chronicle.com/article/an-academic-bestiary-for-the/63478

[235] Whitaker, M. (2017, November 20). The job market: The campus interview. *The Chronicle of Higher Education, Vitae.* Available at https://chroniclevitae.com/news/1949-the-job-market-the-campus-interview?cid=VTEVPMSED1

[236] Pleiss, M. W. (2017, March 3). The art of the campus interview. *The Chronicle of Higher Education, Vitae.* Available at https://chroniclevitae.com/news/1720-the-art-of-the-campus-interview?cid=VTEVPMSED1

[237] Jenkins, R. (2018, February 20). What to expect at a community-college interview. *The Chronicle of Higher Education, Advice.* Available at https://www.chronicle.com/article/What-to-Expect-at-a/242578?cid=cc&utm_source=cc&utm_medium=en&elqTrackId=ed58f780194d4f9ea7a0f78e7248dcfa&elq=6f7182d66da848ebba4000b7437084c7&elqaid=17997&elqat=1&elqCampaignId=7986 This essay also provides links to other articles about community college job searches.

[238] Kelsky, K. (2016, October 18). Lunch with your faculty interviewers. *The Chronicle of Higher Education, Vitae.* Available at https://chroniclevitae.com/news/1581-lunch-with-your-faculty-interviewers?cid=pm&utm_source=pm&utm_medium=en&elqTrackId=16e6d15df17a4a2a801bfb0a72a480c1&elq=392d5dc6b76c4607a220e885ccfe568a&elqaid=11164&elqat=1&elqCampaignId=4299

[239] Przybylski, A. K., & Weinstein, N. (2012, July 19). Can you connect with me now? How the presence of mobile communication technology influences face-to-face conversation quality. *Journal of Social and Personal Relationships, 30*(3), 237-246. doi 10.1177/0265407512453827. Available at http://journals.sagepub.com/doi/abs/10.1177/0265407512453827

[240] Mirriam-Webster. (2017). We just added more than 1,000 new words to the dictionary. *Mirriam-Webster.* Available at https://www.merriam-webster.com/words-at-play/new-words-in-the-dictionary-feb-2017?elqTrackId=66da9262ad3b4eabb1fee943b8bfdc84&elq=69ae1612bb10402a9570af08583971ed&elqaid=12484&elqat=1&elqCampaignId=5088

[241] Clancy, A. (2015, September 15). Pivotal moments in coaching: The coach as catalyst in facilitating transformation [Webinar, recording only available to ICF members]. *ICF Coaching Science, Community of Practice.*

[242] June, A.W. (2018, August 9). Sights on the highest-ranked department, and other job-search advice from a professor who's been there. *The Chronicle of Higher Education, Advice*. Available at https://www.chronicle.com/article/One-Drink-at-Dinner-Don-t/244229?cid=pm&utm_source=pm&utm_medium=en&elqTrackId=acd2b0a12e2e494994e2bc02bb0f363e&elq=059358c551ed499daf48c7d04a506f00&elqaid=20074&elqat=1&elqCampaignId=9352

[243] Sell, S. S. (2017, November 2). AP-CNBC poll: Interview questions often run afoul of the law. *Associated Press-NORC Center for Public Affairs Research*. Available at http://www.apnorc.org/news-media/Pages/AP-CNBC-Poll-Interview-questions-often-run-afoul-of-the-law.aspx)

[244] Rivera, L. A. (2017, October 25). When two bodies are (not) a problem: Gender and relationship status discrimination in academic hiring. *American Sociological Review, 82*(6), 1111-1138. Available at http://journals.sagepub.com/doi/abs/10.1177/0003122417739294?elqTrackId=55e9b1386e344e8089fcb2d5983a877b&elq=0d04059302cc4990b437e18a5e0bb966&elqaid=16312&elqat=1&elqCampaignId=7049&

[245] EEOC. (1978, October 31). The Pregnancy Discrimination Act of 1978. *US Equal Employment Opportunity Commission*. Available at https://www.eeoc.gov/laws/statutes/pregnancy.cfm

[246] Whitaker, M. (2018, February 5). The job market: Waiting for the day. *The Chronicle of Higher Education, Advice*. Available at https://www.chronicle.com/article/The-Job-Market-Waiting-for/242396?cid=at&utm_source=at&utm_medium=en&elqTrackId=8af0f1479586443ab5ce2899e2268e6a&elq=f2a516d476a74c9f96909847954c3692&elqaid=17720&elqat=1&elqCampaignId=7805

[247] Perlmutter, D. (2016, May 30). Academic job hunts from hell: Why you weren't picked. *The Chronicle of Higher Education, Advice*. Available at http://www.chronicle.com/article/Academic-Job-Hunts-From-Hell-/236635?cid=cr&utm_source=cr&utm_medium=en&elqTrackId=fce6893ed94742d48f6586df1e058470&elq=555db40cdbd444ec8e9096f1160bc14e&elqaid=9253&elqat=1&elqCampaignId=3233

[248] Whitaker, M. (2018, February 5). The job market: Waiting for the day. *The Chronicle of Higher Education, Advice*. Available at https://www.chronicle.com/article/The-Job-Market-Waitingfor/242396?cid=at&utm_source=at&utm_medium=en&elqTrackId=8af0f1479586443ab5ce2899e2268e6a&elq=f2a516d476a74c9f96909847954c3692&elqaid=17720&elqat=1&elqCampaignId=7805

[249] HigherEd Jobs. (2016-17). Tenured/tenure-track faculty salaries [Survey]. *HigherEd Jobs*. Available at https://www.higheredjobs.com/salary/salaryDisplay.cfm?SurveyID=39

[250] The home page for Mint.com is available at https://www.mint.com/

[251] The home page for LearnVest.com is available at https://www.learnvest.com/

[252] MechCad Software. (2017, December 6). AceMoneyLite [software program for purchase]. *MechCad Software.* Available at http://www.mechcad.net/products/acemoney/free-personal-finance-software-quicken-alternative.shtml

[253] The home page for GnuCash is available at https://www.gnucash.org/

[254] The Pay Scale cost-of living calculator is available at http://www.payscale.com/research/US/Country=United_States/Salary

[255] Harris, M. (2015, May 11). What is the typical teaching load for university faculty? [Blog]. *Higher Ed professor.* Available at http://higheredprofessor.com/2015/05/11/what-is-the-typical-teaching-load-for-university-faculty/

[256] The online amortization calculator from EasySurf is available at http://www.easysurf.cc/samt8n3.htm?ansal=70000&ipcsal=1&time=30

Part 6: Additional Considerations

[257] June, A. W. (2016, August 14). Why colleges still scarcely track Ph.D.s. *The Chronicle of Higher Education, News.* Available at http://chronicle.com/article/Why-Colleges-Still-Scarcely/237412?cid=trend_au&elqTrackId=6adfd106e30c44fbb74e70e1ee1226b7&elq=3f0b2cd6342040ecb2817b59df9064ad&elqaid=10253&elqat=1&elqCampaignId=3832

[258] Carlson, S. (2017). The future of work: How colleges can prepare students for the jobs ahead. *The Chronicle of Higher Education, Special Report*, p. 9 [PDF]. Available at https://www.nacada.ksu.edu/Portals/0/Clearinghouse/advisingissues/documents/The_Future_of_Work_2017.pdf

[259] Carlson, S. (2017). The future of work: How colleges can prepare students for the jobs ahead. *The Chronicle of Higher Education, Special Report* [PDF]. Available at https://www.nacada.ksu.edu/Portals/0/Clearinghouse/advisingissues/documents/The_Future_of_Work_2017.pdf

[260] Schillebeeckx, M., Marique, B., & Lewis, C. (2013, October 8). The missing piece to changing university culture. *Nature Biotechnology, 31,* 938-941. doi:10.1038/nbt.2706. Available at https://www.nature.com/articles/nbt.2706

[261] For an excellent essay on why one academic gave up the job search and went to work at BuzzFeed, see Zamudio-Suaréz F. (2018, April 27). This academic took a job at BuzzFeed. Here's her advice to graduate programs. *The Chronicle of Higher Education, News.* Available at https://www.chronicle.com/article/This-Academic-Took-a-Job-at/243264?cid=pm&utm_source=pm&utm_medium=en&elqTrackId=10ce12a7d0214ddc840b39309dbcd5e2&elq=513b6b621b784b25b72459106e107a37&elqaid=18851&elqat=1&elqCampaignId=8492

[262] Another place to read opinions in the debate about number of new PhDs versus available academic positions is Lenny Teytelman, co-founder of protocols.io, who believes 90% of PhDs will *not* get a tenure track faculty position, with "too many PhDs competing for academic positions in a very destructive manner." Teytelman, L. (2015, February 1). Is the world producing more PhDs than it needs? ¶ 5. *Quora Digest*. Available at https://www.quora.com/Is-the-world-producing-more-PhDs-than-it-needs

[263] Jaschik, S. (2017, August 28). The shrinking humanities job market. *Inside Higher Ed.* Available at https://www.insidehighered.com/news/2017/08/28/more-humanities-phds-are-awarded-job-openings-are-disappearing

[264] The home page for the project may be found at American Academy of Arts & Sciences (2018). *Humanities Indicators, a project of the American Academy of Arts and Sciences*. Available at https://humanitiesindicators.org/

[265] Institute of Education Statistics. Table 318.30. Bachelor's, master's, and doctor's degrees conferred by postsecondary institutions, by sex of student and discipline division: 2014-15 *National Center for Education Statistics, US Department of Education*. Data released on December 6, 2016; the next data release due December 2018. Available at https://nces.ed.gov/programs/digest/d16/tables/dt16_318.30.asp

[266] Hamrick, K. (2018, March). 2016 doctorate recipients from U. S. universities [Annual survey of earned doctorates]. *National Center for Science and Engineering Statistics Directorate for Social, Behavioral and Economic Sciences*. Data available at https://www.nsf.gov/statistics/2018/nsf18304/data.cfm

[267] Allum, J.R., Kent, J.D. and McCarthy, M.T. (2014). Understanding PhD career pathways for program improvement: A CGS report [PDF]. Washington, DC: Council of Graduate Schools. Available at http://cgsnet.org/ckfinder/userfiles/files/CGS_PhDCareerPath_report_finalHires.pdf

[268] Pannapacker, W. (2013, June 17). Just look at the data, if you can find any. *The Chronicle of Higher Education, Advice*. Available at http://chronicle.com/article/Just-Look-at-the-Data-if-You/139795/

[269] Flaherty, C. (2016, October 28). New effort to track careers of humanities Ph.D.s *Inside Higher Ed, #Quick Takes*. Available at https://www.insidehighered.com/quicktakes/2016/10/28/new-effort-track-careers-humanities-phds?utm_source=Inside+Higher+Ed&utm_campaign=04c0732966-DNU20161028&utm_medium=email&utm_term=0_1fcbc04421-04c0732966-197426605&mc_cid=04c0732966&mc_eid=9ab110d608

[270] Hazelrigg, K. (2016, October 27). CGS announces multi-university project to collect data on career pathways of humanities PhDs [Press Release], *Council of Graduate Schools*. Available at http://cgsnet.org/cgs-announces-multi-university-project-collect-data-career-pathways-humanities-phds

[271] American Historical Association (2017). Where historians work: An interactive Database of History PhD Career Outcomes [Database]. American Historical Association, Career Diversity for Historians. Available at https://www.historians.org/wherehistorianswork

[272] The Stanford PhD alumni employment project [Database]. *Institutional Research & Decision Support (IR&DS),* in collaboration with the Office for the Vice Provost of Graduate Education (VPGE). Available at http://web.stanford.edu/dept/pres-provost/irds/phdjobs.

[273] Cook, B. (2013). The Stanford PhD alumni employment project [Database]. *Institutional Research & Decision Support (IR&DS),* in collaboration with the Office for the Vice Provost of Graduate Education (VPGE). Available at http://web.stanford.edu/dept/pres-provost/irds/phdjobs. See also PPT presentation slides, available at https://cair.org/wp-content/uploads/sites/474/2015/07/19_Cook.pdf

[274] Chesley, K. (2015, October 13). New website reveals PhD career paths for Stanford alumni. *Stanford News.* Available at https://news.stanford.edu/2015/10/13/phd-career-site-101315/

[275] Wood, L.M. (2016, December 2). Who lands tenure track jobs? *Lilli Research Group.* Available at https://lilligroup.com/research/

[276] Wood, L. M. (2013, December 16). Vital questions about tracking placement data. ¶ 9. *The Chronicle of Higher Education, The Ph.D. Placement Project.* Available at http://www.chronicle.com/blogs/phd/2013/12/16/vital-questions-about-tracking-placement-data/

[277] Turk-Bicakci, L., Berger, A., & Haxton, C. (2014, April 1). The nonacademic careers of STEM Ph.D. holders. *AIR Brief.* Available at https://www.air.org/resource/nonacademic-careers-stem-ph-d-holders

[278] Bradburn, N. M. (Project Director), et al. (2017, August). Advanced degrees in the humanities, humanities indicators. *AAAS, Higher Education.* Available at https://humanitiesindicators.org/content/indicatordoc.aspx?i=44

[279] National Science Foundation, National Center for Science and Engineering Statistics. (2016, January). Survey of doctorate recipients (1993–2013), Table 3-16. National Science Board, Science and Engineering Indicators. Available at https://www.nsf.gov/statistics/2016/nsb20161/#/table/tt03-16

[280] Hendrix, S. (2014, September 2). Should I become a professor? Success rate 3%! [Blog]. *Smart Science Career.* Available at http://www.smartsciencecareer.com/become-a-professor/

[281] Main, J. B., Prevnovitz, S., & Ehrenberg, R. G. (2017, December). In pursuit of a tenure-track faculty position: Career progression and satisfaction of humanities and social sciences doctorates [PDF, Working Paper], p.1. Ithaca, NY: CHERI (Cornell Higher Education Research Institute). https://www.ilr.cornell.edu/sites/ilr.cornell.edu/files/CHERI%20WP180.pdf

[282] Flaherty, C. (2017, December 18). Where the grass is greener. *Inside Higher Ed, #News.* Available at https://www.insidehighered.com/news/2017/12/18/study-humanities-and-social-

science-phds-working-outside-academe-are-happier-their?utm_source=Inside+Higher+Ed&utm_campaign=39cce06ca0-DNU20171218&utm_medium=email&utm_term=0_1fcbc04421-39cce06ca0-197426605&mc_cid=39cce06ca0&mc_eid=9ab110d608

[283] Main, J. B., Prevnovitz, S., & Ehrenberg, R. G. (2017). In pursuit of a tenure-track faculty position: Career progression and satisfaction of humanities and social sciences doctorates [PDF, Working Paper], p.1. Ithaca, NY: CHERI (Cornell Higher Education Research Institute). https://www.ilr.cornell.edu/sites/ilr.cornell.edu/files/CHERI%20WP180.pdf

[284] Kerr, E. (2018, February 11). For scholars of women's studies, it's been a dangerous year. *The Chronicle of Higher Education, Faculty*. Available at https://www.chronicle.com/article/For-Scholars-of-Women-s/242521?cid=at&utm_source=at&utm_medium=en&elqTrackId=8d7d4c8dcbf049568e48edda9365be38&elq=204e9f0d5208426e936a5dd3d0a86ad5&elqaid=17855&elqat=1&elqCampaignId=7899

[285] Frequently graduate students find actually admitting to advisors that they want to leave academia frightening. See, for instance Reis, R. (2017, February 23). Having "the conversation" – telling your advisor you don't want to be a professor. *Tomorrow's Professors* [Blog]. Available at https://tomprof.stanford.edu/posting/1617.

[286] Kelsky, K. (2017, January 10). How to shorten a CV. *The Professor is In* [Blog]. ¶ 3. Available at https://chroniclevitae.com/news/1662-how-to-shorten-a-cv?cid=pm&utm_source=pm&utm_medium=en&elqTrackId=dba01e31ff8044cbafe1cf4a56a479a1&elq=ad228f8f78134a2992b6bcc997ef3145&elqaid=12074&elqat=1&elqCampaignId=4873

[287] Yoder, J. (2017, April 24). I found a tenure-track job. Here's what it took. *The Chronicle of Higher Education, Vitae*. ¶ 10. Available at https://chroniclevitae.com/news/1775-i-found-a-tenure-track-job-here-s-what-it-took?cid=VTEVPMSED1#sthash.UJ0NeckS.dpuf

[288] Yoder, J. (2017, April 24). I found a tenure-track job. Here's what it took. *The Chronicle of Higher Education, Vitae*. ¶ 23. Available at https://chroniclevitae.com/news/1775-i-found-a-tenure-track-job-here-s-what-it-took?cid=VTEVPMSED1#sthash.UJ0NeckS.dpuf

[289] Yoder, J. (2017, July 20). I found a tenure-track job: The big picture. *The Chronicle of Higher Education, Vitae*. Available at https://chroniclevitae.com/news/1859-i-found-a-tenure-track-job-the-big-picture?cid=pm&utm_source=pm&utm_medium=en&elqTrackId=9c9a6d58fb8545c580c28a8066190df0&elq=5152cef4c91448d595e6b0804a8b2ba2&elqaid=14821&elqat=1&elqCampaignId=6266

[290] Tonelli, M. (2016, December 13). Job-market diaries: An English professor. *The Chronicle of Higher Education, Vitae*. ¶. 20. His online interview of Brian Goedde is available at https://chroniclevitae.com/news/1639-job-market-diaries-an-english-instructor?cid=pm&utm_source=pm&utm_medium=en&elqTrackId=aefa6bdfaaa3497cbbd320e461265886&elq=94b8730d1f9e4e429725590f5d528e45&elqaid=11816&elqat=1&elqCampaignId=4722#sthash.giPr8FMX.dpuf

[291] Flaherty, C. (2018, February 22). Lego Graduate Student is now an assistant professor. *Inside Higher Ed, #Quick Takes.* ¶ 4. Available at https://www.insidehighered.com/quicktakes/2018/02/22/lego-grad-student-now-assistant-professor?utm_source=Inside+Higher+Ed&utm_campaign=cba0b4d1a6-DNU20180111&utm_medium=email&utm_term=0_1fcbc04421-cba0b4d1a6-197624989&mc_cid=cba0b4d1a6&mc_eid=6081602244

[292] Editors, Chronicle of Higher Education (No names given). (2016, February 29). *An Executive Summary* [PDF, p.3]. Washington, DC: The Chronicle of Higher Education, Special Reports. Available at http://www.chronicle.com/article/An-Executive-Summary/235454?cid=cp32

[293] Dishman, L. (2016, March 21). Best and worst graduate degrees for jobs in 2016. *Fortune.* Available at http://fortune.com/2016/03/21/best-worst-graduate-degrees-jobs-2016/

[294] WorkplaceDiversity.com. (2105). The truth about tenure in higher education. *Diversity in Higher Education.com.* Available at https://diversityinhighereducation.com/articles/The-Truth-About-Tenure-in-Higher-Education In Canada, the estimated number of candidates to tenure track jobs is one-in-five; see Polk, J. (2018, March 7) Transition update: Jared Wesley, associate professor. *University Affairs.* https://www.universityaffairs.ca/career-advice/beyond-the-professoriate/transition-update-jared-wesley-associate-professor/

[295] The Chronicle of Higher Education. (2017, August 13). Tenure status of full-time and part-time faculty members, Fall 2015. *Almanac 2017.* Summary available at https://www.chronicle.com/article/Tenure-Status-of-Faculty/240511

[296] The Chronicle of Higher Education. (2017, August 13). Tenure status of full-time and part-time faculty members, Fall 2015. *Almanac 2017.* Summary available at https://www.chronicle.com/article/Tenure-Status-of-Faculty/240511

[297] Wood, M. (2018, February 2) Who lands tenure-track jobs? Join our crowdsourced research project [Blog]. *Beyond the Professoriate.* Available at https://community.beyondprof.com/blogs/view/35/who-lands-tenure-track-jobs-join-our-crowdsourced-research-project. To participate go to https://community.beyondprof.com/pages/academic-jobs.

[298] "First generation" is a loosely defined term, generally used by educators to mean students who complete college when neither one of their parents has a college degree. Here, the NSF was indicating that these numbers refer to those "first generation" students who then went on to complete a doctoral degree.

[299] National Science Foundation, National Center for Science and Engineering Statistics. (2015). *Doctorate recipients from U.S. universities: 2014* [PDF, p.12]. Arlington, VA: Special Report NSF, 16-300. Available at http://www.nsf.gov/statistics/2016/nsf16300/

[300] Wood, L.M. (2016, December 2). Who lands tenure track jobs? L. Maren Wood, PhD [Blog]. Available at https://lilligroup.com/research/ Note: This blog entry is based on research that Wood did for a project funded by *The Chronicle of Higher Education* from 2014-15.

[301] Flaherty, C. (2017, April 6). Where the faculty jobs are. *Inside Higher Ed, #News.* Available at https://www.insidehighered.com/news/2017/04/06/new-cupa-hr-study-looks-faculty-hiring-pay-chairs-and-adjuncts-and-more?utm_source=Inside+Higher+Ed&utm_campaign=002af6c135-DNU20170406&utm_medium=email&utm_term=0_1fcbc04421-002af6c135-197426605&mc_cid=002af6c135&mc_eid=9ab110d608

[302] Jackson, R. & Super, B. (2018, February 1). *2016-2017 APSA graduate placement survey: Placement report* [PDF]. Washington, DC: American Political Science Association. Available at http://www.apsanet.org/Portals/54/APSA%20Files/Data%20Reports/Employment%20Data/Graduate%20Placement%20Report%202016-2017.pdf?ver=2018-02-02-103603-070 The Piktochart is available at https://create.piktochart.com/output/27113553-january-cotm-graduate-placement#.Wmvc1AT--qo.twitter

[303] Jaschik, S. (2017, August 28). The shrinking humanities job market, ¶ 6. Available at https://www.insidehighered.com/news/2017/08/28/more-humanities-phds-are-awarded-job-openings-are-disappearing

[304] Weissman, J. (2103, February 20). The Ph.D bust: America's awful market for young scientists—in 7 charts. *The Atlantic.* Available at https://www.theatlantic.com/business/archive/2013/02/the-phd-bust-americas-awful-market-for-young-scientists-in-7-charts/273339/

[305] McKenna, L. (2016, April 21). The ever-tightening job market for Ph.D.s. *The Atlantic.* Available at https://www.theatlantic.com/education/archive/2016/04/bad-job-market-phds/479205/

[306] Gould, J. (2015, February 17). The elephant in the lab [Blog]. *Nature Jobs.* Available at http://blogs.nature.com/naturejobs/2015/02/17/the-elephant-in-the-lab/

[307] Schillebeeckx, M., Maricque, B. & Lewis, C. (2013, October 8). The missing piece to changing the university culture. *Nature Biotechnology, Careers and Recruitment.* 31, 938–941. doi: 10.1038/nbt.2706 Available at https://www.nature.com/articles/nbt.2706#f1 Full-size figure is available at https://www.nature.com/articles/nbt.2706/figures/1

[308] Schillebeeckx, M., Maricque, B. and Lewis, C. (2013, October 8). The missing piece to changing the university culture. *Nature Biotechnology, Careers and Recruitment.* 31, 938–941. doi: 10.1038/nbt.2706 Available at https://www.nature.com/articles/nbt.2706#f1

[309] Offord, C. (2017, January 1). Addressing biomedical science's PhD problem: Researchers and institutions seek to bridge the gap between emerging life science professionals and available positions. *The Scientist, Careers.* ¶ 1. Available at https://www.the-scientist.com/?articles.view/articleNo/47732/title/Addressing-Biomedical-Science-s-PhD-Problem/

[310] Jaschik, S., & Lederman, D. Evolving faculty careers [Webinar, PPT Slide 4]. *Inside Higher Ed.* Available at https://www.insidehighered.com/audio/2018/03/05/evolving-faculty-careers?utm_source=Inside+Higher+Ed&utm_campaign=4764e508c9-

webcast_Evolving_Faculty_20180412&utm_medium=email&utm_term=0_1fcbc04421-4764e508c9-197426605 To download the slide deck, click here.

[311] Berlinerblau, J. (2016, June 29). This guy got tenure. You probably won't. *The Chronicle of Higher Education, The Chronicle Review*. ¶ 4 & 5. Available at https://www.chronicle.com/article/You-Probably-Wont-Get-Tenure/236957?cid=trend_au&elq=b1c623ca383f4b9cbec6cdc6adcd2b4f&elqCampaignId=3459&elqTrackId=f75633065a1047ae967a918145c67970&elqaid=9697&elqat=1

[312] Flaherty, C. (2017, April 6). Where the faculty jobs are. *Inside Higher Ed, #News*, ¶ 25. Available at https://www.insidehighered.com/news/2017/04/06/new-cupa-hr-study-looks-faculty-hiring-pay-chairs-and-adjuncts-and-more?utm_source=Inside+Higher+Ed&utm_campaign=002af6c135-DNU20170406&utm_medium=email&utm_term=0_1fcbc04421-002af6c135-197426605&mc_cid=002af6c135&mc_eid=9ab110d608

[313] McKenna, L. (2016, April 21). The ever-tightening job market for Ph.D.s , ¶ 9. *The Atlantic, Education*. Available at https://www.theatlantic.com/education/archive/2016/04/bad-job-market-phds/479205/

[314] Potts, Chris. (2012, December 2). Linguistics dissertations and academic jobs. Data from Chart ¶3, quote from ¶ 5. *Language Log, The Academic Scene* [Blog]. http://languagelog.ldc.upenn.edu/nll/?p=4349

[315] Oprisko, R. (2012, December 3). Superpowers: The American academic elite. *ISPA (International Political Science Association)*. Available at https://www.ipsa.org/news/news/superpowers-american-academic-elite-robert-oprisko

[316] Oprisko, R.L., Dobbs, Kristie L, & DiGrazia, J. (2013, August 29-September 1). *Honor, prestige, and the academy: A portrait of political science tenured and tenure-track faculty in Ph.D.-granting institutions*, p. 48 [PDF]. Paper prepared for delivery at the 2013 Annual Meeting of the American Political Science Association, Chicago, IL. Link to pdf available at https://www.google.com/search?q=Robert+L.+Oprisko+universities+11+percent&oq=Robert+L.+Oprisko+universities+11+percent+&aqs=chrome..69i57.24681j0j7&sourceid=chrome&ie=UTF-8

[317] Warner, J. & Clauset, A. (2015, February 23). The academy's dirty secret. *Slate, Education*. Available at http://www.slate.com/articles/life/education/2015/02/university_hiring_if_you_didn_t_get_your_ph_d_at_an_elite_university_good.html

The full study by Clauset, A., Arbesman, S. & Larremore, D.B. (2015, February 12). *Systematic inequality and hierarchy in faculty hiring networks* [PDF]. Washington, DC: Science Advances. Available at https://www.researchgate.net/publication/276441411_Systematic_inequality_and_hierarchy_in_faculty_hiring_networks

[318] The coalition is composed of presidents or chancellors of nine universities and one research center: University of Wisconsin-Madison Johns Hopkins University, Fred Hutchinson Cancer Research Center, University of Pennsylvania, University of California-San Francisco, University of Maryland, Cornell University, Duke University, Massachusetts Institute of Technology, University of Michigan-Ann Arbor. The names of these participants are available at http://science.sciencemag.org/content/358/6369/1388

[319] Flaherty, C. (2017, December 15). Bottom line up front, ¶ 1. *Inside Higher Ed, #News*. Available at https://www.insidehighered.com/news/2017/12/15/new-calls-clear-easily-accessible-data-phd-program-outcomes-life-sciences

[320] Blank, R., et al. (2017, December 15). A new data effort to inform career choices in biomedicine. *Science, Life Sciences Careers, 358*(6369), 1388-1389. Available at http://science.sciencemag.org/content/358/6369/1388

[321] Horowitz, W. & Rosenthal, L. (2010, April 23). For grad students, a grim job market. *Yale News*. https://yaledailynews.com/blog/2010/04/23/for-grad-students-a-grim-job-market/

See also Robinson, J. (2016, October 10). The academic job market is tottering, but nobody's telling graduate students. *The Martin Center for Academic Renewal, Governance*. Available at https://www.jamesgmartin.center/2016/10/academic-job-market-tottering-nobodys-telling-graduate-students/

[322] Greteman, B. (2107, February 22). Don't blame tenured academics for the adjunct crisis, ¶ 2. *The Chronicle of Higher Education, The Chronicle Review*. Available at http://www.chronicle.com/article/Don-t-Blame-Tenured/239268?cid=pm&utm_source=pm&utm_medium=en&elqTrackId=993e3b22426045e5a500f2580c90f0a9&elq=8b8b0dff90b741c680def323972a3b75&elqaid=12685&elqat=1&elqCampaignId=5193

[323] Weber, S. (2017, August 26). Academia is in crisis—And it's political. *AlterNet*. Available at http://www.alternet.org/academia-crisis-its-political

[324] Gannon, K. (2017, July 24). Fixing our job-market problem, ¶ 1. *Chronicle Vitae*. Available at https://chroniclevitae.com/news/1861-fixing-our-job-market-problem

[325] Platts, T. K. (2014, April 9). Successful and unemployed. *Inside Higher Ed, #Career Advice*. Available at https://www.insidehighered.com/advice/2014/04/09/essay-being-unemployed-young-scholar-social-sciences#sthash.DqzoqlsO.dpbs

See also: Iber, P. (2014, March 10). (Probably) refusing to quit. *Inside Higher Ed, #Career Advice*. https://www.insidehighered.com/advice/2014/04/09/essay-being-unemployed-young-scholar-social-sciences#sthash.DqzoqlsO.dpbs

[326] Kelsky, K. (2014, April 18). Job market PTSD, ¶ 3 [Blog]. *The Professor Is In*. Available at https://theprofessorisin.com/2014/04/18/job-market-ptsd-2/

[327] Fitzpatrick, K. (2018, March 4). Not here to make friends, ¶ 11. *The Chronicle of Higher Education, The Chronicle Review*. Available at https://www.chronicle.com/article/Not-Here-to-Make-Friends/242731?cid=at&utm_source=at&utm_medium=en&elqTrackId=4a714fc28a70426da6a94f97e9db5624&elq=3e906cc02b394a888de4c11431ae8a52&elqaid=18158&elqat=1&elqCampaignId=8098

[328] Jaschik, S. (2013, February 19). Tenure track as alt-ac. *Inside Higher Ed, #News*. Available from: http://www.insidehighered.com/news/2013/02/19/research-aaas-meeting-notes-difficult-job-market-academic-science Jaschik cited Paula Stephan, a professor of economics at Georgia State University who specializes in the intersection of economics and science, who said referred to tenure track jobs as "alt-ac" positions (or alternative academic careers) because they are not the norm anymore. Confusion with terminology arises because usually "alt-ac" refers to jobs outside of the academy.

[329] Weissman, J. (2013, April 10). The ever-shrinking role of tenured professors (in 1 chart). *The Atlantic*. Available at https://www.theatlantic.com/business/archive/2013/04/the-ever-shrinking-role-of-tenured-college-professors-in-1-chart/274849/

[330] Hoeller, K. (2014, February 16). The Wal-Mart-ization of higher education: How young professors are getting screwed, ¶ 13. *Salon*. Summary available at https://www.salon.com/2014/02/16/the_wal_mart_ization_of_higher_education_how_young_professors_are_getting_screwed/ This article was excerpted from Hoeller K., ed. (2014). *Equality For Contingent Faculty: The Two Tier System*. Nashville, TN: Vanderbilt University Press.

[331] Kezar, A., & Maxey, D. (2013, May/June). The changing academic workforce. *Trusteeship Magazine*, a publication of the Association of Governing Boards of Universities and Colleges. Available at https://www.agb.org/trusteeship/2013/5/changing-academic-workforce

[332] Shulman, S. (Chair), et al. (2016, March-April). *Higher education at a crossroads: The economic value of tenure and the security of the profession*, from *The annual report on the economic status of the profession, 2015–16* [PDF, p. 14]. Washington, DC: Academe. Available only o AAUP members at https://www.aaup.org/issue/march-april-2016-compensation-survey

[333] Hoeller, K. (2014, February 16). The Wal-Mart-ization of higher education: How young professors are getting screwed, ¶ 14. *Salon*. Summary available at https://www.salon.com/2014/02/16/the_wal_mart_ization_of_higher_education_how_young_professors_are_getting_screwed/

[334] The US refers to part-time or adjunct instructor positions as "contingent" labor; other parts of the English speaking world refer to these jobs as "casual labor," a term which reflects the idea that these jobs are not meant to provide any sort of full time employment.

[335] Baker, K.J. (2016, February 23). Academic waste, ¶ 6. *Chronicle Vitae*. Available at https://chroniclevitae.com/news/1301-academic-

waste?cid=at&utm_source=at&utm_medium=en&elqTrackId=74c9af333a4c4d92a3247244e8739323&elq=e9abc34316404a4dab9e1c448349d19d&elqaid=8027&elqat=1&elqCampaignId=2530

[336] Morgan, K. (2017, Feb. 26). Cultural divide: Colleges respond to the complaint that they're liberal bubbles, ¶ 18. *The Chronicle of Higher Education, Special Reports.* Available at https://www.chronicle.com/article/Cultural-Divide/239276?cid=db&elq=d4e5220d422d423d9e2b667f369c39fc&elqCampaignId=5217&elqTrackId=7f2055e7f71f4943b9e39a07448e6b9e&elqaid=12736&elqat=1

[337] Yakoboski, P.J. (2015 June). *Understanding the faculty retirement (non)decision*, [PDF], p.1, ¶ 2. New York, NY: TIAA-CREF Institute. *Available at* https://www.tiaainstitute.org/sites/default/files/presentations/2017-02/understanding-the-faculty-retirement-nondecision.pdf

[338] Behling, J. (2015, December 22). UW tenure reforms provide flexibility, accountability. *Milwaukee-Wisconsin Journal Sentinel, Opinion.* Available at http://archive.jsonline.com/news/opinion/uw-tenure-reforms-provide-flexibility-accountability-b99638891z1-363304611.html/

[339] June, A. W., and Newman, J. (2013, January 4). Adjunct project reveals wide range in pay. *The Chronicle of Higher Education, Faculty.* https://www.chronicle.com/article/Adjunct-Project-Shows-Wide/136439 Although the original project was meant to create a separate data base for adjuncts all data is now searchable at https://data.chronicle.com/

[340] Myers, B. (2016, February 14). Where are the minority professors? *The Chronicle of Higher Education, Data.* Available at http://chronicle.com/interactives/where-are-the-minority-professors?cid=at&utm_source=at&utm_medium=en&elqTrackId=25bfd8eb6894461092bf46c126a9b7fe&elq=eacde9bc5dfa4aae89fd27b0953d6eac&elqaid=7887&elqat=1&elqCampaignId=2440

[341] Leiter, B. (2018, January 30). Academic ethics: 'Hidden' hiring criteria, ¶ 1, 2 & 3. *The Chronicle of Higher Education, Advice.* Available at https://www.chronicle.com/article/Academic-Ethics-Hidden-/242381?cid=trend_right_a

[342] Brown, S. (2018, February 15). She wrote a farewell letter to colleagues. Then 80,000 people read it. *The Chronicle of Higher Education, The Chronicle Interview.* Available at https://www.chronicle.com/article/She-Wrote-a-Farewell-Letter-to/242564?cid=db&elqTrackId=91bd25d2aace47c69ba109d0b45c0419&elq=6a9d77e129a048b6982c0d37658236e6&elqaid=17873&elqat=1&elqCampaignId=7911

[343] Rodwell, E. (2017, January 12). Look what they make you give, ¶16. *The Chronicle of Higher Education, Chronicle Vitae.* Available at https://chroniclevitae.com/news/1664-look-what-they-make-you-give

[344] For more information on the academic advising hiring process, see Edwards, T. (2007, March). Practice what we preach: Advising and the hiring process. *Academic Advising Today*, 30(1) Available at http://www.nacada.ksu.edu/Resources/Academic-Advising-Today/View-Articles/Practice-What-We-Preach-Advising-and-the-Hiring-Process.aspx

[345] Home page for NACADA available at https://www.nacada.ksu.edu/

[346] Furlong, J. S., & Vick, J. M. (2016, December 18). From doctoral study to ... administration. *The Chronicle of Higher Education, Advice.* Available at https://www.chronicle.com/article/from-doctoral-study-to-/238708?cid=gs&elq=4014d473fe60427ea743f90518be0c17&elqCampaignId=4784&elqTrackId=78bbeda378f945d5b7783bb2c99850d7&elqaid=11913&elqat=1&utm_medium=en&utm_source=gs

[347] Permutter, D. D. (2017, June 16). Administration 101: Getting your name in the real pool, ¶ 10. *The Chronicle of Higher Education, Chronicle Vitae.* Available at https://chroniclevitae.com/news/1830-administration-101-getting-your-name-in-the-real-pool

[348] Bogel-Burroughs, N. (2016, December 29). Foreign government-sponsored hackers breached ILR School in 2014 to exact 'revenge' against U.S. *The Cornell Daily Sun, News.* ¶ 1. Available at http://cornellsun.com/2016/12/29/foreign-govt-sponsored-hackers-breached-ilr-school-in-2014-to-exact-revenge-against-us/?elqTrackId=6d1e95cd10304dd99a0932eafcfb6c41&elq=15a7a5de098540a08e35106ac73d8de0&elqaid=11966&elqat=1&elqCampaignId=4811

According to an unidentified senior IT official quoted for this article at ¶ 41: "Every research university is subject to these sort of state-sponsored attacks. Unfortunately, they're increasing in frequency and sophistication."

[349] Historically, NASPA stands for the National Association of Student Personnel Administrators. The name was updated to Student Affairs Administrators in Higher Education, but the organization keeps the old acronym for continuity purposes. NASPA [Website]. (Copyright 2008-2018). Frequently asked questions. *NASPA.* Available at: https://www.naspa.org/about/faqs

[350] Roach, M., & Sauermann, H. (2017, September 18). *The declining interest in an academic career* [PDF]. San Francisco, US & Cambridge, UK: PLOS ONE. Available at http://journals.plos.org/plosone/article/file?id=10.1371/journal.pone.0184130&type=printable

[351] Kelley, S. (2017, September 18). One-third of Ph.D.s lose interest in academic careers, but not for lack of jobs. *Cornell Chronicle.* Available at http://news.cornell.edu/stories/2017/09/one-third-phds-lose-interest-academic-careers-not-lack-jobs?elqTrackId=d63a10162d8b44b99c5630974369fbb6&elq=912f02a9953c4a42a847e417c3ff7eb7&elqaid=15793&elqat=1&elqCampaignId=6788

[352] Flaherty, C. (2017, September 29). Rejecting academe, ¶6 & 7. *Inside Higher Ed, #News.* https://www.insidehighered.com/news/2017/09/29/study-challenges-common-belief-most-science-and-engineering-phds-leave-academe?utm_source=Inside+Higher+Ed&utm_campaign=c595b91e33-DNU20170929&utm_medium=email&utm_term=0_1fcbc04421-c595b91e33-197426605&mc_cid=c595b91e33&mc_eid=9ab110d608

[353] Golde, C., & Hartman, S. (2017, February 23). Having "the conversation" – Telling your advisor you don't want to be a professor [Blog]. *Grad|Logic*. Reprint with permission available at https://tomprof.stanford.edu/posting/1617

See also Patel, V. (2018, March 4). Rebranding the Ph.D. *The Chronicle of Higher Education, Special Reports*. Available at https://www.chronicle.com/article/These-PhD-Programs-Pay-More/242666?cid=at&utm_source=at&utm_medium=en&elqTrackId=9d856ee6a34f4e88b898e7f64c81d295&elq=c02d143a172f42e5af9fdcf3bf391975&elqaid=18106&elqat=1&elqCampaignId=8065 and Scharff, V. (2018, March 4). Prepare Your Ph.D.s for Diverse Career Paths. *The Chronicle of Higher Education, Special Reports*. Available at https://www.chronicle.com/article/Advice-Prepare-Your-PhDs/242667?cid=rclink

[354] Moravec, J. (2015, July 13). The future belongs to nerds, geeks, makers, dreamers, and knowmads [Post]. *LinkedIn*. https://www.linkedin.com/pulse/future-belongs-nerds-geeks-makers-dreamers-knowmads-john-moravec/

[355] Moravec, J.W., et al. (2013). *Knowmad Society*. Minneapolis, MN: Education Futures. Moravec encourages readers to rearrange the information to suit themselves and share any ideas at infor@knowmadsociety.com.

See also Moravec, J.W. (2013, October 5). Rise of knowmads [YouTube video]. Available at *https://educationfutures.com/* and *https://www.youtube.com/watch?v=hOtlMaczY0g*

[356] Moravec, J.W. (2013, October 6). Rise of the Knowmads: John Moravec at TEDxUMN. [TEDx talk synopsis]. Available at https://www2.educationfutures.com/john/2013/10/06/rise-knowmads-john-moravec-tedxumn/

[357] Chaya, K. (2018, February 8). When you're a 'digital nomad,' the world is your office. *The New York Times Magazine*. Available at https://www.nytimes.com/2018/02/08/magazine/when-youre-a-digital-nomad-the-world-is-your-office.html

[358] The *Chronicle Vitae* has created an interactive Excel list of essays about quitting academia and where to find them on the internet, available at https://docs.google.com/spreadsheets/d/1OODoiZKeAtiGil3IAONCspryCHWo5Yw9xkQzkRntuMU/edit#gid=0

[359] Bartram, E. (2018, February 15). Why everybody loses when someone leaves academe. *The Chronicle of Higher Education, Opinion*, available at https://www.chronicle.com/article/Why-Everybody-Loses-When/242560?cid=at&utm_source=at&utm_medium=en&elqTrackId=acde54e3677e4f78b2838c258ff407b8&elq=651c3d71c5d3404e9161546ccdd23c92&elqaid=17872&elqat=1&elqCampaignId=7910

[360] Brown, S. (2018, February 15). She wrote a farewell letter to colleagues. Then 80,000 people read it. *The Chronicle of Higher Education, The Chronicle Interview*. Available at https://www.chronicle.com/article/She-Wrote-a-Farewell-Letter-

to/242564?cid=at&utm_source=at&utm_medium=en&elqTrackId=bc816ff34f8c4b52b21d276f9117609c&elq=651c3d71c5d3404e9161546ccdd23c92&elqaid=17872&elqat=1&elqCampaignId=7910

[361] Cassuto, L. (2018, February 25). The grief of the ex-academic. ¶ 16 *The Chronicle of Higher Education, Advice.* Available at https://www.chronicle.com/article/The-Grief-of-the-Ex-Academic/242612

[362] Bartram, E. (2018, February 15). Why everybody loses when someone leaves academe. *The Chronicle of Higher Education, Opinion,* available at https://www.chronicle.com/article/Why-Everybody-Loses-When/242560?cid=at&utm_source=at&utm_medium=en&elqTrackId=acde54e3677e4f78b2838c258ff407b8&elq=651c3d71c5d3404e9161546ccdd23c92&elqaid=17872&elqat=1&elqCampaignId=7910 Quotes are from ¶s 7 & 8.

[363] Bartram, E. (2018, February 15). Why everybody loses when someone leaves academe. *The Chronicle of Higher Education, Opinion,* available at https://www.chronicle.com/article/Why-Everybody-Loses-When/242560?cid=at&utm_source=at&utm_medium=en&elqTrackId=acde54e3677e4f78b2838c258ff407b8&elq=651c3d71c5d3404e9161546ccdd23c92&elqaid=17872&elqat=1&elqCampaignId=7910 Quotes are from ¶s 18 & 26.

[364] Brown, S. (2018, February 15). She wrote a farewell letter to colleagues. Then 80,000 people read it. *The Chronicle of Higher Education, The Chronicle Interview.* Available at https://www.chronicle.com/article/She-Wrote-a-Farewell-Letter-to/242564?cid=at&utm_source=at&utm_medium=en&elqTrackId=bc816ff34f8c4b52b21d276f9117609c&elq=651c3d71c5d3404e9161546ccdd23c92&elqaid=17872&elqat=1&elqCampaignId=7910 Quotes are from ¶s 15, 16, 33, 37, & 38.

[365] Thomason, A. (2017, February 7). Your daily briefing [email list], ¶ 8. *The Chronicle of Higher Education.* Available only to subscribers at https://www.chronicle.com/subscribe or write directly to andy.thomason@chronicle.com

[366] Sinche, M.V. (2016). *Next gen PhD: A guide to career paths in science* [Book Synopsis, About this book. ¶ 2]. Boston, MA: Harvard University Press. Available for purchase at http://www.hup.harvard.edu/catalog.php?isbn=9780674504653

[367] Neutill, R. (2015, December 20). Sixteen years in academia made me an a-hole, ¶ 31. *Salon.* Available at https://www.salon.com/2015/12/20/sixteen_years_in_academia_made_me_an_a_hole/

[368] Hall, L. (2015, June 22). I am an adjunct professor who teaches five classes. I earn less than a pet-sitter, ¶ 1 & 2. *The Guardian, US Edition.* Available at https://www.theguardian.com/commentisfree/2015/jun/22/adjunct-professor-earn-less-than-pet-sitter

[369] Lupupa, J. (2017, January 15). Scholars more likely to leave UK post-Brexit. *The Boar.* Available at https://theboar.org/2017/01/scholars-likely-leave-uk-post-brexit/

See also Petrow, C. (2017, January 6). Brexit higher education bill survey [PDF]. London, England: YouGov. Available at http://www.ucu.org.uk/media/8436/YouGov_Brexit_HE_bill_survey/pdf/YouGov_Brexit_HE_bill_survey

[370] Croxall, B. (2014, January 25). Introduction: This is not the help you're looking for. *#Alt-Academy, a media commons project.* Available at http://mediacommons.futureofthebook.org/alt-ac/pieces/introduction-not-help-youre-looking-0

[371] Richards, E., & Terkanian, D. (2013, December) Occupational employment projections to 2022 [PDF]. Washington, DC: US Bureau of Labor Statistics, Monthly Labor Review. Available at https://www.bls.gov/opub/mlr/2013/article/pdf/occupational-employment-projections-to-2022.pdf

[372] Schuman, R. (2014, September 18). "Alt-ac" to the rescue. *Slate.* Available at http://www.slate.com/articles/life/education/2014/09/a_changing_view_of_alt_ac_jobs_in_which_ph_d_s_work_outside_of_academia.html

[373] Henry, C. (2017). CLIR Annual Report, 2016-17 [PDF]. *Council on Library and Information Resources (CLIR).* Available at https://www.clir.org/pubs/annual/

[374] Sayre, M. B., Brunner, M., Croxall, B., & McGinn, E. (2015, September 10). *Toward a trackless future: Moving beyond "alt-ac" and "post-ac"* p. 103. [PDF]. Washington, DC: CLIR (Council on Library and Information Resources). Available at https://www.clir.org/wp-content/uploads/sites/6/trackless.pdf

[375] Patel, V. (2017, January 29). Opening doors for the Ph.D. *The Chronicle of Higher Education, Graduate Students.* Available at https://www.chronicle.com/article/Opening-Doors-for-the-PhD/239031?cid=db&elq=67dd7ee1d8ac4c3a9f207a00049e8686&elqCampaignId=5076&elqTrackId=e52f7ca2a81a46f493ef5f3fe09d13d0&elqaid=12468&elqat=1

[376] Patel, V. (2017, January 29). Helping history Ph.D.s expand their job options. *The Chronicle of Higher Education, Graduate Students.* Available at https://www.chronicle.com/article/Helping-History-PhDs-Expand/239019?cid=at&elq=52b3867e3cb1425b92a9a2964fde2539&elqCampaignId=5075&elqTrackId=66fe8b65bb5f43bcbfc26a934ecf8156&elqaid=12467&elqat=1&utm_medium=en&utm_source=at

[377] Mellon, L. (2016, Spring). The career diversity five skills [adapted from posts originally published in *AHA Today*]. *American Historical Association.* Available at https://www.historians.org/jobs-and-professional-development/career-diversity-for-historians/career-diversity-resources/five-skills

[378] Flaherty, C. (2018, January 8). The history Ph.D.: Beyond 'alt-ac,' ¶ 2. *Inside Higher Ed, #News, #Teaching and Learning.* Available at https://www.insidehighered.com/news/2018/01/08/historians-urge-departments-enthusiastically-and-substantively-prepare-grad-students?utm_source=Inside+Higher+Ed&utm_campaign=3bcc4f9c28-

DNU20180108&utm_medium=email&utm_term=0_1fcbc04421-3bcc4f9c28-197426605&mc_cid=3bcc4f9c28&mc_eid=9ab110d608

[379] Wood, L. M. (2016, February 22). Academic job market crisis: 1970 – ? [Blog], ¶ 37. *L. Maren Wood, PhD*. Available at https://lilligroup.com/2016/02/22/academic-job-market-crisis-1970/

[380] Flaherty, C. (2014, April 9). So much to do, so little time, ¶ 9. *Inside Higher Ed, #News*. Available at https://www.insidehighered.com/news/2014/04/09/research-shows-professors-work-long-hours-and-spend-much-day-meetings

[381] Bouw, B. (2016, April 19; updated 2018, May 16). More PhDs are leaving academia to launch their own businesses, ¶ 8. *The Globe and Mail*. Available at https://www.theglobeandmail.com/report-on-business/small-business/startups/more-phds-are-leaving-academia-to-launch-their-own-businesses/article29587908/

[382] Flaherty, C. (2017, April 7) GradUCon and beyond, ¶ 3. *Inside Higher Ed, #News, #Teaching and Learning*. Available at https://www.insidehighered.com/news/2017/04/07/how-university-chicago-helping-graduate-students-find-meaningful-careers#.WOhV33QvOJd.linkedin

[383] Wasley, P. (2015, October 5). NEH announces new next generation humanities PhD grant program. *National Endowment for the Humanities*. Available at https://www.neh.gov/news/press-release/2015-10-21

[384] Ortega, S. (Principle Investigator), Engler, J., Kent, J., & Okahana, H., & McCarthy, M. (Co-Principle Investigators). (Grant start date 2017, April 1). Award abstract #1661272: Understanding PhD career pathways in STEM. *National Science Foundation*. Available at https://www.nsf.gov/awardsearch/showAward?AWD_ID=1661272&HistoricalAwards=false

See also Ortega, S.T. (2018, April 2, updated). *Attachment A: Understanding PhD career pathways for program improvement: A survey implementation guide for doctoral institutions* [RFP]. Washington, DC: National Science Foundation. Available at http://cgsnet.org/ckfinder/userfiles/files/Attachment_A-Implementation_Guide.pdf and

Thompson, N. (press contact). (2013, December 6). CGS launches project to study feasibility of tracking phd career pathways. *Council of Graduate Schools*. Available at http://cgsnet.org/node/1790

[385] MLA Commons. (n.d.). Connected academics: Preparing doctoral students of language and literature for a variety of careers. *Modern Language Association*. Available at https://connect.mla.hcommons.org/

[386] American Historical Association. (2014). About career diversity: The pilot phase. *American Historical Association*. Available at https://www.historians.org/jobs-and-professional-development/career-diversity-for-historians

[387] Chambers, P. (Founder and editor). (n.d.). PhD career finder: Non-academic careers of humanities & social sciences; non-academic careers for STEM. *VersatilePhD*. Available at https://versatilephd.com/phd-career-finder/?pk_campaign=201612mmlisted

[388] PhDs at Work. (n.d.). Connecting PhDs working across industries. *PhDs at Work*. Available at http://phdsatwork.com/

Polk, J. (Copyright 2017). From PhD to life: Meaningful careers for Phds [Website blog]. *From PhD to Life*. Available at http://fromphdtolife.com/

Chambers, P. (Founder and Editor). (Copyright 1999-Present). *The Versatile PhD*. Available at https://versatilephd.com/

Centre for Career Management Studies (CCMS). (Copyright 2009-2013). Beyond the PhD—What next after the PhD? [Legacy website]. *Transition Tradition*. Available at http://beyondthephd.co.uk/

[389] Wildcards is a closed group at https://www.facebook.com/groups/wildcards.me/

[390] Hernandez, D., & King, R. (2016, November 24). Universities' AI talent poached by tech giants. *The Wall Street Journal, Tech*. Available at https://www.wsj.com/articles/universities-ai-talent-poached-by-tech-giants-1479999601

[391] Wing, M. R. (2018, January 12) A scholar, but not a professor, ¶ 1. *ChronicleVitae*. https://chroniclevitae.com/news/1979-a-scholar-but-not-a-professor?cid=VTEVPMSED1

[392] NCIS. (Copyright 1989-2018). The National Coalition of Independent Scholars (NCIS) [Website home page]. *The National Coalition of Independent Scholars (NCIS)*. Available at https://ncis.org/national-coalition-independent-scholars-ncis

[393] Attig, D. (2018, July 16). Building an endpoint to your faculty job search. *Inside Higher Ed, #Career Advice, #Carpe Careers*. Available at https://www.insidehighered.com/advice/2018/07/16/how-determine-how-long-continue-faculty-job-search-opinion?utm_source=Inside+Higher+Ed&utm_campaign=ae3d4454c7-CareersInsider_COPY_01&utm_medium=email&utm_term=0_1fcbc04421-ae3d4454c7-197426605&mc_cid=ae3d4454c7&mc_eid=9ab110d608

[394] Sternberg, R. J. (2015, May 26). Career advice from an oldish not-quite geezer. *The Chronicle of Higher Education, Advice*. Available at http://www.chronicle.com/article/Career-Advice-From-an-Oldish/230335

[395] Robison, S. (2013). *The peak performing professor: A practical guide to productivity and happiness*. San Francisco, CA: Jossey-Bass.

[396] Friedman, T. L. (2006, July 5). The age of interruption. *The New York Times*. Available at https://www.nytimes.com/2006/07/05/opinion/05friedman.html

[397] Hallowell, E. M. (2006). *Crazybusy: Overstretched, overbooked, and about to snap!* New York, NY: Ballantine Books.

[398] Surowiecki, J. (2010, October 11). Later: What does procrastination tell us about ourselves? *The New Yorker.* Available at https://www.newyorker.com/magazine/2010/10/11/later#ixzz1OQ0XcL15

[399] Akerlof, G. A. (1991, May). Procrastination and obedience. *American Economic Review, American Economic Association, 81*(2), 1-19. Formerly available at https://ideas.repec.org/a/aea/aecrev/v81y1991i2p1-19.html

[400] Hubbard, B. (2014, February 26). Study finds up to 95% of college students procrastinate. Available at: http://thebluebanner.net/study-finds-up-to-95-percent-of-college-students-procrastinate/

[401] Burka, J., & Yuen, L. M. (2008). *Procrastination: Why you do it, what to do about it.* Cambridge, MA: Da Capo Press. Quotations from pp. 177-189.

INDEX

Academic freedom, 5, 41, 208
Academic Jobs Wiki, 88
Administrative jobs, 89, 107, 209-214
Adjuncting, 8, 65, 73, 200, 202, 209, 216-7, 221
    Salary range, 155
        see also casual labor, contingent hiring, contract hiring
Advertising, 6, 13, 96, 100, 186, 208
    Misleading, 6
Adult education, 210
Alcohol, 178, 211
Alt-ac or Altac, 89, 217
Alternatives to professoriate, 209
    Inside academia, 209
    Leaving academia, 214
Applicants, 6, 35-36, 42, 59, 75, 77, 91, 93, 132, 139, 141, 165, 201-203, 206
    Feedback, 141
    Number of, 201-203
Application portfolio, 91-142
    Cover letter, 91, 93-99, 101-106
    CV, 100, 106-116
    Equity and diversity statement, 137-138
    Evaluations, 139-141
    Recommendations, 116-118, 119-121
    Research job talk, 127-132
    Research statement, 125, 128-131
    Syllabus, 122, 126
    Teaching job talk (sample class), 132-137
    Teaching philosophy statement, 118, 123
Authenticity, 157, 223
AutoHotkey, 87
Benefits, job, 1, 7, 9, 12, 36, 73-74, 188-191, 194-195, 207
Blackboard, 10, 118, 173
Brutality, 1
Bullet journal, 80, 84, 86
Casual labor, 270
Chamber of Commerce, 187
Chronicle of Higher Education, The, 34, 88-89
    ChronicleVitae, 34
Citation services, 66
Classrooms, flipped, 4, 75, 118
Classroom technology, 136
Cluster hiring, 11
Collaborative publishing, 11, 64

Index

Community, learning about the, 187
Community college, 3, 52, 75, 118, 148, 166, 170, 190
    Hiring cycle, 3-4
    Job interviews, 146, 166, 170
    Positives, 202
    Tenure, 4
Compensation survey, 48
Competition with friends or colleagues, 165, 206
Conferences, 57-63
    Affording, 61
    Attending, 59-60,
    Attire, 158, 160, 165
    Networking at, 57-59
    Organizing a panel, 62
    Poster sessions, 62
    Presenting, 60
    Publications from, 66, 69
    Volunteering, 62
Confidence building, 25-27, 156
    see also Imposter Syndrome, 27-32
Confidentiality, 153
Contact us, xv
Contingent hiring, 1, 4, 5, 7, 206
Contract hiring, 6-7, 15, 74, 166, 198, 207
Courses, online, 10, 75, 110, 118, 124, 147, 196, 202, 213
Cross-listing with more than one dept., 64, 99
Curriculum Vitae (CV) 100, 106-116
    Action words, 96, 107, 112-113
    Aspirational, 110
    Formatting basics, 100, 109
    Gapping, 100
    Information to include, 107-109
    Online submissions, 110-111
    Parallelism, 106
CV/resume builders, 112
    Curriculum Vitae (for Android), 112
    CV Maker, 112
    Pocket Resume (for Apple products), 112
    Resumonk, 112
    Your CV Builder, 112
Disappearing job listings, 12-13
Diversity statement, 137-138
Elevator speech, 51-55, 146
Employee assistance programs (EAPs), 211
Equity and diversity statement, 137-139
Exercise, 20, 23

Failure to track PhD employment outcomes, 198-201
Foreign countries as places to work, 36-37
Fulbright Scholar Program, 108
Grief, 215-216
Handling stress, 19-20, 78, 129, 177
Handshakes, 150
Headhunters, 37-39
Hiring cycles, 2-4, 210
Human Resources (HR), 47, 91, 157
Humor, 6, 42, 94, 132
Imposter phenomenon, 27
Imposter syndrome, 27-32, 156
Impression, first, 93, 109, 149, 163, 166, 169
Impression, professional, 98, 125, 151
Inside candidates, 186
Inside Higher Ed, 34
Inquiries, handling, 21, 24
Interview, 143-197
    Alcohol, 178
    Authentic self, 157, 223
    Basic etiquette, 148-152
    Clothing, 158, 160, 165
    Community college, 146, 165
    Conference, 161, 163, 165
    Ending interview/follow-up, 182, 185-187
    General preparation, 143, 146
    In-depth interview considerations, 171-177
    Knowing your institution, 146-148
    Meals, 177-178
    On-campus interview (site visit), 170
    Preliminary, 157
    Questions, illegal, 180-181
    Schedules, 167
    Taking notes during, 150
    Telephone, 157-159, 161
    Traits to project, 156-157
    Types of interviews, 143
    Unpleasant surprises, 179-182
    Video (Skype, Zoom), 159-161
    What not to do, 178-179
Job listings, where to find, 34-41
    Academic Careers Online, 36
    AcademicJobs Wikia, 36
    Chronicle of Higher Education, 34
    Chronicle Vitae, 34
    Conferences, 62

Index

    Higher Education Professionals, 35
    Higher Education Recruitment Consortium (HERC), 34
    Honor societies, 35-36, 50
    Inside Higher Ed, 34
    Journals, specialized, 35
    National Center for Faculty Development and Diversity, 34-35
    Online sources, 34-36
    Print sources, 34-36
    Professional societies, 35
    Times Higher Education, or THE, 35
    Versatile PhD, 90
Job log, 80-82
    Facesheet, 81, 83
    Types, 80
Job offer(s), 188-189
    Considerations, 188-189
    Multiple, 196-197
    Negotiating, 189-196
Job search, 1-48
    Considerations, general, 75-77
    Community college, 3-4, 75
    Cycle, 2-4
    How long to look, 224-227
    Organizing, 78-90
    Overview, 1-2
Leaving academia, 201, 214-215
    Independent scholar, 221-222
    Websites about, 219, 221
Library privileges, 73-74
Mealtime etiquette, 177
Microaggressions, 175
Mind maps, 56-57
Mindfulness, 20, 24
Money worries, 21
    Find work that pays, 65, 72-74
Month-by-month to do list, 13-15
Moodle, 10, 118, 173
National Coalition of Independent Scholars (NCIS), 222
Negotiating, 189-197
Networking as connecting, 48
Networking, general, 48-51
Networking, information links, 55
Note-taking during interviews, 150
Nutrition, 19-20, 22-23
Organizing, 78-90
    Apps, 86-87

    Dropbox, 86
    Evernote, 86-87
    Google Drive, 87
    Text expander, 87
  Bullet journal, 86
  Paper copies, 78-80
  SYSTEM (acronym), 232
  TAFFY (acronym), 231-232
  Tickler files, 228, 230-231
  Overload, tips for handling, 228-230
Overqualified, 155
Persistence, 224
PhD career outcomes, 198-201
Poaching, intellectual, 221
Post-ac, 217
Post academia, 216-222
Postdoctoral work, 10-11
Power poses, 25
Preparation, 156, 165-169
  Background, 146-148
  General, 76, 143-146
  On-campus interview, 166-169
Professoriate, alternatives, 209-215
  Inside academia, 209-214
  Outside academia, 214-215
Professoriate, shrinking, 207
Promotions, 109, 176
Publishing, 65-72
  Academic book proposals, 65
  As graduate student, 64-65
  Citations, 66
  Collaborative publishing, 11, 64
  Determining what to publish, 66-72
  Dissertation, 67, 70
  Planning, 66-72
  Post dissertation, 67, 70
  Titles for articles and books, 57
Quit lit, 215
Recommendations, 116, 119-121
Recruiting firms, 37-41, 47
References, professional, 18, 116-118
Research appointments, 11
Salaries, 48
  AAUW formula, 188
  Calculations, 188-189
  Compression, 189

Index

    Increases, 190, 192
    Minimum, 191, 194
    Resources to determine, 188-189
    Starting, 188, 190, 192
Search committees, 2-3, 13, 15, 36, 93, 100, 148, 154, 165, 179, 186, 223
Self-care, 15, 18-25
Service in academia, 5, 171, 176
Sleep, 19, 22, 169
Social media, 39-47
    As used by academics in their work, 43-47
    Building presence, 42-43
    Problems associated with, 41-42
    Use for job searching, 44-47
Social media platforms, 44-48
    Facebook, 44
    Idealist, 47
    Instagram, 44-45
    Glassdoor, 46-47
    LinkedIn, 45-46
    Snapchat, 46
    Specialized sites (HR offices), 47
    Twitter, 46-47
Social networking, 48-51
Social time, 20, 23-24
Societal pressures, 20-21, 24
STEM, 55, 199-200, 204, 217
Stress, handling, 15, 18-20, 228-234
Teaching, 1, 7-11
    Abroad, 36-37
    As a career, 1, 18, 75
    Load expectations, 4, 6-8, 11, 147, 171, 173, 188, 190, 192
    Methodologies, 4, 75, 118
    Online, 10, 92, 118
    Philosophy, 118, 120, 122-124
    Preparation for teaching career, 18, 75
Tenure, 5-6
    Chance of tenure-track offer, 203-206
    Assistant Professor, 5-6, 196, 202
    Associate Professor, 5, 232-233
    Expectations of hiring institution, 6, 192-193, 224
    Full Professor, 5
    Tenure, possible extinction, 208-209
    Tenure track, 5-6
Text Expander, 80, 87, 142
Thank-you notes, 82, 152
Tickler files. 228, 230-231

Titling your paper or presentation, 57, 169
Tracking your job search, 1-48
    Electronic files, 86-87
    Facesheet, 81, 83
    Log/spreadsheet, 80-82
Transferable skills, 96, 198, 218-220
Visiting Professors or VAPing, 7, 9
Versatile PhD, 221
    Academic jobs, 90
    Nonacademic jobs, 90, 221
Visualization, 26, 32
    Confidence, 26
    Imposter Syndrome, 32
What I want from a job, 1-2, 8, 144
Women, special note to, 152, 181, 192
Working overseas, 36-37
Worksheets, 235-236
Worries, money, 21
Year to year contracts, 7

ABOUT THE AUTHORS

Hillary Hutchinson, MA (social anthropology) and MEd (higher education administration), lives and works near Charleston, SC. She has been coaching academics for over a decade. She helps overwhelmed professors who need to pull it all together and enjoy their academic life. This includes working individually with academics at all stages of their careers to transition to the next phase on a well-defined career path, as well as with those academics that want to transition out of academia.

Mary Beth Averill, PhD, lives and works in Eugene, OR. She's been coaching writers for over 30 years and specializes in working with academic writers. As an academic writing coach, she offers support through both individual sessions and weekly groups for ABD students and for faculty who would like to get articles finalized and submitted or books written. With a doctorate in Biology from the University of Oregon and an MSW several years later, Mary Beth has been an academic writer since the late 1960s herself.

Made in the USA
Middletown, DE
03 September 2021